MESOPOTAMIA, EGYPT, INDUS VALLEY, CHINA, AND PERU ▪ C. 1800 B.C.: KING HAMMURABI OF BABYLON SETS FORTH LAWS GOVERNING CREDIT SYSTEM ▪ ▪

OWN EUROPEAN COINS MINTED IN ANATOLIAN KINGDOM OF LYDIA ▪ LYDIA HAS FREE-MARKET SYSTEM; CITIES FEATURE CENTRAL RETAIL MARKETPLACES ▪ ▪

GION, TRANSPORTED VIA SILK ROAD ▪ 550 B.C.: GREEK CITY-STATES EVOLVE A CIVILIZATION WITH CULTURAL LIFE CENTERED ON MARKETPLACE (AGORA) ▪ ▪

GOVERNMENT, MARKET-DRIVEN ECONOMY, AND FLOURISHING OF ALL THE ARTS ▪ 332 B.C.: ARISTOTLE DESCRIBES USURY AS CRIME AGAINST NATURE ▪ ▪

INA EXISTS ▪ 206 B.C.–A.D. 220: HAN DYNASTY RULES CHINA ▪ CHINA'S CONTACT WITH WEST AND INDIA INCREASES AND TRADE BEGINS TO THRIVE ▪ ▪

MPERORS WILL FOLLOW SUIT ▪ 161–180: MARCUS AURELIUS IS EMPEROR; DURING HIS REIGN, THE ROMAN EMPIRE REACHES ITS GREATEST EXTENT ▪ ▪

ECOMES SOLE RULER OF ROMAN EMPIRE ▪ 330: CONSTANTINE MOVES CAPITAL OF ROMAN EMPIRE TO BYZANTIUM AND RENAMES IT CONSTANTINOPLE ▪ ▪

▪ 476: END OF WEST ROMAN EMPIRE ▪ LATE 5TH CENTURY: WESTERN EUROPE ENTERS DARK AGES; MODERN CAPITALISM BECOMES DORMANT THERE ▪ ▪

■ ■ WESTERN EUROPE'S ECONOMIES REVERT TO AN AGE OF BARTER ■ 622: MUHAMMAD THE PROPHET FLEES MECCA, MARKING THE BEGINNING OF ISLAM

■ ■ ISLAM, FOUNDED BY A MERCHANT, ENCOURAGES MARKET ACTIVITY AND PROFIT FROM FREE TRADE ■ 618–907: MARKET ECONOMY DEVELOPS IN CHINA

■ ■ 1022: SZECHWAN GOVERNMENT PRINTS PAPER MONEY ■ 1066: NORMAN CONQUEST ■ 1096–1291: THE CRUSADES EXPOSE EUROPE TO ARAB CULTURES

■ ■ 1100'S: BILLS OF EXCHANGE ARE INVENTED ■ C. 1100–1300: JEWS ARE CHIEF BANKERS IN MANY CITIES ■ C. 1118: KNIGHTS TEMPLARS ORDER IS FOUNDED

■ ■ 1167: NORTHERN ITALY'S LOMBARD LEAGUE IS FORMED ■ 1183: THE KARIMI, POWERFUL SPICE MERCHANTS, BUILD GREAT WAREHOUSE IN FUSTAT, EGYPT

■ ■ EARLY 1200'S: CATHEDRALS RISE, DRAWING PILGRIMS ■ 1201: VENICE IS EUROPE'S COMMERCIAL CAPITAL ■ 1204: CRUSADERS SACK CONSTANTINOPLE

■ ■ 1250–1350: ERA OF LARGE-SCALE WORLD TRADE 1252: GENOA AND FLORENCE MINT GOLD COINS; FIRST MAJOR EXAMPLES IN WEST SINCE ROMAN TIMES

■ ■ 1271–95: MARCO POLO OF VENICE IS IN ASIA ■ LATE 1200'S: ITALIAN TRADING FAMILIES FORM BANKS; BARDI AND PERUZZI PROMINENT IN FLORENCE

This book is dedicated to all who suffered and died in the terrorist attack on the World Trade Center in New York City, September 11, 2001, and to the courageous men and women who inspired the world by their selfless response to those in need.

Through hope and humanity, may this tragic episode be succeeded by a shining chapter in which tolerance and prosperity prevail throughout the world.

In recognition of the profound sorrow and loss suffered by the international financial community, a portion of the profit from this book is donated to charitable funds established in response to this unparalleled catastrophe.

1290: EDWARD I EXPELS JEWS FROM ENGLAND ■ 1300'S: FLANDERS IS A MAJOR COMMERCIAL CENTER ■ FIRST STOCK EXCHANGE ESTABLISHED IN BRUG

■ ■ 1348: BLACK DEATH WIPES OUT MUCH OF EUROPE'S POPULATION ■ 1350: FLORENCE INSTITUTES LONG-TERM MUNICIPAL DEBT THAT IS TRADED ON ACT

■ 1430: COMMERCIAL OCEAN ROUTES TO INDIA AND FAR EAST OPEN UP TO EUROPEAN MERCHANT ADVENTURERS ■ 1450–1550: FUGGER FAMILY OF BAVA

 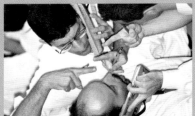  

■ ■ 1500'S: JAPAN'S CASTLE TOWNS EVOLVE INTO COMMERCIAL CENTERS ■ 1509: PORTUGUESE ROUT INDIAN AND EGYPTIAN FLEETS IN PERSIAN GULF; EUR

■ ■ C. 1560: ANTWERP IS ONE OF EUROPE'S BUSIEST MARKET TOWNS ■ 1567: INDOOR EXCHANGE IS BUILT IN LONDON ■ 1576: SPANISH MERCENARIES RA

■ ■ 1600: ENGLAND'S EAST INDIA COMPANY CHARTERED ■ 1602: DUTCH EAST INDIA COMPANY FORMED ■ 1637: DUTCH SPECULATION IN RARE TULIPS CAUS

■ ■ 1673: FRANCE'S COMPAGNIE DES INDES ORIENTALES PURSUES INDIAN OCEAN TRADE ■ C. 1680: THOMAS LLOYD OPENS COFFEEHOUSE THAT EVOLVES INT

■ ■ 1688: DUTCH PRINCE WILLIAM OF ORANGE ASCENDS BRITISH THRONE; LONDON SUPPLANTS AMSTERDAM AS COMMERCIAL HUB OF EUROPE ■ 1689–171

1337-1453: HUNDRED YEARS' WAR ■ 1341: EDWARD III OF ENGLAND DEFAULTS ON WAR LOANS, RUINING ITALY'S BARDI AND PERUZZI BANKING HOUSES ■ ■

ECONDARY MARKET ■ 1397: GIOVANNI DI BICCI DE' MEDICI FOUNDS BANK IN FLORENCE; DYNASTY RULES CITY FOR MOST OF THE FIFTEENTH CENTURY ■ ■

OMINANT BANKERS ■ 1487: SHIPS OF MANY NATIONS BEGIN TO PLY INDIAN OCEAN ■ 1492: COLUMBUS DISCOVERS AMERICA, NEW SOURCE OF WEALTH ■ ■

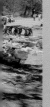

AINS TRADE SUPREMACY ■ 1521: MARTIN LUTHER IS EXCOMMUNICATED ■ 1553: BRITAIN'S FIRST JOINT STOCK FIRM, MUSCOVY COMPANY, IS FOUNDED ■ ■

TWERP ■ 1577-80: FRANCIS DRAKE CAPTAINS FIRST BRITISH SHIP IN INDIAN OCEAN ■ 1600'S: AMSTERDAM BECOMES FINANCIAL CENTER OF EUROPE ■ ■

RST MODERN MARKET CRASH ■ 1652: DUTCH FOUND A COLONY AT CAPE OF GOOD HOPE ■ C. 1662: BRITISH GAIN BOMBAY ■ 1666: GREAT LONDON FIRE ■

YD'S OF LONDON INSURANCE MARKET ■ 1681: DANISH GOVERNMENT ORDINANCE ESTABLISHES THE OFFICIAL GROUND RULES FOR SECURITIES TRADING ■ ■

S THROUGHOUT EUROPE LEAD TO GREAT INCREASES IN NATIONAL DEBT, WITH A CORRESPONDING INCREASE IN TRADING OF GOVERNMENT SECURITIES ■ ■

In memory of my parents, who encouraged me to explore different worlds.

Front cover (central image): Detail, Airbus consortium press conference, June 2000 (see page 215).

Editor: Christopher Lyon
Art Director: Julietta Cheung
Designers: Julietta Cheung, Cheryl Peterka, Misha Beletsky
Design Assistant: John Joseph McGowan
Picture Editors: Lisa Barnett and Robin Raffer
Production Manager: Louise Kurtz

First edition

10   9   8   7   6   5   4   3   2   1

Library of Congress Cataloging-in-Publication Data

Finch, Christopher.
    In the market : the illustrated history of the financial markets / Christopher Finch ; foreword by John M. Angelo.
        p. cm.
    Includes bibliographical references and index.
    ISBN 0-7892-0014-7 (alk, paper)
Investments—History. 2. Stock exchanges—History. I. Title.

HG4521.F563 2001

332.6—dc21   2001041302

THE ILLUSTRATED HISTORY OF THE FINANCIAL MARKETS

IN THE

MARKET

CHRISTOPHER FINCH

FOREWORD BY JOHN M. ANGELO

ABBEVILLE PRESS PUBLISHERS

NEW YORK LONDON

Contents

Foreword

I first walked onto the bond floor of the New York Stock Exchange on January 15, 1966. The room was forty feet square, ringed with telephones. In the center of the room was a fifteen-by-fifteen-foot area surrounded by a brass rail. It was here that members of the Exchange stood to take orders and execute trades.

At 9:30 a.m. each workday, the room was virtually empty. By ten o'clock, when the bell rang to start trading, the place was a madhouse—400 crazed people screaming and yelling in a room that, by law, was allowed to hold only 289. The mob included members of many ethnic groups—Italians, Irish, Jews—citizens with diverse histories, manners, and backgrounds who came together with a single thought: the best possible execution for their clients' trades. The clerk on the phone would get the order and start hollering for his broker's attention. Given the pandemonium, screaming often didn't work and he would be forced to run to the broker, elbowing his way to the brass rail to hand over the order. The smell of sweat and fear was palpable. In the frenzy, fistfights often broke out. Long-standing relationships could end in seconds. Then, suddenly, the day was over. In those days the market closed at 3:30 p.m. Not everyone had had enough. Many of the men would wander off to play gin, poker, or craps.

From the moment I first stepped onto the floor, I knew I wanted to be a trader. I loved it. I seemed to have an ability to hear everything that was happening on the floor. Through the hubbub, I could pick out the important voices and put buyer and seller together. From the intonation of the voice at the other end of the phone, I could tell whether a person was holding back or bidding the limit. I could see in a man's eyes if he was telling the truth. Somehow I could handle two phones at once, watch the ticker tape, and, more often than not, be on the winning side of a trade. It was the free market system at its best—fierce, fast, frenzied; a thing of absolute beauty.

There is something visceral about trading, knowing within seconds whether you're right or wrong. A natural-born trader has the ability to cull all the facts and instantly make up his mind. An analyst likes to weigh decisions; a trader likes to act and it is the action that provides the high. Clarity is also part of the poetry of trading. There are real winners and losers. Every moment of the day you know exactly how you stand. The bottom line is the score card.

Many years ago, I was walking across the floor of the Chicago Mercantile Exchange—the MERC—with its then president, Brian Monnison. As we walked past the pork belly pit, he said to me, "Come on, let's go and trade a few contracts." I told him I didn't know anything about pork bellies. He said, "What do you have to know? They go up and they go down." He was right.

After three years of trading bonds, I was given the opportunity to manage proprietary capital at a major securities firm and left the floor to learn arbitrage—the simultaneous purchase and sale of securities for instant profit. I might buy shares of Royal Dutch in Amsterdam and sell them at the same time in New York. It was an extraordinary business because the New York Stock Exchange considered such trades to be riskless transactions, and as a consequence, the firm was not required to put up any money. This meant that we were able to put on sizable positions that our balance sheet could never support under normal circumstances. Although the spreads were low, and the profits on an individual trade were small, the volume was high and the cumulative returns were enormous.

The middle to late 1970s was a period of explosive growth in the derivatives market. The widespread use and application of products such as options and futures changed the nature of financial markets across the spectrum of equity, currencies, and fixed income in the

United States and other developed markets worldwide. Eventually these markets became efficiently priced, but in the early years, as new products were developed and attracted new buyers, there were huge opportunities for the traders at securities firms and banks.

At about this time, my wife Judy and I began to travel extensively in Europe and Asia, where I had the opportunity to come face to face with colleagues I had traded with and spoken to a thousand times. I met their families and visited their various exchanges, marveling at the handsome and extraordinary buildings that housed each national bourse. I learned too that each exchange had its own peculiar rules and systems, but no matter how different they were from our American exchanges, they all shared a common interest: bringing buyers and sellers together.

Eventually, I came to realize that an exchange is more than just a mechanism for making money. It is the foundation upon which the market system is built, and as such it plays an enormous role in shaping the world. If, in addition to growing corporations, a primary purpose of the market system is to find and finance good ideas, then nowhere does it work better than in the United States. Access to capital and the speed at which capital finds its way into the system are what define us and differentiate us from the rest of the world.

Looking back over thirty-five years on Wall Street, the only constant has been change. During the past half-century, two rule changes mandated by the United States government made the biggest differences to our system. In 1973, ERISA (the Employee Retirement Income Security Act) became law. This obligated corporations to put aside retirement money for their employees. These monies became subject to professional management and were allowed to compound tax-free. At a single stroke, the government added trillions of dollars of wealth to the market and has made U. S. pension funds the largest buyers and sellers of stocks and bonds in the world. It also helped to create and legitimize the mutual fund industry.

The other watershed event came on May 1, 1975, which marked the first day of negotiated commissions on the purchase and sale of stocks. For the first time in two hundred years, the customer could dictate what he would pay a broker. Overnight, commission rates dropped 90 percent; they never rebounded. Customers suddenly found the playing field considerably more level, and the unforeseen result was a violent explosion in volume. In the year 2001, volume on the New York Stock Exchange was one hundred times greater than it was twenty-five years earlier, the daily average exceeding one billion shares.

Back in the 1960s, Wall Street was dominated by a handful of venerable firms, some dating back to the first half of the nineteenth century. It seemed to me then that they would remain in control forever. In reality, few have survived into the new millennium. Those that have done so owe their survival to superior management skills, resourcefulness, and the ability to control greed. However, the survivors bear little resemblance to their former selves. The twenty-first-century firm is much larger and more "bank-like," with tens of thousands of employees and billions of dollars of capital. Successful firms are no longer local or national, but global. They reach to the far corners of the earth and conduct business twenty-four hours a day.

At the same time, the new century offers enormous opportunities for small, highly efficient organizations that can deliver unique products and services as well as superior risk-adjusted returns to sophisticated and demanding clients. In 1988 I co-founded a firm to manage money in a style that generated absolute returns in all types of markets. In the financial world, this approach has come to be known as non-traditional or alternative investing. In the media, and colloquially, "hedge fund" is often used to describe what we do, though the term is something of an oversimplification. Broadly speaking, we manage money in ways that take advantage of inefficient markets and make money in spite of the market.

Technologies, strategies, and numbers change, but one thing remains unaltered: every day, buyers and sellers trade over the telephone, or on the Internet, with people they have never seen or to whom they have never spoken before. Transactions worth trillions of dollars take place without benefit of a lawyer or legal contract. As this book illustrates, the striking of such bargains goes back to the beginning of recorded history, when your word was your bond and a deal was sealed with a handshake.

INTRODUCTION:

The Art of the Bargain

A handshake cements a deal in front of the entrance to the
Wall Street station of the Lexington Avenue subway line.

A thousand years ago, when the Islamic world stretched from Spain to India, Berber tribesmen from the land then known as Maghreb`would head south from settlements like Sijilmassa, on the northern edge of the Sahara, their camels laden with dried dates, sorghum, and other provisions. They also carried trading items such as glass beads and tempered steel blades, the latter required to purchase safe passage through territory controlled by hostile nomads, including the dreaded Tuaregs, the fierce "blue men" of the desert.

Among the chief destinations of these merchants, three weeks or more into the sand dunes, was a godforsaken, snake- and scorpion-infested township named Taghaza, where the blinding Saharan light was intensified by buildings constructed wholly of dazzling blocks of pure white salt. The sole reason for the existence of this hallucinatory suburb of hell was a vast sedimentary saline deposit, just below the surface, which was quarried by slaves brought there from various sub-Saharan regions. The caravan drivers from the north would leave supplies for the slaves and their supervisors, then reload their camels with 250-pound slabs of salt, one strapped to each flank, and set off into the desert once more.

For another three weeks they would head south, until

For centuries, camel caravans like this one, seen in the Egyptian desert, headed across the Sahara to salt mines to acquire precious salt, almost literally worth its weight in gold; today's traders bring millet to barter for salt.

they reached the first stunted trees marking the northern limit of the belt of savannah that spreads out from the headwaters of the Niger and Senegal Rivers. Now the journey became more pleasant, with watering holes and occasional villages to break the monotony. Any baubles left over from the passage through Tuareg territory could be exchanged for fresh food. After a few more days, the caravan would find itself in the modestly fertile area known to the Berbers as Wangara, near where the modern nations of Senegal, Mali, and Guinea meet.

Once there, the caravan would proceed to a pre-arranged location where the traders would unload some of the salt, making a sizable pile of it before withdrawing a discreet distance to bed down for the night. The following morning, they would return to the site to discover a much smaller but nonetheless substantial heap of gold next to the stack of salt. If this reads like the beginning of an African fairy tale, it was in fact the first stage in a tough bargaining process conducted entirely without speech, and often without contact of any kind.

Typically, the Berbers would not accept this first offering of gold as being sufficient to pay for the salt they had unloaded, so they would remove two or three blocks from their stack. Darkness would fall. The Berbers might hear movement near the trading site but, knowing the rules of the game, would refrain from investigating. At dawn they would find that the pile of gold had been modified in size. In response they might return one or two of the salt blocks that had previously been removed from their heap. And so the process would continue, each party adjusting its offer until both sides were content that the exchange was fair. At that point the Berbers would take the gold and move out with an expeditiousness determined by the stately gait of their camels. Once they were safely removed from the area, the gold producers would cut up the salt and carry it back to their communities, where, because of local scarcity, it was

Top: *At Bilma, in Niger, a salt miner stands before neatly stacked 30-pound slabs of salt, ready to be sold.*

Above: *The salt is dug from pits or "harvested" from shallow ponds like those pictured here.*

more precious than any metal.

This silent bargaining practice had already been in use for more than a thousand years (Herodotus had heard rumors of it) and would continue for hundreds more. The secretive miners had devised it so that no one, neither Berber merchants nor local rivals, could follow them and discover the hidden location of the mines.

This c. 2700 B.C. panel, from the Standard of Ur, vividly illustrates the healthy economic life of this major city of Sumer. In contrast to Egypt, where the king was sole owner of all property and land, Sumer's people could own—and trade—land, cattle, and property. Contracts of all kinds quickly appeared, and Sumer became a cradle of civil law.

BANKERS AND BAZAARS

Man has been defined as a tool-making animal. He could just as well be described as an animal that makes bargains. The negotiated bargain is at the root of all legal systems and all systems of government. It is basic to religion, since the rites and dogmas involved in the observance of any form of pious belief imply that a bargain has been struck with a superior being. The bargain is also central to the way man obtains food and shelter. To advance beyond a subsistence level he must make contractual bargains, however informal, that involve the barter of goods, the trading of goods for money, or the exchange of promises.

In the chapters that follow, it will be seen how different types of bargains shaped the financial institutions of emerging cultures, and how the development of the marketplace has been intrinsically intertwined with the evolution of government and religion. Archeological finds from around the globe, in Iron Age Europe and pre-Columbian South America alike, suggest that early man often carried on commercial transactions in places that were also shrines to the prevailing local deities. Later, in both the Old World and the New, formidable civilizations evolved, dominated by god-kings heading

societies in which priestly bureaucracies appear to have regulated most forms of conduct so thoroughly that they even dictated the distribution of the basic commodities of life. Afterward came feudal systems in which commercial contracts between ordinary individuals still had no great significance, since most surplus goods and services were owed to the lord of the manor, who in turn owed goods and fealty to his sovereign in a strictly vertical system of tribute that left little room for free enterprise. Markets might exist within such worlds, but the social structure did not allow for the development of market-driven economies.

Where such economies did emerge—around the Aegean Sea a few centuries before the birth of Christ, and again in Western Europe in the late Middle Ages—it was still common to find the worlds of commerce, law, government, and religion crowded together. In the Athens of Plato and Pericles the central marketplace, or agora, was flanked by temples and the law courts, and was also an important venue for political oratory. Centuries later, as the medieval world merged into the Renaissance, markets chartered by church or liege lord thrived in the shadows of castles and cathedrals, the architectural symbols of the men who made and applied the law.

The most important commercial bazaars of the Middle Ages were the great fairs, large markets that were held on a regular basis, perhaps once a quarter or annually. The greatest lasted for weeks, and were so vital to the economy that in some instances church laws regarding usury were suspended for the duration of the fair. In twelfth- and thirteenth-century France, Champagne—then the crossroads of Europe—hosted a year-long cycle of fairs at Troyes, Provins, Lagny-sur-Marne, and Bar-sur-Aube, the first two towns being visited twice during the annual sequence.

In the Anglo-Saxon world in that period the most celebrated of these events was London's Bartholomew Fair, which survived long enough for Wordsworth to describe it in a poem composed at the dawn of the nineteenth century:

> *. . . What a hell*
> *For eyes and ears! What anarchy and din . . .*
> *. . . Albinos, painted Indians, Dwarfs,*
> *The Horse of knowledge, and the learned Pig,*
> *The Stone-eater, the man that swallows fire,*
> *Giants, Ventriloquists, the Invisible Girl,*
> *The Bust that speaks and moves its goggling eyes,*
> *The Wax-work, Clock-work, all the marvelous craft*
> *Of modern Merlins . . .*[1]

Entertainment had always been one element of the great fairs, but their primary purpose was to provide a location for merchants from all over the known world to hawk their wares: stud bulls, firkins of malmsey, honeycombs, dried figs, bolts of silken damask, Syrian glassware, and devotional objects trimmed with fool's gold. Barber-dentists and bloodletters would set up shop on the fairgrounds, and inevitably there would be miracle workers supported by battalions of shills drumming up business for sexual restoratives and cures for the dropsy, while pickpockets and cutpurses worked the crowd with quiet efficiency.

These affairs were rowdy and boozy and we can be sure that the bargaining was loud and furious. To find the modern equivalent you would need to travel to the Djemaa el Fna marketplace in Marrakech, where yogurt, sheepskins, cheap carpets, and chromolithographic likenesses of Mu'ammar al-Qaddafi and Saddam Hussein are noisily touted while snake charmers provide thrills for the tourists, dervishes dance themselves into a state

This painting of a village fair—known in the Low Countries as a kermesse—was painted by Jacob Savery I (1545–1602), a well-known Flemish painter based in Antwerp.

of ecstasy, and clusters of now somewhat domesticated Tuaregs, in from the desert, listen to the inspired ravings of mad holy men.

In medieval markets merchants traded only in commodities, and then only for spot cash. It was behind closed doors, in houses hung with painted signs advertising the money changer's trade, that the ancestors of today's investment bankers began to deal in securities—bonds written with quill pens on sheets of parchment and authenticated with wax seals applied by commoners and princes alike, perishable documents drawn up to finance voyages of exploration and holy wars, as well as more commonplace commercial undertakings.

Initially this world was in the hands of a relatively small number of powerful banking families, who handled every aspect of these elaborate transactions themselves, sometimes acting as tax collectors for church or state, occasionally underwriting the economy of an entire nation. Soon after the European discovery of the New World, this began to change as an increase in high-risk, long-distance trade led to the formation of joint-stock companies in which speculators of relatively modest means could invest. At about the same time, it became commonplace for European governments to float bonds to be supported by public subscription. Intermediaries between buyers and sellers were needed, and so a new profession came into being: brokering.

At first, the brokers who frequented the taverns and coffeehouses of cities like Amsterdam, London, and, in time, those of New York and Philadelphia, were a raffish lot, looked down upon by respectable bankers and polite society in general. This did not stop financiers and the gentry from availing themselves of the brokers' services, however, and the profession gained respect, if not respectability, as it began to regulate itself, abandoning at

Morrocco is a country of markets, ranging from the teeming souqs *of Tangier and Meknes to weekly gatherings in the isolated villages of the Rif Mountains that attract people from miles around. In this image, Berbers gather at a livestock sale.*

least some of the dubious practices that had been the norm at a time when insider trading was looked upon as felicitous rather than felonious. The fact that brokers proved capable of making fortunes for investors did nothing to hurt their cause.

Despite the rise of the broker, however, big bankers remained major players in the evolving securities markets. They were, after all, the main source of capital. And the story of the rise of stock exchanges cannot be told without reference to the growth of industry and the evolution of politics. If investing is compared, as it sometimes is, to wagering on racehorses, stockbrokers are the bookies (though traders execute the bets), big business provides the mounts, CEOs are the jockeys, and institutional investors are the heavy bettors. Their worlds are interdependent.

POWERS OF PERSUASION

It can be taken as a rule of thumb that market-driven economies lead, during the course of time, to greater and greater specialization of mercantile activity. The agora in Athens was the focus for every kind of commercial transaction, from selling olives by the jug to underwriting trading expeditions to Andalusia or the Black Sea. But by the time the great modern financial centers came to prominence, cities were becoming huge and the complexity of commerce was making it impracticable for butchers, fruit sellers, and money changers to meet in one place.

Often, however, the specialized marketplaces that emerged remained clustered together in adjacent neighborhoods. In New York City, for example, the principal stock exchanges have long been located at the southern tip of Manhattan, on a toe of land that is historically

Below: *In the 18th century, London's coffeehouses served as clubs and places of business where securities traders and others received their mail and attempted to sniff out bargains. This 1798 print shows one of the most famous gathering places, Lloyds, a favorite of insurance underwriters and the ancestral home of the most celebrated of all insurance companies, Lloyds of London.*

Opposite: *This 1908 photograph captures activity at the old curb market on Broad Street, near Wall, in New York City—sidewalk traders gathering to trade unlisted "over-the-counter" stocks. Eventually this market would move indoors and evolve into the American Stock Exchange (the AMEX).*

The Curb Market
Broad & Wall St. New York City
October, 1908

Modern markets are dependent upon electronic technology but still need the intervention of human traders. Here a currency dealer flashes a signal at a Tokyo foreign exchange brokerage.

famous for providing hospitality to markets of all kinds. Today the Fulton Fish Market still nestles in the shadow of the Wall Street skyscrapers, as does Chinatown, with its Cantonese merchants selling chicken gizzards and lotus roots. Nearby, a modified version of the old Orchard Street market—established a century ago by Jewish immigrants—offers bargains on everything from baby clothes to Palm Pilots, while the sidewalks near the World Trade Center are home to an informal gathering of street vendors offering fake Rolex watches, umbrellas, and incense.

In the first half of the twentieth century, the sliver of land to the west of Lower Broadway was home to the spice district, the wholesale shoe district, the fireworks district, and many other localized points of sale, including the huge Washington Retail Market—where you could find caviar, larks' tongues, and grizzly bear steaks—and the even larger Washington Wholesale Produce Market, which sprawled along the waterfront for more than a dozen blocks.

These were places where finding a bargain meant having to use one's powers of persuasion to the fullest. In the traditional marketplace, to make a sale or a purchase was to provide proof that all members of the human race are inherently endowed with histrionic talent. Mini-dramas were enacted whenever a chicken or a dozen eggs changed hands. If the ownership of a fat sow or a silk shawl was at stake, voices were likely to be raised, pleas to the gods might be uttered, eyes would be rolled heavenward. Toward the conclusion of such a transaction, terms like "bandit" and "highway robbery" were apt to be employed. At the end of a successful performance, both parties would come away feeling elated and victorious.

The art of hard-nosed bargaining persists in some parts of the world, but in most of the advanced industrial nations it is no longer an everyday necessity. With their institutionalized, chainwide sale prices, supermarkets and department stores have blunted the bargaining instinct. To find a bargain today, the customer goes to a discount store—or, increasingly, to a discount site on the Internet—where the terms are predetermined and not negotiable. Auctions, it's true, preserve some of the excitement of the traditional marketplace, but even at Christie's and Sotheby's, where Picassos and Rembrandts change hands for millions of dollars, the verbal give-and-take of the master haggler is missing.

Securities exchanges have followed the wider trend with regard to both specialization and eyeball-to-eyeball bargaining. Financial markets today are broken down into many components—treasury bonds, blue-chip stocks, low-cap companies, futures, options, et cetera—each with its own trading machinery. Back in the era of the coffeehouse exchanges, histrionic bargaining was the norm, and for centuries it remained so on most of the world's trading floors, where transactions were negotiated by sweating individuals packed shirt-front to shirtfront in pseudoclassical halls, all viscerally involved in closing the deals that moved the market. Some of these frenzied environments have survived the computer revolution and are celebrated in this volume. Others have disappeared forever.

As in the days of the Medici, market-shaping bargains of vast resonance are still struck behind closed doors by venture capitalists, merchant bankers, and buyout specialists. For most investors, however, the increasing complexity and automation of the markets has meant that profits are made by studying statistical trends and using a combination of experience and guesswork to determine when a given instrument should be bought or sold. In the digital age, this can come down to basing decisions upon elaborate, ever-changing computer models, or even handing over to the computer the decision to buy or sell.

Although retrofitted with the gadgetry of the information age, the New York Stock Exchange remains dedicated to the traditional trading-floor system in which bargains are struck face-to-face, just as they have been for thousands of years.

All this is a long way from the agora in Athens, yet it generates its own kind of excitement as institutional investors snap up vast quantities of shares in a few electronic gulps. And, as the price of Internet stocks helps drive the market, the Internet itself brings the securities marketplace into the office and into the home.

Marshall McLuhan forecast the advent of the global village as a by-product of modern communications. Deep-seated historical grudges and ethnic and cultural differences have prevented anything like a village pub atmosphere from developing, but the Internet has given us something that is beginning to approximate a global marketplace, in which billions—individuals as well as industrialists—can participate. Potentially it is our agora, the cyberplace in which art and ideas can flourish alongside commerce.

Whether the marketplace is in cyberspace, on the floor of the New York Stock Exchange, at a garage sale, in a European village square, an Arab *souq*, or Sotheby's auction rooms, it is always rooted in the concept of property. Someone has something to sell or exchange and some-

The big art auction houses, such as Christie's and Sotheby's, attract major headlines when paintings or other valuable objects are sold for seemingly outlandish sums. Here Christie's employees take telephone bids during a sale of Marilyn Monroe memorabilia, at which $1,267,000 was paid for the dress worn by the movie star while serenading President John F. Kennedy on the occasion of his birthday in 1962.

one else wants to become the owner of that something.

Property is actually a complex concept, a synonym for capital in the sense of wealth expressed in terms of possessions in the most far-reaching sense. For example, it is often remarked of a beautiful woman, "her face is her fortune." In the context of the entertainment industry or the world of high fashion, this can be true quite literally, physical beauty serving there as a form of property. Similarly, athletes and artists can build lucrative careers upon various kinds of talent, which too can be seen as property. And in this "information age," much is made of the highly refined concept of intellectual property: the ownership of ideas.

At the other extreme, on all continents and during many historical periods the notion of property has included the appalling treatment of human beings as possessions. For the most part, however, the concept falls between these extremities, and in its basic form, is easy enough to understand. The property for sale may be a castle or a cottage, a truck or a tricycle, a pig or a picture. The basis of the system's success is that everyone has something to sell and that potential buyers are to be found everywhere and anywhere.

Granted, not everyone starts from an equal position of ownership. Defenders of the free-market system like to point out, however, that anyone who is willing to exchange a fair day's work for a fair day's pay is a property owner, the property involved being the ability to perform a given task in return for payment. Thus, a person entering the workforce is provided with some degree of recompense that permits him or her to acquire other forms of property, on however modest a scale. This in turn creates a basis for establishing credit, another crucial market economy concept.

Relatively free of class-based, historical preconceptions about inherited wealth, America is a country that has been built on the presumption that every individual has the right to enjoy ownership of property. Today this principle is expressed in everything from government-backed mortgages to the powerful influence on the economy of pension funds that bring trillions of dollars into the market—wealth that is managed on behalf of the workers who are the beneficiaries of these funds, and who have thereby become to a significant extent the primary owners of American industry. This is a far cry from the liege and vassal situations from which modern capitalism evolved, and from the pro forma abuse of labor that marked the rise of industrial capitalism. The market system remains imperfect, but it works far better than any other we have seen since the Industrial Revolution. (The planned economies of totalitarian governments, though posing as benevolent collectivisms, have in fact been monopolies of a scope far beyond anything that has been known in democratic societies.)

The ungraspable complexity of the market economy guarantees that it will constantly evolve, and the pressures exerted by increased public participation in the higher reaches of the marketplace inevitably guide that evolution toward greater egalitarianism. Where practical economics is concerned, evolution is revolution from within, and it is precisely this that makes "in the market" an exciting place to be.

No corner of the globe remains entirely untouched by market activity. This satellite dish, capable of instantaneously downloading stock quotes from exchanges around the world, sits next to an old church in a quiet corn field in Raisting, Germany.

1 : The Beginnings of Financial Markets

3500 B.C. – 1000 A.D.

Once the site of a colossal statue, one of the Seven Wonders of the ancient world, the harbor of Rhodes—the namesake capital of an island celebrated in the early history of Mediterranean culture and commerce—is now guarded by the fort of St. Elmo and flanked by delicate sculptures of deer.

A marble statue in the collection of the Uffizi Gallery in Florence portrays the Roman deity Mercury as a muscular young athlete—naked except for his traditional winged cap and a discreet fig leaf—casually leaning against an ornamental tree as if determined to appear nonchalant while pausing briefly for breath during the course of a hectic day. Give him a pair of Nikes and he might almost be a young Wall Street warrior dallying in the locker room of the New York Athletic Club.

Dangling from one of Mercury's arms is a purse. This has nothing to do with fashions current at the Baths of Trajan during the period in which the statue was carved. Rather, it symbolizes the god's dominion over the world of trade and finance, an attribute of his that has been largely forgotten or overlooked by our culture, even though words like "merchant," "commerce," and "market" all derive from the same root as the name Mercurius.

Early in its history Rome suffered a series of severe grain shortages. Seeking a god who, properly propitiated, would put an end to this unhappy state of affairs, citizens of the burgeoning capital adopted Hermes— well established in the Greek world as a warrantor of luck and fecundity—and gave him a new name derived

For the Romans, Mercury, seen here in his traditional winged cap, was the protector of merchants.

from the Latin *merx*, meaning merchandise. A suitably handsome temple to Mercurius was built on the Aventine Hill, in the southern part of the city, and it became a gathering place for the local grain dealers. Eventually Mercury came to be recognized as the protector of merchants in general, not just traders in corn, and statues celebrating his potency as the patron of retailers and entrepreneurs were raised in business centers throughout the Roman world.

Potency is a key word here, since a glance at the origins of Mercury's Greek counterpart tells us that he was closely identified with sexual prowess at its most primal. Homer, it's true, had made Hermes somewhat respectable, transforming him into a kind of Olympian FedEx delivery man, sometimes assigned the additional task of conducting the dead across the river Styx. These duties had not always been part of his curriculum vitae, however. Long before Homer, Hermes had been perceived as belonging, like Priapus and Dionysus, to the cheerfully lewd gang that lived off the fruits of the land in Arcadia—a

Archeologists have calculated that the Colossus of Rhodes, destroyed by an earthquake in 226 B.C., was 156 feet high. It served as a beacon to sailors bringing cargoes into the Aegean Sea, but the belief that it stood astride the harbor entrance, as shown in this engraving by Fischer von Erlach, was the product of medieval myth.

sort of Aegean Appalachia—dallying with acquiescent wood nymphs and plying hillbilly girls with fortified beverages. Hermes was venerated as the protector of cattle and sheep. He was far less protective of shepherdesses.

It was Hermes' reputation for machismo that caught the attention of the Romans when they needed a prototype for a supernatural being to guarantee their harvests. Hermes/Mercurius was also understood to possess the gift of eloquence. Famously, too, he was a patron of music (its inventor, some claimed) and the protector of travelers. He was supposed to have possessed influence over dreams, and on top of all this, there was a strong tradition—ignored by the pious but celebrated by poets and storytellers—that Hermes/Mercurius was the god of thievery.

This last attribute aside, Mercury, then, was the embodiment of the archetypal money manager: a mensch capable of begetting huge profits; a silver-tongued salesman able to induce in clients Technicolor visions of the good life; and a tireless worker who still finds the time to exercise taste and civic responsibility as a fervent supporter of the arts.

EARLY TRADE

In his role as a patron of commerce, Mercury was the product of a place and time in which merchants were attaining new levels of power and prestige. That place was the Mediterranean basin in the millennium before the birth of Christ.

This is not to say that trade was unknown elsewhere or lacking in adherents before that era. About eight thousand years ago, soon after the ice sheets had receded from much of Europe, Asia, and North America, tribes of former hunters and foragers began to settle down here and there—in Anatolia, Mesopotamia, and parts of India and China—in order to cultivate crops and domesticate animals. Undoubtedly, these early farmers

bartered goods with their neighbors, perhaps even naming certain days—the eve of the full moon, say—and specific locations as fixed marketplaces.

The domestication of pack animals, the advent of pottery, and the ability of humans to work metals such as copper led to the rise of new kinds of trade over relatively long distances. Entrepreneurial adventurers opened up land routes over dangerous terrain to gain access to valuable natural resources, while others took to rivers, inland seas, and even the oceans in primitive boats in order to transport their wares from one place to another.

This satellite photograph shows the Tigris and Euphrates rivers draining into the Persian Gulf. Their flood plains nurtured the world's earliest cities.

All of this activity accelerated when clusters of farms evolved into villages, and again when, around 3500 B.C., the first cities appeared on the floodplains of the Tigris and Euphrates Rivers. The cities took root where they did because of their arable hinterlands, but the urban lifestyle could not be sustained by farming alone. It required imports and exports to support its needs.

By the third millennium B.C. it was commonplace for copper to be shipped, by sea and land, from Cyprus to Aleppo; timber and tin were carried by donkey caravan from Syria to the Sinai and beyond, while silver and textiles were hauled across the deserts of Mesopotamia to the great cities of the Euphrates. Merchants in Sumer and Babylon acted as middlemen between farmers and townspeople, dealing in wheat or date-sweetened beer, receiving payment in standard-size ingots of gold or silver. In the evolution of market economies, this form of payment was a major advance from the days in which barley was bartered for fish eggs and lapis lazuli for jade, but it had its limitations.

We all learned in grade school that salt was once used as money (the word "salary" is derived from the Latin word for salt), and all cultures seem to have employed commodity money at some time in their development. In parts of Southeast Asia, for example, measured quantities of rice were commonly used as currency. In other parts of the world, commodities as varied as dried fish, butter, cacao beans, and, of course, slaves have been employed as instruments of exchange. Every continent except Antarctica has seen cattle understood as an

From the time man first learned to domesticate animals, livestock have been looked upon as a form of wealth. This remains the case in places like Mali, in West Africa, where the cowherds seen here lead their cattle.

expression of wealth—dowries were often calculated in terms of so many head of oxen or reindeer—and this persists to the present in parts of Africa. (The importance of cattle as wealth has given us the word "chattel.")

Commodity cash reappears from time to time. For example, under wartime conditions, when coins and paper money lose the governmental underpinnings that sustain their value, easily portable goods such as chewing gum and chocolate are often called upon to replace them. In the latter phases of the Soviet Union's decline, blue jeans provided a more reliable form of exchange than rubles, and it is said that in Nicolae Ceausescu's Romania, cigarettes were the true coin of the realm.

The drawback with most commodity money is that it is perishable. Rice, for example, can be stored for a while but will rot unless consumed. Various cultures attempted to overcome this shortcoming by employing more durable items such as shells and sharks' teeth as mediums of exchange. The problem with most of these tokens was that they had no currency outside a relatively limited cultural and geographic orbit. The cowrie shell, acknowledged as a token of exchange from China to parts of Africa, was a partial exception to this. However, its value varied depending on geographic location. The farther you were from the beaches where the shell was found, the greater its purchasing power.

From the earliest times certain commodities—jewels, precious metals, and the like—were recognized almost everywhere as possessing intrinsic value. Ivory, amber, lapis lazuli, pearls, turquoise, jade, silver, and gold were commodities of this kind. Even if it had been possible for some Scandinavian chieftain to accumulate a treasure house full of dried cod, it would have done him very little good when it came time to doll up his eldest daughter so she could catch the eye of the most eligible bachelor in that neck of the fjord. Precious substances were another matter entirely. They could be employed as adornments and very visible symbols of wealth, and they could be stored indefinitely, subject on the downside only to the all-too-real threat of theft and pillage.

Since they were durable and their intrinsic worth was

recognized throughout the known world, gold, silver, and other quantifiable valuables were crucial to the evolution of the earliest market-driven economies. They did not guarantee the existence of such economies, however. In many places in ancient times, markets either did not exist beyond the rudimentary level of local barter, or else were tightly controlled by totalitarian regimes in which the ruler was sometimes considered to be a deity or descended from the gods, and thus above the petty restraints of such notions as fair trade. God-kings relied on military conquest and the forced or willing tribute of their subjects, which might be demanded in the form of crops, services, or even, in some places, the offering up of a family member for human sacrifice, the latter being thought an honor rather than a duty.

There were, of course, merchants—and wealthy ones—in the ancient Middle East. They were needed to import treasures to embellish the temples and palaces, as well as to provide the everyday necessities that sustained the state. However, they appear to have occupied relatively lowly, fixed positions on the caste ladder and had little influence on the evolution (or deliberate lack of evolution) of the culture, which typically was hierarchic and controlled from the top by the royal household and its attendant priesthood. The prevailing form of economic

(continued on page 36)

The Stele of Hammurabi, of which this is a detail, is famous as the repository of the earliest known legal code, much of which is concerned with matters such as credit and permissible rates of interest. Here Hammurabi, lord of Mesopotamia and Sumeria, is shown receiving a draft of the law from the sun god.

SPOT CASH:
TRADING IN TRADITIONAL AND MODERN MARKETS

In today's world of credit cards and electronic commerce, the notion of purchasing goods or services with coins or bank notes has come to seem almost quaint. It remains, however, the concept that underlies all business transactions. Credit in all its forms is just a way of postponing the day when the terms of a financial agreement must be met.

In the market squares of the ancient world, and at the fairs of the Middle Ages, barter and spot cash were the normal way of doing business, whether you wished to purchase a bushel of dates or have a tooth pulled. Cash payment is still the preferred way of doing business at millions of *souqs* and bazaars in developing nations around the world. Even in New York or Hong Kong there are still times when cash is needed to meet the exigencies of everyday life. For example, most fast food franchise operators see credit cards and checks as a nuisance—a way of holding up the line. Flea market dealers, like others with merchandise to sell in an informal setting, are apt to offer discounts in exchange for spot cash and the implicit opportunity to withhold the details of the sale from the scrutiny of the tax authorities. Back-room bookmakers and narcotics dealers of all stripes are said to

This busy corner of the Djemaa-al-Fna market, at the heart of the Moroccan city of Marrakech, gives some idea of what the great fairs of the Middle Ages must have been like: vibrant gatherings of merchants, food vendors, and street entertainers all battling for attention.

prefer payment in old-fashioned greenbacks, and the same goes for kids selling lemonade at the intersection of Pacific and Elm.

In the world of wholesale commerce, however, rolls of banknotes are seldom encountered today. Occasionally, spot payment will be demanded in order to guarantee immediate delivery of goods or commodities, though an unblemished reputation usually provides assurance of credit. In the great commodity exchanges of the world, cash on the barrel-head—once accounting for a significant portion of all trades—now plays a minor and almost insignificant role, with futures and options contracts making up the great majority of transactions.

Right: *Taken in the late nineteenth or early twentieth century, this hand-colored photograph of the* groote markt *in Nijmegen, Holland, shows a typical busy country market in the days when produce was still brought in on horse-drawn wagons and in hand carts.*

Below: *In this photograph from the 1940s, sidewalk merchants haggle over the price of diamonds in New York's Bowery district.*

Below right: *For a Mother's Day event, schoolchildren sell potted flowers to their contemporaries.*

Top: In France, soon after World War II, a young woman buys tickets for the National Lottery. Kiosks like this are a familiar sight in every French town.

Middle: This historic stereoscopic slide shows sidewalk fish sellers in Huai An, China, during the nineteenth century. It represents the kind of basic, spot cash market that might have been encountered at almost any historical period, and—despite the advent of canned food and convenience stores—street trade of this sort persists in many parts of the world.

Bottom: For all the sophistication of bar codes, debit cards, and industralized farming, a country as developed as the United States retains a strong grass-roots trading tradition. Within living memory, the Great Depression tested the resilience of that tradition as wholesale and retail customers alike gathered to buy from truck farmers at places like the Minneapolis Central Market, seen here in the 1930s.

Could the day be approaching when coins sweaty from the palm, or crumpled paper bills, will be disdained by street vendors of ice cream and hot dogs? Futurists predict that even small transactions of this sort will be replaced soon by some kind of electronic barter in which a snow cone with sprinkles will be exchanged for a digitized portion of your estimated net worth, perhaps with the aid of a bar code tattooed across your wrist.

In the meantime, when you're leaving the house, be sure not to forget those quarters, drachmas, francs, or rupees. Parking meters don't take plastic—yet. ■

Above: *Dot-coms, such as the auction site ebay, have brought the marketplace to the personal computer.*

Above center: *In Gouda, Holland, a cheese-maker and a customer seal a bargain with a handshake.*

Above right: *This aerial view of a floating market, in Bangkok, Thailand, illustrates the fact that markets are not always static places, defined by handcarts and stalls in fixed locations. Often, as in this case, merchants stay on the move, seeking out their customers rather than vice versa.*

Right: *The Fulton Fish Market is one of several traditional-style markets that thrive on the streets and quaysides of New York, within a few blocks of the banks and brokerages of Wall Street.*

Top: *Almost as old as commerce itself, the auction remains a popular way of selling everything from livestock to Impressionist paintings. Here an auctioneer is seen taking bids at the Humboldt County Fair in Northern California.*

Middle: *In the small villages of Malawi there is often not enough business in one locale to support the cost of maintaining a small shop. Traders pictured here set themselves up with a package of goods—used clothing, salt, sugar, maybe bicycle parts—and travel throughout a district. On Mondays the market is in Mtakataka, pictured here; on Wednesdays it is Kalindiza; and Fridays it will be held in Golomoti. Each market is ten to fifteen kilometres from the next— just far enough to ensure a new crop of potential customers.*

Bottom: *A bookmaker notes the details of a bet being placed at the Acadiana Downs racetrack in Lafayette, Louisiana.*

structure in many of these societies is thought to have been centralized redistribution, meaning that everything produced was owed to the ruler, who employed his court bureaucracy—typically ecclesiastical in character—to return pittances to his subjects.

Still, in at least some of these early Middle Eastern civilizations, there was room for the evolution of that prototypical capitalist, the moneylender. The earliest set of laws that we know of, prepared by or for King Hammurabi of Babylon around 1800 B.C., was largely concerned with credit and the rates of interest that could be charged on loans. (For the most part, these loans were made by individuals to other individuals, though sometimes they were issued on behalf of religious institutions such as temples.) On loans of silver, the maximum legal rate was 20 percent per annum. On loans of grain, the maximum approved rate was 33$\frac{1}{3}$ percent. To be legitimate, the agreements attending such loans had to be witnessed by a member of the court bureaucracy and recorded in writing on a clay tablet. Collateral would normally be in the form of property, but a borrower could also pledge his slaves, or even his wife and children. If someone pledged his eldest son, for example, this meant physically surrendering the child to the creditor until the loan was paid off. Should the boy die before the debt was settled, the creditor had the right to take back whatever he had loaned. Protection was provided to the borrower as well as to the lender, however. If, for example, the borrower was a farmer whose crop failed because of a natural disaster, such as a flood or a drought, interest on his loan would be automatically canceled for that year.

The system of credit was so advanced in Hammurabi's Babylon that the laws he laid down permitted the development of two financial institutions—named for the Egibi and Muradsu families—that were to all intents and purposes banks in the modern sense. They not only made loans, but also accepted deposits (on which they paid interest), transferred funds between accounts, and issued bills of exchange and letters of credit. All of this activity was, of course, subject to strict governmental control.

There is reason to think that similar financial institutions may well have evolved elsewhere in the region—in Assyria, for example. The one major exception was Egypt, where the political structure was so monolithic and the economic bureaucracy so authoritarian that there seems to have been little breathing room for commercial enterprise involving personal credit.

THE FIRST MARKET ECONOMIES

The early seagoing trading rivals of the Mediterranean region were the Phoenicians—whose political, cultural, and economic ties were to the monolithic civilizations of the Middle East—and the Hellenic peoples of the Aegean area, not only those who populated mainland Greece and the smaller Greek islands but also those who occupied the coastal regions of Anatolia, in what is now Turkish Asia Minor. Homer's *Odyssey* tells us about their skills and daring as seafarers, though nowhere does that epic hint that these brave mariners might ever have engaged in anything so banal as commerce. The *Iliad* explains why. Homer was writing about a feudal world that, in its way, was every bit as conservative as Egypt or Assyria, a world in which honor depended upon bravery in battle, warriors habitually interacted with gods, and trade was the province of lesser mortals who were not a fit subject for poetry.

In reality, commerce—in which cattle provided the standard unit of value (with gold considered a secondary currency)—played a crucial role in this world.

Among the great early sea-going Mediterranean merchants were the Phoenicians, who left amphorae and ointment jars such as these wherever they settled or traded.

A bridle made from cowrie shells is seen here on the skull of a horse in the chariot pit burial of a Chinese nobleman of the Western Zhou dynasty (1027–771 B.C.) excavated near Xi'an, China; cowrie shells were used as money in this period.

This Tjimba woman in Namibia wears a cowrie shell necklace, a sign of her senior status. Cowrie shells, once used as money by the Tjimba, are now seen as symbolic of wealth.

Disputes over fishing rights and the ownership of territory (the ultimate commodity) were translated into disputes of honor that provided the basis for invasions and sieges in which patriotic young men could perform feats of valor that would win them, or so they were encouraged to suppose, a niche in posterity's pantheon.

Despite their fundamental conservatism, however, early Aegean settlements differed greatly from the monolithic kingdoms that had evolved along the Nile and the Euphrates. For the most part, they were smallish states located in the fertile valleys and basins, which in that part of the world are separated from one another by moun-

tain ranges and arms of the sea. The society described by Homer (thought to be writing around 800 B.C.) was to a large extent rooted in the heroic Mycenaean period, which flourished from about 1550 B.C. to 1150 B.C. Homer might be compared to a later writer, Sir Thomas Malory, who, when spinning the story of King Arthur and the Knights of the Round Table from his vantage point in the fifteenth century, was recording an age of chivalry that was almost a living memory yet had, in fact, disappeared forever. And Homer, like Malory, was living on the threshold of an era that would see dramatic changes in values brought about by maritime exploration fueled by both the spirit of adventure and entrepreneurial capitalism.

In Homer's descriptions of the siege of Troy, we learn that even in that period of feudalism, small nations were ready to join together when faced with a common foe and bound by debts of honor. Small wonder, then, that a few centuries later, Aegean rulers and statesmen saw the advantage of forming alliances between newly emerging political entities that would facilitate the growth of trade throughout the region and beyond. There were conservative holdouts such as Sparta, but for the most part the leaders of city-states like Athens, Corinth, and Thebes—along with their neighbors across the Adriatic in Anatolia and Greek colonists in Southern Italy—saw the value of such alliances. They were linked by culture, by language (with some exceptions), and by the common need to present a united front when dealing with large and powerful neighbors to the east and across the Mediterranean.

In Homer's day and even later, kings still ruled some of the city-states. In other instances the monarchs had been supplanted by hereditary castes of nobles. With regard to both cases the small size of these political units, combined with the desirability of each collaborating with its neighbors, conspired to undermine tendencies toward monolithic totalitarianism. Despots were common enough, but it would have been almost impossible for an entity like Egypt to have arisen around the Aegean. Everything about the way Egypt had evolved pointed to the development of a society that, however sophisticated and refined it was in certain ways, remained essentially static. Everything about the evolution of civilization around the Aegean pushed it toward what might be called controlled instability. The battles for local dominance led to that instability. The need to come together in times of threat from superpowers to the east provided the incentive for control. The result was a dynamic culture that knit the squabbling city-states together,

This third century A.D. *Roman mosaic depicts Odysseus lashed to the mast as he listens to the seductive song of the Sirens. Homer's* Odyssey *never mentions commerce, seeing it as vulgar and anti-poetic, but Greek sailors took to the treacherous waters of the Mediterranean as much in search of wealth as of adventure.*

a culture that invited change (though always within the bounds of reason). This, combined with the necessity of encouraging expanded trade to supply the fledgling civilization with its growing material needs, created the ideal set of circumstances for the rise of a merchant class such as the world had not seen till then, and with that came the rise of democracy as we know it.

One crucially important innovation provided the final impetus that made all this possible, and that was the introduction of coinage, which was to become the keystone of future economic systems. (Interestingly, the word "coin" derives from the Latin *cuneus*, meaning wedge, as in the wedge-shaped form of the keystone of an arch.)

Small pieces of metal, precious and otherwise, had seen limited use as currency since prehistoric times, and some archeologists believe that true coinage was invented before 1000 B.C. The first European coins we can identify with certainty, however, were minted around 640 B.C. in Lydia, an Anatolian kingdom that had as its capital the city of Sardis, located on important trade routes and not far from several Aegean ports. The Lydians are thought to have been of mixed Aryan and Near Eastern stock. They spoke a European language and had strong cultural ties with their Greek neighbors, though there were important differences. Visitors from Greece were astonished, for example, by the freedom and autonomy enjoyed there by the women, who not only were permit-

Originating in Hellenic Sicily, this vase—a krater used to mix wine and water—is decorated with a scene depicting a fish merchant slicing a tuna for a waiting customer.

ted to have a say in the selection of their husbands but also worked as prostitutes to earn their dowries.

Lydia was blessed with large tracts of fertile land that had ensured its early prosperity, but around 687 B.C. King Gyges set out to turn his country into a maritime power. His descendants implemented his ambition, taking the port city of Smyrna for their own and launching raids against neighboring Greek cities in Asia Minor, so that soon the Lydians had amassed a considerable empire. They were not harsh masters, however. Rather than massacring the hard-working Greeks (except when absolutely necessary) or enslaving them, they permitted them to retain their own customs and internal rule, and to continue with their profitable Aegean trade, in return for which the vassal states were expected to pay a substantial tax.

The Lydians also began to extend their own trading activities and in this were greatly facilitated by the introduction of coins, minted at the royal workshops in Sardis. The first were made from electrum, a naturally occurring alloy of silver and gold. Carefully weighed slugs of this metal, each about the size of a large olive, were stamped with a lion's head, a process that produced an ovoid disc. These coins had two great advantages.

This gold coin, one of the earliest known, comes from the Anatolian city of Lydia on what is now Turkish soil. Dating from about 550 B.C., it may well have been struck during the reign of King Croesus, famous for fabulous riches and for the decadence that went along with them.

Because they represented a guaranteed standard, they discouraged cheating by unscrupulous merchants, who had learned to cut gold and silver with base metals. More importantly, they offered for the first time reliable units of precious metal that were small enough to be used for minor transactions—the payment of day wages, for example, or the purchase of grain by the bushel rather than by the shipload. Lydian coins were worth a fraction of a single percent of the smallest silver ingots previously in use. What the kings of Lydia did was in some ways comparable to (but far more radical than) what the brokerage firm Merrill Lynch succeeded in doing in the latter half of the twentieth century: they enabled the small investor to enter the marketplace. In doing so they created the first truly modern economy and proved that it could work.

Another significant innovation of the Lydian kings was the establishment, in the seventh century B.C., of a central retail market—an organized gathering of merchants in a single place where the public could find stalls that sold specialized goods—fruit, oil, incense—in quantities that suited the needs of individual families. Informal gatherings in which goods were bartered had

existed for thousands of years, but the architectural prominence given to the retail area in Sardis was an acknowledgment of the arrival of a market-driven economy.

The most famous of the Lydian monarchs, King Croesus, attained legendary status. By the time he ascended the throne, in 560 B.C., his empire was the most powerful in the region and, for its size, probably the wealthiest in the world. There is reason to suppose, too, that it was entering a period of advanced decadence. Always famous for their love of singing and dancing, the citizens of Sardis had become enamored of gambling (they are credited with the invention of dice), an activity that was greatly facilitated by the introduction of coins. And coins transformed the existing Lydian tradition of prostitution, which hitherto had had a religious basis, into a moneymaking institution that previously had been unknown to the ancient world. The first secular, full-service brothels of which we have any record were established in Sardis, apparently catering largely to the merchant classes. Along with sporting houses and games of chance, the Lydians developed a hunger for luxury goods. Croesus himself built richly decorated

In 1843 Ippolito Caffi depicted the gate of the agora in Athens, practically all that remained visible of the ancient world's most celebrated marketplace.

Dating from around 480 B.C., a short time before the Parthenon was built, this silver tetradrachm is symbolic of the wealth that underwrote the heroic age of Athenian civilization, that wealth being derived in large part from rich silver deposits found near the city.

palaces and celebrated his own reign by issuing coins of pure gold and silver. Eventually, though, he succumbed to the expansionist virus, launching an ill-conceived war against Cyrus of Persia. The Persian armies crushed the Lydian mercenaries and the state of Lydia ceased to be a political force. The influence of its pioneering culture, though, would continue to be felt.

The Greeks were great assimilators and lost no time in adopting Lydian innovations such as coinage and the concept of the centralized retail market. By the end of the sixth century B.C., coins of gold, silver, or electrum were being struck in many of the Greek states, and as their cities grew and prospered, cultural life became centered on the marketplace, known as the agora. In Athens it was a bustling place, incorporating several temples, the law courts, a library, and the mint. It was there that Socrates and other philosophers discussed ethics and ontology with their disciples. For a while it served as the meeting place for the city council, and it was the forum for debates and votes that decided whether or not citizens who had engendered the ire of their fellows should be subjected to banishment.

As time passed, the Athenian city council came to be democratized, largely because of the influence of commerce. Originally, noble birth was a requisite for holding office. By the sixth century B.C., that right became based on the size of one's landholdings. Although this sounds reactionary in today's terms, by the standards of the era

it was a huge step toward democracy, since it permitted successful merchants to have a say in government even if they were not descended from the nobles of the feudal era. That was significant because Athens, like other Greek states, had become a mercantile power. Its people still placed great stock in military prowess, and in times of war its armies were as fierce as those of their ancestors, but the wealth of the state was built primarily on trade rather than military conquest. In the era of Socrates, the trading status of Athens was guaranteed by a strong currency based in extensive deposits of silver discovered near the city. Throughout the Hellenic world, in what we now refer to as the classical period, it was a market-driven economy that financed the means and leisure time that permitted the evolution of a culture that could produce the poems of Sappho and Pindar, the plays of Sophocles and Aristophanes, the sculptures of Praxiteles, the philosophical writings of Plato and

This hull of a Greek sea-going ship from the 1st century B.C., in remarkably good condition, was raised from the bottom of the Mediterranean at Kyrenia.

The Temple at Delphi was among the most sacred of Greek holy places. It was also a repository of wealth that enabled its priests to function as officers of a kind of high-end investment bank.

Aristotle. None of these works was created for a god-king, or even for the exclusive enjoyment of an aristocratic elite. They were made available to everyone.

This is not to say that the Greek city-states—Athens included—were without major failings. Their economies depended upon slavery, which, though relatively benign in its implementation, was still appalling in its implications. And serfdom did not cushion these economies from the seesaw patterns of inflation and deflation that are familiar to the modern world. Credit was abused in ancient Greece, just as in contemporary Europe and America. The interest charged on loans was often astronomical, though

the laws of Solon, introduced in sixth-century B.C. Athens, did at least prohibit the use of citizens as collateral. Among the principal lenders were the priestly castes associated with various religious sites. The temple at Delphi, for example, perhaps the most famous in the Hellenic world, functioned as something resembling a central bank, the priests there using its wealth to make large loans to various political and commercial entities.

Still, trade was elevated to a new level of respectability, and the sense of honor that had once applied only to the values of the warrior caste now became attached to business too. A man's good name was as important to the merchant as it had been to the soldier. (And given the frequent skirmishes between states, not to mention the wars against the Persians, a merchant on one day might be a soldier the next.) Whether the owner of a fleet of trading ships or a walnut seller in the agora, a businessman would not survive for long if his word could not be trusted.

The success of coinage as a basis for trade was resisted for a while by conservative cultures such as Egypt and Phoenicia. The conquests of Alexander would put an end to that, and by the time his armies were sweeping through the Middle East, the use of coins was becoming established in other areas too.

MARKETS UNDER THE ROMANS

When those Roman grain merchants adopted Mercury as their patron god, around 500 B.C., they were probably familiar with Greek coins, but for a hundred years longer fines in Rome would be exacted in the form of cattle. The first Roman metallic coins were not issued until the fourth century B.C.; however, once the citizens of the

Juno Moneta was the principal Roman goddess and her responsibilities included issuing currency. Her temple in Rome doubled as the mint.

A shopkeeper, kept company by a couple of monkeys on the counter, hands bread, perhaps, to a child in this charming Roman relief from the second century A.D., found at Ostia, Rome's busy port at the mouth of the Tiber.

FINANCING THE GOVERNMENT:
TAXATION AND BONDS

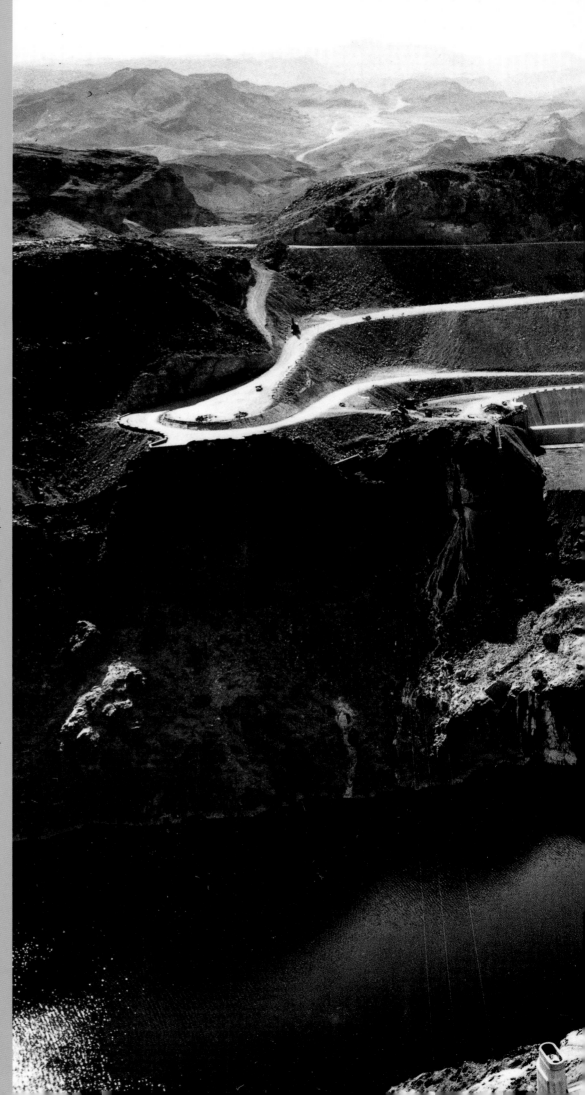

The principal means by which modern governments raise the capital to run the state is taxation, direct or indirect. Taxes on income, commerce, commodities, and so forth, are employed to sustain the various arms of government, as well as to supply services and infrastructure of all kinds. National budgets are based on estimates of tax revenue. Many kinds of unexpected circumstances can cause shortfalls, however, and when national debt arises the government is obliged to borrow from the private sector.

There is nothing new about this. In the Middle Ages, kings and princes went to bankers and moneylenders to finance wars and lavish lifestyles. Having exhausted their credit with one financier, it was not uncommon for sovereigns to exercise their monarchial rights by declaring themselves bankrupt before turning to another lender.

By the time proto-democracies began to emerge, there was ample precedent for governments to indulge in public borrowing, and, despite occasional hanky-panky, they generally did so with a reasonable degree of responsibility. When taxation did not cover their needs, the parliaments of nations like Britain and Holland—and later the United States Congress—turned to the moneyed classes for supplemental income, most often by floating bond issues. These were promissory notes by which the government contracted to pay back the amount borrowed, plus interest, at a specified future date. Sometimes the money raised was assigned to specific uses, and sometimes it was applied to the national debt.

726 feet high, 1,200 feet across, 660 feet thick at the base, Hoover Dam was one of the great engineering feats of the 1930s, a symbol of hope in the middle of the Great Depression, and a prime example of how investment by the U.S. Government—as represented by the Federal Bureau of Reclamation—could create jobs in the private sector, some five thousand men being employed when construction was at its peak.

Roman military triumphs meant that the empire could acquire wealth by pillage. This relief, from the Arch of Titus in Rome, depicts spoils being carried off after the Sack of Jerusalem.

Eternal City got started, they minted coins on a scale never seen before, and during Rome's long period of domination, its aurei and denarii became standard instruments of exchange from the British Isles to North Africa and parts of Asia. As the republic became an empire, however, and the empire declined, Roman coins lost much of their real value. Interest rates climbed, too, starting soon after the death of Augustus in A.D. 14 and continuing till the collapse of the empire. The Romans had developed the most sophisticated economy of the ancient world, but they did not discover any way to prevent inflation.

Although Mercury was the god of merchants, the goddess Juno was responsible for cash flow as such. As Juno Moneta (Juno the Warner) she was the principal goddess of the Roman state and thus in charge of important matters such as the issuing of coins. These were actually struck within the precincts of her temple, and it is from the word *moneta* that we derive the terms "mint" and "money." During the period of the republic, Roman coins were for the most part used with reasonable wisdom, though there were recurrent crises involving public and private debts. (One element contributing to the mood that precipitated the assassination of Julius Caesar was that he had provided relief to debtors, thus arousing the ire of upper-class loan sharks who also happened to be members of the Senate.)

The Romans may have lacked the Greeks' natural flair for commerce, but they pursued it assiduously and proved themselves to be able merchants on an international scale. The republic was built on markets and money.

(continued on page 52)

In modern times, almost the only time government bonds catch the imagination of the general public is when a nation is confronted with a major military conflict. During the First and Second World Wars, entertainment personalities went on the road to sell U.S. war bonds. Purchasing these became a patriotic duty, and it was partly with the capital raised by these issues that American industry was able to transform itself, twice in twenty-five years, into a war machine capable of producing armaments on an unprecedented scale.

In quieter periods, government issues generate few headlines outside of the business pages, although they are considered as solid an investment as any kind of security can be, for which reason they are sometimes referred to as "gilt-edged." Despite this colorful sobriquet, they are about as exciting as glue—but like glue they hold things together—in this case

important structural elements in the fiscal armature that supports the nation's economy.

U.S. Treasury bills are short-term securities issued at a discount and redeemable upon maturity at face value. Treasury notes—which have maturities of from two to ten years—are issued at face value, or close to it, and may be redeemed at face value upon maturity, but pay interest in the interim. Treasury bonds resemble notes but have longer maturities. When a new bill, note, or bond is issued, it is initially made available at an auction run by the Federal Reserve. The purchasers—mostly banks and other large financial institutions, domestic and foreign—then establish a retail price at which the securities are offered to smaller investors. The profits accruing from this resale can be considerable.

Dealers in government securities also trade among themselves, often for purposes of risk

Below left: Governments turn to citizens for voluntary investment in the state—usually in the form of bonds—in order to finance the national debt or, more dramatically, to help combat some major crisis such as all-out war. World War I was marked by horrific trench warfare and unprecedented carnage, the wounded receiving rough and ready treatment in field hospitals that were not always as hygienic as the one shown here. When it came to selling war bonds, the posters issued by the governments of combatant powers tended to emphasize patriotism and the "nobility" of warfare.

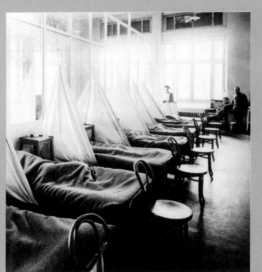

Above: *World War II saw millions of young men and women entering the armed services. Room and board for these recruits, along with training and transportation to the front, were among the many unusual expenses that war bonds helped pay for. Another was the cost of building billions of dollars worth of ships, tanks, and airplanes of all kinds, such as these Stearman trainers aboard which thousands of American and allied pilots won their wings. And millions of women entered the work force, taking on the task of helping fulfill government contracts for everything from parachutes to ammunition.*

Near left: *As in World War I, bond posters were not ashamed to play on the emotions of those who remained on the Home Front.*

Left: *The Doric façade of the Sub-Treasury Building at Wall and Broad Streets was draped with flags and bunting for this World War II Liberty Bond rally. The photograph was taken from the upper stories of the New York Stock Exchange.*

management. Speculators get in on the act by taking up positions in the Treasury futures and options market in the hope of making a killing on the shifts in value that occur as various issues move toward maturity.

From the retail investor's point of view, then, "Treasurys" offer an unparalleled degree of financial stability. From the market professional's point of view they have a special role to play as an indicator of confidence in the economy. When prudent investors sense an economic slowdown, they tend to turn to Treasurys, sending prices up and yields down in the process.

Under certain circumstances, large institutional investors may actually be able to use their positions in Treasurys to influence government policy by importuning the Federal Reserve Board to raise or lower interest rates. Such a situation is reputed to have arisen in the 1990s, during President Clinton's first term in office, when a loosely allied group of fund managers, referred to on Wall Street as the bond vigilantes, are said by some observers to have been able to pressure the Fed—quite legally—by buying and selling Treasurys on a scale that had alternately inflationary and deflationary implications. Advocates of this theory argue that the Clinton administration was persuaded by such pressure to adopt the prudent policies that led to a balanced federal budget. When a government enters the marketplace, then—and despite the fact that it sets many of the rules—it may become subject to some of the same influences that are brought to bear on any business in the private sector.

The money raised by the sale of Treasurys also brings the government into contact with the private sector in that it is used—along with revenues from taxation and other sources—not only to directly support the various branches of government, the military, and the civil service, but also to enter into transactions with private and joint stock companies in order to purchase everything from trucks for the postal service to medical supplies to meet states of emergency at home and abroad. Government funds go towards underwriting

certain kinds of mortgages, as well as to supporting college research programs that are likely to have a future bearing on innovation in many fields of business, from medicine to communications.

Most controversially, the government is the principal client of the companies that make up the aerospace and defense industries. These companies are vital to the overall health of the economy, and their products are crucial to the security of the nation and its allies. There will always be disagreement, however, about just how much defense is enough.

As early as the 1950s, President Eisenhower warned of the dangers implicit in the co-dependencies of the military-industrial complex. Abuses of the relationship between military officials and commercial entities—big and small—within the aerospace and defense industries continue to be a problem. The nature of the beast, however, is such that both the armed services and the branches of industry they deal with are subject to the scrutiny of elected representatives of the people. Ultimately, governmental spending policies can be addressed with votes. ■

Above: *In peacetime, defense spending and military research remain a government priority. Here S-3 Vikings of the U.S. Navy are seen flying in formation during a training exercise.*

Top *The U.S. Government has the responsibility of maintaining scores of National Parks, National Beaches, and National Recreation Areas. Seen here, Bryce Canyon National Park in Utah.*

Near right: *This gigantic wind tunnel was built for the National Aeronautics and Space Administration (NASA) to test large aerodynamic forms involved in supersonic flight.*

Right: *Government participation, in the form of technical support from the Department of Energy's Sandia National Laboratories, has made it possible for the Navaho Tribal Utility Authority to utilize photovoltaic generating systems to bring clean electrical energy to isolated parts of the Navaho reservations.*

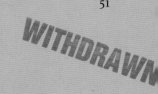

Below: *The U.S. Space Program involves the participation of hundreds of companies and thousands of individuals in the private sector, but is essentially dependent upon government funding.*

Bottom center: *The National Weather Service helps the economy in many ways, such as providing long-range forecasts for farmers and issuing warnings of potentially catastrophic storms.*

Bottom right: *The U.S. Interstate system was funded largely with federal money made available under legislation passed during the Eisenhower administration.*

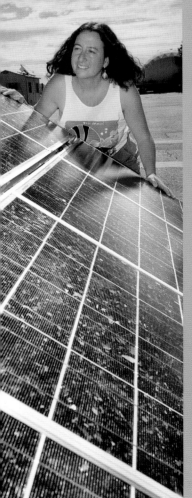

With the Colosseum at its center, this view of Rome at the height of imperial power, in the first century A.D., helps us visualize the commercial and military strength that made her a world capital for a full quarter of a millennium.

Even as the old constitution broke down, Julius Caesar was still very much in favor of encouraging a market economy, but it was the success of his campaigns of conquest, and those of Pompey and the other generals, that turned the tide against the Roman continuation of the Greek mercantile tradition. As Rome's legions swept through Europe and beyond, it became apparent that, by comparison with honest trading, looting and pillage offered a more direct route to the acquisition of wealth and luxuries. And most of the emperors who followed Julius Caesar were thoroughly addicted to wealth and luxuries, as were their more affluent subjects.

The Roman world never entirely abandoned the idea of a market-driven economy. During the period of the empire, however, the concept became subordinate to the workings of an imperial dominion that in many ways was similar to those that had existed in old-style monolithic kingdoms. (Some emperors, including Caligula and Diocletian, followed the example of the pharaohs by declaring themselves god-kings.) When conquest could not be relied on to supply wealth, there was always tribute and taxation, the latter often levied on the merchants and small manufacturers upon whose commercial vitality the state depended.

The emperors could not do away with metal coinage—it was far too well established by then—but they certainly had the power to interfere with it. Nero began that trend when he cut the silver content of the denarius from 100 percent to 90 percent, and he did much the same with the gold content of the aureus. Later emperors debased the coinage even further, often in order to pay the army on whose support their authority depended. Each debasement caused a corresponding rise in the real price of goods and services—in short, inflation.

By the time Constantine I came to power, in A.D. 324, the empire's economy was in ruins. Constantine not only permitted the practice of Christianity, till then subject to violent persecution, but also made it the official religion of the state. This provided him with an excuse

Rome's network of roads, which stretched from the British Isles to the Persian Gulf, was built in order to enable the Roman legions to maintain control throughout the empire. The roads also served as a tremendous stimulus to trade.

This colossal marble head of the Emperor Constantine I is a fragment of a statue that once stood more than 35 feet high. It was Constantine who made Christianity Rome's official religion and moved the capital to Constantinople, laying the foundations for the Byzantine Empire.

to plunder the immensely wealthy pagan temples that existed all over the Roman world, thus replenishing the imperial coffers and helping provide himself with the means to carry out successfully his plan of moving the capital of the empire east to Byzantium, henceforth to be known as Constantinople. Long an important trading center, Constantinople would thrive for more than a millennium as the capital of the Byzantine Empire. Meanwhile, marauding Germanic hordes, aided by continued Roman mismanagement and the collapse of the currency, would plunge Europe into the so-called Dark Ages, giving rise to another feudal era from which modern capitalism would not begin to emerge for almost a thousand years.

China developed independently of the chain of civilizations that arose around the Mediterranean, in Mesopotamia, North Africa, and Europe. For centuries, contact between the two worlds was limited to tenuous links such as the Silk Road—the name given to the harsh and dangerous route across central Asia by means of which precious commodities were transported between Luoyang and centers such as Damascus and Constantinople.

CHINA AND SOUTHEAST ASIA

Chinese civilization had its origins on the fertile plain between the mountains edging the Mongolian plateau and the Yellow Sea. Shang China, where a single dynasty ruled from about 1800 B.C. until sometime in the eleventh century B.C., seems to have come into existence with very little, if any, contact with the great civilizations to the west. Doubtless there was considerable trade within the borders of the state—which occupied only a tiny portion of modern China—but the world ruled by the Shang kings was remarkably self-contained, its artifacts already distinctly Chinese in character. The name

they gave their land was Chung-kuo, which can be translated as "the Place at the Center of the Universe."

One form of import in demand was the cowrie shell, which was brought by the ton from the South China Sea, several hundred miles away. Said to have been valued because of their resemblance to female genitalia, these shells were used as money. When there was a shortage of actual shells, facsimiles were made from bronze, jade, and other materials.

Around the sixth century B.C., during the Chou period, Chinese silks began to appear in the Mediterranean region. It is assumed that they were carried there along what came to be known as the Silk Road. This forbidding highway ran north of the Himalayas through dauntingly bleak terrain controlled by the nomads of the steppes, whose speedy horses, war chariots, spears, and bows and arrows made them feared opponents. The merchant who was prepared to brave contact with these characters earned every *wuzhu* or drachma that came his way.

In the early days the Chinese were not, in fact, shipping silk west to realize a profit. Rather, they were using it, along with food and the occasional princess, to barter with the barbarians who menaced their northern and western borders. The bargain struck was silk, rice, and highborn maidens in exchange for being left in peace, the assumption being that the tribesmen of the steppes might be distracted from sacking and plundering if they were bought off. It seems probable, therefore, that the nomads themselves initiated the trading process.

Chinese silk became highly valued in Europe. Spices, furs, and bronze objects also traveled from the Far East to the Mediterranean lands. It is surmised that in return, Westerners traded gold and silver, along with ivory, gemstones, and glass vessels.

Also during the Chou period, the first true Chinese coinage was introduced.[2] Made of bronze, the earliest coins took the form of tiny spades and knives. Before long, these rather awkward shapes, which must have ripped the silk lining of many a purse, were replaced by circular coins with holes in the center and etched with calligraphic markings, a type that would survive for more than two thousand years.

China remained essentially inward looking, but by the Han dynasty (206 B.C.–A.D. 220) it could not avoid increased contact with the West and with India, which was exporting Buddhism along with a variety of exotic commodities, such as incense and ivory. During this period a highly centralized government, which had exercised tight control over the economy, gave way to a more relaxed system that permitted trade within China to thrive. In particular, merchants began to exploit the resources of the southern sections of China, sending pearls, gingerroot, cinnamon, and tortoiseshells north by river and by coastal routes. Others traveled along the portions of the Silk Road that were being colonized by China to bring back jade and horses. By now the commercial possibilities of trade with the West were becoming appreciated. One Han envoy, Chang-Chi'en, managed to travel as far as Bactria, just short of the Caspian Sea. A healthy entrepreneurial tradition had been born.

Merchant adventurers were not confined to China. European demand for the spices of the East and other luxuries led Indian maritime traders to undertake expeditions to the tropics of Southeast Asia, visiting Thailand, Cambodia, Vietnam, Sumatra, Java, and the Philippines, each round-trip taking more than a year to complete because of dependence upon the seasonal prevailing winds.

Although visited from time to time by Chinese explorers, especially after Han dynasty influence spread into Korea, the islands of Japan remained relatively isolated, a land of squabbling fiefdoms that would not be unified until the seventh century A.D. Essentially, though, the key Asian trading routes were already in use by the end of the Han dynasty if not before, and patterns of commerce would not change greatly until European explorers found their own routes to the Far East, by way of the Cape of Good Hope, fifteen hundred years later.

To a large extent the sociopolitical climate of Asia did not change much during those centuries. Islam spread into India and the Mongols invaded China, but the underlying cultures did not undergo radical changes. In India a strictly codified caste system had emerged, and well-delineated class systems existed in most parts of Asia. Almost everywhere, room was found for the establishment of a merchant class, which, while perhaps not accepted on equal terms by the nobles and lesser aristocrats, was able to distance itself from the peasantry that constituted the vast majority of the populace. Access to capital left these merchants relatively free to create highly stratified social mores of their own, comparable to but quite distinct from those associated with hereditary privilege.

Coinage was introduced in China simultaneously with its invention in Europe. This early example combines knife symbolism—long associated with wealth—with the Chinese tradition of circular coins pierced with square holes.

S. GIORGIO. M

2 : The Rise of Traders, Bankers, and Merchant Princes

1000–1720

This seventeenth-century panorama shows Venice toward the end of its golden age as one of the great trading and banking cities of Europe, a bustling port where the exotic commodities of the Orient were brought for distribution to the burgeoning market economies of the West.

The final collapse of the Roman Empire, during the fifth century A.D., left Europe fragmented and divided up among a motley array of petty rulers—Saxons, Visigoths, Jutes, and the like—each of whom controlled his own territory, usually by means of brutal displays of force. The great road network built by the Romans fell into disrepair. Only the bravest dared use the established trade routes, because bandits infested the highways and the seas were swarming with pirates. In addition, by the seventh century the rise of Islam had cut Europe off from direct contact with Africa and much of the Middle East.

Lacking the guarantees a strong central government could provide, coinage, with the exception of the gold solidus of Byzantium, lost much of its utility as a form of international exchange. The Roman gold pieces that remained were hoarded for their value as bullion. Many were melted down to create jewelry for the nobility or ornamental objects for the increasingly wealthy churches. The crude coins that were minted in various European principalities were generally struck from silver or base metals such as copper. With cash playing a greatly diminished role in the economy, many people were reduced to serfdom, since there was no established way of paying for their services. Under these circumstances, the market system that had been built up in the West over the previous twelve hundred years was virtually destroyed. Luxury goods were still in demand by both earthly rulers and princes of the cloth, and doubtless there were men prepared to take any risk in order to supply that demand; but for the most part, trade regressed to the age of barter as a new feudalism took hold.

This feudal age would give rise to historical figures of heroic proportions—Charlemagne, for example (who introduced an important currency based on a silver coin that evolved into the penny)—but the great majority of its leaders were concerned with conquests and power struggles rather than with encouraging commerce.

A strong influence on the rebirth of trade during the Middle Ages was the cult of the pilgrim. Sacred sites such as Canterbury (its cathedral shown at left) drew legions of worshipers, who in turn attracted merchants of all kinds. A stained glass window from the church (below) shows pilgrims en route, c. 1280, about a century before Chaucer wrote his Canterbury Tales.

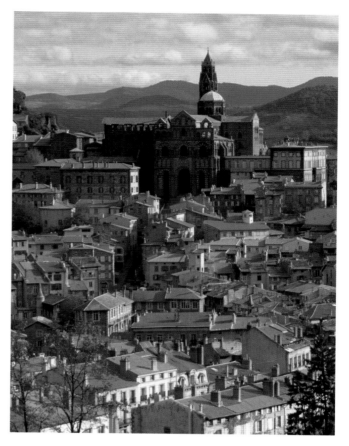

Above: *This open-air market in Florence is a reminder of the restless energy that made the city such a dynamic commercial center as the Middle Ages gave way to the Renaissance.*

Right: *High in France's volcanic Massif Central, the cathedral city of Le Puy-en-Velay was another major pilgrimage site.*

Trade between distant places persisted, though in a marginalized way, until, slowly, starting around the eleventh century, it began to regain something of its former importance. This resumption of mercantile activity had a good deal to do with the fact that the peoples of Europe shared a common church and beliefs (and common enemies too). Glorious cathedrals were rising, some housing holy relics that became the objects of pilgrimage, so that throngs of the faithful would descend every year on the sites of major shrines, such as Santiago de Compostela in northwestern Spain. Pilgrimages encouraged rulers, whose authority depended on upholding the faith, to offer travelers some degree of protection. This in turn helped make it possible to reestablish trade routes, and it encouraged the consolidation of institutions such as the great annual and quarterly fairs, which lasted for days and even weeks at a time, to provide venues for commerce of all kinds.

Feudal lords were not opposed to trade. They were simply uninterested in it except to the extent that it could be taxed and could supply them with luxuries. Their wealth was dependent upon land and the tribute due to them from their serfs and vassals. The church itself had become a great landowner and expected to receive tithes from nobles and commoners alike. Trade and mercantile adventure became the province of a new middle class that was beginning to emerge in towns like Florence, Genoa, Milan, Ulm, Nuremberg, Hamburg, Bergen, Ghent, Bruges, Antwerp, London, and Venice (the latter being one of the first to emerge because of its easily defensible location and its special relationship with Byzantium). Tiny by today's standards, these urban centers grew in importance largely as a consequence of the inability of the feudal world's basically rural economy to find a useful place for everyone in a population that was increasing rapidly. In some cases, towns were founded by royal or noble families looking for a way to utilize this manpower surplus. In other instances, they were sanctuaries where runaway serfs could find refuge from their former masters.

One of the first great Italian banking centers was Siena, which reached the peak of its power and influence in the latter part of the twelfth century, before being eclipsed by Florence. Pictured in a painting by Vincenzo Rustici is the procession to celebrate Palio, *a semiannual horse race, which continues to be a major tourist attraction today.*

Gradually these overgrown villages, surrounded by defensive walls, evolved into economic and political entities that could not be ignored as their citizens made themselves useful by becoming weavers and coopers and masons and merchants of various sorts. Larger towns were often the seats of bishoprics, so that during the great age of cathedral building the church provided a considerable impetus for trade. At the same time, city fathers and ecclesiastical leaders often found themselves at odds over the degree of liberty that should be allowed to ordinary citizens, and over the ultimate allegiance of those townspeople.

Certain cities, Venice in particular, profited from the most conspicuous of all feudal follies, the Crusades. At the end of the twelfth century, as the Fourth Crusade was being planned, the doge of Venice promised a fleet of ships on condition that the Crusaders take time out to subdue some troublesome Dalmatian neighbors. This was agreed to, so that when, in 1204, the Crusaders elected to postpone their sacred campaign against Islam in favor of sacking Constantinople, the Venetians were on hand to exploit the situation, taking on a large portion of the commercial interests of the Byzantine Empire, including access to the profitable spice routes to the east.

Venice had the military clout to declare itself a republic, independent of royal masters. Most medieval towns were subject to some feudal lord who had granted a charter and limited political privileges. In time, though, many were permitted to exercise a good deal of autonomy, becoming largely self-governing. Like the city-states of the classical Greek world, they evolved distinctive cultures and formed alliances for mutual protection, often organizing themselves into confederations such as the Hanseatic League, which for centuries dominated mercantile activity around the Baltic. These confederations sent out paramilitary forces to keep the trade routes open, taxing traffic to pay for this basic law enforcement.

Up to a certain point, cities were permitted to grow because neighboring feudal lords learned to overlook a modest degree of independence in exchange for the services the townspeople could provide, especially as the residences of nobles evolved from fortified wooden halls into grandly appointed stone castles. As urban centers grew richer and more independent, however, many feudal lords became concerned and attempted to suppress the liberty of the townspeople by force. The more powerful cities could raise their own armies and were prepared to resist. In the twelfth century, for example, a fierce campaign was waged between the forces of the Holy Roman Emperor Frederick Barbarossa and the already well-established towns of Lombardy. Barbarossa was never able to completely subdue the townspeople and, in 1183, was obliged to grant a great deal of independent authority to the Lombard League. He recognized the confederation as what might be described as a nominal fiefdom, an entity promising fealty, but little else, to the empire—a compromise that satisfied honor on both sides.

Northern Italian towns, such as Florence, Siena, Pisa, Mantua, Milan, and others (along with port cities like Genoa and Venice), were on the verge of establishing a full-fledged mercantile culture, with a dominant merchant caste at the helm. They were, in short, evolving into modern cities with identities that depended on their commercial specializations rather than on being the site of a shrine or the seat of a bishopric.

One of the commercial specializations that arose in the Italian cities was banking. At the most basic level this consisted of moneylending and money changing. On a higher plane, however, came the emergence of what we would now call investment bankers, or venture capitalists—entrepreneurial figures who discovered new ways to use money to expand existing forms of commerce into areas that would permit true market-driven economies to take shape.

These Italian bankers were successors to Jewish merchants, who had played a significant role in the financial world in the early Middle Ages, and to the Knights Templars. In many parts of Europe Jews had been driven to earning a living by lending money and demanding interest because other forms of trade were forbidden to them. In England, for example, Jewish bankers came to prominence in the eleventh century, following the Norman Conquest. For almost two hundred years they were the leading source of credit in London and other English cities. Propaganda associated with the Crusades turned public opinion against them, however, and they became subject to ruinous taxes and organized anti-Semitism. In 1290 Edward I expelled all Jews who would not submit to conversion to Christianity.

The Knights Templars were members of a feudal order, forged in the Crusades and headquartered in Jerusalem, who from the twelfth century acted as treasurers and money brokers to the courts and nobility of Europe. Dealing with the Templars, a member of the landed gentry could take out a mortgage in France and

In the Middle Ages and early Renaissance, cities with common political and commercial interests often formed confederations such as northern Germany's Hanseatic League. Shown here are the seals of several important German trading centers affixed to this document setting down the terms of their association.

pick up Byzantine gold coins guaranteed by that bond in Cyprus or Palestine—wherever the credit was needed. The Templars did much to protect the trade routes along which they transported bullion and other valuables to their castle strongholds. They also served as accountants and financial advisers to kings and princes.

Despite the fact that all members of the order took vows of poverty and chastity, the Knights Templars eventually became too wealthy for their own good, a sitting target for a ruler with an eye for easy money. In 1295 Philip IV of France—Philip the Fair—decided to manage his financial affairs without the advice of the Templars and removed his reserves from their safe-keeping to the Louvre. This was a prelude to a ruthless campaign to destroy the knights and seize their assets. Since the order's strongholds were spread all over the known world, from England to the Near East, Philip decided against waging war and instead employed the expedient of arresting the Templars' leaders on trumped-up charges that included encouraging ped-erasty, engaging in sex with the corpses of noblewomen, consorting with Muslims, and, worst of all, usury. On a spring day in 1310, fifty-four elders of the order were taken to the outskirts of Paris and burned at the stake.

THE RISE OF BANKING

The vacuum left by the demise of this financial empire provided an opportunity for entrepreneurs of a less exalted social status to exploit. By the late thirteenth century, families of Italian speculators, such as the Bardi and Peruzzi of Florence, had begun to make their mark in the world as merchant bankers, dealing in cash, commodities, and bills of exchange that guaranteed the payment of accounts in distant markets without the necessity of shipping coin or bullion. Usually these mer-chant bankers were exporter-importers themselves, with representatives scattered along various trade routes. The greatest of the Italian banking houses had offices—often run by family members—in a dozen or more urban centers, from London and the burgeoning cities of the

Low Countries to Venice in the east. This facilitated their ability to perform a variety of financial services on an international scale, for both merchants and feudal lords. In 1317, for example, the pope contracted with the Bardi and Peruzzi families to have monies due to the Vatican from the Apostolic Chancery of England deposited at the banks' London branches. The actual cash remained in London, to be used as capital there, while a bill of exchange was forwarded to Rome, where the pope was paid in cash from the banks' Italian reserves.

The use of guaranteed bills of exchange made for a more secure way of transferring money over distances, given that, although safety of travel had improved, highway bandits were still very much a fact of life, as we know from the Robin Hood legends. At the same time, bills of exchange functioned as a precursor of paper money and had the effect of helping put more cash into circulation.

The way it worked was as follows. Funds deposited with the bank for safekeeping created a pool of assets. The bank drew upon this reservoir of liquidity to make loans to other customers. Those loans circulated (at a

With the rise of banking in Italy came the beginnings of modern bookkeeping practices, facilitated by the adoption of Arabic numerals. Shown here is a register kept by the Milan branch of the Medici bank in the fifteenth century.

Independent banking centers like Florence and Venice (the latter seen here in an 1982 aerial view) achieved a level of political power rivaling that of hereditary monarchies.

premium) from city to city by means of bills of exchange. In effect, then, several different parties were able to utilize the bank's reserves at the same time. As long as the pool of assets remained relatively stable (meaning that sufficient deposits must be retained in order to cover probable withdrawals), then the bank was in a position to continue to issue credit, often in the form of its own paper. Thus, by financial sleight of hand, 20 ducats could be made to do the work of 100.

This was an enormous stimulus to trade. The bankers themselves frequently took advantage of the equity in their reserves to deal in commodities of all kinds. They also charged for safeguarding a depositor's wealth and for facilitating the transfer of credit from one place to another.

Bills of exchange had another important function. They enabled bankers, on a technicality, to maneuver around the church's strict prohibitions against usury, an offense punishable by excommunication. According to Roman Catholic doctrine, usury occurred only when a profit was made on the repayment of a loan. Bills of exchange, it was argued, were not loans. They were contracts between businessmen that enabled transactions of all kinds. Profits were deemed to be from foreign exchange fees and from payment for the bankers' services in facilitating the transfer of funds. Any suggestion that interest was being paid on a loan was thus circumvented.[3]

The growing confidence of the emerging merchant class was symbolized in the thirteenth century by the minting of the first universally accepted gold coins to be issued in the West since Roman times. Not surprisingly, these were put into circulation by the three most prosperous market economies of the day, Florence, Genoa, and Venice.

The medieval merchant banker, then, was a person of some consequence. He could afford to live in a fine house—a palace, even—and his family could dress in silks from the East, his wife's fingers adorned with gold rings, his daughters' hair sewn with pearls. As mercantile activity thrived, the wealthiest cities became architectural jewels such as had not been seen in the West in almost a thousand years. In Florence, Genoa, Venice, and Pisa, too, as well as in Valencia and Barcelona, the new buildings included halls specially erected to house trading floors. There were as yet no joint-stock companies, no shares to be traded (most of the commerce was in everyday commodities), but it was in places like these that the modern exchange had its roots.

Feudal lords might still despise the banker as a parvenu, but nobles and monarchs alike were quick to grant him an audience when they suspected that the traditional tributary system might not be generating sufficient rev-

Florence's wealth was rooted in its importance as a manufacturing center, especially of fine cloth. Its banking families learned to parlay the credit implicit in this wealth into an entirely new concept of finance that helped shape modern market economies.

enue to satisfy the increasingly expensive requirements of keeping up with the neighboring princelings on the fields of chivalry. Dealing with the mighty of the feudal world could add luster to a banker's reputation, but it could also lead to ruin, since kings and princes were apt to renege on their debts without fear of retribution. For that reason, the rates of interest demanded of royal borrowers were often far higher than those asked of commercial borrowers. To give a single instance, when Charles VIII of France decided to launch an attack on the kingdom of Naples in 1494, the only bank that would provide him with credit was the house of Sauli, a prominent Genoa firm. The loans they offered are said to have carried interest rates as high as 100 percent per year.

Lombard bankers financed the military adventures of Edward I of England, enabling him to build a chain of castles to keep the unruly Welsh in place. In return, these bankers were given special privileges that enabled them to gain a dominant position as exporters of English wool, the nation's single most important commodity. Edward, however, was adept at playing one Italian against another, so that some banker was always primed to ante up

Like other great banking families of the period, the Fuggers of Bavaria became industrialists on the side, investing heavily in enterprises such as this labor-intensive Bohemian silver mine.

Painted in 1529 by Hans Maler von Schwarz, Wolfgang Ronner was a gifted protégé of the Fuggers, representing them in Carinthia and the Tyrol, where the family had extensive mining interests. The upside-down letter in his hand shows the Fugger trademark.

the requisite funds for the next fortress, however slim the chance of being repaid might be. Banking families whose members balked at this treatment, such as the Frescobaldi—former royal favorites—were simply banished from the realm and thereby driven out of business.

This did not discourage the next generation of Italian bankers from providing Edward's grandson, Edward III, with the means to pursue the opening skirmishes of the Hundred Years' War. Despite their generous support, the young king promptly exceeded his means, extricating himself from this predicament by the simple expedient of declaring himself bankrupt. Within a half dozen

years, this act of feudal arrogance had totally destroyed the great Florentine banks of the Peruzzi and the Bardi.

The demise of these institutions corresponded with the arrival of the Black Death, which swept through Europe, climaxing in 1348 and wreaking its greatest devastation in towns and cities where people were crowded together under horribly unsanitary conditions. It would take years for the burgeoning merchant society to recoup its strength and recover its chutzpah, but when it did so it would help inaugurate one of the greatest periods in the history of Western culture.

One innovation that would contribute greatly to the evolution of the Renaissance had been seized upon and enthusiastically propagated by investment bankers and merchants as early as the thirteenth century. This was the

(continued on page 72)

DIRECT INVESTMENT:
VENTURE CAPITALISTS

The business plan that the fledgling Sun Microsystems team presented to John Doerr was just three pages long, but it contained all the information he needed in order to make a decision, and the cash-hungry startup was soon the recipient of the funds it needed to take its first step towards Nasdaq stardom.

Doerr is the most celebrated partner in Silicon Valley's best-known venture capital operation, Kleiner Perkins Caulfield & Byers. Sun is just one of his success stories. Other companies he has backed include Compaq, Lotus, Genentech, Netscape, Amazon.com, Excite, Google, WebMD, and Handspring. How does he pick winners like these? "Find the right team," is the answer he regularly offers to interviewers. In a market saturated with talent, technology, ideas, entre-preneurs—and even available funding—a viable niche and the right mix of people, he believes, are what really count.

There was a time, not long ago, when it seemed all too easy to come up with that magic combination. The Internet in particular had spawned business conditions in which infant companies receiving the proper nurture were putting on corporate muscle so fast they were evolving almost overnight into, well, very big toddlers—rug-rat Gargantuas capable of terrifying the traditional financial world with their unco-ordinated muscular power. The nurture they needed came from a very special kind of care provider known as a venture capitalist. If the CEOs of the dot-coms were the geeky princes and princesses of the New Economy, the VCs were the glamorous and slightly mysterious powers behind the throne.

Independent equity funding is not limited to the kind of high tech startups that attract speculative venture capital. Independent businessmen turn to sources of private equity funding for businesses as varied as fishing, long-distance trucking, and investment-intensive resorts, like the Whistler ski resort in British Columbia pictured here.

The Singer sewing machine and the Kodak box camera were Victorian precursors of the late twentieth-century tech revolution inspired in part by the first Apple computers. Apple is an example of a company that benefited from the early attention of venture capitalists. Today it remains a favorite of enthusiasts such as the couple encountering a new iMac at a Tokyo exposition (right). *Early in 2001, Apple co-founder Steve Jobs introduced the company's G4 Titanium notebook computer* (bottom).

Sun Microsystems is one of a number of high-tech companies to benefit from venture capital provided by Kleiner Perkins Caulfield & Byers, one of Silicon Valley's most famous independent equity companies. Here (top center) *Sun's co-founder Andy Bechtolsheim is seen in 1985, amid a roomful of the workstations he designed. Founders of Microsoft, Bill Gates and Paul Allen* (opposite right), *pictured in the mid-1980s, remain the most famous entrepreneurs of the personal computer era. Amongst Internet retailers, Amazon.com remains one of the top stories. In Amazon's British distribution center* (opposite center), *employees prepare books from the Harry Potter series for shipment. Meanwhile, in Japan, Amazon founder Jeffrey Bezos* (opposite bottom) *spreads the gospel at a Tokyo news conference.*

For centuries, individuals and financial institutions have advanced money to business adventurers embarking on potentially profitable enterprises. It was just such a loan that got Antonio into trouble in Shakespeare's *The Merchant of Venice*. and it was independent equity funding that fueled the wave of innovation that drove American industry to world prominence in the second half of the nineteenth century. In the past, though, most businesses were started by individuals who had prior experience in the commercial arena in which they hoped to make their mark. That changed with the technological revolution brought about by the personal computer. Nobody had experience in this arena because it hadn't existed till then. Software and Internet startups were fronted by young men and women with ideas to spare but without commercial pedigree. This represented a kind of risk that traditional financial institutions were not in the habit of accepting. It also represented an opportunity for imaginative venture capitalists with the willingness to speculate. Not surprisingly, perhaps, many of the most successful VC concerns are private companies, and thus able to take the kind of chances that make the shareholders of joint stock companies very nervous. More and more, however, companies listed on various stock exchanges have been drawn into the VC field.

Venture capital is just one aspect of independent equity funding. The VC specialist invests at the grass roots level—sometimes called first round funding—assuming that a few at least of his investments will produce near astronomical returns. At the other end of the independent equity

Jeffrey P. Bezos
Founder & Amazon

spectrum are corporations like J. W. Childs, Allied Capital, Heller Financial, and TA Associates that pursue more conservative strategies (although they often have VC divisions), investing in established or semi-established companies, often at the "mezzanine" level, providing emerging businesses with a final push towards the level of liquidity that enables them to go public or else entering into partnerships with the management of mid-size businesses. Other relatively safe loan activities for independent equity include backing for commercial mortgages and for investment in hardware of various kinds on the part of creditworthy borrowers. In these areas, independent equity offers an alternative to the credit supplied by large banks.

This form of independent equity is well known around the world. Until recently, the aggressive, risk-taking model of the venture capitalist has been a largely American phenomenon. Despite its tradition of merchant banking, Europe was a little slow to follow the VC lead of Silicon Valley companies like Kleiner Perkins, Menlo Ventures, and Hummer Winblad, though Britain, France, Germany, Switzerland, the Netherlands, and Scandinavia now host significant venture capital activity. Japan is home to ambitious VC concerns like Softbank Corp. and Hikari Tsushin, though these companies have been frustrated by deep-seated business prejudices and the fact that listing standards on Japanese stock exchanges have prevented public offerings of companies that, within the American

system, would be seen as having great potential.

Even in America, however, tales of venture capital miracles have become less common. Recently, Alan Patricof, who might be considered the dean of American venture capitalists, addressed the question of why so many VC-driven dot-com companies went belly-up so quickly once the New Economy boom passed its peak. As the founder of Patricof & Co. Ventures, he was in a strong position to offer an opinion. Founded in 1969, his New York-based company has been involved in the launching or development of scores of major businesses, ranging from Apple Computer to Office Depot.

In his talk, Patricof blamed his contemporaries for such things as making faulty assumptions about the readiness of inexperienced management teams to perform within a demanding environment; encouraging the expenditure of too much money on marketing without having a viable product; failing to recognize the capital intensity of building a business/brand name; and launching IPOs before startups had demonstrated readiness. His recommendations included a return to core values; recognition that companies cannot be built overnight; and acknowledgment that the Internet is not a business unto itself, but actually a new and key part of almost every existing business.

Good common sense, and well worth bearing in mind, but as Patricof's own unrivaled record would suggest, venture capital remains an exciting and sometimes enormously profitable field because—however diligent the individual investor may be in terms of research and practical spade work—it is dependent on the spirit of adventure that is implicit in its name. A venture capitalist is someone who goes out on a limb and sometimes manages to grab the golden apple. ∎

A company needing to expand an existing manufacturing facility, or to buy expensive heavy equipment, such as the floating cranes seen here in Tampa Bay **(top left)** or new trucks for its delivery fleet **(opposite bottom left)**, may well prefer to deal with an independent equity company rather than with a bank. Independent equity companies have even had an important role to play in establishing Advantage Schools **(center right)**, a concept launched in 1996 to set new standards in public education. In the realm of independent equity investing, it is the venture capital area that produces the most spectacular results, however, and the importance of its contribution can be gauged from the impact upon our everyday lives of companies like Microsoft that did not even exist just a few years ago. A contemporary company that may have such an impact fifteen years hence is Kymata Ltd. **(center bottom left)**, a high-tech firm headquartered in Scotland's "Silicon Glen," which manufactures components essential to the Dense Wavelength Division Multiplexing industry.

Not all these companies are from the high tech regions of the economy. The lifestyle sector is also strong, as can be exemplified by the success of Martha Stewart's several enterprises **(top right)**. But new technologies still hold out the promise of limitless growth, and despite recent setbacks, investors remain focused on areas such as telecommunications—represented here by Handspring's Visor Prism with Visorphone **(below)**—and human genome research, like that carried out in the laboratories of Celera **(center left)**. Nor is the impact of these new industries merely local, as can be judged by the photograph **(below left)** of a Vietnamese woman cycling past a huge billboard advertising computer giant Compaq in Hanoi.

adoption of the use of Arabic numerals. The influence of Islamic scholarship on the West had been growing since the time of the Crusades.[4] In the court of the kings of Sicily, for example, Muhammadan scholars discussed Aristotle and Averroës with their Christian and Jewish counterparts. Arabic translations of Greek classics prompted Europeans to take note of their own glorious but forgotten past. Islam had produced great mathematicians, and in 1202 a Pisan named Leonardo Fibonacci published an essay titled *Liber Abaci*, in which he argued for the benefits of using the Arabic numeral system. The church and other conservative authorities resisted such an idea, asserting the primacy of the traditional Roman characters. Bankers and merchants ignored this, realizing that the Arabic system (actually borrowed from India) was far more efficient for the crucial purpose of bookkeeping. It would prove ideal too, of course, for the needs of scientists like Copernicus and Galileo, and as such would help change man's picture of the universe.

MERCHANT PRINCES

The fifteenth century saw the rise of a number of major merchant banking families, such as the Fuggers, a Bavarian clan whose services to the pope and other rulers earned them elevation to the nobility. In the style of the period, the Fuggers not only acted as bankers but also traded extensively in silk, wool, and spices and controlled significant holdings in the silver mines of the Tyrol as well as the Hungarian copper fields.

Destined for even greater fame was the mightiest of all the Florentine banking families, the Medici. This dynasty was a product of the feuds between guilds that were ongoing throughout the city's golden age. The rise of guilds, each devoted to the promotion and welfare of a single trade or profession, was an important by-product of the reestablishment of a market-driven economy. They existed throughout Europe, and in Florence the *arti,* as they were known there, were thoroughly caught up in the often violent squabbles that characterized the political life of the city. The first im-

Like other banking families of the period, the Fuggers were considerable patrons of the arts. This portrait of Jakob Fugger II (1459–1525) is by Albrecht Dürer.

Cosimo de' Medici (1389–1464), seen here in a posthumous portrait by Jacopo Pontormo, was one of the most influential bankers of his or any other period, and a patron of the arts who did much to shape the culture of Florence during its greatest era of brilliance.

BRVGÆ, FLANDRICARVM
VRBIVM ORNAMENTA.

An early sixteenth-century map of Bruges by Godfried Kempesen. From the late Middle Ages this city was one of the principal commercial centers of Flanders. According to tradition, the first regular securities exchange came into being here in the thirteenth century when traders in bills of exchange began to meet in front of the home of the van Buerse family.

portant Medici was Salvestro, a leader of the wool-carders guild (a blue-collar organization) who in 1378 helped instigate a riot in which the so-called lesser guilds rose up against the greater guilds, whose members made the fine cloth on which the Florentine economy depended. Not long after, Giovanni di Bicci de' Medici founded an upstart bank that provided him with the means to become a power within Florence, his popularity rooted in the family's continued identification with proletarian sentiments.

Giovanni had two sons, Cosimo and Lorenzo. The branch of the family sired by Lorenzo would later play a major role in Tuscan public life, but first it was the turn of Cosimo and his grandson Lorenzo, known as the Magnificent. Not only did Cosimo enlarge and enrich his father's already successful banking and trading empire, he also became the de facto ruler of Florence without ever holding fixed public office and without attempting to suppress the existing trappings of republican government. He survived a period of political exile (for fomenting a war that helped fill the Medici coffers) and was a major patron of the arts and the new learning, building magnificent palaces and churches, commissioning works from seminal Renaissance artists such as Donatello, Ghiberti, and Luca della Robbia, founding public libraries, collecting Greek and Latin manuscripts, and commissioning the first modern translation of the works of Plato.

It would be difficult to find a figure that better represents the historical relationship between mercantile activity and the promotion of art and scholarship at the highest level, yet Lorenzo the Magnificent did manage to exceed the achievements of his grandfather in this respect. Not only did he provide patronage for Leonardo da Vinci and Michelangelo, not to mention Botticelli, Pollaiuolo, Verrocchio, Filippino Lippi, Ghirlandaio, and scores of lesser but still gifted artists and craftsmen, he was himself an intellect of the first order, able to debate with experts on any subject, a stylish prose writer, and one of the most talented and innovative poets of his day.

He was also a tyrant, dominating Florence with far less discretion than Cosimo. Riding roughshod over the city's constitution, Lorenzo was prone to spite and addicted to revenge, on occasion having his rivals hanged by the neck from their palaces or hacked to pieces and dragged through the streets. He was excommunicated by one pope but was able to persuade another to make his son Giovanni a cardinal. Giovanni—who later became Pope Leo X—was fourteen years old at the time. (It was Martin Luther's dispute with Leo X, over the sale of indulgences and church corruption in general, that sparked the Reformation, an event that would have devastating repercussions in every aspect of European life, including the business world.)

THE FLEMISH TRADITION

Some great banking families, then, were beginning to act like feudal lords themselves. That was less the case, however, in Flanders, another center of both commerce and the new learning. Cities like Ghent and Bruges had long been active in the rapidly evolving European market economy. In Bruges there seems to have been trading in commercial bills of exchange as early as the thirteenth century. Merchants there used to gather in front of a house belonging to the commercially prominent van Buerse family (also known as the de Bursa family) to make deals. Because of this, the name Buerse became synonymous with commerce involving securities, and

most scholars contend that this is the true origin of the term "bourse," meaning a stock market. (The fact that *bourse* happens to be the French for "purse"—from the Latin *bursa*—doubtless contributed to the acceptance of the term outside the Flemish-speaking world.) Etymology aside, Bruges has a strong claim to being thought of as the site of the first stock exchange, however informal its organization.

In many ways the bankers and merchants of Bruges and other urban centers in the Low Countries were much like those of Tuscany and Lombardy, but their style was different. The ornate mansions of Ghent, overlooking the city's canals, were handsome by any standards, but less grandiose than the palazzi of Florence and Milan. Comparatively speaking, the emphasis of wealthy Flemish merchants was on luxurious domesticity rather than pomp. The ideal emerging in Flanders and the Netherlands was that of *haut bourgeois* comfort, then something of a novelty.

In the sixteenth century the agreeable lives of these Flemish merchants, and of those in all the burgeoning urban centers of Europe, were shaken up by the repercussions of three major socioeconomic events. One was the opening up of the Americas and other distant markets; another was the revival of centralized authority in the hands of a few powerful monarchs; the third was the emergence of the Reformation as a force capable of changing the religious and political allegiances of half the continent.

The discovery of the Americas and of new sea routes to Asia offered vast opportunities to merchant adventurers. At the same time, it threatened the clout of certain cities, Venice in particular, that had depended for their commercial preeminence on privileged access to the traditional overland trade routes to the east. Meanwhile, treasure from the Americas and elsewhere was enriching the coffers of huge neofeudal entities like Spain, enabling them to use strong-arm tactics against cities within their orbits, long perceived by kings and courtiers as being too wealthy and having too much independence. When Ferdinand and Isabella dispatched Columbus to find a

As the age of exploration opened up trade with the Far East and the New World, and Counter-Reformation armies overran the great Flemish banking centers, Amsterdam became the commercial capital of Western Europe. This painting of about 1520 by an unknown master shows the city's harbor thronged with ships of many nations.

maritime route to the Indies, Spain had just ended Moorish domination. Soon it would be annihilating civilizations across the Atlantic, but that did not divert religious zealots associated with the Spanish monarchy from conducting holy wars in Europe. Thus Charles V of Spain, born and raised in Flanders, continued and completed the defeat and humiliation of the great Flemish commercial centers which his kinsmen of the duchy of Burgundy had begun a few years earlier.

Similar events were happening all over Europe, with many independent, or quasi-independent, urban centers being subdued or marginalized by resurgent royalist forces. Systems of tribute reasserted themselves, supported now by elaborate bureaucracies. Even so, major Italian centers like Florence, Venice, and Milan managed

to survive and even thrive as the capitals of small but still powerful states, while cities like Antwerp, Amsterdam, London, and Bristol began to gain in commercial prominence, in part because of the political divisions created by the Reformation.

As Bruges and Ghent were overrun, the commercial focus of the Low Countries shifted to Antwerp, which for a few years around 1560 was probably the busiest market town in Europe. Over a thousand foreign merchants were resident there, and a Florentine visitor reported that as many as five hundred ships passed through the port in a single day. By 1531 (while Henry VIII was on England's throne) Antwerp had a building—dubbed the Bourse—that was used as an exchange for commercial bills and notes. Many of those who frequented the Bourse were followers of Luther and other reformers, and anti-Protestant fervor contributed to the savagery of a devastating 1576 raid on the city by mercenary armies employed by the Spanish. The chief cause of this pitiless attack, however, was that the Spanish crown faced crippling levels of debt, having acquired the habit of spending the treasures of the Americas (or using them as collateral for loans from Italian bankers) before they arrived in Europe. Because of this the mercenaries had not been paid, and they took out their rage on the citizens of Antwerp, at least six thousand of whom were killed during an orgy of destruction that also saw the sacking of the Bourse. This "Spanish Fury" started the city's downward spiral.

AMSTERDAM AND THE EAST INDIA COMPANY

By the mid-1580s Amsterdam had assumed the mantle of chief marketplace of the Low Countries. Many Protestant refugees from Antwerp and other Flemish cities had made their way there, and despite claims on her by Spain and other powers, Amsterdam clung to independence and thrived as an autonomous mercantile center, trading with European neighbors and sending expeditions to distant lands. It was there, at the dawn of the seventeenth century, that one of the first great modern commercial institutions came into being.

By the late 1590s Dutch boats were rounding the Cape of Good Hope and staking out trading bases along the Malay Archipelago, known in those days as the Spice Islands. Within a couple of years, merchants organized into small companies were sending dozens of vessels to exploit the rich possibilities of this new trade. Once beyond home waters, crews often found themselves subject to the hostile attention of Spanish and Portuguese rivals. Dutch sailors even fought one another, each company seeking the trading advantage.

It was because of this that the Dutch East India Company was established, founded by a charter from the Netherlands States-General in 1602. This combined all the small companies together into one large entity charged with upholding the interests of the Netherlands in the Far East. Among other things, that meant that

With its network of canals and handsome rows of burghers' houses, many built by merchants during the heyday of the Dutch East India Company, Amsterdam retains much of the character it must have possessed when it was sending galleons to forge trading ties with the Spice Islands and to colonize North America.

The stone walls of Fort Amsterdam on Ambon, in the Moluccas, now part of Indonesia, stand witness to the colonial ambitions of Dutch traders.

Nutmeg, native to many parts of what is now Indonesia, was one reason European seamen and merchants risked their lives sailing to the tropical archipelago known as the Spice Islands.

In Indonesia's Banda Islands, local dancers perform in armor brought there centuries ago by Portuguese adventurers who, by the end of the fifteenth century, were active in the Indian Ocean as well as in Africa and South America.

captains and crews were granted the right to wage war on behalf of the government when engaging with enemy ships on the high seas. In this respect, the Dutch East India Company was a military institution as well as a commercial entity. It was capitalized to the extent of approximately 6.5 million florins, a huge amount for the period, raised by national subscription in shares issued at a value of 3,000 florins apiece. These were made available in all the principal Dutch cities, but the largest quantity was handled by the Amsterdam exchange, which as a consequence became the most important stock market of the day and, in many ways, the first of the modern era, being the pioneer in responding to a market-driven environment in a flexible and innovative way. Trading was conducted in a handsome Renaissance-style building, in the courtyard of which sober, black-suited burghers out of a Rembrandt painting could be found consorting with swashbuckling sea captains and brightly robed emissaries from the Malabar coast. No people were more involved in exotic trade than the Dutch, yet it was those black-suited burghers who set the tone for mercantile life in the Netherlands, establishing a mood of bourgeois propriety that was exported to the New World with mixed success when the Dutch settled in Brooklyn and Manhattan.

TULIPOMANIA

In the mid-1500s the Hapsburg emperor Ferdinand I dispatched a special ambassador, Ogier Ghiselain de Busbecq, to the Turkish court of Suleiman the Magnificent, grand sultan of the Ottoman Empire. There, de Busbecq discovered that the great glories of the court included massive displays of a kind of brilliantly hued flower he had never seen before, the tulip, which had arrived at the Golden Horn a few centuries earlier, having originated in the steppes of Asia. When he returned to Vienna the diplomat brought with him a selection of bulbs, which he passed on to Carolus Clusius, director of the Imperial Herb Garden. Some years later, at the time of the Counter-Reformation, Clusius, a Protestant, was forced to flee Vienna, seeking refuge in Holland. There, his reputation as a botanist led to his appointment to a position at the University of Leiden, where in 1593 he planted some of the tulip bulbs he had brought with him.

By then Clusius had been cross-breeding tulips for more than three decades. His primary interest in the genus *Tulipa* was to explore its medicinal properties. The people of Leiden, however, were taken with the gorgeous blossoms, and soon wealthy citizens were cultivating them for their aesthetic value, which was heightened by their rarity. The stems of these early varieties were somewhat shorter than those of most modern hybrids, but the heads of the flowers were large and often multicolored, with contrasting fields of scarlet and saffron, deep purple and milky white, bleeding together to create spectacular marbled effects.[5]

Tulips became the rage among Dutch aristocrats and rich merchants, who were prepared to pay huge sums for bulbs that promised to yield especially magnificent blossoms. At first the trade was restricted to the limited number of wealthy individuals who had privileged access to the bulbs, but before long, gardeners and groundskeepers began taking bulbs home in their pockets. Soon the middle classes and peasants, too, were able to experiment in their backyards, propagating new varieties that were bought by speculative merchants, who sold the bulbs by the pound to the nobles and plutocrats from whose landscaped grounds the previous generation of plants had been stolen in the first place. By the 1630s the entire country was gripped by Tulipomania.

Theft had its limitations as a reliable source of supply, and after a while everybody was forced to buy from the merchants, who, more than anyone else, were able to take advantage of the craze. For a few years profits were phenomenal, with single bulbs sometimes changing hands for the equivalent of more than $1,000 in modern terms. Families mortgaged their homes and sold their most precious possessions to capitalize their speculative fantasies. A few sober politicians tried to introduce legis-

During the 1630s the Dutch economy was almost ruined by runaway speculation in tulip bulbs. Nonetheless, Holland retains its renown for tulip cultivation. This boatload of blooms is being transported on a canal near Amsterdam.

*This map of London, by Braun and Hogenberg, was published in 1572,
fourteen years into the reign of Queen Elizabeth I, during which period
the city was a rising force in the world of international commerce.*

lation to prevent things from getting out of hand, but nothing managed to bring down the fever until, in 1637, a group of dealers staged one of their periodic tulip auctions and nobody bid.

Within two months the entire pyramid had collapsed. Thousands of people were made bankrupt, which in turn had a devastating impact on the Amsterdam bourse, causing the first great crash in modern stock-market history. As word of the collapse spread throughout Europe, people assured one another, "That could never happen here."

More untrue words were never spoken, though it took almost ninety years for the English and the French to discover that no nation is immune to epidemic gullibility when the promise of easy money is dangled in front of its citizens' noses.

THE RISE OF ALBION

For all its problems with Spain and Portugal, and with France, too, for that matter, the biggest economic thorn in Holland's side was England. From a mercantile point of view England was much like the Netherlands: a small but relatively affluent country, hostile to the papacy and with a maritime tradition that made expansion of trade to both the New World and the Far East a predictable ambition. London had been a secondary center of international banking since the thirteenth century, largely as a base for foreign bankers. (It was no accident that one of the city's chief financial thoroughfares was known as Lombard Street.) In the seventeenth century London began to evolve into a major independent banking

After the fire of 1666 London was rebuilt with handsome stone buildings, including Christopher Wren's masterpiece St. Paul's Cathedral, in whose shadow London's financial district began to take shape.

center. Its domestic bankers, many of whom had been goldsmiths, benefited from England's break with the Vatican, since the country was no longer subject to the Catholic church's laws against usury. London's citizens were extremely savvy when it came to European politics and the new global economy, as were the nation's monarchs. Henry VIII had proved himself more than adept at handling international crises, facing down the pope and declaring himself head of the Reformed Church of England. His daughter Elizabeth I proved to be at least as skilled in diplomacy, and easily as strong-willed. Never less than regal, she still managed to work effectively with the sometimes rough-and-ready nouveau-riche commercial elite. The British navy that defeated the

Spanish Armada was made up in large part of armed merchant ships captained by men whom many in other parts of Europe called pirates. These patriotic rogues, more properly called privateers, helped enrich crown and citizenry alike by crisscrossing the Atlantic to plunder Spanish colonies and treasure ships.

Under Elizabeth's successors, the Jacobeans, the British began to colonize North America, and—despite the distractions of a civil war that saw Charles I lose his head along with his throne—the nation's wealth and worldly influence continued to increase. Provincial ports such as Bristol benefited from this, but increasingly that wealth was centered in London, which, by the time of the restoration of the monarchy in 1660, was on its way to

Sir Thomas Gresham (1519–1579), one of Elizabeth I's top financial advisers. Said to have been the richest commoner in England, he sponsored several institutions that contributed to London's rise as a financial center, most notably Gresham College and the Royal Exchange.

child of Sir Thomas Gresham, cloth dealer, merchant adventurer, and agent for the crown. In 1570 it received an important boost, as was reported by John Stow, author of the Elizabethan classic *The Survey of London*, first published in 1598:

> . . . on the 23rd of January, the queen's majesty, attended with her nobility, came from her house at the Strand, called Somerset House . . . to Sir Thomas Gresham's in Bishopsgate Street, where she dined. After dinner her majesty returning through Cornehill [*sic*], entered the burse on the south side; and after she had viewed every part thereof above the ground . . . she caused the same burse by an herald and trumpet to be proclaimed the Royal Exchange, and so to be called from thenceforth, and not otherwise. [6]

In part, the granting of the royal imprimatur was in recognition of Sir Thomas's service to the crown, but it was also an acknowledgment of the growing importance of London's merchant community in national affairs. With revenues earned from the exchange, Sir Thomas—said to be the richest commoner in England—set up a bequest to launch Gresham College, a novel kind of educational institution that called on leading members of the London commercial community to deliver free lectures, in English rather than Latin, to clerks and apprentices and anyone else who cared to attend. A special emphasis was laid upon practical lessons that could be learned from the latest developments in science and technology—mapmaking, for example, and the application of astronomy to the art of celestial navigation. Gresham College played an invaluable role in preparing Londoners for the realities and possibilities of a changing commercial world. It also gave birth to the Royal Society of London, the learned association before which some of the greatest scientific propositions of all time were first presented.

As for the Royal Exchange in Cornhill (rebuilt after the 1666 fire), it served for almost a hundred years as the primary site for the trading of commercial paper, and

becoming Europe's most prosperous city. The great 1666 fire briefly slowed this growth, but the city was quickly rebuilt, medieval half-timbered buildings that had burned like tinder being replaced by handsome brick terraces and parklike squares. Thus, London emerged as a wholly changed and startlingly modern city—another instance of the mutually beneficial interplay between capital and culture—crowned by Christopher Wren's masterpiece, St. Paul's Cathedral.

An indoor exchange, modeled on the Antwerp bourse, had been erected in London as early as 1567, the brain-

also as a retail marketplace. A London buck could spend the morning buying or selling shares in the Muscovy Company (the world's oldest joint-stock company, founded in 1553), then enjoy a plate of curds and cream with his mistress, or perhaps purchase a cameo pendant for his wife from one of the shops lining the courtyard that served as a clearinghouse for gossip, commercial and otherwise. In the 1690s, however (not 1660, as sometimes reported), a group of about 150 stock traders was asked to cease doing business in the polite environment of the Royal Exchange because of rowdy behavior. Later, brokers were also banned from the rotunda of the Bank of England—another favorite gathering place—for much the same reason.

The surrounding area had become known as Exchange Alley (usually abbreviated to 'Change Alley), and it was there that these brokers continued their haggling and gossip in coffee and chocolate rooms such as Garraway's, the Jerusalem Coffee House, Lloyd's (which gave birth to Lloyd's of London, the world's most famous insurance

(continued on page 90)

When the original Royal Exchange was destroyed in the 1666 London fire, it was replaced by a more substantial building, shown here in an eighteenth-century engraving by William Tite.

BIG DEALS:
THE CHANGING WORLD OF MERGERS

To any American car owner old enough to have grown up in a world dominated by the Big Three Detroit auto manufacturers, it came as something of a jolt when, in 1998, the venerable company founded by Walter Chrysler was acquired by the even more venerable Daimler-Benz Corporation. It was a deal that brought home the fact that mergers and takeovers have become international in scope, even in a sphere such as the automobile industry, traditionally nationalistic to the point of chauvinism.

Over the years, Europe has seen its fair share of mergers and acquisitions, but still the concept of the "takeover"—with its suggestion of gun-slinging banditry—has been looked on as something of an American specialty, an inevitable by-product of the frontier mentality endemic on Wall Street (or so Europeans have chosen to believe).

This attitude goes back to the middle of the nineteenth century, when there was a frontier and European investors—though anxious to cash in on America's booming economy—were appalled by what they perceived as the piratical ethics of the American business community. This reputation was a concern for the American robber barons who were coming to the fore about then and who were eager to have access to European capital. When orchestrating the flotation of a bond issue in London, Andrew Carnegie was careful to have the financial editor of the *Times* publish an article disassociating Carnegie and his allies from American rogue traders like Jay Gould and Jim Fisk, whose recent manipulations of Erie

There is nothing new about the concept of the merger. Back in 1881, the two great circus entrepreneurs of the Victorian era—Phineas T. Barnum and James A. Bailey—joined forces to create the Greatest Show on Earth. In 1907 that extravaganza was taken over by John Ringling, becoming Ringling Bros. and Barnum & Bailey Circus.

Railroad stock had cost naïve English investors a bundle. When it came to shotgun mergers and brute force takeovers, Carnegie and fellow tycoons like John D. Rockefeller were, in fact, every bit as rapacious as Gould and Fisk, but they had the good sense to make sure that they were not perceived as expanding their empires at the expense of shareholders.

One way of managing this, as Rockefeller demonstrated, was by keeping would-be investors at arm's length. In 1870 Rockefeller, along with four partners, incorporated Standard Oil, a joint stock company in which the partners controlled all shares issued at the time, either directly or indirectly. This concentration of stock meant that no Wall Street speculator would have the opportunity to attempt a takeover of what otherwise might have provided a very attractive target.

Meanwhile, Rockefeller organized a cartel of Ohio oil refiners to make deals with local railroad companies that had the effect of doubling haulage rates for refiners outside the group. Threatened with bankruptcy, the majority of these refiners were forced to accept buyout bids from Standard Oil. Rockefeller carried out similar coups in New Jersey and Pennsylvania, and by 1878 Standard Oil controlled more than 90 percent of all the refineries in America.

Having become a virtual monopoly, Standard Oil began to attract the attention of government at both state and federal levels, leading to the institution in 1890 of the Sherman Anti-Trust Act. In the short run, the new law did nothing to prevent the growth of the biggest trust of all—the so-called money trust—which for a couple of decades dominated many aspects of American commerce, playing a leading role in scores of mergers and takeovers. The money trust was a loosely organized (and unacknowledged) association of major financial institutions such as J. P. Morgan,

Kuhn Loeb, and First National Bank and National City Bank, whose officers had the knack of being elected to one another's boards. Like heads of Mafia families, the principals in these operations, such as Jacob Schiff and J. P. Morgan himself, were often at odds with one another, but they knew when to pull together for their own good—even acting as an informal central bank in times of crisis—and by doing so achieved tremendous power that was often expressed in terms of financial pressure to engineer mergers and buyouts. It was by way of such methods that Morgan came to replace Carnegie as the dominant figure in the U.S. steel industry.

Every era—and especially every bull market—has it own character when it comes to mergers and buyouts. The period that followed World War I and climaxed with the boom of the mid- and late 1920s, was characterized by a merger mania that had a strong impact on many industries, from retailing to auto manufacture. The mergers of the 1920s also saw the beginnings of the

media conglomerate when, in 1928, the Radio Corporation of America (which owned the patents on Photophone sound equipment), the Keith Albee vaudeville circuit (which owned theaters) and Joseph Kennedy (who owned a small production company and was acknowledged as one of the shrewdest operators on Wall Street) joined forces to create RKO, which overnight became one of the Big Five movie studios.

The 1960s hosted the beginning of the conglomerate craze in which aggressive companies began to acquire other corporations, often from outside their traditional market segment, so that a business with its roots in heavy industry might find itself controlling entities that produced underwear or baby food. This policy meant that a company could grow without running into anti-trust difficulties, but it often found that it was facing new challenges at management level because of the diversity of expertise required.

The 1980s proved to be the heyday of the hostile takeover. The targets were often the

Today's entertainment industry is dominated by huge conglomerates like AOL-Time Warner, built on acquisitions and mergers, but show business mergers have a long history. An early example was the creation of RKO—an amalgamation of the Radio Corporation of America (RCA), whose showcase Radio City Music Hall **(left)** was built in the 1930s; the Keith-Albee-Orpheum vaudeville chain, whose flagship theatre, the Palace, is seen below right, and the film booking office of Joseph P. Kennedy **(below)**—which overnight came to be a force to be reckoned with.

Many of the American industrialists of the late nineteenth century built their businesses with the help of mergers and takeovers—often of the hostile kind. John D. Rockefeller **(above)** enlarged his burgeoning oil empire **(left)** by organizing a cartel that pushed rivals to the brink of bankruptcy by forcing up haulage costs. When a company began to falter, Rockefeller would move in and snap it up. Famously, the American steel industry **(opposite)** was dominated for decades by Andrew Carnegie, himself no stranger to the art of the takeover. In the early years of the twentieth century, however, J. P. Morgan engaged in a series of acquisitions that made him the dominant figure in steel.

conglomerates that had been painstakingly assembled during the previous couple of decades. A typical example was Beatrice Foods, a huge and complacent commercial empire involved in many industries besides its core business. Beatrice Foods fell to Kohlberg, Kravis, Roberts, one of the buyout specialists of the period, working in conjunction with Drexel Burnham Lambert, the corporate raider's favorite investment bank. Once taken over, Beatrice was broken up and its parts sold off at a handsome profit.

KKR was far from being the only takeover specialist of the period. Others included Carl Icahn, Sid Bass, Sumner Redstone, Ronald Perelman and Irwin Jacobs. Their favored method of attack was the leveraged buyout, which involved making an offer backed with borrowed capital (much as an investor might buy stock on margin). Often high yield "junk" bonds were issued as part of the takeover strategy. Initially, at least, these were usually underwritten by Drexel's high yield bond department, headed by Michael Milken, the acknowledged mastermind behind the wave of leveraged buyouts. This subsided at about the time Milken was indicted under federal racketeering and fraud laws, an event that contributed to the demise of Drexel, which in 1990 was forced to file for bankruptcy.

A by-product of the leveraged buyout era was the legal but arguably less than ethical practice known as "greenmail," made famous by corporate raider T. Boone Pickens. This elegantly nasty way of getting rich would have delighted the rogues of the Daniel Drew era. It involves mounting an apparent buyout bid that appears serious enough to put the present management of the target company on the defensive. The greenmailer does this by acquiring a significant position in the stock of the target company. In a defensive move, the target company begins to buy back its own shares. The value of the stock rises dramatically. The greenmailer waits for the optimal moment then sells his shares at a handsome profit.

It is the perception of many business leaders today that—from a purely commercial point of view, at least—bigger is not only better, it is in fact the only way to survive. The long-term evidence for this is not in place yet, but if everyone else is acting on that assumption, then you'd better be prepared to play the same game, and one sure way to get big quickly is to be on the lookout for suitable mergers. So it is that the recent past has been marked by blockbuster mergers such as AOL/Time-Warner and Travelers/Citibank. Certainly the executives involved are hardnosed and ambitious, but their motivation is very different from that of the corporate raiders of the 1980s, or for that matter from the rogue traders of the 1860s. Like the robber barons of the Victorian era, they are interested in strength through consolidation rather than in buccaneering raids on unsuspecting victims.

In all probability, though, it is just a matter of time before some Captain Kidd of the buyout world spots a weakness in the way the global mega-corporations are capitalized and launches a successful attack on one of the new and seemingly invincible financial dreadnaughts. In the world of mergers and takeovers, what goes around comes around. ▪

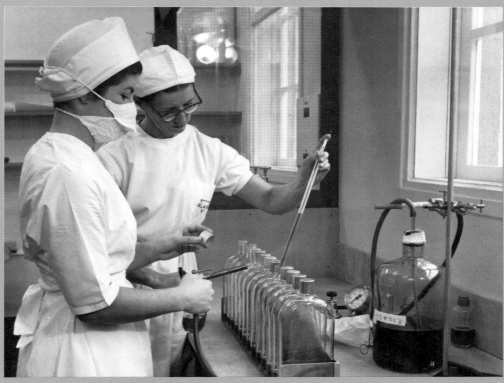

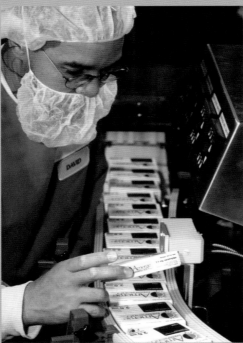

Above and left: *Since the 1990s, there has been a trend towards mergers between already large companies in order to create even larger entities that can compete more readily in the global marketplace. Based in England, GlaxoSmithKline is a major player in world healthcare and pharmaceutical markets. It was incorporated in 1999 as a merger of Glaxo Wellcome and SmithKline Beecham, themselves the products of earlier mergers.*

Left bottom and left center: *Perhaps the most astonishing merger in recent years is the one that saw America Online (AOL)—the Internet giant, huge but barely out of its cradle—purchase Time Warner, creating a media/communications/entertainment company of gargantuan proportions. The acquisition was celebrated by AOL Chairman and CEO Steve Case (arm raised) and Time Warner Chairman and CEO Gerald Levin. It soon led to a striking synergy between different divisions of the new entity as when AOL is used to promote Warner Brothers movies.*

Opposite top and top left: *Although mergers are far more common, it is not unheard of for a company to be split up into smaller units. In the case of AT&T, the American telephone giant, the breakup occurred because of government intervention and was intended to open the industry to competition. Occurring as the age of the hand-operated switchboard gave way to the era of fiber optics and digital telecommunications, the breakup proved a great success, with the regional so-called "Baby Bells" and other entities spun off from the parent company able to thrive alongside AT&T and newly created rivals.*

Opposite bottom left and far left: *A merger that shocked many observers was the deal that brought Daimler Benz and Chrysler Corporation under the same umbrella. As these photographs of a 1955 Chrysler 300 classic and a Mercedes 300 SL of the same era show, the component companies had espoused very different design philosophies, one expressing European elegance, the other quintessentially American.*

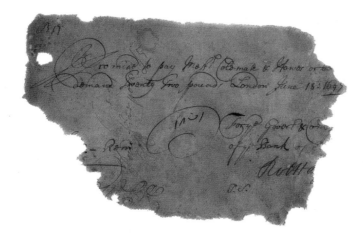

This tattered fragment is what remains of the earliest known banknote, put out by the Bank of England, which began issuing such notes in 1694.

The flagstones and coffeehouses of 'Change Alley were for many years the focus of British financial life. This painting, by the Victorian artist Edward Matthew Ward, is an imaginative reconstruction of the scene in 'Change Alley in 1720, at the height of South Sea Bubble speculation.

company), and especially Jonathan's, which was to become the cradle of the modern London Stock Exchange. A merchant would list one of these gathering places as his office address, receiving mail and visitors there. Business in these noisy social centers (alcohol was served as well as coffee) was brisk, thanks in part to the fact that the British government, like others, was turning increasingly to bond issues as a way of raising revenue. And they were not just places for trading securities. At Garraway's, for example, every kind of commodity, from dye to real estate, was auctioned. The very first sale known to have been held there, in January 1672, was of beaver pelts shipped from Canada by the Hudson's Bay Company.

Institutions like Garraway's also served as clearinghouses for news and gossip, domestic and international—much of it considered seditious and threatening to the ship of state, thus attracting the attention of government spies and informers such as the notorious Henry

Muddiman, described by Samuel Pepys as "an arch rogue." Many coffeehouses, including some that were outwardly respectable, were notorious as centers of illegal gambling, and often of prostitution too. Frequently they served as the headquarters of quack doctors and bunco artists of various persuasions. It was, therefore, in an atmosphere tinged with intrigue, charlatanism, and even lewdness that the modern stockbroker came into being.

In 1694 a hint of respectability was brought to 'Change Alley by the establishment, on Threadneedle Street, of the Bank of England, set up by government fiat as a central clearing bank—the world's first national bank and the first to issue banknotes guaranteed by the state. (Thirty-three years earlier, Sweden's Stockholm Bank had become the first to issue banknotes of any

This wood engraving depicts the frenzied activity outside Garraway's Coffee House, on 'Change Alley, as the South Sea Bubble is about to burst.

kind.) This helped set the stage for a boom in stock trading, both in government securities and annuities and in newly created companies. A mini market crash in 1696 led to the introduction of a code of conduct that attempted to place some modest ethical restrictions on brokers, who till then had not been above indulging in blatant insider trading and other forms of chicanery. This code did nothing, however, to prevent a disaster that was to bring stock speculation in Britain into disrepute for many years.

THE SOUTH SEA BUBBLE

That disaster was the South Sea Bubble, a classic example of the consequences of gullibility on the part of investors beguiled into taking financial risks with no basis in reasonable expectations. A bubble, whether blown from soapy water or from promises of untold wealth, is something that eventually bursts. Until that dreadful moment, however, everyone admires the beauty of the fragile, liquid envelope—its prismatic sheen, its ability to refract everyday reality into something that seems magical. Bubbles are real, but their existence is so tenuous that they are utilized as metaphors for unreality.

Decades before the South Sea Bubble, British authors, including John Dryden, used "bubble" as a verb to describe the act of perpetrating a swindle, and as a noun to designate the victim of a scam. This usage does not do full justice to investors duped by the typical stock-market bubble, however. Where financial speculation is concerned, the victim is often capable of cheating himself without any outside assistance from helpful hucksters. The hucksters are usually in evidence, of course, but they are apt to become victims too, because many of them get carried away by their own rhetoric.

As had been the case with Tulipomania, there is always an invigorating overture and a first act that promises great things to come. So it was with the South Sea Bubble. The first chords of the overture were heard in 1711, when the newly incorporated South Sea Company was granted a monopoly on trade to South America and the Pacific

When the London Stock Exchange finally found a permanent home, it was discreetly tucked away behind surrounding buildings, access being by way of one of the narrow alleys that abound in the City of London.

Islands. In return for this, the tycoons behind the enterprise, led by Robert Harley and greatly encouraged by the earl of Oxford, agreed to pay off a sizable chunk of the national debt accumulated as a consequence of Britain's involvement in the War of the Spanish Succession (1701–14), which was then winding down. The perceived value of the monopoly depended on the widely touted belief that Britain would be given considerable trading privileges in the Spanish colonies once the war was over. In fact Harley, an ardent Whig, and his partners were probably every bit as interested in employing the South Sea Company as a domestic financial institution that could divert business from the Bank of England, founded by their Tory political rivals.

The South Sea Company did engage in some trade, however—mostly supplying slaves to South America—and generated enough profit to attract shareholders. In 1718 King George I lent prestige to the company by becoming its governor. The following year, the directors of the company proposed to the government that their shareholders take over the bulk of the national debt in return for additional concessions. Most of that debt was owed to individual citizens to whom state annuities were due. The company proposed to offer these disappointed creditors the opportunity of exchanging their annuities for South Sea Company stock.

Getting a scheme as bold as this one accepted was not easy, of course, especially since England and Spain were at war once more, thus taking some of the shine off the proposed monopoly. Politicians like Robert Walpole warned of the follies implicit in the whole enterprise, but the directors of the South Sea Company distributed bribes to prominent members of the Whig establishment and to other useful figures, such as the duchess of Kendal and Madam von Platen, the king's mistresses. (The fact that these bribes took the form of stock in the company can be seen as ironic.) In April 1720 the government accepted the proposal, and the stage was set for a fiasco of heroic proportions.

For a few brief months, the prospects seemed glorious. Almost immediately, half of the annuitants agreed to the company's terms, presumably believing that they were cutting their losses by gambling on the rosy future portrayed by the South Sea confidence men, who obviously had the government in their pocket. This convinced many otherwise sane investors that they could not afford to miss out on a good thing. Trading at Jonathan's and the other 'Change Alley coffeehouses reached manic levels. Shares that had traded at £175 at the end of February peaked at over £1,000 in June. And the rise of this stock encouraged entrepreneurs of dubious scruples to float new joint-stock companies claiming to be in a position to exploit everything from Greenland fisheries to insurance policies on female chastity and, in one famous case, "an undertaking of great advantage, but nobody to know what it is." (This latter scheme was well subscribed to before the perpetrator took off for the Continent at very short notice.)

Eventually the euphoria began to fade, and credulity gave way to suspicion. The rumor that directors of the South Sea Company were surreptitiously unloading stock did nothing to restore public confidence, and as the summer of 1720 wore on, share prices began to descend and then to plummet, falling to a value of £135 in September. Some smaller start-ups crashed even more violently, but none did more damage than the South Sea Company itself, which caused thousands of bankruptcies and wrecked tens of thousands of lives. A mob bent on revenge descended on Westminster, but by then

many of the chief culprits had taken off for friendlier climes, having destroyed crucial records. When Lord Stanhope, one of the conspirators' chief political allies, was accused in Parliament of wrongdoing, he worked himself up into such a state of righteous indignation that he passed out on the floor of the House. A doctor was called in to let blood, but Stanhope soon gave up the ghost, becoming one of the less lamented victims of the South Sea Bubble.

One thing that helped sustain this particular bubble was that useful research into the actual potential of the South Sea Company was virtually nonexistent. Common sense might have told investors that there were probable limits to its possibilities, but hard information was difficult to come by in an age when it took months for the fastest ship to cross the ocean and return. In addition, there was no obligation upon the joint-stock companies of the time to make any serious show of disclosure. Information was spread, and controlled, by leak and

The speculative climate surrounding the South Sea and Mississippi Bubbles was sustained largely by the expected profits to be derived from the slave trade, considered a normal commercial activity in the first half of the eighteenth-century. Pictured here is a slave trading post at Fort des Maures on Moyella Island, off the coast of West Africa.

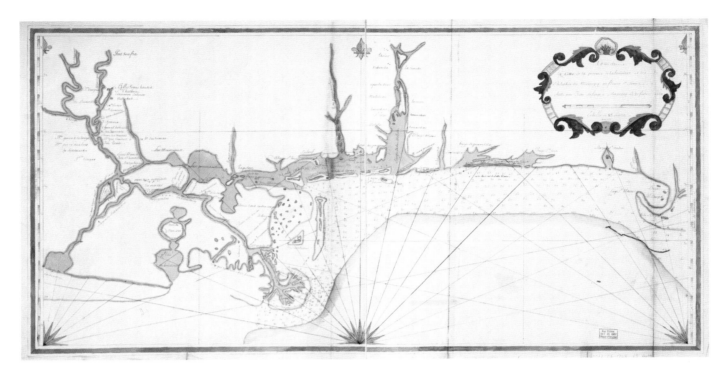

Top: *The Mississippi Bubble was the consequence of wild speculation based on the potential of the slave and tobacco trades, linked at the time to French colonial territories in North America. This eighteenth-century map shows the Mississippi Delta and a section of the Gulf Coast, with New Orleans and Natchez marked as still tiny settlements.*

Above: *Scottish by birth, John Law (1671–1729) was a brilliant financial theorist who took virtual control of the French economy; the Mississippi Bubble destroyed his reputation and forced him to flee the country.*

Left: *When John Law's scheme to exploit the wealth of the American territories collapsed, fortunes were destroyed overnight and angry crowds poured into the streets of Paris and other European cities.*

innuendo. Anyone wanting to float a scheme involving overseas speculation, therefore, was presented with a distinct advantage, at least in the short run.

This did little for the reputation of brokers, and it was during this period that Samuel Johnson, in his great *Dictionary of the English Language* (1755), defined the professional stockbroker, or "stockjobber," as "a low wretch who gets money by buying and selling shares in the funds."

The denizens of Jonathan's were undeterred by scares, scandals, or unkind definitions, however, and in 1773 pooled their resources to build themselves a more commodious meeting place alongside the old Royal Exchange. They dubbed these still modest premises New Jonathan's, but they were also known as "the Stock Exchange." Anyone intent on doing business there was charged sixpence a day.

THE MISSISSIPPI BUBBLE

Virtually simultaneous with the South Sea Bubble was another speculative scheme that was to become equally notorious. This one was perpetrated in France, masterminded by a remarkable Scotsman named John Law.

Law possessed great charm and forcefulness, along with a genius for practical economics and an equal talent for getting into trouble. In his youth he killed a man in a duel and was forced to take refuge in Amsterdam. In 1705 he published a book titled *Money and Trade Considered, with a Proposal for Supplying the Nation with Money*. His theories found no immediate application at home but came to fruition in France, where he had talked his way into a close friendship with the duc d'Orléans, the regent.

In 1716 Law was granted the authority to launch the Banque Générale, and with it the right to issue banknotes. That same year, he established the Compagnie d'Occident (renamed the Compagnie des Indes in 1719), for which he obtained virtually monopolistic privileges in the tobacco and slave trades and in developing the French territories in North America, which then included much of the area drained by the Mississippi River. On top of this, Law took over the collection of taxes throughout the kingdom and had himself placed in charge of the French mint. For a brief period, John Law *was* the French economy.

Certainly he had no difficulty in finding investors willing to purchase stock in the Compagnie des Indes. The demand was such that the price of a single share shot up from 500 livres to 18,000 livres, an amount that bore no relationship to the company's earnings, which were modest to say the least. As in the case of the South Sea Bubble, people persuaded themselves of the vast potential of the enterprise. When Law merged the Compagnie des Indes with his quasi-official Banque Générale, public confidence received a further boost.

Law—who was certainly an overreacher but probably not a crook—intended to pay off the public debt of the French crown by trading shares in his merged companies for government securities. This drove up the value of these *billets d'état*, thus contributing to the boom, which by now had spread to other parts of Europe. The French government attempted to retire more of its debt by printing additional paper money, which was readily accepted by speculators who were anxious to increase their holdings in the Compagnie des Indes.

It was a beautiful bubble, but like all bubbles it was bound to burst. In 1720, just as the South Sea Bubble was popping across the Channel, it became apparent that the earnings of the Compagnie des Indes did not in any way justify the valuation that had been placed on its stock. In addition, the way in which the company's finances were intertwined with those of the state spelled disaster for the economy as a whole. Overnight, it seemed, the scales were lifted from investors' eyes. The fatal deficiencies in John Law's scheme, till then invisible, suddenly were startlingly obvious. Stock markets all over Europe crashed.

Despite his good intentions, Law was assigned the blame for the entire disaster and by the end of 1720 was forced to flee the country. The French government assumed his business debts and bailed out the economy in the conventional way, by raising taxes.

3 : From Trading Posts to the Emergence of Wall Street

1650–1850

A replica of Christopher Columbus's ship, the Santa Maria, *lies at anchor in 1996, almost in the shadows of the World Trade Center towers in New York's financial district.*

Many of the stocks bought and sold at the newly established London Stock Exchange and at sibling exchanges on the Continent were issued by companies involved in colonial trade, which along with the Industrial Revolution was the motor of the securities business from the sixteenth-century heyday of the Amsterdam Bourse until World War I. The Americas had been exploited by European powers since Columbus's accidental discovery of the New World, and the Dutch had settled the southern tip of Africa as early as 1652. As for Asia, parts of it had been subject to European influence since Alexander's armies marched into the Punjab in the fourth century B.C. During the Middle Ages Islamic traders were active all over the Indian Ocean, and the Chinese undertook extensive maritime expeditions throughout the region too, though by the fifteenth century these were severely curtailed, leaving the field clear for newcomers. Starting in 1487, junks, dhows, and Arab galleys were joined by the caravels of Portuguese explorers and merchants, which were followed by galleons flying the flags of half a dozen nations; then came British frigates, Baltimore clippers, and the exquisite, metal-flanked tall ships of the tea trade, which in turn gave way to piston-powered gunboats,

Considered to be the world's oldest printed shares, "actiën" like this one, issued by the United East India Company of the Netherlands, quickly became the object of highly speculative trading.

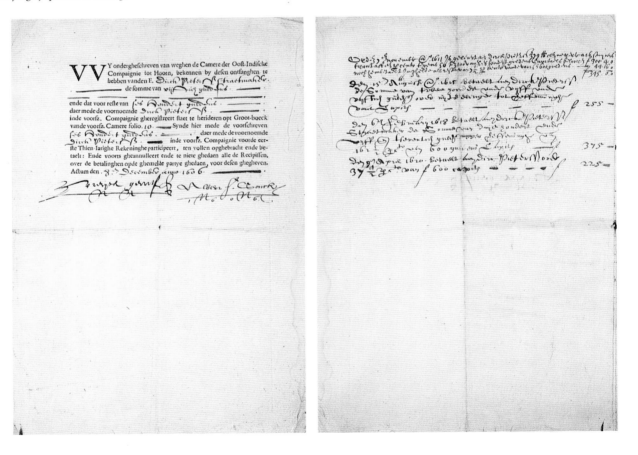

This view of a Dutch East Indies Company squadron under full sail, painted by Ludolf Backhuyzen in 1675, conveys the power of an organization that dominated the lucrative spice trade during the 1600s.

raffish tramp steamers, and, finally, sleek cruise boats.

At the beginning of the sixteenth century the Portuguese were the most active of the European colonists in the region, securing their position by seizing the port of Socotra, which controlled the entrance to the Red Sea. This meant that Arab traders no longer had unchallenged access to the Indian Ocean from Egypt (which was about to fall into the hands of the Turks, who themselves were threatening expansion into Asia). In 1519 the Portuguese viceroy of the Indies, Afonso de Albuquerque, took possession of Goa, on the Indian coast, and used this as a base for further exploration, setting up fortified trading settlements as far away as Malacca, on the Malay Peninsula. The coastal peoples around the Indian Ocean were used to trading posts catering to overseas merchants, but the concept of a self-contained and defensible strong point controlled entirely by an

alien power was new to most of them, as was the religious intolerance that went along with the Portuguese colonial concept. Not surprisingly, then, the Portuguese often had to fight to protect their gains, battling not only the Turks—who sought to regain Muslim trading superiority—but also well-armed Hindu armies and navies. In the end Lisbon was never able to control the Indian Ocean, though it remained a force to be reckoned with as other colonialists set out to grab a piece of the action.

The role of the Dutch in the Indian Ocean can be gauged from the tremendous boost given to commerce in the Netherlands by the formation of the Dutch East India Company (see chapter 2). Ships underwritten by investors in Amsterdam set out in 1595 for Java, where the Dutch persuaded the locals that they were there to help keep Portuguese gunboats and Roman Catholic missionaries at bay. By the time the East India Company

Spices brought Portuguese traders to the port of Malacca in 1511. Prized for flavor and believed to cure everything from venereal disease to the plague, they were worth their weight in gold. Spices remain essential commodoties in Indonesia, as in this market in Sweta in the Lesser Sunda Islands.

was founded, in 1602, a toehold had been obtained in Ceylon and the Portuguese had been driven from some of their Indian settlements. Soon the Dutch also held the principal Spice Islands.

Sir Francis Drake captained the first British ship to enter the Indian Ocean during his 'round-the-world privateering expedition, which lasted from 1577 to 1580. The British did not become active in the region, however, until their own East India Company was incorporated a few years after its Dutch rival. At first, despite their victory over the Spanish Armada, British crews were wary of the firepower of their Dutch opponents, and with good reason, since it soon became clear that the latter were not about to give up their dominance in Indonesia without a titanic struggle. Realizing this, the British concentrated on establishing themselves in India, where at first they made slow progress. Although they acquired Bombay (part of the dowry of the Portuguese princess

Catherine of Braganza, who married Charles II of England), they discovered that trading in India was not as profitable as they had hoped it would be. The Indians had little use for British products, such as heavy wool cloth, so British merchants were forced to buy Indian goods in order to barter them for the spices that were their chief objective. This same scenario held for other early European traders in the region, too. The peoples of the Indies were prepared to do business, but on their own terms. Pressured by their stockholders back in London, Amsterdam, and elsewhere, the Europeans wanted cheap goods. It soon became apparent that to obtain these they would have to take political and military control of the areas where business was done, thus beginning the process of colonial capitalism.

Danish would-be colonists were part of the story; so were the French, spearheaded by the Compagnie des Moluques, established in the walled seaport of Saint-Malo in 1616 and superseded in 1664 by the Compagnie des Indes Orientales, which competed with the Dutch, Portuguese, and British around the coasts of India. One French beachhead was established on the Bay of Bengal in 1673. This brought them into contact with the king of Siam (now Thailand), who at the time was waging war against the Dutch. To obtain the French as allies he offered them the cities of Mergui (now part of Myanmar) and Bangkok. The French accepted this bargain but botched the opportunity and were soon evicted. After that, the French were quiescent in the region until Joseph-François Dupleix, the great rival of the British general Robert Clive, tried to overrun southern India in the middle of the eighteenth century. Thanks to Clive's superior military aptitude the Frenchman failed, but in doing so showed how colonialism could be advanced by becoming parasitic upon the politics and society of the host culture (Dupleix assumed the mantle of a Mogul prince), applying the rule of divide and conquer, and using indigenous troops to fight on behalf of the European power, binding them to the Imperial cause.

(The biggest success of the French in Asia would come with the annexation of the countries now known as

Laos, Cambodia, and Vietnam, which derived from the efforts of the politically astute missionary Pigneau de Behaine at the end of the eighteenth century.)

Through victory at Plassey in 1757 over the nawob of Bengal, Great Britain became the supreme colonial force in India. The British had learned from Dupleix to play prince against prince, and at the same time introduced as many British institutions as could be approximated on the subcontinent. As the Industrial Revolution progressed, India came to be seen less as a source of exotic commodities—spices and such—and more as a potential market for British manufactured goods. Soon it would be embraced, too, as a source of basic raw materials needed by the new industries to satisfy the appetites

of the rapidly expanding British middle-class population. (The same pattern emerged elsewhere as other colonial powers became caught up in the era of industrialized capitalism.) In 1813 the trading monopoly of the East India Company was rescinded, and although the firm remained a major force for several more decades, the character of the Raj—British rule of the Indian subcontinent—changed dramatically, with the old-style merchant adventurers being replaced by traveling salesmen and civil servants. European-style speculative investment had taken root, and eventually, in 1875, the Native Share and Stockbrokers Association came into being in Mumbai (known to Westerners as Bombay).

This was Asia's first stock market.

(continued on page 108)

British entrepreneurs found that Ceylon (now Sri Lanka) provided ideal conditions for growing tea. In this photograph, sacks of tea are attached to a pulley system for transportation to the drying house.

BUILDING INFRASTRUCTURE:
STATE AND LOCAL FINANCE

In the United States, as in some other countries, local government—at the state, county, city, and even school board level—plays a considerable role in defining the character of the marketplace, at least on a regional level. It does so by its involvement in projects as dramatic as building new stadiums for major league sports franchises, and as mundane as maintaining sewage systems. Developments of the former sort often rely upon somewhat untraditional forms of financing. The State of Michigan, for example, made a substantial contribution to building the Detroit Tigers' new home, CoAmerica Park, with funds deriving from gambling revenues. Elsewhere, such newfound sources of revenue as gaming and lottery profits are used to supplement education budgets and the like.

For the most part, however, state, county, and city governments provide the services required by their citizens by way of conventional means such as taxation and the floating of notes and bonds. Municipal bond issues often arouse far more public interest and controversy than Treasurys since they involve local concerns and, in many cases, have to be voted upon by the electorate before they can be implemented. Alert citizens, therefore, are very aware of the fact that the revenue from such and such a bond issue is intended to rehabilitate playgrounds, build jails, maintain country roads, hire more police officers, erect

A project of the Port Authority of New York and New Jersey, the John F. Kennedy International Airport AirTrain system—seen here while under construction—is designed to link airline terminals with one another and with public transportation.

a new senior center, or whatever, and such decisions tend to provoke debate.

Not all municipal issues fall into this category. Managing the budget of even a small community is no easy matter, so that often a municipality finds itself faced with a temporary shortfall. An upcoming bond issue or next year's taxes may promise relief, but there remains the question of what to do in the interim. It may be as simple as going to a bank and asking for a loan, but an alternative is to issue short-term promissory notes for which the principal and interest is secured by the issuing authority's credit and perceived ability to tax its constituents (which in some places is limited by law).

Credit ratings for local governments are issued regularly by recognized institutions such as Standard & Poor's and Moody's. If a city's rating goes down, it will have to offer potential investors a higher yield on future notes, making them, in extreme instances, the municipal equivalent of junk bonds.

Municipal bonds and notes are of special interest to investors—both private and corporate—who find themselves in high tax brackets, the reason being that the interest earned on this type of security is exempt, wholly or in part, from federal taxes, and often from local taxes too. This gives them a distinct advantage over Treasurys and other kinds of bonds, but occasional debacles on the grand scale demonstrate that municipal securities are not necessarily the rock-steady investments they were once thought to be.

One such debacle was New York City's flirtation with bankruptcy in the mid-1970s. In the end, a worst-case scenario was averted, but only narrowly, and the brush with disaster was enough to make many investors decidedly nervous. Two decades later came a full-fledged catastrophe in the form of the bankruptcy of Orange County, California, one of the nation's wealthiest and till then most fiscally responsible-seeming municipalities.

In the early 1990s—like many private and publicly owned companies, and a significant number of municipal entities—Orange County took a deep plunge into the derivatives market, theoretically as a form of risk management. The fund in question had been entrusted to the supervision of county treasurer Robert

Citron, who built up an $8 billion portfolio consisting substantially of complex packages of derivatives. So well did the fund perform at first that Orange County found itself entrusted with capital by 180 other municipal treasuries, some from out of state. Before long, however, problems began to surface. Interest rates rose, adversely effecting the derivatives markets, and the portfolio began to leak money, eventually

SUSPENSION BRIDGE OF TRIBOROUGH BRIDGE FROM ASTORIA TO WARD'S ISLAND, NEW YORK CITY

© INTERNATIONAL NEWS PHOTOS

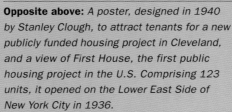

Opposite above: *A poster, designed in 1940 by Stanley Clough, to attract tenants for a new publicly funded housing project in Cleveland, and a view of First House, the first public housing project in the U.S. Comprising 123 units, it opened on the Lower East Side of New York City in 1936.*

Opposite below: *Motorcycle policemen lead the motorcade at the opening in 1940 of California's first freeway, the Arroyo Seco Parkway, now the Pasadena Freeway, connecting downtown Los Angeles with Pasadena.*

Left: *The stately University Hall on the campus of Ohio State University is a replica of the school's first building, where classes were first held in September 1873 for 24 students. The building is a reminder of the essential role of public funding in building the "land grant" colleges that became the state university system in the U.S.*

Above left and right: *Robert Moses, seen here in 1938, has been called a modern-day pharaoh for the astonishing extent of public works projects he created through the agencies he controlled. These projects included the Triborough Bridge, which connects Queens, Manhattan, and the Bronx.*

Above: *The entrance to a typical New York City high-rise public housing project* **(left)** *and a father, with his son, seen in a contemporary inner city housing project of low-rise townhouses.*

losing close to $1.5 billion. As a result, Orange County bonds defaulted on their interest payments and court-appointed investigators found that Citron's fund had been, to say the least, poorly designed.

This crisis came as a jarring shock to bond traders. Orange County recovered, however, and the market recovered too.

Although the Orange County disaster was caused by poorly considered trading in derivatives, municipal bonds themselves have not given rise to active futures and options markets such as those that derive from Treasury bills. The reason for this is that investors generally hold onto municipal notes in order to benefit from the tax advantages that accrue. In addition, the tax-free status of the interest on municipal securities makes it tricky, from a legal viewpoint, to practice certain kinds of derivatives trades that could be perceived as permitting an improper profit

to be made on untaxed income. The special and even unique role of municipal bonds is thus protected, and they remain among the basic building blocks of the economy. ■

Above: *This spectacular structure is the Skybridge carrying the rapid transport system Skytrain across the Fraser River in New Westminster, British Columbia.*

Right: *This council estate (public housing project) at Thamesmead in London, built about 1971, displays an aggressively modern appearance and concern for security.*

Top center: *Festooned with laundry, this high rise public housing block is in the Aberdeen section of Hong Kong.*

Top right: *The light rail system in downtown Detroit, here shown crossing above the Skywalk, is part of a locally-funded "renaissance" in the Motor City.*

Middle left: *Known as the "Big Dig," the Boston Central Artery Project is an enormously ambitious construction scheme that was supposed to have been financed by toll fees from the Massachusetts turnpike system. Innumerable complications and delays have clouded the picture considerably.*

Middle right: *CoAmerica Park, the new home of the Detroit Tigers baseball team—seen here in April of 2000, on opening day of its inaugural season— was built in part with funds that the State of Michigan derived from a tax on gaming.*

Bottom: *America's state-funded university systems are amongst the finest in the world. Seen here is the Fine Arts Center of Arizona State University.*

THROGMORTON STREET AND THE PLACE DE LA BOURSE

By the end of the eighteenth century the commercial world was making rapid adjustments to deal with the new kind of global economy created by colonial expansion. The old philosophy of mercantilism, in which every nation looked out only for itself, was gradually being replaced by the kind of macroeconomy foreseen by the great Scottish economist Adam Smith in his seminal book *The Wealth of Nations*, published in 1776. The theory he challenged was an archetypal example of oversimplification: export as much as you can, its advocates proclaimed, and import as little as possible—adding that the balance of trade reflected by this principle could be expressed properly only in terms of the value of goods measured against gold, or against the worth of other precious metals.

Smith argued that the true wealth of a nation was to be found in such things as an able labor force, and insisted that the acceptance of paper money would have the effect of liberating any economy. He also expressed a strong belief in the benefits of a free trade system, uncluttered by the protectionist restrictions that were an inevitable consequence of the old mercantilist beliefs.

A free trade movement began gaining strength in England soon after Smith's book was published, and the nineteenth century saw many steps—such as the repeal of the Corn Laws—toward the removal of tariffs, all of which benefited the London stock market and helped it attract foreign capital.

Before that could happen, however, British markets had to deal with the consequences of the French Revolution and the Napoleonic Wars, both of which interfered with Britain's trade within Europe. This interruption in trade came on the heels of Britain's loss of her American colonies.[7] In the long run, however, all this was offset by imperial expansion, by the nation's deplorable but lucrative participation in the slave trade (abolished by law in 1807), and by Britain's pioneering role in the creation of the Industrial Revolution.

In 1801 the London Stock Exchange reorganized itself as a private club with 550 members and moved to handsome new premises on Throgmorton Street, hard by the Bank of England. This was a practical expression of its growing strength, much of which derived from the investment climate generated by the "satanic mills" (so described by William Blake), which by then had been polluting England's fair and pleasant land for several decades. The age of steam had led to the proliferation of mechanized factories where men, women, and children spent twelve-hour shifts threading bobbins and stoking furnaces. The growth of manufacturing industries created a demand for coal and iron. The need to move heavy goods from one place to another led to the digging of a network of canals, the grading of new turnpikes, and eventually, starting in the 1820s, the development of the world's first railway network. Vast amounts of capital were required to achieve all this, and the stock market was on hand to see that it was raised. London became the first great city to be swept up in the age of industrial capitalism, and by the time Queen Victoria came to the throne it was the wealthiest place on earth.

Like any other stock market, the London exchange did

The poet and artist William Blake wrote of the "Satanic mills" of the Industrial Revolution. Despite such expressions of sincere disgust, however, factories such as this English bleach mill, depicted by William Hicks in about 1791, helped make Britain the wealthiest nation of the early modern period.

In Europe, America, and elsewhere, railroad stocks were the volatile high-tech stocks of the Victorian era, creating boom and bust conditions that could hardly be inferred from this photograph of a peaceful English train station in Saltash, Cornwall. An incidental consequence of the "railroad revolution" was a golden age of bridge building, typified here by Isambard Kingdom Brunel's Royal Albert Bridge spanning the River Tamar.

suffer occasional panics, such as the crash of 1847, which was caused by speculative practices on the part of the Bank of England, combined with the public's mania for railroad stocks. (The Internet stocks of their day, railway shares provided an opportunity to invest in state-of-the-art technology and dominated the London market for three-quarters of a century.) Essentially, though, nineteenth-century London was a very safe place to do business, thanks largely to Britain's political stability and avoidance of major wars. This was in stark contrast to the turmoil that disrupted life in much of Europe. Also, the British government was in the hands of a

democratically elected house generally sympathetic to commercial interests, and the stock exchange itself was self-governing and not subject to parliamentary control. To be a British subject was a requirement of membership in the exchange, but there was nothing to stop anybody, wherever they were from, from investing there. From the end of the Napoleonic Wars to the start of World War I, the London Stock Exchange was preeminent in the field. Its nearest rival in Europe was the Paris Bourse—officially known as the Compagnie des Agents de Change de Paris—which differed from the LSE in that, like many exchanges on the Continent, it was subject to tight governmental control and supervision.

Although preceded by bourses in Lyon and Toulouse, the Paris Bourse is a venerable enough institution, having won the official recognition of Louis XV in 1724. It was forced to suffer through the hyperinflation of the

revolutionary period and began to recover only when Napoleon put dampers on the economy. Like the London Stock Exchange, it began to take on its modern form in 1801—the year the Bank of France was established—and moved into its present quarters, the Palais de la Bourse, seven years later. There it settled into its singular and characteristically Gallic way of doing business, which saw trading divided into various categories.

A limited number of official *agents de change* (only sixty prior to 1898) were licensed by the government to operate on the *Parquet* ("floor"), a section of the trading floor located within an enclosure called the *Corbeille* ("basket"), where no one else was permitted. Otherwise, access to the trading floor—open six days a week from 12:30 P.M. to 3:00 P.M., while most Frenchmen were eating lunch—was the privilege of all French citizens "in full enjoyment of their civil rights," a definition that excluded undischarged bankrupts and women.

To become an *agent de change* it was necessary to be nominated by a decree countersigned by a financial minister of the current administration. These traders were awarded a variety of privileges, including the exclusive right to negotiate transfers of public funds as well as a distinct advantage when it came to handling what we would call blue-chip stocks.

Members of the *Coulisse* ("wing")—a term used to describe traders working within the Bourse (sometimes on its steps) but outside the Parquet—were for the most part limited to trading in the securities of more obscure and emerging companies, as well as in overseas issues. Eventually, however, the Coulisse developed its own advantages precisely because that was where foreign stocks were traded. Fortunes were made speculating in Russian railroad bonds, South American mining securities, and other overseas issues. Fortunes were lost, too, in reckless speculations such as those generated by the frenzy surrounding French efforts to build the Panama Canal.

The Paris Bourse seen in a photograph from the 1880s. In those days, members of the Coulisse—traders in the stocks of small and emerging companies and overseas issues—often conducted business on the steps of the exchange, beneath the imposing portico.

Plagued with disease and fraught with technical shortcomings, a French attempt to dig a canal through the Isthmus of Panama was one of the great investment disasters of the nineteenth century.

The Bourse's third market, known as the *Hors-Côté* ("outside"), was made up of over-the-counter brokers dealing in unlisted securities. This was similar to New York's curb exchange (the ancestor of the American Stock Exchange), operating on the sidewalks around the Bourse, often after hours (the *Petite Bourse*) and even in the evenings (the *Bourse du Soir*). In the 1930s, however, the curb market was assimilated into the Coulisse, which in turn merged with the Parquet in 1961.

As already noted, the nineteenth-century Paris Bourse was at a disadvantage as compared with the London Stock Exchange, in part because of the social and military upheavals of that century—the defeat of Napoleon, a major uprising in 1848, and, in 1870 and 1871, the disastrous Franco-Prussian War and the revolt of the Communards. In addition, the French middle classes were basically conservative when it came to financial

matters, while most representatives of the aristocracy were snobbish to the point of utter disdain in the face of vulgar commerce, which meant that an important source of potential capital went virtually untapped. In England, by contrast, members of the landed gentry, while perfectly capable of snooty behavior, were far more likely to participate in mercantile endeavors of all kinds.

THE ORIGINS OF WALL STREET

It may not have seemed important at the time, but the other great market story of the late eighteenth and early nineteenth centuries was the emergence of stock trading on the eastern seaboard of North America. Since they were primarily of British and Dutch descent, the early colonizers of New England and the Middle Atlantic region were the heirs of established trading traditions. They helped pioneer the use of paper money, starting in 1690 when the Province of Massachusetts Bay issued notes to pay for a military expedition in Canada. Other colonies followed suit. Officially the notes were called Bills of Credit, because the British Crown had not granted the settlers the right to issue money. Functionally, however, these bills could be used in exactly the way banknotes are used, and they contributed to a serious inflation problem that reached its peak around 1750. The British Parliament tried to bring this under control by introducing some sensible measures to prohibit the casual printing of paper money to meet the rising expenses of colonial assemblies. This attempt to put a damper on Yankee profligacy merely irritated the colonists, thereby helping precipitate the Revolution.

As long as North America remained a collection of colonies, cities such as Boston, New York, and Philadelphia functioned as outposts of empire from which merchants sent the riches of the Americas back to Europe. Those riches were astonishing. The British colonies might not have been important sources of gold, but they offered a wealth of other raw materials as well as seemingly limitless tracts of wilderness suitable for transformation into arable land—land on which to grow both produce for the expanding American population and cash crops that could be shipped across the Atlantic and redeemed in London or Liverpool.

Prior to 1776, the economy of the future United States was essentially uncomplicated (inflation aside), especially because the British government and its representatives in North America did all that could be done to restrict the rights of the colonists to trade with nations other than the United Kingdom and its other colonies. Such restrictions sometimes could be circumvented, were always resented, and eventually would be brushed aside by public uprising.

When independence was attained, Americans found themselves immensely rich in land and resources but lacking a universally recognized national currency, as well as key elements of the infrastructure needed to sustain the public sector of the economy. So far as cash was concerned, it took quite some time for the dollar to fully establish itself, and in the early years of the republic it had to compete with various European denominations, including the pound sterling, which remained legal tender. This meant that trade within the United States sometimes took on a quasi-international flavor.

When the short-lived First Bank of the United States was launched in 1792, it issued notes with the intention of establishing a national currency. Anti-federalist opposition to the idea of a central bank doomed the enterprise to failure.

As for the public sector, the U.S. Treasury Department was established in 1789, and it was followed two years later by the First Bank of the United States, with headquarters in Philadelphia. This institution functioned reasonably well but was dissolved in 1811 because of hostility from state-chartered banks, and because it had proven attractive to European investors—British investors in particular—raising the specter that the new nation's central bank could fall under the control of foreigners.

Certainly, the British had no intention of cutting their financial ties with America, to whatever extent they could be sustained under the circumstances, and they were greatly reassured when British subscriptions to the dissolved First Bank of the United States were returned despite the fact that the two nations were on the verge of war once again. This display of good faith did much to convince financiers in London that they had little to fear by investing in the former colonies. Meanwhile, speculators from other countries were all too eager to partake of what they perceived as limitless possibilities that in the colonial era had been unavailable to them. This alone

might have encouraged the emergence of independent American securities exchanges. Further stimulus came from the federal government and various state and local authorities, which floated bonds to avoid the imposition of unpopular taxes in the financing of public programs of various kinds.

The emergent nation had three principal banking centers, Philadelphia, New York, and Boston, with Philadelphia being at first the most powerful of the three. It was almost inevitable, then, that securities trading should spring up in these cities. Boston lagged behind a little, not establishing a formal exchange until 1834. The real battle for dominance was between Philadelphia and New York.

In Philadelphia the need for a formally constituted exchange had been suggested as early as 1746 when a retiring mayor had donated a sum of money to establish such an institution. The realization of his dream would have to wait almost half a century, but by 1754 merchants and brokers were meeting regularly at the London Coffee House to trade in securities and conclude other kinds of business. This coffeehouse later became one of the cradles of the Revolution and, consequently, was closed by the British during the War of Independence. Stock and bond traders simply moved to the City Tavern and continued their activities there until, in 1790, they formed themselves into the Philadelphia Board of

Left: *The London Coffee House, at the southwest corner of Market and Front Streets in Philadelphia, was home to America's first stock market.*

Right: *Located a stone's throw from today's New York Stock Exchange, the Tontine Coffee-House, built in 1794, was an early gathering place for Manhattan securities traders. Shown here is its constitution and an issue of* The New York Prices Current, *the indispensible business journal of its day.*

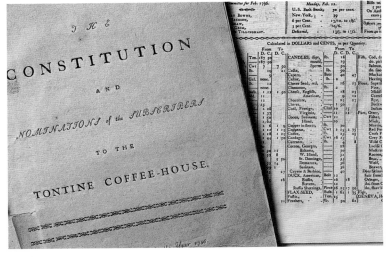

Brokers, the first organized American stock exchange.

New York was not far behind, though the traders who did business on the sidewalks of Wall Street and in the Tontine Coffee-House seem to have been a shade less scrupulous than their rivals to the south. Certainly they were quick to exploit any advantage they could discover, such as the fact that New York was significantly closer than Philadelphia, by great circle routes, to major ports in countries like England, France, and Holland. Happenings in European markets and politics were of vital importance to American brokers, and in those days, before the transatlantic cable and oceangoing steam packets, the only way for news to cross the Atlantic was by sailing ship. Typically, the crossing to Philadelphia took as much as a day longer than the crossing to New York. This meant that New York brokers, including the agents of foreign banks and investors, had the opportunity to digest the arriving information and head for Philadelphia by land—on horseback or in a fast post chaise—arriving in time to use their advance information to the disadvantage of the Philadelphians.

The Pennsylvanian merchants fought back, erecting a series of semaphore signal towers on hilltops across the state of New Jersey. Signalers manning these were capable of transmitting information, such as coded stock prices and lottery numbers, between New York and Philadelphia in as little as ten minutes, and this must be considered one of the first great experiments in modern communications technology.[8] The system worked so well that it remained in place till the coming of the telegraph in 1846. For a somewhat shorter time, it helped sustain Philadelphia's preeminence in the field of trading securities.

The embryonic New York exchange was not about to fold its tents, however. Nor would it allow itself to be undermined by scandals such as the bankruptcy of William Duer, a prominent British-born and -educated trader who was a close friend of Alexander Hamilton, a member of the Continental Congress, and a signatory to the Articles of Confederacy. Duer's flamboyant lifestyle had been supported by speculations that at first seemed

This painting by Vincent Maragliotti is an imaginary portrayal of the famous 1792 meeting beneath a buttonwood (sycamore) tree where twenty-four brokers and merchants signed the Buttonwood Agreement, considered the origin of the New York Stock Exchange.

inspired but in the long run proved foolish, and possibly rooted in felony.

Then as now, New York brokers were proud of their moxie, and setbacks had the effect of providing them with motivation. They did realize, however, that they could strengthen their position if they abandoned their extravagantly freewheeling ways in favor of a more organized style of business.

In May 1792 a group of two dozen New York brokers and traders met under a buttonwood tree that shaded the lot on which 68 Wall Street now stands. There they entered into an agreement to establish a formal exchange with prescribed methods of doing business that excluded the rigged auctions that till then had regularly occurred in securities trading in Lower Manhattan. Even so, there was still no bricks-and-mortar exchange, as such. For a decade and a half more, brokers would continue to ply their trade in coffeehouses and taverns, and often

(continued on page 122)

BUILDING HOMES:
GOVERNMENT AGENCIES IN THE MARKET

The Great Depression was a watershed in U.S. economic history, not only because of the misery it caused at the time, and the way in which it shook the nation's pride and confidence, but also because it saw the federal government entering the marketplace in wholly unprecedented ways. The government had always been a major employer by way of the military and the civil service. During Franklin D. Roosevelt's New Deal administration, however, the president determined to jumpstart the economy by using the government to create jobs in the private sector. The Civilian Conservation Corps (CCC) rounded up more than 2.5 million unemployed young men and paid them $30 a month to dig ditches, do forestry work, clear trash from national parks, and generally make themselves useful wherever there was a need for them. The government-financed Public Works Administration (PWA) transformed the American landscape by investing in projects that included a massive inventory of bridges, tunnels, dams, and public buildings of every description, many conceived on an heroic scale. The Works Progress Administration (WPA) even found work for artists and writers, creating murals for post offices and researching guidebooks, some of which remain in print today as key documents of the age.

Levittown, New York, neatly laid out in this 1949 aerial view, was one of the so-called "exurbs" that sprang up in the wake of World War II. The housing needs of many returning servicemen were met with the aid of so-called Fannie Mae mortgages, issued by the government-backed Federal National Mortgage Association and guaranteed by the Veterans Administration.

Among the government agencies created during this period was the Federal Housing Administration, voted into existence by Congress in 1934. It was intended to help everyone involved in the lower end of the housing market—homebuyers and home-builders alike—by providing federal insurance that would protect mortgage lenders from default. In 1938 the Federal National Mortgage Association (FNMA)—otherwise known as Fannie Mae—was created by the federal government and authorized to buy FHA

insured mortgages, thereby ensuring a secondary market (a market for trading in securities after they have been issued).

In 1944 Fannie Mae's charter was modified to permit it to buy mortgages guaranteed by the Veterans Administration, and as GIs returned to civilian life, it played a major role in the real estate aspect of the postwar recovery. In 1954 Fannie Mae became a "mixed ownership" corporation, its preferred stock still owned by the government but its common stock available to private investors. In 1968 the Fannie Mae charter was amended again and the company was split into two, Fannie Mae becoming an entirely privately owned entity, now permitted to purchase conventional mortgages (those not insured by the FHA or the VA). The publicly owned side of the agency became the Government National Mortgage Association (GNMA)—immediately dubbed Ginnie Mae—a wholly owned government association

*During the Great Depression of the 1930s, the U.S. government flew in the face of conventional wisdom by stepping in to create jobs for the unemployed, establishing for that purpose agencies such as the National Recovery Administration (NRA), the Public Works Administration (PWA), the Works Progress Administration (WPA), and the Civilian Conservation Corps (CCC). It was the PWA, for example, that financed the building of New York City's Triborough Bridge **(top right)**, connecting Manhattan, Queens, and the Bronx. The WPA helped keep the nation's culture alive, sponsoring theatrical events **(top)** along with mural projects and posters such as the example seen here **(right)**, originating in Chicago and promoting the work off the CCC. The latter, in slightly less than a decade, found employment for 2.5 million young men **(center right)**, who were paid $30 a month to perform a variety of useful tasks, from digging irrigation ditches to cleaning up national monuments.*

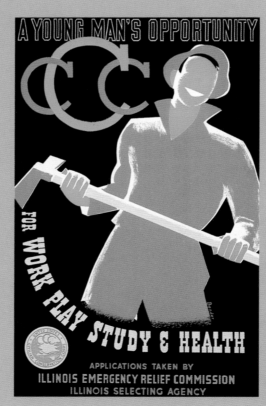

Below: *President Franklin Delano Roosevelt's efforts to create a "new deal" for the American people were avidly and actively supported by his wife, Eleanor, here seen visiting a WPA site in Des Moines, Iowa.*

Bottom: *A Native American view of the "taming" of the Old West is being created by Navaho mural artist Gerald Nailor in a photograph taken in Window Rock, Arizona, in 1943.*

operating within the Department of Housing and Urban Development (HUD) and dedicated to ensuring that mortgage funds are available throughout the U.S., especially in economically deprived areas where loans are more difficult to obtain.

Two years later, the Federal Home Loan Mortgage Association—Freddie Mac—was chartered. This government-sponsored private corporation is designed to purchase mortgages from financial institutions in order to repackage them as securities for sale to private investors, thus creating funds for home loans.

As vestiges of the New Deal, these agencies have contributed hugely to the growth of home ownership among low- and middle-income families. In the sprawling suburbs of the Levittown era, in rural communities by-passed by the Interstates of the Eisenhower years, and in once blighted urban streets on their way to being reclaimed from poverty and crime, the progeny of the Federal Housing Administration have brought opportunity to millions of American families. ∎

During the Great Depression and the World War II period, housing was a major concern of the U.S. government, with millions of people, like these Brooklyn residents **(below)***, living in substandard conditions. It was the aim of the United States Housing Authority to wipe out slums, as expressed in a 1941 poster* **(bottom left)***. The war period saw the government mobilizing its resources to create temporary accommodations, such as an estate* **(bottom right)** *in St. Paul, Minnesota, for both military personnel and defense industry workers.*

Cross Out Slums

Top left: The rush to build housing during World War II led at times to something like a revival of the barn-raising tradition. Here, in 1941, a construction crew raises the framework for a building in the Franklin Terrace defense housing project in Erie, Pennsylvania.

Top right: As this example from Annapolis, Maryland, demonstrates, by the 1980s public housing projects had moved far away from the monotony of row upon row of nearly identical buildings that had made the defense projects of the war years, and even the exurbs of the postwar era, so dreary.

Above: Today the government has a hand in the operation of several kinds of mortgage programs. The Federal Home Loan Mortgage Association—better known as Freddie Mac— is a federally sponsored private corporation charged with purchasing mortgages from financial institutions and then repackaging them as securities in order to generate the funding for new home loans.

Left: Government-supported mortgages and loans also contribute to the renovation of existing homes, contributing to the rebirth of run-down inner-city neighborhoods and to the preservation of small-town and rural America.

in the open air, where they shared the sidewalks with hawkers of sweet corn and buttermilk and with the vagrant pigs who lived off the plentiful garbage.

In those early postcolonial days, trading was almost entirely in government bonds, but by the end of the eighteenth century a few new commercial issues began to appear, notably those of banks and insurance companies, as Manhattan moved briskly toward becoming the nation's principal banking center. (This came about in part thanks to the Pennsylvania legislature's decision to outlaw private banks, which drove several important financiers to move their business operations away from the City of Brotherly Love and into the Big Apple.) Commercial activity increased after the War of 1812, and by 1817, when the New York Stock & Exchange

Board was established, with new rules and a new constitution, thirty stocks were listed. "Board" was included in the name to honor the so-called Board Room of the Tontine Coffee-House, where the members met. Membership cost $25.

The War of 1812 had been financed partly by means of government bonds that at first were dangerously undersubscribed, until a small syndicate that included John Jacob Astor—the German-born immigrant who had built a fortune upon fur trading, land speculation, and commodity dealing—stepped in to informally underwrite the issue. By buying the surplus at a considerable discount, then reselling it at close to face value, Astor made a profit of approximately 100 percent.

Once the war was over, the U.S. economy began to gain momentum on the strength of an expansionism that saw the frontier pushed back again and again and American industry on the rise, its progress driven by ambitious and often ruthless men who recognized the

Completed in 1825, the Erie Canal was a major factor in establishing New York as the prime commercial hub of the United States. This in turn ensured that Wall Street would be recognized as the national center of securities trading, usurping the role of its greatest rival, the Philadelphia exchange.

potential involved in tapping the nation's enormous natural resources. There were economic downturns, but the periods of recovery more than offset these interruptions in the upward trajectory. Investment in new turnpikes and canals helped boost the stock markets in both New York and Philadelphia, which ran neck and neck until the opening of the Erie Canal in 1825 confirmed Manhattan as the nation's commercial capital. As in Europe, the emergence shortly afterward of railroads as a practical means of transportation prompted a new round of investment and speculation, strengthening the position of the New York brokers still further.

This period was marked by the rise of investment banking companies designed specifically to raise capital for the many new enterprises that were being launched. One of the first was Prime, Ward & King, founded in New York in 1826 by Nathaniel Prime, a Wall Street veteran. Others, such as Thomas Biddle & Company of Philadelphia, were established in various other financial centers but still channeled much business into New York. Foreign investors, too, set up merchant banking operations that would have a powerful impact on the evolution of Wall Street. The House of Rothschild—then by far the world's most powerful private banking concern—was strongly represented in the form of August Belmont & Company; Belmont, a protégé of the Rothschilds,

In the early 1820s, the securities traded on the New York Stock & Exchange Board consisted chiefly of shares in local banks and insurance companies, along with federal, state, and local government bonds.

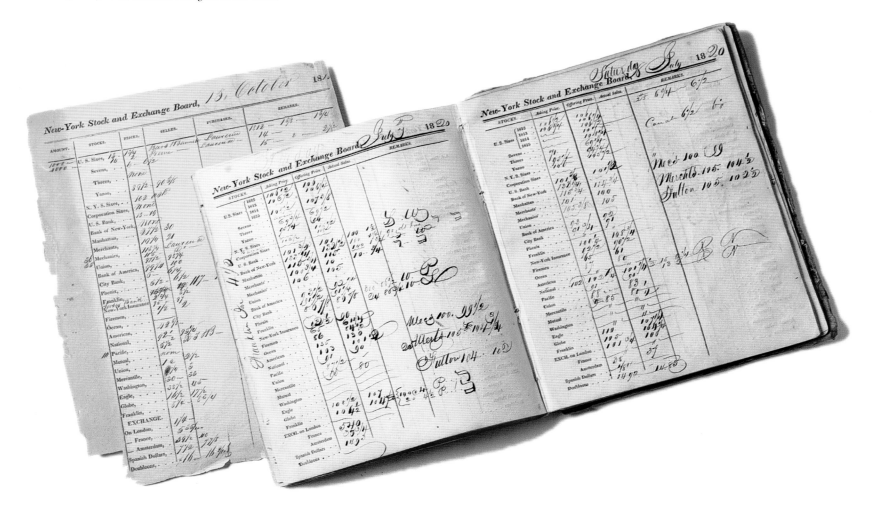

LAYING THE ATLANTIC CABLE.

The laying of the first transatlantic cable—a task completed in 1866—meant that Europe and America could now be in virtually instantaneous contact, which had immense consequences for securities trading on both continents.

Compact and easy to use, the telegraph was the Internet of the nineteenth century. Its impact on stock markets was enormous since it permitted quotes to be transmitted rapidly to distant locations.

From 1842 to 1854, the New York Stock & Exchange Board gathered in this large hall where, following each of its two daily sessions, the "authentic news of the stock speculators" was announced.

became the family's de facto agent in America. Possessed of an astute business mind and considerable charm, Belmont, despite the social disadvantages implicit in his Jewish origins, became a prominent figure around New York and did much to strengthen the commercial ties between the United States and Europe.[9] Jewish financiers in general had strong connections in the Old World, and played an important role in the evolution of Wall Street almost from the very first.

The invention and rapid acceptance of the telegraph in the 1840s was another stimulus to activity on Wall Street, both attracting investment and permitting the more rapid dissemination of information about happenings in the market. (The coming of the Atlantic cable in 1866 would allow, for the first time, virtually instantaneous communications between the United States and Europe.) Also in the 1840s, the Exchange Board moved the scene of its daily activities to a large rented hall at the corner of Wall and William Streets. Membership in the organization now cost $400 a year.

A colorful account of the Exchange as it was during this period was published by the journalist George G. Foster in his 1853 collection *Fifteen Minutes Around New York*. There he describes the "inner red-canopied sanctuary of the Exchange" and notes the arrival of members of "the mercantile old fogy class . . . [who] pause to blow, at every three or four paces, as they hoist their heavy and unwieldy persons slowly and toilingly up the granite steps."

He goes on to build a word picture of the scene in the rotunda as members and clerks hold sotto voce conversations that, amplified by the acoustics of the interior, accumulate into a "confused, perpetual murmur, like the swarming of bees," which eventually "becomes thunderous in your ear, and almost crazes you." Overheard by an outsider, he reports, the talk—all half phrases and broken sentences, supplemented by enigmatic gestures and signs—is as mysterious as anything that might be encountered in a Chinese temple.

Here Foster depicts the Exchange at the moment known in the parlance of the day as "High Change," the time when, after a "two shilling dinner at Brown's," traders met to discuss the morning's business, attempting to analyze the strategies of the "big bugs" in order to lay plans for tomorrow. It was the period, too, when the commercial reporters of the daily papers prowled for tidbits of gossip that might hint at who was going short, who was lame, and who was being cornered. Conveyed in whispers, shrugs, and innuendos, these tidbits would be rushed to the telegraph office "as soon as the last cat was hung," to be transmitted to the provinces, where they would be "trumpeted forth the next morning as if the Delphian oracle had spoken."

When the hour of three chimed from the spire of Trinity Church, all this activity came to an end:

> The banks have already their shutters closed, though now and then some belated customer steals out from the door and rushes wildly off with a bit of paper in his hand, which he savagely crushes up with his fingers, lest it should escape his grasp and have to be taken up over again tomorrow. The street grows rapidly vague and silent—footsteps echo but rarely along the pavement—the omnibuses cease to stop at the head of the street to wait for passengers—the clock points to ten minutes after three and Wall Street has locked up and gone home.[10]

In 1842 the New York Stock & Exchange Board moved into the spanking new Merchants' Exchange at the intersection of Wall and William Streets. Mellowed by time, the structure still exists, now being known as the Old Custom House.

4 : The Victorian Era and the Opening of Global Markets

1850–1900

In 1878–79, Edgar Degas painted Portraits à la Bourse, *depicting activity on the trading floor of the Paris Stock Exchange. The artist had good reasons to be interested in the subject matter, his own family having been almost ruined by reckless speculation in cotton.*

The Victorian era saw the rise of stock markets all over Europe, few of them competitive with London or Paris on a global scale but each important within its own sphere of influence, and several of them acquiring a broad international significance.

With the formation, in 1871, of the German Empire, Prussia's dominance of the German-speaking world led

In 1857, a financial panic originating in the California gold fields and known as the "western blizzard" hit Wall Street, forcing some banks and dealers into bankruptcy. This painting by Charles G. Rosenberg and James H. Cafferty is titled Wall Street, Half Past Two O'clock—October 13, 1867 *and portrays the scene when the panic was at its peak.*

to the recognition of Berlin as the capital, and during the decades of prosperity that followed, the Berlin Börse rose to considerable prominence. (Its cousin in Frankfurt was also of some significance and would come fully into its own a century later.) As with the Paris Bourse, however, German exchanges were subject to government control; in 1896 legislation was enacted that placed restraints on activities such as speculation on stock futures. This drove many major German investors to shift the focus of their activity to overseas exchanges such as those in London, Amsterdam, and Brussels.

The original rules of the London exchange had been based on those of the old Amsterdam exchange. In 1876 the tables were turned when the Amsterdam Bourse was reorganized roughly along the lines of the London Stock Exchange—though certain British peculiarities, such as the division of members into brokers (intermediaries with the public) and jobbers (market makers), were not adopted. This ushered in a period when Amsterdam became once more an important center for the trading of international securities of all kinds, with a particular emphasis on oil stocks.

The Brussels Bourse, founded by Napoleon in 1801, became another prominent market, upholding the traditions of the Flemings who had helped create the brokerage business five hundred years earlier. The most interesting nineteenth-century development in Belgian finance, however, came in 1822 with the launching of a new kind of bank: the Societé Générale pour favoriser l'industrie nationale, which not only loaned money to Belgian industry but also played an active role in actually directing many industrial endeavors, from mining to transportation. In this respect it served as a model for the so-called universal banks that came to dominate the neighboring German economy three decades later, and also played a major role in France. Such universal banks

Above: *In this 1889 photograph, visitors crowd the gallery overlooking the Gothic Revival splendor of the New York Stock Exchange's main trading floor.*

Right: *By the late nineteenth century, Wall Street had become an international force, its potency symbolized by financiers like J. P. Morgan and Jacob Schiff, whose names carried as much weight in Europe as in America. The focal point of this power nexus was the New York Stock Exchange, whose building is seen at the center of this photograph from about 1887.*

tend to usurp, to a large extent, the role of capital markets. In Brussels, however, the Bourse continued to play a significant role, and in 1874 it moved to a suitably grand Louis XIV–style building.

Various Swiss cities, such as Zurich, Basel, and Geneva, housed important exchanges. Not surprisingly, given Switzerland's strong banking tradition going back to the late Middle Ages, these tended to be dominated by the local banks. In Austria, too, bankers played a controlling role; the country's premier bank, Creditanstalt, was founded in Vienna in 1855 and for decades functioned as a classic example of the universal bank.

Stockholm and Copenhagen were host to securities markets of some international significance, as was Milan, though the Italian economy remained predominantly agrarian. In most Eastern European countries the local bourses were of relatively little account beyond their own borders, and they frequently doubled as commodity exchanges, where the house business was likely to be dominated by trading in the local agricultural staples.

As the nineteenth century wore on, all of these European markets—even London and Paris—were increasingly forced to take note of what was happening across the Atlantic, where Wall Street was becoming a formidable power in the world of international commerce.

PASSION AND PANICS

Wall Street's global prestige was not won easily. Certainly postcolonial America's brave new world bubbled with commercial energy, and the seemingly endless supply of raw materials bred tremendous confidence in the future of the American economy. At the same time, and perhaps because of that energy and confidence, the New York financial and securities markets seemed to attract rogue speculators by the bushel, making Wall Street a sometimes risky place to invest your money, as was made apparent by the frequent panics that came to characterize life in the investment jungles of Lower

Manhattan. (Americans preferred the frenetic term "panic" to the more sedate British "bubble.")

During the 1840s the New York Stock & Exchange Board was at the hub of a rather quiet financial scene, the American commercial securities market being dominated by banking stocks, though toward the end of the period an increasing number of far more volatile railroad shares was beginning to cause tremors of excitement. The 1850s, in contrast, were marked by a series of scandals and a major panic. The scandals involved the issuance of fraudulent shares, mostly on the part of the heads of railroad companies who took advantage of slow communications with Europe, where American railroad stock was popular. (No one on the far side of the Atlantic, it was assumed, would notice a few legal discrepancies.)

The major panic was precipitated, at least in part, by the most sensational of all the ore strikes ever made in America. This was the 1849 discovery of gold at Sutter's Creek, which drew hundreds of thousands of men and women from all over the world to California. One result of the gold rush was the spawning of many small banks in the western boomtowns. Over a period of several years, the sheer quantity of ore passing through their hands encouraged some bankers to become reckless in

Left: *Referring to traders who speculate in rising or falling prices, the terms "bull" and "bear" had been current for at least thirty years when, in 1879, William Holbrook Beard painted this fantasy of financial warfare, set at the hallowed intersection of Wall and Broad Streets.*

Below: *In the era of the California gold rush, banks were free to issue their own notes, such as this example, redeemable for "twenty five cents in gold dust."*

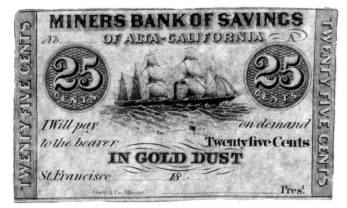

the quantity of banknotes they issued. (At the time, it was the right of any chartered bank to issue paper money.) This triggered a cycle of inflation that led to the failure of a number of insurance companies and other financial institutions. When the buzzards came home to roost, the result was the Panic of 1857, sometimes called the "western blizzard." Many traders on Wall Street managed to benefit from it, correctly anticipating the course events would take and selling short at just the right moment. Others lost their shirts. The market soon bounced back, however, and was in a generally healthy condition at the outbreak of the War Between the States in 1861.

On Wall Street the war arrived on April 17 in the form of an angry mob that rushed in from Broadway, headed for the offices of the *Journal of Commerce*, a mildly pro-slavery publication. The staff there was forced to raise the Union flag, whereupon the rabble raised a cheer, then set off to pay friendly visits to other newspapers thought to be sympathetic to the Confederate cause.

The Civil War period witnessed the issue of the first "greenbacks": non-interest-bearing notes, popularly said to be backed by nothing more than the green ink they were printed with, that had the status of legal tender in the North. It also saw the rise to fame of an obscure Philadelphia investment banker named Jay Cooke, who was engaged by Secretary of the Treasury Salmon Chase to help float a series of massive government bond issues required to finance the Union cause. Cooke sold these bonds with the aid of a network of as many as 2,500

On the eve of the American Civil War, the federal government began to issue so-called greenbacks, a form of paper currency not tied to the value of gold or any other precious metal; skeptics claimed it was backed by nothing more than the green ink used by the printers.

Howard Pyle illustrated The Rush from the New York Stock Exchange on September 18, 1873, *the day on which the great investment banking house of Jay Cooke & Co. was forced to close its doors, precipitating a major panic.*

agents scattered throughout the northern states, with whom he communicated by telegraph, thus establishing the world's first "wire house."

Financing the Civil War added greatly to the stature of the New York stock market. In 1863 the New York Stock & Exchange Board changed its name to the New York Stock Exchange, plain and simple. In 1865, as the war ended, the exchange moved into its own premises, a five-story building at 10-12 Broad Street (just south of Wall Street), which was enlarged and remodeled twice during the next three decades. In 1869 the New York Stock Exchange and its Government Bond Department

(continued on page 140)

Right: *When Edward A. Calahan invented the stock ticker, in 1867, it transformed the securities industry by permitting share prices to be transmitted almost instantly throughout the Wall Street financial district, and soon to brokers in other cities, too. This handsome example dates from the mid-1870s.*

Below left: *Seen here demonstrating his recent invention, the telephone, Alexander Graham Bell is one of the men who came to symbolize an age of American technological innovation that was driven by the stock market, which in turn drove the market to new heights.*

Below right: *Bell's great rival, Thomas Edison, is seen here with one of his most celebrated inventions, the phonograph.*

CLOSELY HELD:
INVESTMENT IN PRIVATE COMPANIES

"If you can't trust a man's handshake, you can't trust his signature."

— Warren A. Bechtel

Levi Straus. Publix Super Markets. Bechtel. The Trump Organization. Suntory. Seiko. Bertelsmann AG. Enterprise Rent-A-Car. Mars, Inc.

What do these giant corporations have in common?

Each is privately held, which is to say that they are not listed by any stock exchange, their shares never having been made available to investors through the medium of a public offering. In America and most developed markets, they are subject to strict financial disclosure requirements and other government regulations, in much the same way as listed companies. On the other hand, they are not vulnerable to shareholder uprisings, hostile takeovers, or greenmail, as is the case with companies whose stock is traded to the public.

Not only are these companies privately held, they tend to be private in every way. Mars, Inc., for example, is noted for the atmosphere of extreme discretion that cloaks its candy bar and cat food empire, which is hardly surprising given that the company is controlled by a tight group of family members, including John Franklyn Mars

---

When the British handed over sovereignty of Hong Kong to the People's Republic of China in 1997, the transfer included the nearly completed Hong Kong International Airport. In 1998 Bechtel Group, Inc., one of the most prominent privately-held companies in the world, completed the bridges and roads connecting Hong Kong Island to the site of the new airport. The construction project is part of a remarkable $20 billion infrastructure development effort called the Hong Kong Airport Core Programme, led by an integrated Bechtel-government team.

(President and CEO), his brother Forrest Mars Jr., and their sister Jacqueline Mars Vogel.

Many prominent privately held companies are essentially family businesses. The largest in America is Cargill, Inc., the widely diversified Minnesota-based giant that is the nation's largest exporter of grain, at the same time being a major player in several other commodity fields, as well as having large-scale involvement in financial markets, food processing, feed and fertilizer production, and the slaughter of cattle. Although close to 85 percent of the corporation's stock is held by direct descendents of the founder, this is no mom-and-pop operation.

The company's sales in 2000 amounted to well in excess of $47 billion.

The concept of the family business is as old as commerce itself, with fathers, sons, brothers, and cousins coalescing into organizations that naturally take on the shape of hierarchies. Marriages sometimes bring in new partners, as do common interests that draw two or more of these hierarchical units into the same orbit (a situation than can stimulate competition or cooperation).

Such closely held businesses are sometimes started with savings, sometimes with borrowed money. Some are built on a single good idea,

and some on a combination of vision and gambler's luck. The Ford Motor Company, a family business in the glory days of the Model-T and the Model-A, had its roots in Henry Ford's concept of an automobile for everyman; but that dream might have come to nothing if he had not been ready to risk his life for it, as happened in 1904 when he took his Arrow Special out onto a frozen lake and drove it to a world speed record.

Whatever its beginnings, a closely held corporation depends from day one upon private equity investment. As the company grows, it may need to borrow, but essentially

Above: *Henry Ford shows off his first automobile—dubbed a quadricycle—on Bagley Avenue in Detroit in 1896.*

Top center: *Founded in 1969, DHL Worldwide Express was a pioneer in the field of express delivery services. Here DHL President Robert M. Kuijpers (left) shakes hands with Boeing Europe Chairman Dick Jones on the 1999 purchase of 44 Boeing 757 aircraft.*

Top right: *The largest privately held company in America is Minnesota-based Cargill, Inc., a conglomerate that, among other things, is the nation's largest exporter of grain. Here Cargill workers are seen raking a grain pile in Wood River, Nebraska.*

Bottom right: *Another large privately held corporation is Koch Industries, Inc., whose multiple interests include the production (seen here) of pollution control equipment, a specialty of its John Zink subsidiary.*

Bottom left: *During the company's heyday, when Model T's like these rolled off the production line, Ford Motors was a privately held corporation. The first public offering of Ford stock did not occur until the 1950s.*

it survives and expands by returning profits to its corporate coffers.

While businesses like Cargill have built their fortunes by concentrating upon the basic building blocks of the economy, this type of company lends itself well to the ambitions of individuals with a flair for self-promotion. Donald Trump inherited a significant real estate business, but it was his personality and ability to generate media publicity that transformed it into something far more substantial.

In an era when the entertainment industry is dominated by a half-dozen media conglomerates, it's easy to forget that show business—especially the movies—was built largely on the enterprise of closely held companies dominated by families or individuals. Names that spring immediately to mind are the Warner Brothers and Walt Disney. Like so many movie pioneers, the Warners—Harry, Sam, Albert, and Jack—began their careers soon after the turn of the century by operating nickelodeons, then moved on to theater ownership and film production. Theirs remained a family business for a couple of decades largely because no Wall Street house was prepared to underwrite such a motley crew involved in so dubious an enterprise.

Coming to Los Angeles in 1923, after the failure of his first business in Kansas City, Walt Disney joined with his brother Roy to launch the tiny animation studio that five years later would have its first big hit with *Steamboat Willie*, the sound cartoon that launched the meteoric career of Mickey Mouse. Throughout the 1930s, as Disney added Donald Duck, Pluto, and Goofy to his stable of stars, the company

remained a private entity. And despite his success, Disney had to struggle to find backing to produce his great first animated feature, *Snow White and the Seven Dwarfs*.

Walt Disney's reason for having the company remain private was that he was determined to control every aspect of every frame of film that emerged from his studio. Eventually, however—in 1940—he was forced to go public in order to capitalize the ambitious expansion program that would see the production of films like *Pinocchio* and *Fantasia*.

Today's Walt Disney Company is the epitome of the entertainment mega-corporation. This does not mean that the age of the significant private show biz company is dead, however. Anyone who thinks otherwise need only look at the businesses spawned by *Star Wars* and *Indiana Jones* maestro George Lucas. His Lucasfilm Ltd. has produced five of the twenty top grossing films of all times. His special effects house, Industrial Light and Magic, is the industry yardstick, while Skywalker Sound and the THX Group are leaders in sound recording and sound systems respectively.

The Lucas empire epitomizes everything that is positive about the concept of the privately owned company. The writer/producer/director's success and business savvy have enabled him to remain in full creative control of an enterprise that depends upon avoidance of the kind of ritualized compromise that has become the norm in the film industry. Like his acknowledged hero, Walt Disney, George Lucas has used his independence to remain true to his vision. ■

Top left: *Although his company eventually went public, Walt Disney was a classic example of a filmmaker who used the concept of the closely held private corporation to permit himself the kind of creative independence shareholders might have balked at.*

Top center: *In 1919, movie luminaries Douglas Fairbanks, Mary Pickford, Charles Chaplin, and D.W. Griffith (left to right) incorporated United Artists, a closely held distribution company intended to give them control of their artistic destinies.*

Right: *Claudette Colbert and Clark Gable starred in the 1934 hit* It Happened One Night, *produced by Columbia Pictures, which had been launched a decade earlier as a private company backed by the Giannini brothers of the Bank of Italy.*

Top right: *The tradition of creative independence through control of a closely held company has been maintained by writer/director/producer George Lucas.*

Middle right: *The prerogatives of private ownership have permitted Lucas to be the absolute auteur of the Star Wars films.*

Bottom right: *Independent producer Albert "Cubby" Broccoli, originator of the James Bond movies, visits a huge sound stage under construction for* The Spy Who Loved Me.

Bottom center: *Film still from Dr. No, with Sean Connery as Agent 007.*

Christmas Carnival in the New York Stock Exchange, *an 1885 engraving for* Harper's Weekly, *captures the mood of ebullience of the market in the Gilded Age.*

(formed in 1867 to deal solely in U.S. government securities) joined forces with the Open Board of Brokers—one of several rival groups—thereby doubling its membership to become America's preeminent securities exchange.

The NYSE now embarked on its most dynamic period of expansion. The half century between the Civil War and World War I was an era of investment banking on the grand scale, in which often colorful and always ruthless financiers like Jim Fisk, Jay Gould, Daniel Drew, E. H. Harriman, Jacob Schiff, and J. P. Morgan provided the capital for "robber barons" like Andrew Carnegie,

Henry Frick, and John D. Rockefeller to carve out vast industrial empires. Wall Street was the catalyst.

Railroads crossed the continent, bringing many new territories into the national mainstream, all to the benefit of the NYSE. This was a great age of invention, too. Alexander Graham Bell and Thomas Edison were only the most visible symbols of technological fecundity in a period that saw the introduction of the light bulb and the telephone, and also the typewriter, the phonograph, the trolley car, the Linotype machine, the mimeograph, the pocket camera, the motion picture camera, the rotogravure, the bicycle, the cash register, the electric punch-card system, the fountain pen, the sewing machine, and hundreds of other useful novelties, including, eventually, the automobile and the airplane. Each of these gave rise to an industry that would be embraced by the brokers at 10-12 Broad Street. Technology had an impact on the workings of the NYSE itself, which benefited from such innovations as the ticker-tape machine, first seen on Wall Street in 1867, and the telephone, first installed on the trading floor in 1878.

Still, there were crises, often of operatic proportions. The real fun began soon after the conclusion of the Civil War, when the New York financial world fell into the hands of a small group of gifted manipulators with the moral scruples of undernourished piranhas.

The war and its aftermath provided an unstable social climate in which both young rogues and veteran raiders could flourish. Among the latter were "Commodore" Cornelius Vanderbilt and Daniel Drew, and among the former, Jay Gould and James Fisk. Together they would manage to create panics that would put Wall Street in the big leagues.

Remembered today as the architect of the New York Central Railroad, Vanderbilt—brought up in extreme poverty on Staten Island—made money in shipping and many other fields before, in his sixties, he turned his attention to the iron horse. Drew, a rigid, born-again Christian and former circus performer, also made a fortune in shipping before deciding that the future lay in the railroads. He and Vanderbilt were natural rivals, especially because Vanderbilt was bullish by nature and conviction, while Drew was a master manipulator of the bear market.

In the early 1850s Drew gained control of the run-down Erie Railroad, had himself appointed treasurer, then began to speculate in the company's shares, managing to squeeze millions out of the Erie over a period of several years despite the fact that the company was virtually wiped out during the "western blizzard" panic. His avowed piety and Scrooge-like appearance notwithstanding, Drew was a con artist of the most blatant sort. Selling cattle on the hoof early in his career, he practiced an old wrangler scam that involved denying the animals water until just before they were about to be sold, then

For much of the nineteenth century, railroad stocks dominated American securities markets. This stereoscopic image shows a Union Pacific locomotive pushing flat cars across Devil's Gate Bridge over Weber Canyon, Utah.

feeding them salt and letting them drink as much as they wanted, so that when a steer stepped on the scales his weight was artificially inflated, sometimes by forty or fifty pounds. On one legendary occasion, when Drew needed to create a bull market for his prize investment, the Erie, he came up with the startlingly simple trick of pulling a kerchief from his pocket, thereby "accidentally" depositing a slip of paper on the floor in front of a group of known speculators. When the paper was surreptitiously retrieved, it appeared to be an order to purchase a large quantity of Erie stock. The speculators hurried off to find their brokers and enjoyed a few days of bliss before they discovered that they had been outsmarted yet again, as Drew took his profits and cheerfully watched the stock tumble.

Among the new arrivals on Wall Street in the post–Civil War period were two young reprobates whom Drew, drawn to his own kind, took under his wing. One of these was Jim Fisk, a flamboyant New Englander who, like Drew, had enjoyed a brief fling in the carnival world, traveling with a small circus-menagerie before discovering the vastly more rewarding joys of manipulating money. When the War Between the States broke out he learned how to grease palms in Washington to win contracts on behalf of the Boston retailer Jordan,

In an image that owed more to wishful thinking than reality, political cartoonist Thomas Nast portrayed the derailing, by "Justice," of ruthless speculators Jim Fisk, Daniel Drew, and Jay Gould, infamous for their manipulation of Erie Railroad stock.

Seen here in a daguerreotype by Mathew Brady, Cornelius "Commodore" Vanderbilt was a self-made man and one of Wall Street's most ruthless operators.

Jim Fisk loved wine, women, and song as much as he enjoyed outwitting rival speculators. He was shot dead by a failed investor who had become the lover of his ex-mistress.

Driving one early partner to suicide and ruining many other lives, Jay Gould earned the right to be called the most hated (and feared) man on Wall Street.

Marsh & Co. to supply blankets to the Union Army. Learning that cotton was selling for twelve cents a pound in the beleaguered South, while the asking price up North was two dollars a pound, Fisk began to amass the beginnings of his first fortune by smuggling cargoes of cotton through the lines. When the war was almost over he chartered the fastest vessel he could find and had it waiting off Halifax, Nova Scotia, the most easterly point on the continent that was connected to the telegraph. (This was a year before the transatlantic cable came into service.) When the captain of the ship received Fisk's one-word message—"Go!"—he called for a full head of steam and took off for Europe, arriving well ahead of the regular mail boats so that Fisk's agents in London had time to unload $5 million in Confederate bonds before news arrived that the Confederacy was a thing of the past.

Setting up in New York, Fisk promptly lost all his ill-gotten gains to veteran stock sharks who knew how to shake down greenhorns, however cunning and avaricious. Within months, though, he had found new backers and set up in the burgeoning financial district as a partner in the company Fisk & Belden. It was at this point, in the winter of 1865–66, that Fisk performed the unlikely feat of winning the trust and protection of one of the most feared men on Wall Street, Daniel Drew. Shortly after, he introduced Drew to another driven young scoundrel, Jay Gould.

How Fisk and Gould became friends is one of the great mysteries of Wall Street. Sometimes described as verging on the effeminate, Gould was as dour and laconic as Fisk was flashy and garrulous. It was a classic instance of the attraction of opposites, and friendship might not be the right term to describe their relationship. Rather, they were drawn together into a sort of symbiotic unholy alliance.

Born poor (like Vanderbilt, Drew, and Fisk), Gould began his professional life as a bookkeeper in the Catskill Mountains. After persuading Charles Leupp, an elderly leather merchant, to float a sizable loan, Gould, then age twenty, built and operated a tannery. It did well for a

while but went under during the 1857 crash. Devastated, Leupp killed himself, a tragedy for which some members of the business community held Gould responsible for the rest of his life.

In fact, Gould had been using company funds to indulge in speculative activity on his own behalf and had squirreled away enough cash to move his base of operations to Lower Manhattan, where he became involved in stock manipulation, though on a modest scale prior to his alliance with Fisk and Drew. Soon, Drew shocked the Street by taking on the two younger men as partners to help him tend his personal cash cow, the Erie Railroad. Possibly Drew felt the need for fresh blood to handle the dirtier side of the business. In any case, he quickly taught his protégés the secrets of watering stock and selling short. They demonstrated their willingness to learn by conducting a series of corporate raids characterized by precise planning and merciless execution. The epitome of paunchy panache, Fisk used his newfound clout to indulge his taste for nine-course dinners, flashy jewelry, comic-opera military costumes, and fleshy showgirls. Gould stayed at home and counted his money.

As it happens, Commodore Vanderbilt—then a venerable but still ruthless figure, well into his sixties—had begun to cast greedy glances at the Erie Railroad, which he thought would make a pretty pendant for his New York Central. Relying on his well-honed predatory instincts, he set out to corner Erie stock. At first things went well; so well, in fact, that Drew tried to reach a compromise with Vanderbilt—or perhaps only pretended to. As soon as an agreement had been made, Drew went back to planning, with the aid of Fisk and Gould, a way of undermining the Commodore. Just when Vanderbilt thought he had the Erie in his pocket, he discovered that Fisk and Gould, as directors of the company, had voted themselves $10 million in Erie bonds. These were earmarked for "improvements," but a clause in the prospectus made them immediately convertible into stock. Soon the Street was flooded with Erie certificates that were so freshly printed it was said that the ink came off on your fingers.

For the moment Vanderbilt was stymied, but he fought back. Earlier, he had persuaded Judge George Barnard to slap Fisk and Gould with a bouquet of writs and injunctions intended to prevent bond-to-stock conversions of precisely the sort he had just been burned by. Now he demanded that the judge swear out arrest warrants for Gould, Fisk, and Drew, claiming that the use made of the bond issue had clearly violated the law.

The three conspirators fled across the Hudson River to New Jersey and, from Taylor's Hotel in Jersey City, defied the authority of New York City. Sporting one or another of his many Ruritanian uniforms, Fisk took to strutting along the banks of the Hudson, where he had installed cannons pointed at the spires of Manhattan. More practical, and quickly bored with exile, Gould headed for Albany, where he mounted a campaign designed to persuade New York State legislators to pass a bill legalizing the making of bond-to-stock transactions of the sort he and Fisk had indulged in. Representatives

This illustration from Harper's Weekly *purports to show the chaos at the New York Gold Exchange on Black Friday — September 24, 1869, the day that Jay Gould's attempt to corner gold reached its climax.*

of the people did not come cheap when doing favors for citizens as well-heeled as Gould, Fisk, and Drew. Many palms had to be greased, sometimes more than once, since Vanderbilt had sent his own agents to lobby, armed with satchels overflowing with cash. In the end, though, the Commodore concluded that he was throwing good money after bad and decided to cut his losses, which were said to be in the region of $6 million. The Gould-sponsored bill was allowed to pass through the legislature and the members of the Erie Gang, as the press liked to call them, returned to the Big Apple.

Old and tired, Drew attempted a reconciliation with Vanderbilt, which was grudgingly accepted on the Commodore's terms. (In other words, the chronically misused stockholders of the Erie unknowingly shelled out enough cash to salve Vanderbilt's wounded pride.) Faced with this betrayal, Fisk and Gould felt it their bound duty to ruin their former patron, which they managed to do in a new round of sleight of hand involving Erie stock. Then, after toying profitably with some other railroads, they turned their attention to bigger things.

BLACK FRIDAY

It was Gould who came up with the notion of cornering the market in gold, a commodity vulnerable to manipulation at that time because during the Civil War, the Union had issued paper money (those famous greenbacks) that was not redeemable for bullion. This led to hoarding of the precious metal and speculation on the part of traders, most of which took place in a short-lived exchange dubbed Gilpin's Gold Room. Considered decidedly unpatriotic, that exchange was closed by Congress in 1864, the year that saw Sherman's army marching through Georgia. A few months later it was replaced by the New York Gold Exchange — referred to colloquially as "the Gold Room" — a cavernous chamber described by contemporaries as resembling a rat pit (a place in which rats were set upon by dogs for the amusement of spectators), full of smoke and

An affluent American family in despair after a Wall Street crash.

foul vapors, with an incongruous fountain at the center and a large dial for showing the current asking price against one wall.

Once the Civil War was over, gold speculation was further encouraged by the importance of the close relationship between the value of the metal and the cost of grain, a major export. A British merchant wanting to import a shipload of wheat would be expected to pay in dollars, which, more often than not, he would acquire locally in exchange for gold. If the price of gold was high, then the foreign importer got more dollars for his bullion and could afford more grain, which would be good for farmers and the American economy as a whole.

This, it can be presumed, was the argument presented to President Ulysses S. Grant by Jay Gould when they dined alone aboard the *Providence*, flagship of Jim Fisk's Narragansett Steamboat Company, in June of 1869. The speculator, known by now as the Mephistopheles of Wall Street, was attempting to persuade the president that it was an act of patriotism to permit him to run up the price of gold by maneuvering to corner the market. Success of such a plan would depend on the U.S. Treasury's not releasing gold from its reserves to stabilize the market. According to Gould (there were no other witnesses), Grant did not offer any reason to anticipate support from his administration. Gould was not discouraged, however, especially since he had the ear of Abel Rathbone Corbin, Grant's brother-in-law, whose enthusiasm for Gould's plan was heightened by the fact that he had been promised a place in the cartel that would benefit directly from any gold corner. With Corbin's assistance Gould managed to arrange for another ally, General Daniel Butterfield, to be named to an important Treasury post.

At the outset of September that same year—for unstated reasons that later aroused suspicion—the president ordered an end to auctions of gold from the Treasury. Until then, these had been regular events. On September 1, it took a fraction over $131 in greenbacks to buy $100 worth of gold (as estimated at pre–Civil War levels that served as a standard measure). Gould and the carefully selected members of his syndicate began to buy, pushing the price upward but not as fast as he had hoped for, because a pool of bears was going short at the time, anticipating that prices were sure to fall as they usually did at that time of year. Frustrated, he called on Jim Fisk to stir things up. Fisk had been skeptical about this scheme from the first. Now, though, Gould managed to persuade him that the fix was in place, probably by intimating that the president and the first lady had been suitably recompensed in return for Grant's keeping the Treasury out of the action.

Fisk promptly lent his larger-than-life presence to proceedings in the Gold Room, loudly placing orders for gold on a scale that suggested, given his known track record, that he must be acting on inside information of some kind or another. The bears backed off and the price began to rise. By September 23, it closed at just beneath

$144. Gould and his cartel were in possession of $40 million in gold contracts, close to double the amount that was available in bullion in the New York area. Gould was poised to strike, and to secure his position, he asked his bought man Abel Corbin (who had already been amply rewarded) to write to the president asking him to keep the Treasury from releasing gold. The letter backfired. Either Grant realized for the first time what was going on, or else he decided he could no longer go along with the conspiracy. Through his wife, he warned Corbin to get out of the gold market. Corbin went to Gould, warning him of the situation, asking for his pound of flesh (which he valued at $100,000) and demanding to be released from the cartel. Gould let him go on condition he tell no one else that the president was now certain to order the release of gold from the public coffers. For his part, Gould allowed Fisk in on the secret, and the pair planned their strategy for the few hours of trading that were left to them before the Treasury acted. The corner might be doomed, but there was still money to be made.

As soon as the Gold Room opened on Friday, September 24, Fisk—through various agents—began to bid up the price at a seemingly reckless pace. Almost immediately gold was trading at $155, as those who had been selling short days earlier snapped up gold from a Gould broker in order to cover their positions. As duped speculators pushed the price up further and further, a scenario orchestrated by Fisk and his gang, Gould unloaded more and more of his accumulated hoard at vastly inflated prices. The Gold Room had become a scene out of bedlam as some shorts, unable to raise the funds they needed to cover, became hostile and threatening, while others fainted or collapsed in hysterics. Meanwhile, on the trading floor of the nearby New York Stock Exchange, prices dropped like bricks as investors dumped securities in order to cover what appeared to be disastrous short positions in the Gold Room.

A little after noon, gold reached $161. At that point the price began to fall. Some believe this happened because news of the Treasury's intent to release gold reached the room. Others suggest that the market had turned on its own, before the story broke. In any case, amid continued chaos, gold prices slid as rapidly as they had soared and by day's end had settled at just over $131.

September 24, 1869, became known as Black Friday and spawned its fair share of suicides and stories of families reduced to penury. The shock waves emanating from the gold bubble devastated the economy as a whole, the value of some blue-chip stocks falling as much as 25 percent in the next few weeks.

As for the men behind the panic, it has been estimated that Gould's cartel profited to the tune of somewhere between $40 million and $50 million—equivalent to close to a billion in today's currency. (By analogy with the modern phenomenon known as "greenmail," this might be called "goldmail.") Gould himself was the main beneficiary, of course. As for Fisk, he had made sure that none of the contracts his agents had assumed were in his name, so he came out of the deal even, though it's assumed that Gould compensated him handsomely for his assistance. Some of those Fisk agents were in fact ruined in the debacle, and Albert Speyers, the broker most involved in bidding up prices, was so overwhelmed by the experience that he lost his mind.

With his wilder schemes behind him, Jay Gould went on to become the respected éminence grise of Wall Street. Jim Fisk was not so fortunate. Soon after the attempted gold corner, he found himself being blackmailed by Edward Stokes, the current boyfriend of his former paramour, Josie Mansfield. Stokes had access to some damaging letters that Fisk (who had a wife stashed away in Boston) had written to Josie. For a while, Fisk paid up. When he refused to continue these payments, however, Stokes made the contents of the letters public, which led to an acrimonious court case, a field day for the gutter press, and eventually to a confrontation on a landing of the Grand Central Hotel, off Washington Square, which resulted in Stokes shooting Fisk, who died hours later.

CRASH CONTROL

The next disaster came just four years after Black Friday, precipitated by that hero of the early 1860s, the investment banker Jay Cooke. During the Civil War period, Cooke's bond-selling exploits had brought him only modest profits. With the coming of peace, he had plans to enrich himself on a grander scale. In the immediate postwar period, transcontinental railways were perceived—especially in overseas markets—as prime investments, leading as they did to land grants with all the attendant possibilities of creating real estate monopolies. Cooke, the consummate bond salesman, became the exclusive agent for the sale of bonds floated by the Northern Pacific Railroad. He was paid for this in quantities of Northern Pacific stock that made him the virtual

The development of transcontinental railroads, linking the Atlantic with the Pacific, created many new business opportunities, and at the same time provided a battleground for epic struggles between rival corporate raiders.

As railways opened up the West, settlers followed, and so did capital to build new businesses and communities.

owner of the company. Unfortunately for Cooke, he had failed to recognize a change in the mood of investors, especially European investors, who by 1873 were beginning to respond to the disappointing returns that resulted from the irresponsible dumping of American railroad stocks in their markets. Cooke quickly discovered that Northern Pacific instruments had become difficult to move. Stuck with much of the operating cost of the railroad, his company was bleeding money and lost many depositors who wanted to distance themselves from what they perceived as a lost cause. The bank was forced to close its doors, triggering the crash of 1873, which saw more banks and brokerages ruined and the market in chaos. George Templeton Strong, a Wall Street lawyer and investor of the era, recorded the progress of the panic in his diary:

September 18. Going into Wall Street, I found crowds standing about and general excitement. The great house of Jay Cooke & Company, with its affiliations and auxiliaries, had hauled down its flag; so had Robinson and Suydam—also Richard Schell. Their example will probably be followed by many others tomorrow . . . and things look squally . . .

(continued on page 154)

EXPLORING NEW WORLDS:
EMERGING MARKETS

Economists and business journalists often talk about "emerging markets," a euphemistic blanket term for what might more accurately be called undeveloped or underdeveloped markets. These come in many different social, political, and fiscal shapes and sizes. Economies such as those of Brazil and Mexico are home to major companies that play a role in the big global picture, yet they are described as emergent because they are, or recently have been, subject to destabilizing forces capable of causing currency fluctuations and market volatility on a scale unknown within developed markets. Some longtime industrialized nations, emerging from decades of state control—such as those in the former Soviet bloc—are often called emergent because they have not yet completed the process of fully adapting to market economy conditions. The term is applied to a range of economies, varying from those of countries that might take their place in the developed world in the near future to others that are so destitute as to be in a state that is less about emergence than about chronic emergency. In the latter category are many of the nations of sub-Saharan Africa, and some, such as Haiti, in the Caribbean/Central American zone.

With the exception of a couple of East European examples, all emerging markets suffer from the dry rot of chronic poverty. Even where

In July of 2000, a quarter century after the end of the Vietnam War, a landmark trade agreement was signed between the governments of Vietnam and the United States, a pact that permitted scenes such as this in which women in traditional hats stack crates of empty bottles in a Coca-Cola plant located at Ngoc Hoi.

there is a thriving middle class or a rising meritocracy—in India, for example, and many Latin American countries—a huge underclass still exists. In more extreme instances, only a tiny wealthy minority, often identified with a corrupt and oppressive government, stands apart from the hungry masses.

Many of these emerging markets have a colonial past, and with the rise of multinational conglomerates, they still find themselves dependent to a greater or lesser extent upon the developed world and upon investment that originates in distant financial centers like Osaka, Amsterdam, or Toronto. Businesses in the capital-rich countries look to the less-well-endowed nations to assist the implementation of their agendas in two basic ways. They see these countries as a source of inexpensive labor for work in manufacturing plants and other labor-intensive tasks. In some cases, they also see them as a source of raw materials, such as petroleum and minerals of all sorts. Both of these factors are vital to the Japanese economy, for example, where labor costs are high and there is little domestic availability of key raw materials.

It is theorized that businesses from the developed world help the economies of the poorer nations by creating jobs that in turn enable workers in those countries to buy necessities—

perhaps even create a demand for consumer goods. This pattern seems to manifest itself most effectively in the more advanced underdeveloped countries, where there is already an economic infrastructure that can support and justify the existence of, for example, automobile factories such as Volkswagen has established in Brazil and Mexico.

In an attempt to foster economic progress and stability in underdeveloped areas, the industrialized powers have underwritten organizations such as the International Monetary Fund (IMF) and the World Bank, both headquartered in

---

Top center: *In a St. Petersburg factory, a Russian worker operates a metal lathe.*

Top right: *A Ugandan day worker watches anxiously as the sack of tea leaves he has picked is weighed, determining his take-home pay for the day.*

Bottom right: *In the Ivory Coast city of Korhogo, a center of West African cotton production, a weary employee sprawls on bales of cotton waiting to be shipped.*

Bottom center: *Coffee beans dry in the warm Nicaraguan sun.*

Bottom left: *The Chinese government has made strenuous efforts to encourage its industries to compete in the global market place. The operators of plants such as this cotton mill have found their products to be in demand around the world.*

Washington, D.C. The IMF might be described as the international bank of last resort, responsible for stabilizing troubled economies by providing short-term loans designed to head off regional debt epidemics. The World Bank (also called the International Bank of Reconstruction and Development) was set up to provide funding for long term economic development around the world, its mandate encompassing everything from building dams to fighting epidemics such as AIDS.

Both the IMF and the World Bank have been the target of much highly-publicized criticism and dissent on the part of both moderate and radical groups who see the role of these institutions as being patriarchal at best. Should they be abolished, however, it seems likely that they would have to be replaced by somewhat similar organizations, providing safety nets for plummeting economies.

Recently a good deal of attention has been paid to the notion of encouraging entrepreneurism at a grassroots level in poorer countries. A principal spokesman for this approach is the Peruvian economic theorist Hernando de Soto, who believes that the everyday commerce of any typical impoverished third world country displays many of the fundamental characteristics of the free market system. However poor, people still produce goods—fruits, poultry, handmade baby clothing, whatever—and sell them in public marketplaces, whether estab-

lished or happenstance.

According to de Soto, the problem is that potential entrepreneurs are often stifled in their ambitions both by a lack of legal infrastructure and an excess of bureaucracy. In developed economies, it's difficult to conceive of a situation in which more business legislation is desirable. In some third world countries, however, the concept of property rights—to take an obvious example—is so vaguely defined that the establishment of contracts involving loans secured by collateral is virtually untenable. At the same time, in some of these cultures, the bureaucracy involved in obtaining a license to pursue legally sanctioned commerce is so intimidating as to discourage merchants from operating within the law. Outside the legal system, the merchant may be able to survive, but his potential will be limited.

Seen from this point of view, one way to encourage market economies in underdeveloped areas is to find ways—no easy task—of revising local codes and regulations so as to make it easier for would-be entrepreneurs to live up to their potential. ■

Top left: *In Thabazimbi, South Africa, a giant mechanical shovel probes for iron ore.*

Top center: *Argentinean cattlemen herd Herefords across a river in Neuquen Province.*

Bottom right: *At the end of the twentieth century, stock buying fever spread to places where it had long been discouraged. Here would-be investors jostle to make trades at the Shanghai International Securities Company.*

Bottom center: *Lumberjack steering timber, Abidjan, Ivory Coast.*

Bottom left: *Miner drilling for gold, Gauteng, South Africa.*

September 20. . . . By twelve o'clock, the Bank of the Commonwealth and the Union Trust Company had stopped, and the Stock Exchange had closed its doors. A wise measure, and might that they never be reopened. . . . People swarmed on the Treasury steps looking down on the seething mob that filled Broad Street. There was a secondary focus at Cedar and Nassau streets where people were staring at the closed doors of the Bank of the Commonwealth and at the steady current of depositors flowing into the Fourth National and then flowing out again with an expression of relief.[11]

In the days of Cooke, Fisk, and Gould, and for a few decades more, the American stock market was in the hands of a relatively small number of people, so that panics could be caused by the greed or folly of a single person. This was the case in 1884 when a young man named Ferdinand Ward, the business partner of Ulysses S. Grant Jr.—son of the now retired president—caused a significant crash by using the prestige of the Grant name to borrow money, which Ward then invested recklessly, covering his tracks by paying phony "dividends" that were derived from further borrowings rather than actual earnings. When the inevitable happened and the firm of Grant & Ward collapsed, it brought down the Marine Bank (its chief creditor) and, by contamination, several other financial institutions, some headed by officers who proved to have been taking liberties with bank funds themselves in order to finance speculative schemes. These failures drove down the market and caused panic selling, which was finally halted by powerful Wall Street forces, including the House of Morgan.

On orders from his father, London-based Junius Spencer Morgan, financial tsar-to-be J. P. Morgan orchestrated a revival on the floor of the NYSE, snapping up shares as speculators dumped them until confidence was restored. Morgan would be at the center of most of the financial dramas of the next thirty years, sometimes precipitating crises, sometimes helping resolve them, sometimes managing to do both—becoming the dominant figure of the last era in which the market remained the exclusive domain of a small financial elite.

This 1888 photograph shows miners and supervisors at Republic Gold Mining Company in De Kapp, South Africa.

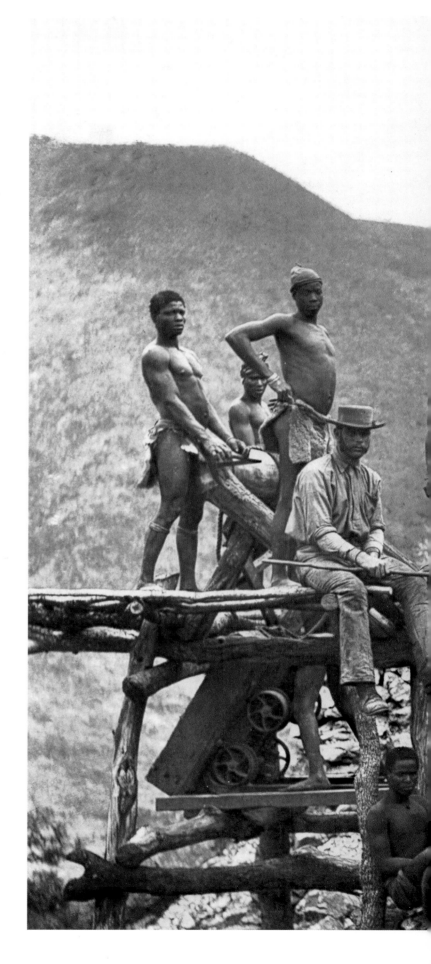

One of the larger-than-life figures of colonial capitalism, Cecil Rhodes made a fortune in gold and diamonds as he promoted a vision of British-dominated southern Africa.

Sorting diamonds in a Kimberley office in South Africa, 1888.

MARKETS AROUND THE WORLD

Wall Street was not the only place in the New World where stock markets had taken root. In the United States itself, there were by the end of the nineteenth century a number of important regional exchanges, in Philadelphia and Boston, as already noted, as well as in cities like San Francisco and Chicago, though the latter city was to gain greater recognition as the home of the world's leading commodities exchanges.

Across the Great Lakes in Canada, the Toronto Stock Exchange (founded in 1852) played a major role in the growth of the Canadian economy, as did another Toronto institution, the Stock and Mining Exchange, and regional exchanges in Montreal (founded 1872) and the western provinces.

As in Canada, securities trading in Mexico began with the offering of mining stocks, which commenced

John Sloan's painting of the Philadelphia Stock Exchange Building, circa 1897.

The Cairo Stock Exchange is one of the oldest and most active on the African continent.

in the 1850s. The Mexico City *bolsa* had its start on the sidewalks when, around 1880, merchants and brokers began to meet on Plateros and Cadena Streets to trade in both shares and commodities. In 1886 the Mexico Mercantile Exchange was established, and in 1895 the Bolsa de México began trading in a new brokerage center, until an economic crisis, precipitated by the depreciation of metal prices on the world market, brought trading almost to a halt. In 1908 the Bolsa de Valores de México came into being; much later, it would swallow up the smaller exchanges that had evolved in Guadalajara and Monterey to become today's Bolsa Mexicana de Valores.

Brazil's first stock exchange was the *bolsa* of Rio de Janeiro (founded in 1845). The São Paulo exchange followed in 1890, and these two dominated nine regional markets that operated independently until a merger that took place in 2000. For many years these exchanges were public entities, linked to the finance departments of state governments, which also appointed the brokers.

From the latter part of the Victorian era until the 1920s the Argentine economy showed great strength, and there was a brief moment when the Bolsa Comercio de Buenos Aires was the sixth-busiest stock market in the world. Political upheavals put an end to that.

Another early exchange in Latin America was Peru's Bolsa Comercial de Lima, which began trading in commodities in 1861. Chile's Bolsa de Comercio de Santiago followed in 1899. Like most South American exchanges, they suffered in this early period from primitive or nonexistent communications, which severely curtailed their activities; thus, they were essentially small, provincial operations until highways were carved out of the mountains and instruments such as the wireless telegraph became commonplace.

Compared with most of Africa, however, South America was positively sophisticated economically during the latter half of the nineteenth century. The only important markets on what was patronizingly referred to as the Dark Continent were at opposite ends of the landmass, in places that were the sites of one of the world's oldest

In the nineteenth century as today, coffee was a key commodity in the Brazilian economy. In this view taken at Santos, Brazil, beans are raked out in the first operation after being brought in from a plantation.

civilizations, and one of the newest. Curiously, it was the latter that gave birth to Africa's first stock exchange, but only by a matter of one year.

The Johannesburg Stock Exchange came into existence in 1887 in what was then an isolated, overgrown boomtown, which had sprung up as the result of the discovery of enormous reefs of gold buried in the veldt of the Transvaal. Like New York, the future South Africa (statehood was then a few years off) had been colonized by settlers of Dutch and British descent. In other ways, though, South Africa could not have been less like colonial New York. The British, who had been a presence there for less

than a hundred years, did bring their merchant traditions with them. The Boers, on the other hand, who had been in Africa since 1652, did not represent the Dutch mercantile spirit. Rather, they were descended from country folk who had left home in search of land. (The word "boer" can be translated as "peasant.") They were deeply conservative and had been at a remove from the European mainstream for two hundred years, so that their attitudes were completely out of keeping with the times. To say that they despised blacks would be an understatement. They looked upon them as belonging to a wholly inferior race. British slave traders had been no better, certainly, but by the latter part of the Victorian era most Britons were liberal by Boer standards, having adopted a somewhat paternalistic attitude toward subject peoples.

The British were all too anxious to exploit the land, however, and the gold strike in the Transvaal, which followed astonishing discoveries of diamond fields not far away, was something that British adventurers like Cecil Rhodes knew how to take advantage of. The majority of the Boers would have preferred to be left alone to tend their land, but the cash flow generated by the mines could not be ignored, and it forced them to enter the modern age in a great rush. Commercial rivalry nurtured their already highly developed distaste for the British, fanning a hatred that in a few years would lead to the Boer War. From the first, then, the Johannesburg Stock Exchange was an exciting place to do business, its trading floor the playground of overnight million-aires sporting rough-and-ready manners that would have seemed familiar on the American frontier.

In 1888, more than two thousand years after Alexander conquered Egypt, a stock exchange was opened in Alexandria, to be followed in 1903 by another in Cairo. In the first half of the twentieth century these markets had a considerable influence throughout the region.

However, sleeping giants were beginning to come to life in Asia. The first Asian stock market, in Bombay, has already been mentioned, and more were to become established on the Indian subcontinent. But it was Japan—after centuries of feudalism—where stock trading would make the most important breakthrough. And it was in Japan's great rival China that Western economic influence would be met with the most complex blend of resistance and acquiescence.

EUROPEANS IN CHINA

In China there were periodic explosions of mercantile activity; in the late eighteenth and early nineteenth centuries, during the Ch'ing period, there was a rapid expansion of banking, as an increase in the volume of long-distance trade, much of it based in Shanghai, called

for large amounts of venture capital. At this time, paper money came into general use in China.[12] It might be thought, in fact, that everything was in place for the emergence of a modern and self-generated Chinese securities market. Working against this, however, was the intense conservatism that existed at the top of the social hierarchy and the determination of Western nations to muscle in on the Far East, just as they had done in Latin America, Africa, and other parts of Asia.

When the European powers and the United States sent envoys to seek diplomatic status and commercial privi-leges in China they were rebuffed, because the Chinese refused to accept any other national entity as an equal. To their way of thinking, all other countries were vassal states and therefore had no franchise to sue for rights of any kind. This was especially galling to the British, who were horrified to find that highborn diplomats like Lord Napier were treated as if they were merely common tradesmen and therefore beyond the pale. The British persisted, however, and among the commodities they imported into China was opium, long illegal there. This called down the wrath of the Chinese rulers and set off a round of warfare in which the Chinese were repeatedly defeated, thanks largely to the superior weaponry that had been developed by the British during the Industrial Revolution. These setbacks led to the Treaty of Nanking, signed in 1842, in which the British were awarded many concessions, including possession of the island of Hong Kong, which they would rule for the next century and a half. Treaties with other Western nations followed, as did more fighting, including a war of rivalry over Korea between China and Japan that broke out in 1894 and resulted in humiliating defeat for the Chinese.

By then, Chinese industrialization—especially the development of a modern armaments industry—had been advocated by some of the generals and other patriots who sought to co-opt the Western barbarians' technology for the benefit of the citizens of the Place at the Center of the Universe. This failed, largely because, despite the nation's merchant tradition, a self-sustaining and self-regulating market economy had never been

In this nineteenth-century image, Chinese workers in the already Westernized seaport of Canton are shown loading a native vessel that will ferry goods to the side-wheel steam packet waiting in the harbor.

permitted to evolve in China. Now, when it was needed, it was found to be too complex and sensitive a vehicle to be created overnight. In particular, the old habits of bribery and corruption, resulting from centuries of dealing with government monopolies, refused to go away. Short-term successes were discovered to have been built on financial quicksands.

The stage was set for the end of dynastic China and decades of violent unrest that would see a Marxist government in power by the middle of the twentieth century. Ironically, it would be this Marxist government, in a somewhat modified form, that would attempt to bring China into the mainstream of the world economy.

JAPAN EMERGES FROM ITS COCOON

The route to the mainstream followed by China's neighbor and intense rival, Japan, was different but equally unlikely, marked by extreme xenophobia, paradoxically combined—during certain periods, at least—with the eager acceptance of outside innovations.

The first known contact between Japan and the West came in 1542 when a Portuguese ship was driven ashore at Tanega-Shima during a storm. The crew was well received, and this led to commercial contacts between Portugal and Japan and the subsequent arrival of vessels from other European nations. Soon, trading privileges were granted to the Dutch, the Spanish, and the British.

Some of their ships carried missionaries, and a significant number of Japanese were converted to Christianity, occasionally at the insistence of their local feudal lords. The Japanese authorities seem to have been tolerant of this situation, until European religious rivalries erupted on their shores. Portuguese Jesuit missionaries did their best to discredit Spanish Franciscans and have them thrown out of the country. The Franciscans, meanwhile, warned the Japanese against Protestants and suggested that a Spanish fleet be sent to burn Dutch boats in Japanese ports. The shogun and his advisers concluded that these religious disputes had serious political undertones, and became suspicious of the motives of foreigners in general. The result was the suppression of Christianity, which involved a number of massacres. The European powers tried to hold on to their commercial privileges, but—except for some very limited rights allowed the Dutch East India Company, under extremely humiliating terms—all trading missions were closed down. The ruling Tokugawa shogunate took an increasingly severe attitude toward all contacts with foreigners, including Japan's Asian neighbors. With the exception of the Dutch, who were allowed to dock one boat a year and were confined to an Alcatraz-like island off Nagasaki, all foreigners were banned from the Japanese archipelago and Japanese citizens were forbidden to travel abroad on pain of death. (Exemptions were provided for occasional diplomatic missions to China and Korea.)

Thus began one of the most extraordinary episodes in the history of any nation, the virtually total seclusion of the Japanese people from the rest of the world. This was to last for almost two hundred years, from the 1670s until 1853, when Commodore Perry sailed into Uraga harbor with four well-armed U.S. naval vessels, carrying the American government's demand for a treaty permitting trade between the two nations.

Traditionally, the great majority of Japanese had lived under a basically feudal economic system in which they paid dues to the local manor and lived off what extras they could grow or produce for themselves, or what they could barter for with neighbors. Many farmers produced

The former Tokyo Stock Exchange, built after World War II; it was the center of the Japanese financial world until a fully computerized trading platform replaced its traditional trading floor.

Commodore Matthew Perry entertains Japanese guests aboard the USSF Powhatan. *Perry's famous expedition to Japan helped to open the country to Western trade.*

silk to generate supplemental income, but that trade was largely controlled by the feudal landlords. At a relatively early date, however, there seems to have been some significant commerce on the part of merchants who served as agents for the chieftains in disposing profitably of surpluses of commodities such as rice. Also, some members of the samurai caste—originally privileged warrior vassals of the

This ukiyo-e print from 1857 shows a woman choosing cloth at the Mitsui department store in Edo (Tokyo). The Mitsui merchant clan would form the basis for one of the great financial and industrial conglomerates of the twentieth century.

aristocrats—began to gain business experience by adapting their skills to managing the affairs of feudal estates, serving as bailiffs for patrician clans. Their descendants would play an important role in establishing the modern Japanese economic system.

By the Tokugawa era (the period of Japanese seclusion from the world), cities had begun to develop their own characteristically urban cultures, in which a rising merchant class was eager to assert itself.[13] Business enterprises—not dissimilar to Western joint-stock companies—appeared in many parts of Japan, marketing products or commodities through representatives in Edo (Tokyo), Osaka, and other commercial centers. Even this kind of activity was highly regulated, though, with the government requiring licenses of merchants who wanted to operate in the capital.

According to the Japanese caste system, people in trade were at the bottom of the social ladder. The shopkeepers and moneylenders of Edo were somewhat like Cockneys in Charles Dickens's London. With diligence they might attain wealth, but they could never escape the stigma of their origins. Until London surpassed it in size, at some point in the first half of the nineteenth century, Edo was the largest city in the world, with a population in excess of one million. Half of these people belonged to the merchant class, but they were confined to about one-fifth of the land, the rest being set aside for the estates of nobles and aristocrats, public buildings, temples, and shrines.

A feature of life in the larger cities was the existence of guilds, which often served as banking institutions. In Edo, for example, there was a brotherhood of fish wholesalers and brokers that made loans to fishermen for the purchase and maintenance of boats and nets. In return, the fishermen agreed to deal with the guild on an exclusive basis, selling their catches at a predetermined price. In Osaka the guilds introduced many kinds of commercial credit. By the time Japan was opened up to the rest of the world again, it possessed the beginnings of the kind of fiscal infrastructure required to compete in the international marketplace.

The city of Kobe, Japan, seen in the 1890s, with Osaka Bay beyond, had already become one of the leading Far Eastern ports in the few decades since it was reopened to foreign trade in 1868.

Though a legacy of centuries of bureaucratic intervention remained something of an impediment, there had been a marked increase in commercial activity of all kinds, from mining to manufacturing, even before Perry's flotilla appeared on the scene. Some local chieftains, sensing the way the economy was changing, became embryonic industrialists within their own domains before the shogunate finally collapsed under military and diplomatic pressure from Europe and America, leading in 1868 to the end of feudalism.

Several of these progressive nobles were deeply involved in the radical political changes that transformed Japan in the period between the late 1860s and the mid-1880s. For hundreds of years the emperor had been kept in isolation in Kyoto, a symbolic head of state but without political clout. The real power lay with the shogun. Now, in what became known as the Meiji period, the post of shogun was abolished and the emperor was given a more active role. As a result, progressive members of aristocratic clans were able to assume important executive positions in the eventual Meiji government, and they used their commercial background to help justify central control of industries such as munitions,

railroads, and shipbuilding. These industries were considered of vital strategic importance to Japan, whose leaders had persuaded themselves that they could protect their heritage only by becoming militarily and industrially strong within the modern family of nations.

Much Japanese wealth became concentrated in the hands of a few powerful financial houses bearing names like Mitsui and Mitsubishi that are still familiar to investors today. These formed the nuclei of trustlike combines known as the *zaibatsu*. As the zaibatsu evolved, they became dependent on intricate networks of commercial and family interests that knit them so firmly into the political establishment that at times they behaved almost as if they were branches of the current administration.

Still, private enterprise evolved rapidly, and stock exchanges were founded in several Japanese cities, including Tokyo (1878), Osaka (1878), and Nagoya (1886). It would take the best part of a century for these exchanges to assume a global significance, but the foundations for the Japanese economic miracle of the post–World War II era had been laid well before the end of the nineteenth century.

5 : Trusts and Tribulations

1900–1939

At the dawn of the twentieth century, inebriated with heady new technologies,
the industrialized nations reached an apogee of economic self-confidence.
A spectacular expression of this was the 1900 Paris Exposition Universelle,
during which the Eiffel Tower was illuminated with tens of thousands of
electric light bulbs.

On May 26, 1896, the *Wall Street Journal* carried the first edition of the Dow Jones Industrial Average. The *Journal*'s publisher and editor, Charles Dow (Edward Jones was his partner), was fascinated by market cycles and devised the index to make these cycles palpable to his readers. The Dow Jones grabbed the imagination of professionals and nonprofessionals alike. It was, of course, the prototype for scores of indexes—Standard & Poor's, the Nasdaq (National Association of Securities Dealers Automated Quotation System), the Nikkei, the FTSE (Financial Times Stock Exchange), the DAX (Deutscher Aktienindex), the Hang Seng, and so on—each of which would not only record market moves but sometimes would help shape them, too.

Only a dozen stocks were tracked by the Dow in the early days. The original twelve were American Cotton Oil; American Sugar Refining Co.; American Tobacco; Chicago Gas; Distilling & Cattle Feeding Co.; General Electric; Laclede Gas Light Co.; National Lead; North American Co. (an ancestor of today's Ameren Corp.); Tennessee Coal, Iron & Railroad Co.; and U.S. Leather (preferred). Taking into account that one crucial sector

In 1904, a bespoke-suited stockbroker consults the ticker tape in his office, surrounded by appurtenances of the Gilded Age.

Immigrants arrive at Ellis Island. America's wealth was built on ingenuity and hard work, but also upon the exploitation of cheap immigrant labor, which, in the early part of the century, sometimes led to violence and bloodshed.

Exploitation also led to the rise of increasingly powerful labor unions. These workers may have made the stylish hats they wear while picketing during the Ladies Tailors strike in New York in February 1910.

of the market—transportation—had its own index, this list gives a pretty good idea of the strengths of American industry at the end of the nineteenth century (though it's worth noting that four steel companies would be added in the next five years).

The overall health of the private sector in those days was still rooted in America's wealth of natural resources, though with manufacturing and heavy industry playing ever greater roles. The expanding economy was fed by a steadily growing workforce as new waves of immigrants arrived, determined to improve their lot. The fact that many workers were underpaid, however, led to the kind of labor unrest that was characteristic of industrial capitalism during the first machine age. Striking workers and union agitators made Wall Street nervous, and were denounced as subversive to the economy. In practice, though, the panics that happened from time to time more often seemed to be an expression of the overweening ambition of a single towering ego, sometimes in temporary alliance with, or else opposed by, one or two other titans from the world of merchant banking.

In 1901, for instance, J. P. Morgan took umbrage at the attempt by his greatest rival, E. H. Harriman—in concert with Jacob Schiff of the banking house Kuhn, Loeb and Company—to gain a controlling interest in the Northern Pacific Railroad (the company that had figured in Jay Cooke's self-destruction), which was now controlled by Morgan's client Jim Hill. Morgan's response to this affront was to bid the price of Northern Pacific stock up to more than $1,000 per share, it being unthinkable that he could have permitted Harriman to succeed. This led to a classic bubble situation, and when the bubble burst there was a minicrash. Meanwhile, oblivious to lives that had been ruined, the Harriman-Schiff forces and the Morgan-Hill forces arrived at a compromise, giving both Harriman and Hill what they wanted (access to a right-of-way into Chicago).

Almost at once the market started to climb again, its ascent interrupted in 1903 by another brief downturn caused by runaway speculation. That correction was overshadowed, however, by the New York Stock Exchange's move to its new building at 18 Broad Street, a colonnaded classical revival structure, designed by George B. Post, with a pediment embellished with reliefs representing Commerce and Industry clustered around a central figure embodying Integrity. Inside the building

Early in the twentieth century, traders associated with the New York Curb Exchange ply their trade near the dignified portals of the NYSE.

was what was to become the world's most famous trading floor: a huge, marbled space occupying an area about half the size of a football field, its elaborately molded and gilded ceiling suspended ten stories above the heads of the traders below.

These grandiose surroundings were a reflection of the tastes and ambitions of the bankers who dominated the market at the time, and the industrialists whose enterprises sustained it. It was during this period that moguls like Morgan, Andrew Carnegie, and Henry Clay Frick were raising great mansions along Fifth Avenue and building art and rare book collections that would rival

The sixty-six-room mansion built by Andrew Carnegie at 93rd Street and Fifth Avenue in New York City.

those amassed by their predecessors and exemplars, the Medici. Unlike the Medici, however, they did not patronize living artists and scholars to any great extent. Rather, they sought out paintings, sculptures, and manuscripts created by the men with whom the bankers and merchants of Florence, Venice, and Flanders had surrounded themselves centuries earlier.

In 1907 the flow of stock trading that underpinned the mansions and collections of Fifth Avenue was threatened once more, and again the culprit was overenthusiastic speculation that had put pressure on the liquidity of the New York banks. In October of that year, a run on the hopelessly overextended Knickerbocker Trust Company precipitated a major panic. Lacking a central bank to fall back on, the financial community found itself in the hands of a small group of the most solvent investment bankers, led by Morgan and his old rival Schiff, who met with Theodore Roosevelt's secretary of the Treasury, George Cortelyou, and procured the release from the Treasury of $25 million in order to prop up the system. Some observers at the time suspected that Morgan and his partners had in fact orchestrated the whole thing— panic and loan alike—for their own benefit. The consensus of opinion today suggests that both the bankers and Roosevelt behaved responsibly in a moment of real crisis (though there's little doubt that the lords of finance did quite nicely for themselves in the process). Despite the economy's underlying strengths, and Wall Street's burgeoning role in world markets, both investors and the nation at large had been threatened with disaster. This unprecedented display of cooperation between the public and private sectors was timely and, in both the short and long run, crucial. Among other things, it had a direct influence on the passage, in 1913, of the Federal Reserve Act, which would provide a safety net in the form of federally funded regional banks, even though many members of the financial community were opposed to that move.

The decision to establish such a reserve system followed 1912 Congressional hearings at which Morgan and other leading bankers were required to respond to the suggestion that a cartel of New York financiers was conspiring to gain control of large sections of the American economy by behaving as a trust.[14] In a rare public appearance, Morgan fiercely repudiated this charge. No wrongdoing was proven against him or any of the other subjects of the inquiry, but the hearings did draw attention to the fact that the officers of organizations such as J. P. Morgan & Co., Kidder, Peabody & Co., the First National Bank of New York, Kuhn, Loeb and Company, Lee, Higginson & Company, and National City Bank of New York were called upon to sit on one another's boards with astonishing frequency.

In this cartoon, President Theodore Roosevelt is portrayed as being Jack the Giant Killer, facing down the ogres of Wall Street, including J. P. Morgan and John D. Rockefeller.

From modest beginnings like this Paine, Webber & Co. office in Boston, seen in 1902, grew many of today's large brokerage houses.

The death of J. P. Morgan in 1913 marked, symbolically at least, the end of an era (though his son, J. P. Jr., known as Jack, was an able successor, playing a leading role in the American financial world for decades to come). The age of the robber barons and their merchant prince underwriters was over. Those financial giants were cosmopolitans who had long been involved in Europe in a variety of ways, but now World War I dragged all of America, however reluctantly, into the international arena. From the point of view of the money markets, this meant that the United States became a creditor nation on a huge scale, with the great powers of Europe deeply in its debt.

(continued on page 177)

BETTER THAN AVERAGE:
BLUE CHIPS

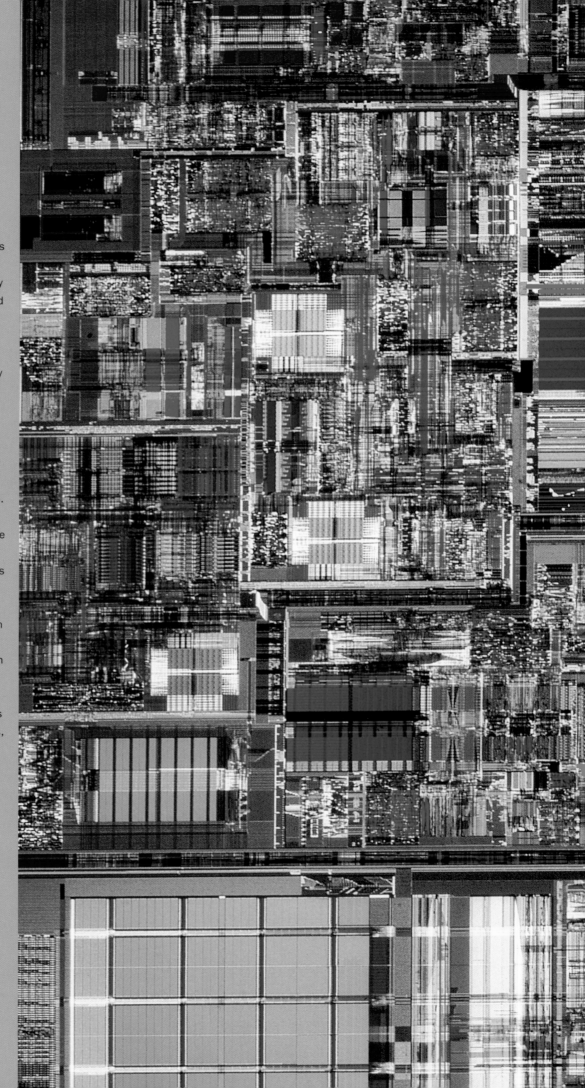

Blue chip stocks are publicly traded equities issued by a company that is a recognized leader in its field; that has a history marked by growth, consistent earnings and regular dividend payments; and that can be presumed to be in a position to continue to demonstrate stability relative to market conditions as a whole. Where American securities are concerned, they are the kind of stocks that find themselves perched among the elite used to calculate the shifts of the Dow Jones Industrial Average.

Of the thirty Dow companies listed at the time of writing, General Electric is the only one that was there when the original dozen Dow companies made their debut on May 26, 1896. Between 1898 and 1901, GE was twice removed from the list, though only briefly. Since November of 1907, it has been a continuous presence on the index, paying regular dividends on stock that has increased in value approximately five hundredfold.

The epitome of blue chip, GE was founded in 1892, when Edison Electric Co. merged with two other power companies. Over its more than a century of existence, GE has become a force to be reckoned with in many industrial arenas including, in its present incarnation, generators and turbines, nuclear reactors, aircraft engines, locomotive manufacture, kitchen and laundry appliances, plastics, entertainment media (as parent of NBC), medical imaging, and financial services. In several of these fields, it holds either the top spot, or the number two spot.

An aerial photograph of Los Angeles? A multimedia wall sculpture recently purchased by The Museum of Modern Art? Neither. In fact, this exquisite and intricate abstraction is a greatly enlarged detail of the die used to produce Intel's Pentium 4 processors. Having dominated its segment of the computer hardware market for years, Intel is a blue chip company in every sense of the term.

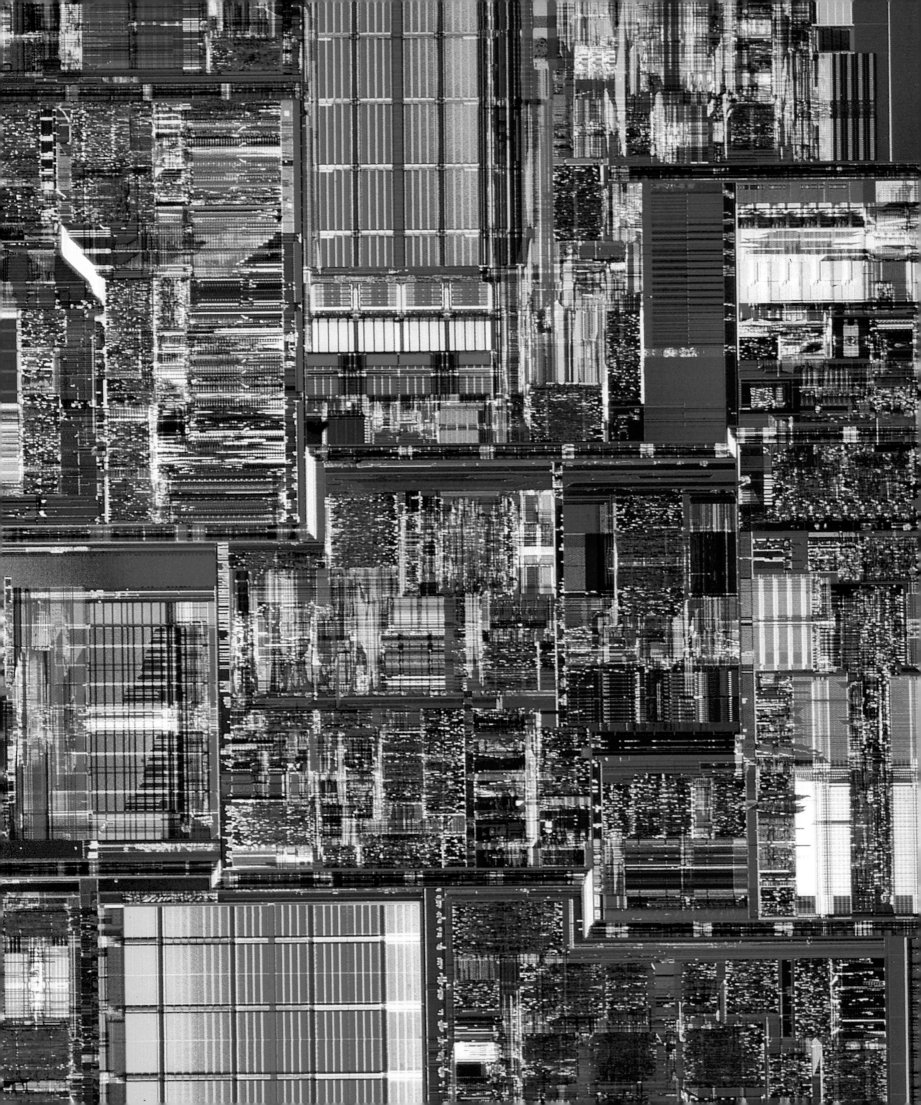

Throughout its early history, GE was perceived as a cutting-edge, high-tech company. Its involvement in developing radio, for example, was revolutionary at the time. Gradually, however, it has come to be seen as a classic example of an Old Economy firm, though one which has positioned itself well to adapt to the demands of the New Economy.

New Economy firms, almost by definition, are too young to have acquired blue chip status. There are a couple of exceptions to this rule, however, one example of which is Intel (appropriately enough the world's largest manufacturer by far of chips for microprocessors) a company that has been around for more than a quarter of a century and which became, along with Microsoft, the first Nasdaq-listed company to become a component of the Dow.

The fact that the great majority of the Dow companies are listed on the New York Stock Exchange is a measure of the NYSE's continuing prestige as the blue chip exchange, but also—from a different standpoint—of the perception that the NYSE is home to the establishment whereas Nasdaq is the exchange of the future.

There is indeed a significant difference between the way the two exchanges do business. Nasdaq is an all-automated exchange, whereas NYSE transactions depend upon a person to person confrontation on a trading floor that has been electronically retrofitted but is otherwise not much different from the trading floors of J.P. Morgan's day. When you buy or sell a block of GE shares, the process if fundamentally different from buying or selling a block of Microsoft shares, a difference that includes the way in which NYSE and Nasdaq "market makers" set prices.

In early stock exchanges, securities were auctioned by lot—much like an auction of furniture. During the nineteenth century, in order to accommodate greater volume of sales, the process known as continuous auction came into favor. Its natural home was the traditional trading floor and at the NYSE, it remains in force today.

When an investor wishes to trade that block

Top: *Any list of blue chip stocks is peppered with names that have been around for decades, and in some cases for a century or more. Coca-Cola, for example, was first tested in 1886 and named the following year.*

Above: *Boeing, which today occupies a commanding position in the American aerospace industry, has roots that goes back to aviation's pioneer era. In 1919, William Boeing (right) and pilot Eddie Hubbard carried out the first American international mail delivery flight between Vancouver, British Columbia, and Seattle.*

Right: *Procter & Gamble registered this trademark in 1889.*

Safe!

IT FLOATS

99 44/100 % PURE

⟦Safe for baby's skin. Safe for mother's complexion. Safe for father's early-morning temper, because he never has to *hunt* for it! Ivory is always on top.⟧

Above left: *Caterpillar Inc. has been in existence since 1925, when it was called the Caterpillar Tractor Company.*

Above right: *The company that became International Business Machines, better known as IBM, was incorporated in 1911 and first appeared on the Dow in 1932 when it was known for its adding machines and office equipment. Later it came to dominate the market in main-frame computers, of which this is a very early example.*

Left: *"It Floats" was a celebrated advertisement for Ivory Snow soap in 1927 when the manufacturer, Procter & Gamble, was already 90 years old.*

Below left: *Although its name has undergone several name changes, DuPont has a history that goes back to 1802. One of the company's greatest hits was nylon, especially in the form of nylon stockings, which caused a sensation when first introduced in the early 1940s.*

Center left: *General Electric was first included on the Dow Jones Industrial Average in 1896, at approximately the time that its engineers designed and built this electric locomotive for a Georgia railroad. GE remains on the Dow today, making it the ultimate blue chip company.*

of GE shares, the following procedures are involved. Orders giving instructions for the purchase or sale are forwarded from a brokerage house to its booth on the trading floor. The instructions are passed on to a floor trader who takes them to the appropriate cluster of "specialists" at a fixed location known as a trading post. Each of these specialists deals in a small number of securities (no more than six) for which he is called upon to "make market," which he does by striking with the floor traders sequential bargains that reflect supply and demand for a given stock. Each specialist must be prepared to maintain fair prices by supporting, with his own assets if necessary, the securities he represents. The net result is a continuous series of mini-auctions taking place simultaneously at each station.

This system grew out of the need for buyers to be able to find sellers, and vice versa, in the crowded context of a large trading floor. This problem does not exist within electronic exchanges such as the Nasdaq since the electronic trading platform allows buyers and sellers to find one another almost instantaneously. Without the need for specialists, Nasdaq's system can accommodate multiple market makers contesting with one another for investor's orders.

This is a so-called dealers' market in which the market makers represent large financial institutions. (Unlike a broker, a dealer is a principal in all transactions, buying and selling for the account of the institution with which he is affiliated.) Like the specialists of the NYSE, Nasdaq market makers have a responsibility to commit their own capital to setting prices in

a fair and open way. The investor wishing to buy or sell Intel shares can find the latest bid and asked prices listed on the screen of his laptop. When he places an order, that information goes directly into the system and modifies, however minutely, the data already there. Dealer-driven markets like this are sometimes called "over the counter" markets because they hark back to the days when unlisted securities were literally sold over the counter, or even by dealers on street corners.

Proponents of the Nasdaq argue that instantaneous data processing enables investors to participate in the market with greater directness and immediacy than where a trading floor is involved. Proponents of the trading floor insist that face-to-face interchange offers a fairer form of making market. Whichever way market making is done, however, it represents a crucial point at which many different cost factors involved in placing any product before the public are established. Stock exchanges are not just about trading shares—blue chip or otherwise. They also have a direct impact upon the price a household pays for food, heating oil, or any other kind of commodity. ■

Above right: *The Walt Disney Company began life as a storefront animation studio back in 1923. Today it is a media and entertainment giant, controlling an empire that includes a major television network, cable channels, Internet interests, and popular theme parks such as Walt Disney World in Florida, seen here.*

Below right: *Today, Caterpillar has progressed from manufacturing tractors to building heavy equipment of many different kinds, thus guaranteeing its continued status as a blue chip stock.*

Opposite above: *Boeing's long-term leadership in the field of civil aviation is all the more remarkable because it has been achieved in one of the most competitive of all industries.*

Opposite far right: *At the GE Lighting Technical Center in Shanghai, workers check testing of energy-saving spiral compact fluorescent lamps.*

Opposite center: *Microchips, like those pictured here etched on a wafer of silicon, have made Intel a true blue chip.*

Left: *Among Boeing's more unusual projects was the Lunar Rover vehicle, built for NASA's moon landing program.*

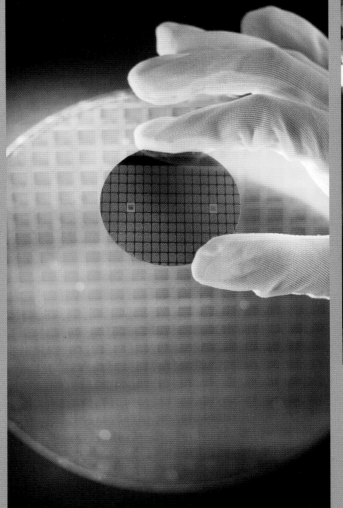

As they had during the War of 1812 and the American Civil War, government bonds played an important part in the financing of World War I.

Silent movie stars made many personal appearances to promote the sale of Liberty Loan war bonds. Here Douglas Fairbanks whips up the enthusiasm of a large crowd.

By the time American troops saw action in France, European nations were already deeply in debt to the United States, having borrowed heavily to finance their own war efforts. This indebtedness would have drastic consequences once hostilities had ceased.

EUROPE BETWEEN THE WARS

The Great War was a watershed in every imaginable way, and its impact on European stock markets and commercial activity in general was devastating. As John Kenneth Galbraith has pointed out, there are three ways of acquiring the means to wage a war. One is the use of governmental force. (The drafting of civilians into various branches of the military is a good example of this, its roots traceable to feudal economies.) The second is taxation, which tends to become punitive during wartime. The third is borrowing. During the 1914–18 period, the belligerent nations exploited all three of these possibilities with a vengeance, and each had economic consequences for the postwar world.

If the wealth of a nation does indeed reside in its labor force, then the killing and maiming of millions of young men in the bloodbath of trench warfare was bound to have a far-reaching effect on the economies of countries like France, England, Germany, and Russia. As for taxation, the drastic increases that were imposed in order to wage the war provided dangerous precedents for the postwar world. Finally, an orgy of borrowing set the stage for inflation on a mammoth scale.

Add to this the fact that the Allies forced on Germany a settlement that called for crippling terms of financial reparation, and it can be surmised that the market miseries of the postwar period were inevitable. (It was by pointing this out, while the terms of the 1919 Treaty of Versailles were still being negotiated, that the influential

In Germany in the aftermath of World War I, inflation reached such astronomic levels that currency was barely worth the paper it was printed on. This housewife is shown using large-denomination bills to light her kitchen stove.

economist John Maynard Keynes first came to the world's attention.) Only America, the principal lender to the Allies, was immune, and then only for a while. Meanwhile, Russia embarked on its Marxist experiment and Germany succumbed to mega-inflation, which at one point saw a pound of butter selling for a trillion marks. Most of Europe was in a technical state of depression long before ordinary Americans came to know the meaning of the term firsthand. This was felt very directly in the bourses and exchanges, even the mighty London Stock Exchange, which—although it managed to retain a good deal of its prestige—fought a losing battle to hold on to its position as the top securities market in the world, a title that eventually had to be conceded to the New York Stock Exchange.

Britain was deeply in the red thanks to the war debts

John Maynard Keynes, a portrait drawing by Gwen Raverat.

it had run up by borrowing in America. The situation was not helped when, in 1925, just as postwar inflation was settling down to manageable levels, Winston Churchill, then Chancellor of the Exchequer, made the blunder of returning the pound sterling to the gold standard, and to the old exchange rate against the dollar ($4.87 to the pound). He was acting, in this instance, with the strong backing of Montagu Norman, the eccentric and very powerful governor of the Bank of England, for whom the gold standard was a kind of Holy Grail. Bolstered by transatlantic loans from the Federal Reserve Bank of New York and the House of Morgan, this move was intended to engender confidence in sterling. In fact it had the opposite effect, making British goods very costly in world markets and driving down exports, until prices were lowered, which in turn led to wage cuts and labor unrest climaxed by the highly divisive and socially catastrophic General Strike of 1926. By then, Britain was already suffering from a state of depression that did not make itself felt in America for another half decade. It has even been suggested that attempts to prop up the British pound — orchestrated by the New York branch of the Federal Reserve in partnership with the Bank of England — contributed to the speculative mood that led up to the Wall Street crash and helped bring about the

Above: *Winston Churchill's great days were far in the future when, in 1925, as Chancellor of the Exchequer, he engineered Britain's return to the gold standard, a move that proved to be disastrous for the economy.*

Left: *The Soviet Revolution saw Russia opting out of the postindustrial market economy that was evolving in the West. Here, on a crisp day in 1917, Red Guards march through the streets of Moscow.*

*A direct consequence of Britain's return to the gold standard was
the General Strike of 1926, which provoked much violence. Here,
a strikebreaker lies in the street after being savagely beaten.*

Great Depression in the United States. In any case, Britain's doomed return to the gold standard lasted just six years.

Some of the appeal of fascism between the wars—an appeal encountered in most European countries, and in America too—was due to the fact that in Germany, and to a lesser extent in Italy, dictatorships proved capable, in the short run, of generating industrial and economic revivals, thereby bringing local depressions to an end. To a large extent, Germany's success was the result of a virtual prohibition on imports, combined with government borrowing to create state-sponsored jobs such as building the autobahns. If this sounds innocent enough, the question that must be asked is, would it have worked in the context of a democracy? Also, could it have been sustained for any length of time given a peacetime economy? The reality is, of course, that Hitler had no interest in maintaining peace.

AMERICA IN THE JAZZ AGE

In the immediate aftermath of World War I, Wall Street slumped as it became apparent that the European powers would have a great deal of difficulty repaying their war loans. The somberness of the mood was deepened by the sight of war wounded on the streets, the advent of Prohibition, and the terrible flu epidemic that ravaged the entire world. But the war to end all wars had been won, in significant part, because of American intervention, and this permitted the nation to pat itself on the back and slip back into the illusion of isolation—though real isolation was gone forever.

Gradually a sense of optimism returned. Movies and radio transformed what was then known as *the* show business, making entertainment accessible to millions who had never entered a concert hall or legitimate theater, and the cocktails, speakeasies, and bootleggers spawned by Prohibition encouraged a cavalier attitude toward lawbreaking, making delinquency the norm. The Jazz Age had arrived, and it found its ultimate expression on, of all places, Wall Street.

Western Europe might be suffering from inflation and unemployment. Russia might have fallen into the hands of ill-kempt proletarian hordes. But suddenly the American stock market was soaring. Behind this boom lay the fact that more Americans than ever were investing in stocks— ordinary Americans with no financial background and often without reliable fiscal advice. It seemed apparent to the man in the street that huge profits could be had for the asking. Speculation was rampant and many new

In America, the 1920s brought Prohibition and prosperity, bootleggers and a runaway bull market. The spirit of the age was epitomized by jazz, flappers, and fast cars.

securities investors bought on margin, which is to say, with credit. Sometimes the proportion of a stock purchase actually covered by the investor's cash was as little as 10 percent, and it's been suggested that some newcomers to the market didn't fully understand how margin buying worked. It was the archetypal bubble situation yet again, and remarkably few people gave any thought to the possibility that this bubble could ever burst.

BLACK THURSDAY

By the time of the most famous panic of all—the Great Crash of 1929—the market had changed radically, the pool of investors having widened to include a significant number of middle-class citizens who, prior to World War I, would never have considered buying stock.

This change should not be exaggerated, however. Some popular histories give the impression that virtually every adult in America, from college professors to short-order cooks, was speculating in the market. As Robert Sobel points out, in his classic study of panics, this was not really so.[15] He quotes an estimate made in 1928 by Joseph McCoy, chief actuary of the Treasury, that approximately three million Americans were shareholders, not counting a relatively small group of hardcore speculators. (The total population of the United States was then closing in on 120 million.) Most of those three million, according to McCoy, were "upper middle class" urban dwellers, in the market for the long haul and looking to receive modest income from dividends rather than to making a quick buck.

Even some of these conservative investors, however, bought on margin, not seeing any real risk, and throughout the 1920s there was a shift from investment in bonds, generally considered safer, to investment in stocks, which tend to be more volatile. One thing that made buying on margin seem almost patriotic was that America had entered the age of credit. Tens of millions of Americans— many times more than were investing in the stock market—were buying cars and refrigerators and radios and appliances of all kinds on time. Why not buy stocks ~

on time too? In a bull market such as the one that characterized the 1920s, it seemed to make perfect sense. To borrow an example quoted by Sobel, if you bought a Chrysler automobile by taking out a car loan, it would have depreciated greatly in value by the time you had paid off the note. If you bought Chrysler stock on margin, on the other hand, it was likely to have appreciated in value by the time you paid off the note—always assuming, of course, that the market kept heading upward, as it had been doing throughout the decade.

The 1920s in America have been mythologized as one long party, its memory perpetuated by images of speakeasies, flappers dancing the Charleston, wing-walking stunt flyers, and gangsters in fedoras. That was only one side of America—not endorsed by the Daughters of the American Revolution and their "dry" allies—but it was an image that many Americans had chosen for themselves. They owned up to being brash and a little rough at the edges; but they were feisty, by golly, and they had know-how to spare. Americans had cleaned up that little mess in Europe and now they were going to show the rest of the world how to have a good time. Americans exuded confidence, as Britons had a generation or two earlier, and that confidence found one arena of expression in the stock market.

Market growth was modest at the beginning of the decade, with a sizable dip in 1923, but from 1924 to 1929 the Dow Jones Industrial Average reached spectacular

While the boom lasted, Americans allowed themselves to be influenced by a heady cocktail of daring and frivolity. Unfortunately, not everyone managed to keep their eyes on the ball.

to repay their war debt, America's recent allies had to make sure that their former enemies, the Germans, paid them the reparations agreed to at Versailles. The Germans could do this only by borrowing from America, thus setting up a self-perpetuating cycle of loans and debts that threatened all of the economies involved.

Then there was that matter of buying on margin. It was not always quite as straightforward as it seemed. To give one example, investors were sometimes taking advantage of margin arrangements to buy shares in closed-end investment trusts that were themselves set up by brokerage houses to buy securities on credit. These then spawned tiers of subsidiaries that could issue more stocks and bonds, which brought in additional margined capital to continue creating financial structures bearing a remarkable likeness to that time-honored archetype, the pyramid scheme. The principle behind this was euphemistically known as leverage. At the same time,

(continued on page 190)

In 1926, when these cloche-hatted beauties demonstrated the Charleston on the roof of the Sherman Hotel in Chicago, more Americans than ever were buying stocks, many of them taking advantage of margin sales that stretched their credit to the limit.

Charles Lindbergh was the son of a U.S. Congressman who was deeply suspicious of Wall Street's excesses. Still, Lindbergh's 1927 solo transatlantic flight only added to the hysteria that fueled the bull market.

new heights every year, entering a particularly giddy phase in 1927. Unemployment was low, as was inflation. Most sectors of the economy were attracting strong investment, especially the high-tech areas of the day, such as airplane manufacture and airlines, their prestige boosted by record-breaking flight after record-breaking flight, culminating in Charles Lindbergh's solo trip from New York to Paris. The automobile industry was popular with investors too, and in 1928 Chrysler and Nash joined General Motors on the Dow's industrial index—Ford at the time was privately owned—which by then had been expanded to track the shares of thirty companies.

Still, there were problems underlying all this. In order

LOOKING TO THE FUTURE:
GROWTH STOCKS

The one thing that can be said with certainty about growth stocks is that they're desirable to have in your portfolio. Defining exactly what they are, however—except by resorting to the redundancy that they're stocks that grow in value—is far from easy.

In the early years of the twentieth century, any broker's list of growth stocks would have included such onetime Dow Jones constituents as the Distilling and Cattle Feeding Company, Baldwin Locomotive, and the Pacific Mail Steamship Co. Each was a well-established corporation holding the promise of long-term fiscal health. In order to anticipate future growth problems—which eventually arrived—the investor would have had to anticipate (a) Prohibition, (b) the eclipse of the railroads as the premier form of land transportation, and (c) the rise of long-distance aviation as a challenge to the predominance of the merchant marine.

More recently, in the late 1960s and early 1970s, brokers talked about a group of growth stocks known as the Nifty Fifty. These were securities issued for the most part by blue-chip companies such as American Express, IBM, Bristol-Myers, Xerox, Polaroid, Proctor & Gamble, Pepsico, GE, and Texas Instruments. "Buy these stocks for the long term," was the brokers' incantation, "and you can't go wrong." The advice seemed to make sense, since these were well-established companies with proven growth records. There was no reason, it was

In the Edwardian era, Baldwin Locomotive—most famous of all American locomotive builders— would have been considered a prime example of a growth stock (if that term had been invented). In reality, however, the rise of the automobile and changing socio-economic conditions meant that the writing was on the wall for the entire industry. Though the last commercially manufactured U.S. steam locomotives were built in the 1940s, examples are still in service in countries including Cuba, Brazil, and the Philippines.

argued, why that growth should not continue. It was a no-brainer to invest in the Nifty Fifty.

Or was it?

In fact, the Nifty Fifty was doomed by its own success. Investors' desire to own these stocks pushed the prices up, and by 1972 a significant number of issues in the group were selling at a nifty fifty times their earnings, or more. In December of that year, Johnson & Johnson shares showed a price/earnings ratio of 57.1. For McDonald's, the ratio was 71.0.

Polaroid's P/E ratio was a phenomenal 94.8. Such discrepancies between price and earnings could have only one consequence 1:1; sure enough 1973 saw a huge sell-off of many of these "surefire" growth stocks, leading to a sharp market decline. Even so, if you had invested $5,000 in Nifty Fifty stocks such as Disney or Bristol-Myers, back then, and held onto them until today, the long term increase in value would have enabled you, by now, to trade in your Gremlin for a Range Rover.

A quarter of a century later, a different kind of growth stock came into vogue. This revolution was spurred by high tech entre- preneurialism and the explosive expansion of Internet related businesses. The companies involved were mostly very new, often having recently been listed for the first time by Nasdaq or some other exchange. Unlike

Around 1970, a group of stocks came to be publicized as the Nifty Fifty. What distinguished them was the fact that they were considered surefire growth stocks. These were not necessarily securities of young and rapidly developing companies. On the contrary, the list included such long-established household names as American Express and Pepsico. The former had been around since 1850, initially as an express delivery service, then later as a *travel company, whose "travellers cheques" became indispensable for Americans abroad—"Don't leave home without them," worried American Express spokesman Karl Malden in 1960s commercial* **(top and above left).** *Pepsi also has roots in the nineteenth century and had long been established in many countries around the world, including Hungary, where the billboard seen here* **(above right)** *was photographed in the early 1970s.*

Other companies that made appearances amongst the Nifty Fifty included McDonald's **(left)**, *Snap-On Tools* **(opposite bottom)**, and *Texas Instruments*, here represented by *Jack Kilby* **(bottom left)**, the Texas Instruments scientist who was co-inventor of the integrated circuit. Two examples of his original 1958 integrated circuits, for which he was later awarded a Nobel Prize, are illustrated **(center left)** along with notes made at the time. At its Palo Alto Research Center (PARC) in the 1970s, Xerox helped ignite the PC revolution with innovative personal computers **(below).** In the early seventies, all of these companies—plus Bristol Myers, IBM, and other familiar names—were so successfully touted as growth stocks that their price-to-earnings ratios were inflated by eager investors to the point where the companies soon became overvalued—quickly putting an end to any advantage to backing the Nifty Fifty. In practice, of course, all of these companies soon recovered from this setback and remained sound long-term investments that did not need gimmicky "growth-stock" promotion.

the Nifty Fifty stocks of the 1970s, they were generally in the low capitalization category, but they were linked to innovative technology and novel fields of endeavor that promised the almost infinite expansion of what came to be called the New Economy. Like the Nifty Fifty, they were the answer to a stockbroker's prayer, and displayed growth patterns that set investors' hearts aflutter—but only for a while. Even more so than their Nifty Fifty predecessors, many of these tech stocks soon found themselves saddled with price/earnings ratios that verged on the astronomical. In August of 1999, for example, America Online stock had an astonishing P/E ratio of 254.3. AOL, of course, was one of the survivors, but soon after the turn of the millennium, many of its weaker tech siblings took a nosedive. A generation of highly touted growth stocks bit the dust.

What then is a growth stock? Cynics might say it is a broker's term designating any stock he's hoping to move. Beyond the sales pitch, however, a growth stock might reasonably be defined as a security that has shown good growth in the recent past and can justifiably be expected to continue that growth pattern into the foreseeable future. Such stocks may be found in any sector of the economy and at any level of capitalization. At the time of writing, for example, IBM is an example of a blue chip that is enjoying a period of significant growth. Many financial advisors and stock tipsters, however, continue to look for growth stocks amongst low and mid cap companies that have recently appeared in the marketplace. In reality, investing in these companies entails a degree of risk that does not fit with the traditional concept of growth stocks, but this is offset by the fact that the businesses concerned have almost their entire potential in front of them. ∎

DU PONT ANNOUNCES LUCITE

New accessories de toilette fashioned from a new material by a new process—created for the modern boudoir

Lucite
A Creation by the Makers of Pyralin

Companies issuing growth stocks can be of any size and description. What unites them is a managerial vision that meets the challenge of the market in a timely fashion. Home Depot **(above)** *met the needs of both do-it-yourself homeowners and small professional construction companies, growing rapidly in the process—here opening its first store in Germany. DuPont is a long-time member of the Dow Jones Industrial Average family that has enjoyed sustained growth built upon major technical breakthroughs such as the invention of Lucite in the 1920s* **(top center)**, *Teflon, and Dacron, and the development of herbicides and pesticides* **(top right)**.

Opposite bottom center: *In recent years, the media and entertainment industry has often been seen as a sector notable for growth stocks, with their development fueled by mergers. Seen here at a preview for a Universal Studios' theme park in Osaka, Japan, Jean-Marie Messier (left)—chairman and CEO of Universal's French parent company, Vivendi—with senior Universal executives.*

Top left and right: *In a period of consolidation, banking is sometimes a sector in which growth stocks can be found. HSBC Holdings plc may not be a familiar name to the man in the street. In fact, HSCB—which owns Hong Kong and Shanghai Bank, Crédit Commercial de France, and several important American banks, as well as 62 percent of Hong Kong's Hang Seng Bank—is Britain's largest banking*

company and a force to be reckoned with. In July of 2000, HSBC group chairman John Bond (center) was able to announce that net profit for the first six months of the year had jumped 31 percent, to 3.53 billion in U.S. dollars. Among the jewels in the HSBC crown is the striking Hong Kong and Shanghai Bank Headquarters, designed by Norman Foster.

Above right: *Like DuPont, Dow Chemical has sustained growth through innovation, especially in the fields of plastics, chemicals, hydrocarbons, and pesticides. Seen here, a Dow plant in Germany.*

Bottom left: *Pittsburgh Plate Glass (now PPG) established its reputation as a maker of plate glass; shown here are the immense grinding disks used to polish the glass sheets in the 1930s.*

manufacturing corporations that were benefiting from the boom—such as Chrysler Corporation—were using cash surpluses to enter the credit market, making large sums available for loans to investors choosing to buy on margin.

Exactly when things began to get out of hand is impossible to determine. The bull market of the 1920s had built gradually. There was no manipulation on the part of a single cartel of greedy speculators. The situation that could precipitate a crisis evolved slowly as the market climbed and private and institutional investors alike saw an opportunity to make money. There are professional speculators in any market, especially the stock market. It must be presumed that they know what they are doing, and understand the consequences of making a wrong guess. Problems arise when the speculative virus begins to spread to those who do not fully appreciate the consequences of that kind of risk taking, or who are temperamentally unsuited to it. The longer favorable market conditions are sustained, the farther the virus can spread and the worse the eventual crash.

This was exactly the situation in the 1920s. As the market rose, conservative investors turned into speculators, and the rewards they gleaned in the short run encouraged

In 1929 the Great Crash finally arrived, and Variety *celebrated the event with this famous headline.*

other people to enter the fray, often with little or no knowledge on which to base their investments. Rumors circulated—some of them true—of fortunes being made overnight. Newspaper columnists became witting or unwitting accomplices to unscrupulous brokers who would load up on a given stock, then have their journalist friends print stories favorable to the company concerned, thereby pushing the price skyward. Major industrialists fanned the flames. John Raskob of General Motors declared in *Ladies' Home Journal* that everyone should be rich. It was a simple matter, he explained. All you had to do was save fifteen dollars a month and invest the money in good common stocks. In twenty years, he calculated, this would create $80,000 of net worth.

Not that everyone was swept up in the mania. Some Street veterans and politicians were skeptical, and the Federal Reserve made feeble efforts to put a cap on speculation by attempting to tighten credit. That failed to work, and certainly few people drew any lesson from the recent collapse of the Florida real estate boom, which had been a pointed example of speculation gone wild. Instead, more and more leveraged investment poured into the market and the upward spiral continued, until the whole wobbly edifice began to crumble beneath its own weight.

The beginning of the end came on October 18, 1929, a Friday, when a number of prime stocks began to fall, pretty much without warning. In those days there was trading on Saturday mornings, and the downward trend continued. Brokers and other professionals tried to convince themselves that the weekend would allow common sense to reassert itself, but enough investors had become jittery to cause a continued sell-off on Monday, a day that saw an unusually heavy volume of transactions. On Tuesday the market rose a little, but on Wednesday it dropped once again, more than canceling out the previous day's recovery and wreaking havoc with many of those closed-end investment trusts as the downside of leverage became obvious.

On October 24—dubbed Black Thursday—the roof fell in. Almost $10 billion on paper was wiped out by 11:00 A.M., at which time the visitors' gallery of the

On October 24, 1929—Black Thursday—Wall Street is flooded with investors who seem overcome with disbelief.

NYSE had to be closed because it was packed, to the point of being a safety hazard, with ruined investors, some enraged, some hysterical. As business on the floor continued at a frantic pace, huge and sometimes unruly crowds gathered outside the exchange.

Meanwhile, a consortium of leading New York bankers met at the offices of J. P. Morgan & Co., where it was decided that the big banks must do something to bail out the market. Shortly after, Richard Whitney, the NYSE vice president, who was understood to represent the bankers, appeared amid the pandemonium of the floor and began to buy large blocks of blue-chip stocks. Trading continued to be frantic, with the ticker unable to deal with the volume of business and falling as much as five hours behind, but the trend was reversed and some stocks actually ended the day on the plus side.

The market seemed to have stabilized, but on the following Monday prices began to plummet again. The bankers had more meetings, but this time the kind of support they had displayed the previous Thursday did not materialize, and rumors began to circulate that leading members of the banking community were actually

Top: *The Great Depression arrived amid widespread unemployment that led to the homeless building shantytowns known as Hoovervilles—a lefthanded tribute to President Hoover, who was held responsible for the plight that the nation found itself in. This example, one of the largest, was in Seattle.*

Bottom: *President Franklin Roosevelt's New Deal was built around government employment programs, such as the WPA, intended to put Americans back to work.*

affiliated with bearish pools deliberately forcing the market down. Tuesday was Election Day, so the market was closed, but on Wednesday the decline continued, and although the curve began to flatten out somewhat, stocks went on falling. Except for a couple of halfhearted revivals, they would go on falling for the next three years.

The stories of suicides provoked by the 1929 crash have probably been exaggerated. The number of people ruined by the collapse was substantial, however. It included many leading Wall Street figures, some of whom had been playing fast and loose with stock belonging to shareholders in their companies. The most conspicuous miscreant was Richard Whitney, the man who led the rally on Black Thursday. Soon after the crash he was elected president of the NYSE. A few years later he was sent to jail, having been found to have made illegal use of customers' accounts and of stealing from the exchange itself.

By pulling America through the Great Depression, FDR earned the gratitude of millions of ordinary Americans. He made more than his fair share of enemies on Wall Street, however, many members of the financial establishment being convinced that government intervention in private sectors of the economy set a dangerous precedent.

During 1921 the Dow Jones Industrial Average had hovered at around 75 points. On the last day of 1928 it hit the 300 mark for the first time in its history. In September of 1929 the Dow peaked at 381.17. After the October crash, stocks headed steadily downward until, in July 1932, the index bottomed out at 41.22. It would be 1954 before the index hit 300 again.

The brief period from the crash until Franklin Delano Roosevelt's 1933 accession to the White House was marked by bank closures, bond defaults, and every imaginable variety of financial disaster. FDR's successful efforts to turn the economy around, however slowly and painfully, were dependent upon the kind of government intervention that was advocated by John Maynard Keynes in his *General Theory of Employment, Interest and Money* (1936). This did not guarantee the president the support of the financial community—the Old Guard was appalled by his presumption—but it did help get Wall Street moving forward again, if only sluggishly, and the public's trust in the market was at least somewhat restored, in part thanks to the provisions of the Securities Act of 1933, designed to ward off circumstances that could lead to a panic as devastating as that of 1929.

6 : From World War II to the OPEC Crisis

1940–1975

On May 8, 1945—V-E Day—crowds thronged into New York's Times Square, where the electrical "brownout" had been lifted to mark the end of the war in Europe. Soon, Americans would begin to enjoy a level of affluence that would sweep away memories of the Great Depression.

When World War I erupted in Europe, the New York Stock Exchange closed down for several days in response to the financial chaos in overseas markets. No such closure marked the outbreak of World War II, because Wall Street no longer felt dependent upon Europe. It was soon discovered, however, that the American economy was not immune to events across the Atlantic. In the spring of 1940, as Hitler's armies swept down through the Low Countries and into France, the Dow Jones Industrial Average plunged, losing 23 percent in one two-week period. America's eventual entry into the conflict, precipitated by the attack on Pearl Harbor, led to another slump, but

Built by the wartime Defense Plant Corporation and operated by Standard Oil of California, this huge refinery near San Francisco went on line in January of 1945, supplying high-octane fuel for B-29 Superfortresses and other military aircraft.

as the tide of war changed, so stock prices began to rise, displaying a vigor they had not possessed in more than a decade, making up much of the ground that had been lost in the wake of the 1929 crash.

In 1945 the market did close down to mark V-J Day. It was an appropriate moment for brokers to pause for breath, since the war had given American industry a massive shot in the arm and the global conflict ended with Wall Street the undisputed financial center of the free world. Other currencies became firmly pegged to the dollar as a result of the Bretton Woods Agreement of 1944, named for the site of a meeting during which the Allies— principally the United States and Britain—mapped out the economic structure of the postwar world.

In the new order of things the free world found itself pitted against the Communist bloc, but that did little to dampen the confidence of U.S. investors. The Dow rose steadily through the 1950s and the first half of the 1960s, fueled to a significant extent by defense spending. There were some temporary downturns, triggered by a variety of events, such as the outbreak of hostilities in Korea (though in the long run the market rose during the Korean War period), the Soviet Union's confidence-sapping 1957 launch of *Sputnik I*, and the 1962 Cuban missile crisis. A more unusual instance occurred in 1955 when Harvard professor John Kenneth Galbraith made an appearance before the U.S. Senate Banking Committee investigating the possibility that the ongoing bull market might be excessively fueled by speculation. Galbraith, who was well known in government and banking circles if not to the general public, happened to be on the verge of publishing a book about the 1929 crash and, while advising caution, ventured to draw some parallels between the situation in the late 1920s and that existing in the mid-1950s. While he was still answering the committee's questions, stocks began to fall. For a few days, until the market rebounded, he became, for millions of investors, the most unpopular man

Women played a large part in the war effort, helping the revival of American industry. In this 1942 photograph, women workers assemble the fuselage of a bomber at a Long Beach, California, plant.

During the war, assembly-line techniques were applied to aircraft manufacture. Here Martin PBM-3 flying boats stand half completed at a Baltimore, Maryland, factory.

In Long Beach women employees inspect bomber nose cones for possible flaws before they are approved and sent to the production line for final assembly.

in America. When, shortly after, he was hospitalized because of a skiing accident, he received scores of telegrams informing him that he was receiving just punishment.

The NYSE itself was changing. Women had been admitted to the trading floor for the first time in 1943, though not until 1967 would there be a woman member of the exchange (three years before the first African American member, and nine years before the first foreign member). Nineteen fifty-three saw the last day in which the daily volume of business was below a million trades. This increase was due largely to the fact that commission houses, trading on behalf of individual clients, were bringing many new small investors into the market. Merrill Lynch was the leader in this regard, soon becoming the nation's largest brokerage house by assiduously pursuing entry-level customers, however modest their means, and providing them with reliable research and advice on which to base their portfolios. Other companies such as Bache, Paine Webber, E. F. Hutton, Dean Witter,

World War II saw women invading the trading floor of the New York Stock Exchange for the first time. In 1943 the rules were changed to permit the hiring of women as clerks and in other lowly roles. It would be almost a quarter century before the exchange admitted its first woman member.

and F .I. du Pont were quick to follow suit.

Another significant development was the rise of the American Stock Exchange (AMEX), an over-the-counter exchange that had begun life as the New York Curb Agency (NYCA). This had been a true sidewalk exchange, competing for the low-end market with the seedy "bucket shops" that thrived around Wall Street for many years. (Bucket shop brokers specialized in such dubious practices as accepting orders for a given security but not executing those orders until the price was more favorable to the broker.) Originally a true sidewalk agency, trading on the streets and sidewalks of Lower Manhattan, this organization moved indoors in 1921 to establish its headquarters at 86 Trinity Place, a couple of blocks west of its bigger cousin on Broad Street. After several name changes, the former curb traders adopted their eventual moniker in 1953. At first the exchange handled primarily what we would now call start-ups, along with smaller companies and others that for various reasons did not qualify for listing by the NYSE. Over the decades, however, many of these newer and smaller businesses grew in scale, so that by 1953 the AMEX listed

(continued on page 206)

Top left: *By 1955, Merrill Lynch, Pierce, Fenner & Beane had become the largest brokerage in America, with 114 offices nationwide. The company's success was built upon giving ordinary people access to investment facilities. The result was a huge volume of business, as can be judged by this scene in the New York wire-order center.*

Top right: *In their largest branches, Merrill Lynch employed huge electrical display boards that anticipated the electronic displays of a later era. Visiting his local office, an investor could inspect the latest quotes from the NYSE almost as if he had access to the trading floor.*

Bottom left: *In order to handle ever greater volume, Merrill Lynch employed all the forms of automation that were available at the time. Here an employee feeds messages into pneumatic tubes that will carry them to their destinations in other offices.*

Bottom right: *In Merrill Lynch's New York wire room, operators receive orders for the sale and purchase of stocks that have been forwarded by Teletype from branch offices in different parts of the country.*

RETAIL INVESTMENT:
MAIN STREET MEETS WALL STREET

It has been estimated that in the year 2001 close to 100 million individuals in the United States either owned stock or participated in the market through mutual funds, retirement accounts, or pension plans of various kinds.

During the past half-century, the democratization of investment has made spectacular strides. Three trends have been largely responsible for this. One was the rise of the so-called "wire house"—a term used to describe a kind of commission brokerage with satellite offices in many parts of the country, connected to Wall Street by telephone, telegraph, and (more recently) computer. Another was the abolition of fixed brokerage commissions, which made investment more attractive to small investors. The third was the widespread public acceptance of the mutual fund and other similar-style entities that permit the retail investor to purchase a stake in a cluster of companies rather than in a single corporation.

The notion of the wire house goes back to the nineteenth-century invention of the telegraph, which made it possible for investors in, say, Seattle to be aware almost immediately of happenings on Wall Street. Essentially, though, the pioneer wire houses did not change the character of investment. They simply provided facilities for investors in far-flung outposts.

Citigroup—whose gleaming headquarters tower dominates the New York skyline in this photograph—is the epitome of the modern financial service company, catering to both retail and institutional investors through subsidiaries that include Citibank (banking and credit card services), Salomon Smith Barney (brokerage), and Primerica (mutual funds and insurance services).

The new kind of wire house, which came to the fore in the wake of World War II, was largely the inspiration of Charles Merrill, who had made his reputation before World War I when he recognized the emerging importance of chain stores and underwrote both Safeway supermarkets and S.S. Kresge (the future K-Mart). He amassed another personal fortune during the stock market boom of the 1920s, but his greatest days did not come until after World War II, when he was already in his sixties.

It was his belief that the future of the stock market lay in opening the world of investment to millions of middle-class Americans who till then had thought of investing as the exclusive province of the rich. His plan was to develop a network of user-friendly Main Street branch offices in any of which a would-be investor of modest means could form a working relationship with a client-oriented personal broker who would provide research that originated at the company's headquarters.

Merrill's plan began to gain traction with the bull market that gathered momentum at the end of the 1940s and lasted until the mid-1950s. By the time of his death, in 1956, his brokerage—Merrill Lynch—was the largest in the world, with more than 400,000 clients. Other houses like E. F. Hutton, Paine Webber, and Dean Witter quickly climbed onto the bandwagon Merrill had set in motion.

Almost two decades after Merrill's demise, in May of 1975, the financial industry received an unwanted wakeup call when brokerage commission rates were deregulated by order of the Securities and Exchange Commission. This meant that commissions could now be negotiated, creating pressure for brokers to offer discounts to their best customers. Charles Schwab went much further than that, launching his discount house in which commissions were a fraction of what had been the norm prior to deregulation. This encouraged small retail investors to play a more active role in the market and led to a vast increase in the number of trades executed every day on the New York Stock Exchange.

Another phenomenon that gathered momentum around the same time was a broadening of

interest in the possibilities inherent in investment trusts and especially mutual funds. An investment trust—sometimes called a closed-end trust (itself an idea that goes back to the 1820s)—is an organization capitalized by publicly offered stock. The capital raised is invested in a diversified portfolio of securities entrusted to a money manager, or a team of money managers. A fixed quantity of shares in the trust is traded in the market. A mutual fund (sometimes called an open-end trust, or unit trust) is similar in that it invests the money provided by its subscribers in a diversified portfolio. The difference is that—instead of issuing a fixed quantity of shares in its own capital—it makes a continuous offering of stock at a price that reflects its

Opposite above: Charles Merrill made several fortunes during his very busy lifetime, but he will be best remembered for opening up the world of investing to far wider participation by creating a chain of brokerages tailored to the needs of the smaller retail investor.

Opposite below: One way in which Merrill Lynch made investing a user-friendly activity was by opening an information booth in New York's Grand Central Station, permitting commuters to learn something about the stock market on their way to or from work.

Above left: The Merrill Lynch system was in part built upon the idea of giving retail investors— whether in New York or New Mexico—access to personal brokers who could provide advice based on the best available research.

Left: In 1954 Merrill Lynch went so far as to launch the "Stockmobile," a motorized brokerage office designed to bring the world of investment directly to Main Street and even the suburbs.

Above: Another way in which investment has been opened up to the man in the street is by way of mutual funds. A company such as Fidelity offers many choices of funds, each of which— through its diversified holdings—permits the retail buyer to hold a stake in varied segments of the market, however modest his budget. Thanks to his sustained success as manager of Fidelity's Magellan Fund, Peter Lynch **(top right)** helped popularize the entire field of mutual funds while earning himself a reputation as a brilliant stock picker.

Left: As a pioneer of the discount brokerage house, Charles Schwab has contributed a great deal to the democratization of the investment business.

current asset value. It is open-ended in that the investor can buy into the fund, or cash in his holdings, with a minimum of fuss.

For the small investor, the advantage of investing in trusts or funds of this sort is that they provide the opportunity to share in a diversified investment program, which is inherently safer than using the same amount of capital to take up positions in the securities issued by a small number of companies.

Mutual funds came fully into their own during the 1970s as more and more small investors began to see them as a relatively safe way of participating in the market in order to defend hard-earned savings against the inflationary trends of the decade. They continued to gain popularity as inflation waned and the bull market of the 1980s showed that the best-managed funds—such as Fidelity's Magellan Fund, with rising star Peter Lynch at the helm—could generate significant profits for investors. Top fund managers like Lynch, George Soros, John Templeton, and Nils Taube took on something of a celebrity status, being perceived as stock pickers with an almost uncanny nose for a winner.

Another kind of mutual fund, less dependent upon the talent of an individual manager, is tied to one or another of the benchmark stock indexes. A typical example of this is the Vanguard 500 Index Fund, which aims to match the performance of the Standard & Poor's 500 Index. This is achieved by investing the fund's principal assets in the 500 securities tracked by the S&P Index (the chart below tracks a recent ten-year period). The very concept of such a fund guarantees diversification of investment and promotes consistency of performance. At the same time, such funds are inexpensive to operate because they do not have to be actively managed, decisions to buy and sell being largely pre-determined by stock movements as analyzed by sophisticated computer programs. Passively managed funds of this sort are designed to take advantage of the fact that the market as a whole—while it experiences downturns—has a solid history of showing significant gains over the long haul. ■

Above: *The concept of investing for the masses has been greatly enhanced by the advent of the personal computer. The fact that stock quotes are available instantly in any home with a link to the Internet has changed the entire investment landscape, both for the professional trader (seen here) and for the retail customer.*

Right: *Diversification and still more diversification is the mantra of the fund manager. Although some mutual funds do specialize to some extent—concentrating, perhaps, on stocks from a particular region or country—there is always a desire to diversify within the chosen parameters. Along with taking up positions in other sectors of the market, a typical fund might well have holdings in government-backed mortgages* **(above right)**, *in industrials* **(opposite above)**, *in financial institutions* **(right center)**, *in health care* **(below right)**, *and in energy production* **(opposite)**. *Today's fund managers also find themselves called upon to make decisions based upon the consequences of multinationalism. The famous "Chain Bridge"* **(far opposite)**, *which joins the twin cities of Buda and Pest in Hungary, was illuminated upon its 150th anniversary by bulbs manufactured by the Hungarian subsidiary of U.S. giant GE. The performance of subsidiaries of global concerns in emerging or developing markets is one of the multitude of considerations that fund managers, and now individual investors, must consider as they make investment decisions.*

Historical Price Performance of Three S&P Indices

- S&P Global 100
- S&P 500
- S&P Global 1200

the stocks of many major corporations, including several large West Coast utility companies, a number of airlines, and various cutting-edge technology concerns. Nonetheless, there were problems. Criticism of management in a staff report ordered by the Securities and Exchange Commission saw a shake-up at the AMEX in 1962, but the exchange was soon back on track thanks to the guidance of a new chairman, Edwin Posner. While never challenging the leadership of the NYSE, the AMEX had become a considerable national and international force, attracting members representing all the chief American investment houses.

The Dow Jones Average flirted with the 1,000 mark throughout the latter half of the 1960s and into the 1970s, finally crossing the line on November 14, 1972. Almost at once, however, the market went into one of its most precipitous postwar declines, the Dow falling to below 600 in 1974, partly in response to the rise of the Organization of Petroleum Exporting Countries (OPEC) and the consequent oil crisis, and partly because of the mood created by the fallout of the Watergate scandal and Richard Nixon's resignation from the presidency. Compounding the situation—thanks to some ill-considered posturing on the part of the Nixon and Ford administrations—foreign money was scared away from Wall Street, which played into the hands of the new eurodollars market that was beginning to thrive in the wake of the 1971–72 collapse of the Bretton Woods system.

One of the economic miracles of the twentieth century was West Germany's recovery from the devastation of World War II. This 1948 photograph shows a Krupp armaments factory in Essen converted to the repair of locomotives.

The Marshall Plan brought these American tractors to a French farm, where a more traditional form of horsepower had previously been used to pull the plows.

EUROPE AFTER THE WAR

In Europe the prolonged hostilities of 1939–45 had resulted in the usual pattern of "economic mobilization for war." Men were drafted from the labor force, many never to return. (As in World War I, this did have the beneficial effect of revealing that women workers had the potential to significantly expand a nation's productivity.) Heavy taxation was imposed, reducing levels of consumption and freeing up materials for military use. And the usual borrowing went on—with the United States once again the chief lender—except that this time it was accepted in advance that there could be no demand for cash repayment. The result was a program, cunningly crafted by Franklin D. Roosevelt and his advisers, under the name Lend-Lease. This enabled American industry to provide guns, airplanes, and essential provisions to the British while maintaining the illusion that some sort of long-term restitution would be made.

Once the Third Reich surrendered, every effort was made to see that Europe did not slip into the same pattern of inflation that had arisen after World War I. The Marshall Plan, named for its initiator, Secretary of State George C. Marshall, pumped $13 billion (worth perhaps four times as much in today's world) into European economies. When this scheme expired, in the early 1950s, American investments and aid continued to pour into Western European markets, in part because the United States saw the need to retain these countries as allies against the Eastern bloc nations that now found themselves, in effect, part of a Soviet empire. Investment in Europe made sense in other ways too, however, since some markets there were showing signs of significant growth.

To the surprise of most observers it was the West German economy that made the most spectacular recovery. In 1950 the German Börse began to operate once more. Because West Berlin was then isolated—an urban island surrounded by Soviet bloc territory—the main trading focus shifted to Frankfurt, a long-established exchange with roots going back to 1585, with Düsseldorf playing a strong supporting role. German industry began to thrive again, helped by its ready acceptance of early moves toward European economic union, notably the establishment of the European Coal and Steel Community. Such acceptance came, in part at least,

The Berlin Börse began to operate once more in the 1950s, but the bulk of trade shifted to the rival exchange in Frankfurt.

Stockbrokers outside the London Stock Exchange, 1949.

because Germany's political and business captains were determined to become leading partners in a new Western alliance. The German stock exchanges, therefore, abandoned the inward-looking habits of the interwar years and became major players on the world financial stage. In this they were greatly aided by the fact that German bankers and brokers were in effect reinventing their role from scratch, and were thus freed from the inhibitions that can be the consequence of fossilized tradition.

This is not to say that tradition—a living tradition—is not sometimes a healthy thing. Problems occur when the antique rituals associated with overwrought traditions take on an importance that outweighs the imperatives of

the moment. Something like that happened to the London Stock Exchange in the wake of World War II. One of the classic sights of London in the years following the war was that of battalions of identically turned-out gents—armed with rolled umbrellas and protected from the demons of modernity by bowler hats—crossing the Thames bridges on foot at approximately 8:45 A.M. en route to "the City," many of them headed for the trading floor of the London Stock Exchange. This spectacle was a great draw for early-rising tourists. For British commerce, however, and especially for the LSE, it was a symbol of the debilitating gravitational pull imposed by the status quo (or what was perceived as being the status quo, since in fact

Postwar England was plagued with strikes, such as this one in which merchant seamen demanded shorter hours and better working conditions.

everything was changing as Britain's empire rapidly dissolved and her influence in the world became diluted).

In certain ways, though, the status quo, perceived or otherwise, continued to have some advantages. There were more banks per square mile in the City of London than anywhere else on earth, and this simple fact attracted capital. On top of this, foreign lending institutions were drawn to operate in Britain because of a relatively relaxed regulatory system. (By the early 1970s more American banks had branches in London than in New York.) And entrepreneurial spirit had not entirely vanished, as is evinced by the fact that in the 1970s London merchants were able to forge a leading position

in the domain of futures dealing and, aided by favorable legislation, in the field of currency exchange. So it was that the City muddled through despite periods of severe labor unrest, the decline of key industries, and the nationalization—frowned upon in business circles— of major sectors of the economy, such as health care, coal mining, and the railway system.

The London Stock Exchange itself continued to chug along at a comfortable pace—far too comfortable in the long run—on the strength of substantial fixed commissions and giving its members a virtual monopoly on trading in British commercial and government securities. The problem was that the controls that ensured the prosperity of its members in these areas worked against the exchange where international business was concerned. This became crucial in the late 1950s and 1960s when, as a result of restraints placed on American capital markets, U.S.-based multinational companies were forced to look for financing abroad to sustain the growth of their foreign subsidiaries. American and European investment bankers joined together to facilitate the issuing of the necessary securities. With this came a renewed emphasis on global finance dominated by large industrial investors. A contributing factor in the trend was that many of the world's industrial nations, such as Canada, Australia, Israel, and Japan, were finding it difficult to raise sufficient capital in their home markets and so were floating securities redeemable in any of several European currencies. More than any other banking community, the City of London was able to take advantage of all this.

Compared with Britain, France made a rather better job of rebuilding its industrial infrastructure and preparing for competition in world markets in the decades following World War II. Indeed, the years from 1945 to 1975 have come to be known in France as *les trente glorieuses*. It could be claimed, in fact, that it was during this period that the French nation finally entered the twentieth century. Paris may have been the cradle of modernism when it came to the arts, but it had remained in the age of Balzac when it came to plumbing and other domestic amenities. The typical Frenchman had made a virtue of being out of step with the rest of the world. Not long after the liberation of Paris, though, this attitude began to change. That same typical Frenchman might still insist on taking an eternity for lunch and demand that his *poularde Joinville* have a pedigree leading back to Bresse, but now he dreamed of having a Citroën DS parked in his driveway.

Introduced in 1955, the DS can be taken as symbolic of the French postwar recovery. With its air suspension system and its flying-saucer profile, it was the most futuristic-looking car of its day, and among the most technologically advanced. And it was not an isolated

In the postwar period French industry underwent radical modernization. Here new automobiles are about to emerge from a Renault factory.

France quickly reestablished its preeminence in the fashion industry, where names like Christian Dior and Jean Patou came to the fore.

Looking to the future without abandoning tradition, the French have managed to combine elegance with technology in projects such as their trains á grand vitesse (TGVs), high speed trains such as the Eurostar that links Paris with London by way of the Channel Tunnel.

instance of changing priorities. The French were building modern expressways to accommodate the DS and other stylish vehicles that poured out of the factories of Citroën, Renault, Peugeot, and Simca. A building boom saw Paris ringed with suburbs that echoed, however distantly, the spirit of Le Corbusier's *ville radieuse* (radiant city). The French love affair with aviation gave birth to a formidable aerospace industry, and French engineers sent *trains à grande vitesse* (high-speed trains, or TGVs) winging from Paris to all corners of the nation and beyond.

All this was achieved with a unique blend of government direction and private enterprise, in which the Paris Bourse played a key role. Especially after the reorganization of 1961 that did away with the antiquated divisions between Parquet and Coulisse, the exchange provided an efficient interface between the state and private sectors, the policy-making Exchange Commission being headed by the governor of the Bank of France.

France's economic revival was achieved without the nation surrendering in any way the independence that Frenchmen of all political persuasions hold so dear. For every move that was made toward internationalism (collaboration with Britain in building the Concorde, for example), a contrary move was made to protect the culture from outside contamination (such as the frequent attempts to ban English and American slang from the lips of French youth). If there was a potential problem in all this, it lay in the fact that the high degree of government involvement in the private sector, which worked well until the mid-1970s, tended to create a lack of flexibility that would prove to be a drawback as world markets changed and became more complex. The need for further reform was noisily debated at cafés and restaurants near the Paris Bourse like Gallopin, L'Aiglon,

(continued on page 218)

GLOBAL VIEW:
INTERNATIONAL EQUITIES

The retail investor who buys stock in Bayer AG may feel he is purchasing a small interest in a manufacturer of that most taken-for-granted and inexpensive of miracle drugs, Aspirin. This is true, but beyond that he is investing in a huge, German-based, multinational conglomerate that encompasses more than 350 companies on five continents, one that is involved in the production of chemicals, fertilizers, medical products, automotive parts and imaging systems, and much else besides. Bayer AG is a major player in what has come to be seen as the global economy.

In the Middle Ages, promissory notes were traded across frontiers throughout Europe and as far East as the Holy Land. In the Age of Colonialism, Western nations established economic bases around the world. By the early twentieth century, a few companies—like Heineken Breweries and Shell Oil—had become genuine multinationals, and they were followed by many others. It was not until the 1970s, however, that the modern version of globalism began to emerge. It did so at the end of the post–World War II period, during which world markets had been in thrall to Wall Street. The phenomenon that heralded the change was the rise of the eurodollar, fueled in part by the reluctance of Soviet bloc nations to entrust their money to American institutions.

At the same time, East European central banks and American corporations alike wanted to see their funds denominated in dollars, the dominant currency.

With more than 350 companies scattered around the world, Bayer is an international conglomerate with interests in scores of industries. Here at a research center in Yuki, Japan, a Bayer employee examines an aubergine plant used in an experiment to test the potential of a new insecticide.

The result was that bankers in London and elsewhere in Europe began accepting deposits in what came to be known as eurodollars; American banks set up branches, or beefed-up existing operations overseas. Simultaneously, new centers of offshore banking activity were established as in Grand Cayman and the British Channel Islands that offered the advantage of low taxation.

This new kind of banking was a great stimulus to worldwide fiscal activity. All of this corresponded with a revival of commerce and national pride in countries like Germany and

Japan that had been devastated during the war. Soon, some European industries had recovered to the point where they were able to compete with their American counterparts—a recovery that was reinforced by steps being taken towards European Union. In South-East Asia, Japan provided the most spectacular economic miracle, but there were other success stories, too, in Singapore, Hong Kong, Korea, and Taiwan (as well as in neighboring Australia), and eventually, Communist China became a player to be reckoned with. Even long–stagnant economies like those in India and some Latin American countries began to stir.

At the same time, the phenomenon of the multinational conglomerate, with commercial interests in scores of different nations, became increasingly commonplace. These mega-corporations tended to have their head-quarters in one of the established business centers, but their operations in Peru or Sumatra were apt to be crucial to their fiscal well-being. In many ways, these companies acted much like their colonial predecessors, except that they did not back up their presence abroad with highly visible military garrisons, and were occasionally subject to the fiats of local regimes, elected or other-wise, that saw fit to nationalize an oil field or some such irresistible asset.

By the final quarter of the twentieth century, then, a new kind of global economy had taken shape and it radically altered the world of

investment. Even companies with no overseas divisions were prone to shifts in international conditions because their goods were sold in foreign markets and a recession in Japan could have an impact upon the demand for goods produced in Norway or Canada. Also, the interdependence of markets around the world led investors to take an ever greater interest in stock listed on foreign stock exchanges. There had always been activity of this kind, of course, especially between America and Europe, but the digital age created a situation in which the dissemination of market information became virtually instantaneous, so that it was as straightforward

Top left: *This rustic advertisement for condensed milk, issued circa 1910, scarcely suggests that Nestlé would become the world's pre-eminent food corporation.*

Bottom left: *Once dominated by American and European companies, automobile manufacture has become thoroughly interna-tionalized, with Japanese and Korean companies establishing production facilities in locations scattered around the globe. Here Toyotas undergo their final inspection in Durban, South Africa.*

Below and below right: *The Anglo-Dutch oil company Shell was one of the first to turn the production and shipping of petroleum into an international business. This production platform in the North Sea is home to Shell workers for weeks on end and is equipped like a small city.*

Top right: *A recent success in multi-national business collaboration has been the European aircraft manufacturing consortium Airbus Industrie. Here, in June of 2000, Jean-Luc Lagardere of the French Lagardere Group, Richard Evans of British Aerospace Systems, and Manfred Bischoff of DaimlerChrysler clasp hands in front of a model of an Airbus A3XX.*

Top left: *A trainload of Volkswagen sedans leaves a production plant in Wolfsburg, Germany, in 1998.*

Left center: *In Beijing, a Bayer employee handles a sheet of "Makrolon," a lightweight glazing material used to create skylights and transparent roofs for large buildings such as train stations and sports arenas.*

Above: *An oil tanker and cargo vessel under construction in the Palermo shipyards of Cantieri Navali Riuniti.*

for a New Zealand investor to place a well-considered put option in Zurich as in Wellington.

A couple of decades ago, an investor interested in civil aviation might have built a hedge into his portfolio by investing in both Boeing and McDonald-Douglas, rivals in the large passenger aircraft field. Today, he would be likely to hedge by investing in Boeing (which has absorbed McDonald-Douglas) and in the European combine that manufactures the competing Airbus line of aircraft.

In a broader sense, a fund manager might attempt to diversify his portfolio by investing heavily in another country or region that he believes is likely to perform well. The challenge here is to guess correctly what will be

happening in the targeted market a year or two years down the line. It is difficult enough to guess what will be going on in the domestic market during the same period, and the further afield the investor looks, the tougher it is to get an accurate sense of where things are going. A computer screen can provide the facts and figures, but it cannot offer an accurate guide to the impact of political shifts and deep-seated cultural influences.

The fact that the market has become globalized offers many new opportunities to the adventurous investor, but only if he is willing to give up his own domestic prejudices and understand that the greater marketplace is influenced by values that are often very different from those of Wall Street. ■

Right and opposite center: *Rupert Murdoch has built his Australian-based News Corporation into an international media giant whose properties include STAR, a pan-Asian satellite and pay-TV operater, and the Fox TV network.*

Opposite top: *The construction giant Bouygues participated in building the Channel Tunnel, here seen at its French entrance.*

Opposite bottom: *The age of digital communications has brought new international giants to the fore. One such company is Finland's Nokia, best known for its mobile telephones but also involved in other areas of the communications field, such as network security systems.*

Below right: *Merger mania reaches every part of the globe: shares of Hong Kong Telecom close lower after it was swallowed up by Pacific Century Cyberworks in March 2000.*

Above: *The fashion industry is increasingly international in its reach. Benetton's engagingly multicultural advertising mirrors the international reach of a company with thousands of boutiques in hundreds of cities around the globe.*

Above right: *Devices that allow one to share what one is seeing or hearing with someone a continent away are part of Motorola's future.*

Right: *Sony Pictures Classics, part of the pioneering multinational corporation, Sony, distributed the critically-acclaimed film Crouching Tiger, Hidden Dragon.*

and La Cave Drouot, where members of the financial community rub shoulders with correspondents from Reuters and the Agence France-Presse. Eventually, the Bourse—now officially known as the Société des Bourses Françaises—was given more freedom to determine its own destiny, though it remained under the vigilant supervision of the Commission des Opérations de Bourse (COB), an entity modeled on the U.S. Securities and Exchange Commission.

Market recovery in Italy was slower than in France, stability there being impeded by changes of political leadership that seemed to occur almost weekly. At the end of World War II, during which it had been a major battlefield, Italy had been unified and independent for less than a hundred years. The great Italian banks of the Middle Ages and the Renaissance were things of the distant past, ruined by disastrous loans to feckless kings and princes. The economy was predominantly agrarian. In the 1950s, however, the country moved rapidly toward

Industry in postwar Italy was dominated by great family clans like the Pirelli and the Agnelli. The latter's empire was based upon the success of Fiat automobiles.

Like the French, Italians new how to market style; one of the great stars of the postwar fashion scene was Emilio Pucci, seen here with one of his models, a display of his trademark scarves, and a distant view of Florence.

a mainly industrial financial base. Since there was little outdated plant to hold things back, a variety of industries, from steel manufacture to textiles, were able to take advantage of state-of-the-art technology. And, like the French, the Italians knew how to export style, almost as if it were a distinct commodity.

Given these developments, the Italian stock markets did relatively well for a while. (As in the Middle Ages, these markets were scattered among a number of regional centers, so that no one city dominated, though Milan was the first among equals.) Political upheavals continued, however—there were well over fifty changes of government between the end of World War II and the turn of the century—and continued to be a drag on the economy as a whole. Scandals in high places, including the upper reaches of the banking industry, did not help. Offsetting these ongoing problems has been Italy's ability to spawn its fair share of major-league companies—including Fiat, Pirelli, and Benetton—that have helped keep the local exchanges moderately healthy.

Many of these top companies have been dominated by the influence of a handful of establishment families. Until the mid-1980s, in fact, clans like the Agnelli (whose Fiat-based empire includes banks, department stores, insurance companies, and many other businesses, as well as motor vehicles) and the Pirelli operated almost like the Japanese *zaibatsu*, sitting on one another's management boards and using their banks and holding companies to control a large sector of the Italian economy. As a group these families were known as the *ala nobile* ("noble chamber").

The Brussels Bourse saw its fortunes rise thanks to the foundation of the European Free Trade Union, which in turn led to the European Economic Community and then the European Union, all of them with bureaucracies centered on Brussels. The Belgian economy did not offer the investor much in the way of major international companies, but because the market there showed steady growth and a notable lack of volatility, it enjoyed a credibility that made it a favorite with cautious professionals.

The health of the Netherlands' postwar economy drew much of its strength from the fact that, although

The Brussels Bourse.

The docks of Rotterdam, one of the engines of the strong Dutch economy.

*The discovery of large oil fields under the North Sea gave a
tremendous boost to several West European economies,
providing them with a measure of protection against fluctuations
in petroleum prices engineered by OPEC nations . . .*

a small nation, it is home to a formidable array of major corporations. Because some of the largest—Royal Dutch/Shell, for example, and Unilever—are half British, there has long been interaction between the Amsterdam and London markets, the stocks of these giant companies being traded on both exchanges. Another multinational giant based in the Netherlands is Philips Electronics. And, since the country is blessed with some of Europe's busiest port cities, it is home to important shipping and hauling companies. All of this has made for a strong national currency, the guilder, and a healthy securities market.

The Scandinavian exchanges, too, can be defined largely in terms of the internationally important corporations they list. Since World War II, for instance, a com-

pany like Volvo has been a huge presence on the floor of the Stockholm exchange. The telecommunications giant L. M. Ericsson and appliance manufacturer Electrolux are further examples of Swedish companies known around the world, but going back to the 1960s, Sweden's economy as a whole has had one of the slowest growth rates among industrialized nations, and this has been reflected in the performance of stocks.

In Norway and Denmark the market has been shaped by the presence of large shipping concerns, gas and petroleum companies with a strong interest in North Sea oil, pharmaceutical companies, and, increasingly, telecommunications concerns. Prior to the emergence of one remarkable telecommunications-based company, Nokia, the Helsinki exchange was dominated by the

... but such discoveries were not enough to shield Western consumers from the OPEC oil crisis of 1973–74. Abandoned gas stations sometimes found other uses; this one, in Potlatch, Washington, became a religious meeting hall.

stocks of forestry companies and paper manufacturers.

The world's wealthiest nation (on a per capita basis), the Swiss Confederation is actually a surviving example of those fraternal associations of cities and regions—like the Hanseatic League—that banded together to encourage trade and offer mutual protection during the Middle Ages. Shielded from potential enemies by mountain ranges, the Swiss evolved a unique economy in which a lack of raw materials was balanced by the development of highly sophisticated and efficient service industries, especially in the areas of banking and insurance. In addition, the long-established Swiss watchmaking tradition led to the nation's developing an unrivaled reputation for precision engineering, which in recent years has been extended to include the field of microelectronics. Other

areas in which Swiss industry excels are the construction of light and heavy machinery and the manufacture of chemicals and pharmaceuticals, while Nestlé is the world's premier food group. Throw in unparalleled political stability and it will be seen that Switzerland is something of an investor's dream. In the decades following World War II, the then-independent stock markets in Zurich, Basel, and Geneva were among the busiest anywhere in Europe.

THE RISE OF THE EURODOLLAR

The character of international banking changed radically in the wake of World War II; a major cause of the transformation was the advent of the Cold War. To the greatest possible extent, the planned economies of the

The food giant Nestlé is one of the cornerstones of the always-strong Swiss economy.

Soviet Union and its satellites were sealed off from the market economies of the West. Virtually no luxuries or consumer goods were imported, but internal problems ranging from crop failures to bureaucratic ineptitude and corruption ensured a frequent need to purchase essential commodities such as grain from outside the Communist bloc. Soviet goods had to be exported to pay for these imports, and the resulting commerce meant that, as a matter of course, reserves of capital had to be maintained in the form of deposits with Western banks. Given that most international business transactions were pegged to the dollar, it was important for those deposits to be denominated in dollars. Ordinarily, the obvious place to keep such funds would have been the United States, but America was the enemy, and Stalin and his successors feared that U.S. authorities might respond to a political crisis by freezing Communist bloc assets.

Given that very real possibility, a far safer bet was to make use of Western European banks. Although the nations in which they were located belonged to the North Atlantic Treaty Organization, their ruling parties lacked the political clout to unilaterally seize the capital holdings of a superpower. Nor were these countries as adamantly hostile to the Soviet Union as the United States, many of them having elected socialist governments and a few, like France and Italy, being home to large and well-organized Communist parties.

The chief beneficiary of this perception was the London banking establishment, which was desperately searching for a new source of income at a time when the pound sterling was taking a beating around the world. The British economy might have a hangdog look, but banking regulations in the United Kingdom were rather easygoing, and the old-school-tie chums who ran London's financial institutions had managed to sustain the aura of confident expertise earned by their great-great-grandfathers when Victoria was on the throne and the Royal Navy ruled the Seven Seas. Sipping port in the clubs of St. James, many of these Savile Row–upholstered gentlemen may have been inclined to toast the demise of Stalin's "Evil Empire." In boardrooms overlooking Lombard Street and Cornhill, however, they were happy to shake hands with Eastern European bankers in off-the-rack suits, and to accept from them sizable deposits in the form of what came to be known as eurodollars. Not to be confused with the euro, the term eurodollar was a banker's usage meaning simply that a deposit was entered in dollars even though it was held by a European bank.

Among other factors playing into the growth of the eurodollar market were a number of regulations imposed on American banks that made it advantageous for them to deposit certain funds with their London branches (generally so as to be able to pay valued clients higher interest rates). The penultimate stage in the rise of the eurodollar was precipitated in 1968 when the U.S. government placed limits on the amount of credit that could be extended by American banks to underwrite foreign investments. This encouraged many U.S. banks to establish full-service European subsidiaries (as opposed to customer-service branch offices) through which they could offer unlimited eurodollar loans. The shortsighted federal restrictions were removed after a few years, but by then the subsidiaries were well established and thriving. They became even more important in 1974 when OPEC orchestrated the crisis that sent oil prices soaring. Like the Soviets a couple of decades earlier, the leaders of the OPEC nations decided it would be safer to deposit their new-found wealth in Europe rather than the United States, as President Nixon had made thinly veiled threats suggesting that he might seize OPEC assets if America was "held hostage" again. The crisis also caused other nations to turn to London and other eurodollar centers in search of loans to finance oil imports sufficient to tide them over. This strengthened the eurodollar market still further.

Long before the 1974 oil crisis, London was firmly established at the center of eurodollar activity. By the mid-1970s, however, the term eurodollar had become something of a misnomer, because the eurodollar market

Changes in the patterns of international finance during the 1970s saw the rise of offshore banking, often in quasi-independent political entities such as Guernsey in the Channel Islands. Guernsey's capital, St. Peter Port, is home to scores of banks from all over the world.

stretched from the Caribbean to Hong Kong. New York financial institutions were major participants, both through their London subsidiaries and through branches established in offshore banking centers such as Grand Cayman in the West Indies and the islands of Guernsey and Jersey in the English Channel. Located in small, independent or quasi-independent political entities, these offshore operations were able to provide tax breaks on profits while "booking" loans that had actually been brokered in London, New York, or even Hong Kong or Tokyo.

Japanese bankers, in fact, had quickly become major players in the eurodollar market. Due to tight financial regulations, Tokyo itself was not in a position to challenge London as a center for eurodollar activity, but Japanese banks overcame that by setting up offices in Britain and the United States. They also developed their own offshore market, though it was of limited global significance.

The result of all this was that the eurodollar market became the world's primary source of capital, a truly international market with no domestic territory. As such, it set the stage for a new era of global banking, and for the inauguration of a new spectrum of financial markets.

In Bretton Woods, New Hampshire, in July of 1944, the United Nations met at the Mount Washington Hotel to discuss postwar economic cooperation and established a monetary system that remained in effect until 1972.

It was at this time that the Chicago futures markets came fully into their own. Founded in 1848, the Chicago Board of Trade (CBOT) had begun life as a grain exchange. The Chicago Mercantile Exchange (the "Merc"), established in 1919, had built its reputation on trading many kinds of commodities, from butter and eggs to copper and lumber. As was normal with commodities exchanges, they had made a specialty of trading in futures, since dealers could attempt to manage their risks by speculating on the possible price of lumber or pork bellies at some given future date. (By betting both ways—for an anticipated rise in price, and for a possible matching fall in price—uncertainties can be minimized, a strategy known as hedging.)

With the 1971 collapse of the Bretton Woods international monetary system and the subsequent situation in which currencies could shift in value against one another, it seemed obvious to smart Chicago traders that money could now be treated like any other commodity subject to market fluctuations, and they were the people with

the experience and know-how to do it. In 1971 an entity known as the International Monetary Market (IMM) began to deal futures and options on foreign currencies. In 1973 CBOT launched a subsidiary, the Chicago Board Options Exchange (CBOE), based on the notion that if it was appropriate to deal options on currencies, then why not deal options on stock prices? Or stock indexes? Or on any kind of financial paper, for that matter?

The answer to these rhetorical questions transformed the financial world. It had not been unknown in the past for stock options to be traded in an informal kind of way, gentleman to gentleman, and there had even been a number of small brokerages that specialized in such trades, though on a rather modest scale. The idea of an organized, high-powered options market was something else entirely. It was a boon for institutional investors seeking to hedge their positions, and it was a challenge for speculators. Almost overnight, derivatives trading (trading in contracts that derived their value from underlying securities, currencies, or commodities) became a universal hit, with futures and options markets taking root in every major market center around the world.

Options trading was sexy. It brought an element of excitement that would make being "in the market" a hot ticket for the generation that came of age in the 1980s.

Another major development of the period where Wall Street was concerned was precipitated by a change in SEC regulations that occurred on May 1, 1975. For a decade or so there had been much discussion about the fat fixed commissions on trades that were standard in the industry at the time. It was the SEC's argument that commissions should be negotiable. This was strenuously opposed by most members of the NYSE and AMEX, who habitually saw the SEC as being the enemy—a body made up of outsiders who did not understand the market. If fixed commissions were outlawed, they protested, then their profits would be eroded.

There were pressures for change, however, one of which was a product of the information age. When the fledgling Nasdaq market began operations in the early 1970s, it took advantage of the computer to post prices electronically in brokers' offices. Although only low-cap stocks were involved at first, this proved popular, as did the fact that Nasdaq offered negotiated commissions, giving especially favorable terms to its best customers. In 1971 the NYSE was forced to accept negotiated commissions for trades involving $500,000 or more. On May Day 1975, fixed commissions were abolished altogether.

Most NYSE and AMEX member companies responded by trying to keep their commissions as high as possible, though they were of course forced to be flexible. Some firms took a different approach. One was the commission house recently formed by Charles Schwab. Schwab's idea was to lower commissions as far as was feasible and count on making his profits by increasing the volume of business. The Street was skeptical, to say the least, but Schwab succeeded. Providing the opportunity to play the market for as little as a nickel a trade, his discount house (soon copied by others) drew millions of new investors into the market.

More importantly, negotiable commissions also led to an enormous increase in trading activity on the part of what became known, around that time, as institutional investors. There had always been institutions in the market, of course—pension funds, insurance companies, and so forth—but the high price of fixed commissions had tended to reinforce their innate conservatism, so that fund managers had an excuse to sit on stocks as long as possible. The new situation changed that attitude and encouraged institutions to become far more aggressive and creative in their approach to the market.

This attitude would have come to nothing, however, if it had not been catered to by a new kind of investment bank. Prior to 1975, such banks had been able to get along quite comfortably with rather little capital—$50 million or less, in most cases. Salomon Brothers broke the mold by going public and raising the kind of capital required to facilitate the trading of huge blocks of shares on behalf of institutional investors. Other houses followed suit, and block trading quickly became the norm.

On Black Thursday, during the 1929 crash, the NYSE had traded almost thirteen million shares, a record that stood for decades. By the late 1970s and early 1980s, daily volume routinely surpassed one hundred million, a fact that can largely be attributed to negotiable commissions, the subsequent evolution of institutional investing, and the success of discount brokerages.

On a February day in 1948 at the Chicago Board of Trade, the "board marker" notes the plunging price of May wheat.

The Chicago Mercantile Exchange is home to the eurodollar futures pit, seen in this 1997 photograph.

7 : Junk Bonds, Big Bangs, and the Rise of the Nasdaq

1975–1990s

In 1981 the venerable trading floor of the New York Stock Exchange received a high-tech makeover. A suspended tubular steel space frame was installed to distribute power, communications cables, and air conditioning to trading posts outfitted with large video screens to display market data.

The rapid evolution of the eurodollar market, and the subsequent explosive development of trading in options and other derivatives, had a wide variety of consequences. Approached wisely, derivatives trading provided institutional investors with a valuable new tool for handling risk management. Used without due care, derivatives trading offered the opportunity for traders to crash in devastating fashion. An early victim of this transformed business climate was the Franklin National Bank, which in 1974 failed due to huge losses in foreign-exchange speculation. The mid-1970s was, in fact, a bad period for Wall Street in general. New York City's 1975 brush with bankruptcy did nothing to steady investors' nerves, already frayed by rampant inflation.

The "go-go" 1980s saw a wild cycle of boom and bust on Wall Street, punctuated by nightlong revelry at discos like Studio 54, caught here in one of its more decorous moments.

In 1975, New York found itself on the brink of bankruptcy. President Ford declined to bail the city out, and was rewarded with this classic Daily News *headline.*

The Dow managed to creep up to 1,000 toward the end of 1975, but only briefly. The period from 1976 to 1981 was essentially one of market stagnation, but change was in the air as the antibusiness attitudes of the Woodstock generation gave way to a more pragmatic spirit that brought new blood to Wall Street.

The days when the great investment bankers lived in mansions on Fifth Avenue were long over. Some of the new Wall Street warriors (as they liked to be called) followed the example of New York artists and moved into downtown loft buildings, converting former industrial spaces into palatial apartments conveniently within walking distance of the financial district. This was emblematic of the fact that Wall Street was developing a bourgeois-bohemian[16] wing made up of men and women whose priorities, aside from getting filthy rich, had little to do with the conservative values that had been espoused by the financial community earlier in the century (though these young lions may have had something in common with the rowdies who created the New York exchange back in the eighteenth century). Suddenly it was commonplace to see money managers in gaudily hued suspenders and Wall Street lawyers in microminiskirts dancing into the small hours at discos like Studio 54 and the Palladium.

Above: *The 1980s rise of telecommunications entrepreneur Craig McCaw, seen here in the Seattle facility of McCaw Cellular One, was fueled in part by junk bond financing.*

Below: *Ted Turner, in 1987, and the central newsroom of Cable News Network (CNN), in 1994, part of his Turner Broadcasting empire, created with the help of junk bond financing arranged by Michael Milken of Drexel Burnham Lambert.*

In 1989 Michael Milken, then under indictment on fraud and racketeering charges, spoke at a forum in Mexico. One of the stars of the 1980s boom, he showed a generation of corporate raiders how junk bonds could be used as leverage in buyouts and takeovers.

Not surprisingly, then, the period encompassed by the bull market that commenced in 1982 was nicknamed the "go-go eighties." It was a banner period for New York restaurants as young "arbs" (arbitrageurs), in the process of becoming "foodies," spent their bonuses on *soufflé de homard* and *faisan en daube en gelée*, washed down by amusing clarets with serious price tags. A variety of peripheral enterprises, from the fine-art auction houses to suntan parlors, participated in the boom. In December of 1985 the Dow passed the 1,500 mark, and on January 8, 1987, the unthinkable happened as the index broke the 2,000 barrier.

Fueling this vertiginous rise was a wave of mergers and the inventive exploitation of what became known as the junk-bond market (essentially, the market in high-yield bonds issued by companies with low credit ratings that have no other way of raising money). The mastermind behind both was Michael Milken of Drexel Burnham Lambert, who persuaded many institutional investors, including the officers of a significant number of savings and loan and insurance companies, that junk bonds were not as risky as they might at first appear, and that their impressive yields made them worthwhile investments. These bonds could also be effectively used, he demonstrated, as leverage in big-time takeovers. For a while, in fact, his theories worked astonishingly well, but the late 1980s crisis in the savings and loan industry demonstrated that building a portfolio that placed too much trust in junk bonds was a very risky business.

Junk-bond speculation was not the only reason for the crash of 1987; other factors, including rising interest rates, were involved. But what happened on October 19 of that year caught everyone by surprise.

On the day following Black Monday, 1987, traders at the New York Stock Exchange pored over newspaper reports of the crash.

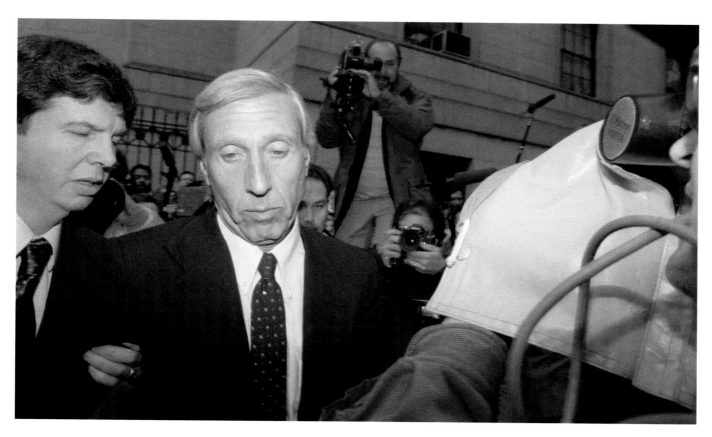

Facing a possible five years in prison, Ivan Boesky arrives at Federal Court on April 23rd, 1987, to plead guilty to charges stemming from insider trading.

BLACK MONDAY

In the annals of Wall Street, October is the cruelest month—the time of year when the memories of earlier crashes come to a simmer just below the surface, awakening fears and superstitions. October of 1987 arrived with several years of bull market in its wake and optimism tinged with raw nervousness in the air. This was no ordinary bull market. It was one of the headiest bull markets of all time.

Robert Sobel has suggested that the final ingredient in creating a great bull market is the excitement caused by a new, glamorous industry that promises to change our lives for the better. According to his theory, in the case of the bull market of the 1980s, that glamour industry was the investment business itself.[17] For the new "yuppie" MBAs of the 1980s, a high-paying job with an investment banking firm like Goldman Sachs or Salomon Brothers was positively glamorous, and their arrival on Wall Street followed closely upon radical changes in the industry that opened up all kinds of new possibilities and seemed to cry out for creative risk-taking. Deregulation had made fixed commissions a thing of the past, stimulating competition. Money-market mutual funds had drawn millions of small investors into the arena, adding greatly to the coffers of financial institutions, which could now indulge in block trading on a hitherto unknown scale. (The demise of fixed commissions helped make trading in large blocks of shares all the more attractive.) Derivatives activity continued to gather momentum, with speculation rather than hedging dominating the mood.

Takeover fever began to spread, with borrowed capital being used to make hostile bids for long-established companies. When those bids succeeded, companies were often broken up so that their components could be sold

(continued on page 238)

IN AT THE GROUND FLOOR:
SMALL COMPANIES AND LOW-CAPS

Agreat moment in the history of any startup occurs when its stock is considered ready for an initial public offering (IPO). To reach this point, the company must have proved that it has made good use of the venture capital used to launch its commercial life and that its business plan is working as promised. It must be ready to show that it has reached a sufficient level, in terms of capitalization and liquidity, in order to warrant listing on one of the world's stock exchanges. Since major exchanges like the New York Stock Exchange and the Frankfurt Börse have listing standards that are extremely difficult to meet, many countries now have special exchanges for start-ups, sometimes called low-cap or alternative markets. (It was as an alternative market that Nasdaq first established itself, though now it has adopted a two-tiered system in which its established and better capitalized companies are distinguished from the newcomers.)

Having met the necessary standards for listing, the startup must find an investment bank that is willing to underwrite its IPO. The investment bank sets the price at which the stock is offered, but that price is no more than a starting point—like an auctioneer's first call for a bid ("Do I hear fifty?")—and the bid and asked prices begin to change the moment the stock enters the secondary market, which is to say, when it is formally listed by the exchange in question and thus becomes open to public trading.

Relatively small companies can make a big splash, as has been the case with Pixar Animation Studios—headed by Apple Computer co-founder Steve Jobs—which has used proprietary software programs such as Marionette and RenderMan to create computer-generated movies such as Toy Story, A Bug's Life, *and* Toy Story II. *Seen here, Woody and Buzz Lightyear, stars of the* Toy Story *movies.*

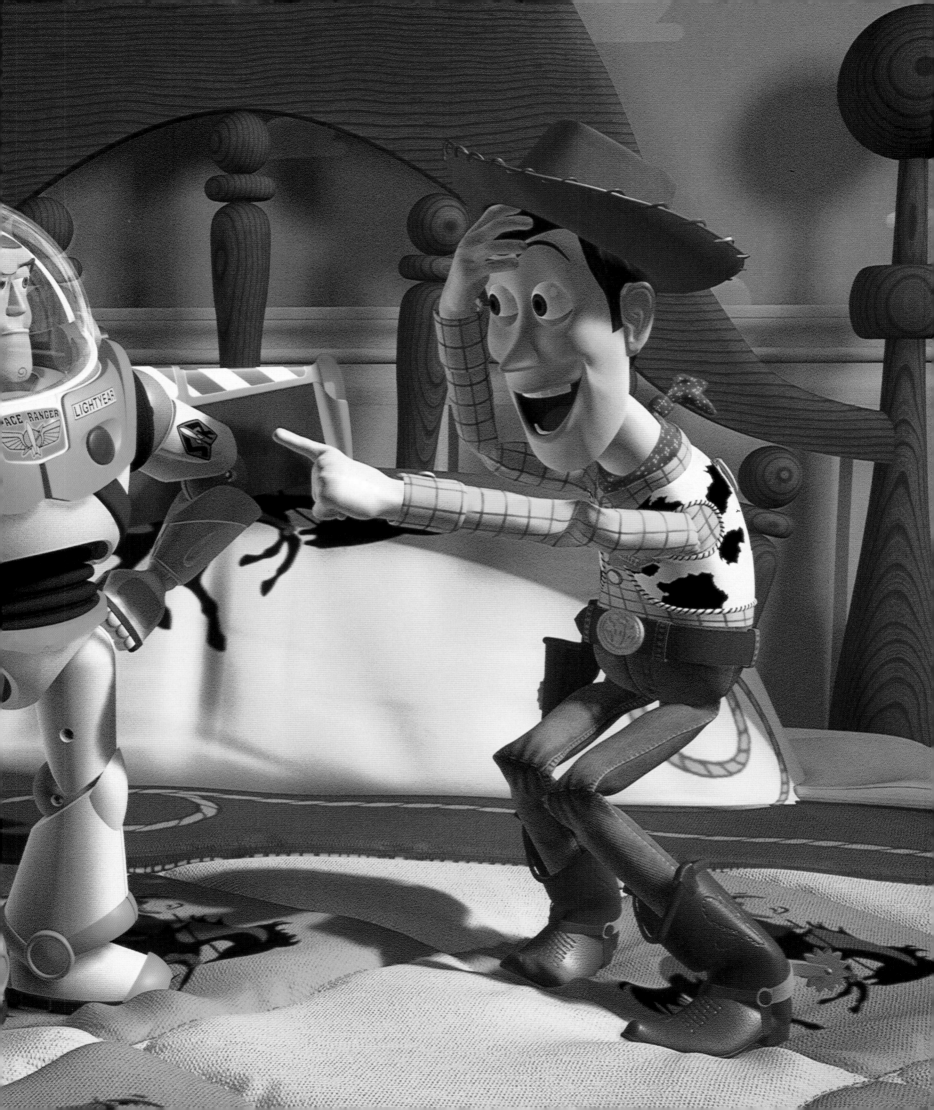

There was a time when IPOs were relative rarities that occurred only when companies had achieved a certain maturity. Until a couple of decades ago, startups that chose to go public generally did so through the medium of the so-called over-the-counter market, which did not require listing by an exchange. This took different forms at different times. In New York, for example, over-the-counter stocks were once traded at the old Curb Exchange—literally a sidewalk exchange in the shadow of the NYSE. The Curb Exchange evolved into the American Stock Exchange (AMEX) and its role as the principal marketplace for over-the-counter shares was assumed by the National Association of Securities Dealers (NASD), the organization that gave birth to the Nasdaq exchange.

The success of the Nasdaq is a reflection of the fact that the recent past has been a period of technological innovation of a sort that has had a great impact upon the world of commerce in general, and securities trading in particular—a period in which important new companies sprang up almost overnight. The precipitous decline in tech stocks that followed the wreck of the dot-coms should not blind anyone to the fact that the future of the market still lies largely in the hands of the visionaries and entrepreneurs

who are developing tomorrow's technology. The dot-coms that failed did so because of strategic management errors, or because they arrived too late in a field that quickly became overcrowded. Where they were *not* mistaken was in attempting to capitalize upon the potential of the Internet and the new information technology.

Information technology is a field that is far from exhausted, and a rapidly expanding sector within this field, well represented in the low-cap markets, is information storage, the digital age having generated a glut of data that is overwhelming existing storage systems. This is an example of an area in which a startup with sound technical qualifications might have a good chance to succeed. It has become apparent, too, that the Internet has an insatiable appetite for content—from original editorial matter to games and imagery of all kinds—and this is another instance of an area where newcomers can prosper, so long as they have original ideas.

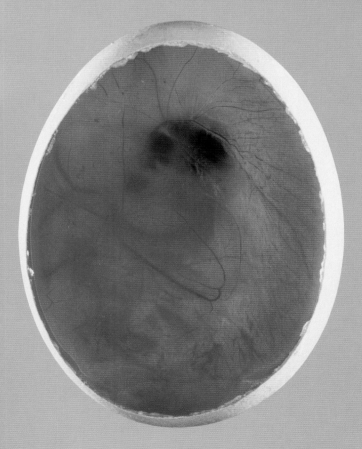

Opposite top: *It is a century since railway stocks dominated stock markets, yet there is still a place for small, well-run railway companies such as Genesee & Wyoming, which operates specialized freight operations in ten U.S. states, as well as railroads in Australia (seen here), Canada, Mexico, and Bolivia.*

Left: *When the subject of energy comes up, most people think in terms of global giants like Shell, but in fact there are many viable smaller energy concerns such as Evergreen Resources, Inc., an independent Denver-based company concerned with oil and gas exploration and operations that include development of a 2.4 million acre tract in Northern Chile.*

Opposite bottom left and far left: *Describing itself as "a leader in safety from field to fork," Neogen is a small but active company specializing in food safety and animal health. Its products range from a vaccine that prevents botulism in horses to kits that food manufacturers employ to check for the presence of harmful bacteria, as well as tests designed to detect pesticide residues in crops such as sweet corn.*

Above, left to right: *An unusual success story is that of the Curtiss-Wright Corp., once one of the largest aircraft manufacturers in the world, which has survived attrition in the aerospace industry by retooling itself as a smaller and highly specialized entity. With roots going back to the Wright Brothers and Glen Curtiss, Curtiss-Wright designs and manufactures high-tech systems such as the motion control mechanisms for the leading edge flaps of the F-22 Raptor.*

Left: *Embrex, Inc. knows what happens within a hen's egg as the embryo chick is developing. This expertise has led to the development of a system for inoculating the embryo against poultry diseases while still in ovo.*

There also are great opportunities for entrepreneurs who are able to offer improvements in the telecommunications field. Admittedly, there is virtually no chance for a startup to challenge hardware giants like Nokia and Ericsson, let alone network access providers like AT&T and Deutsche Telekom, who have to invest billions to lease radio wavebands. There is plenty of possibility, however, for a newcomer to contribute to the software or chip design that would help bring greater efficiency to the wireless communications field, especially where it intersects with the Internet. To give a single example, conventional Internet web pages are written in hypertext markup language (HTML). The tiny screens of handheld devices require displays written in an alternate language known as wireless markup language (WML), a system that might well be improved upon by a savvy newcomer. The success of NTT DoCoMo's I-mode mobile telephone service in Japan—where more people use their handhelds to access e-mail than make use of PCs—both demonstrates the potential of the system and serves as a test bed in which its early shortcomings are becoming apparent. Those shortcomings will keep aspiring tech CEOs busy for years to come.

Other fields in which future startup activity can be expected are the biotechnology and genetic engineering sectors. Both are in their infancy, and thus are ripe for entrepreneurial activity. Admittedly, companies like Celera Genomics, Genset, IMPATH, and Incyte Genomics have already (and in a very short time) established dominant positions, but there is still plenty of room for innovation by newcomers.

This is not to say that high-tech startups are the only ones worth watching. Energy-related IPOs have attracted favorable attention in the recent past, and from time to time someone will think up a new way of marketing frozen yogurt. The fact remains that, ever since the Industrial Revolution, technology has driven market expansion, and there is no reason to suppose that this will change at any point in the near future. ∎

Right: *There are small companies whose names are known around the world. One of these is Velcro—the maker of hook and loop fasteners, based on nature (those burrs that cling to your clothes) and patented by Swiss inventor George de Maestral in the 1950s. In Seattle, Velcro has given rise to a bar sport in which contestants spring from a trampoline and attempt to stick to a Velcro wall.*

Opposite top: *Trex is a company that prides itself upon being America's largest manufacturer of alternative decking products. Its specialty is a wood-plastic composite that has the appearance and convenience of wood while offering many advantages in terms of durability and maintenance.*

Below: *The drive-in restaurant, with car-hops dispensing burgers and sodas, is emblematic of the 1950s, yet the concept thrives today in the form of the Sonic Drive-Ins.*

Bottom center: *Dover Downs Entertainment caters to fans of many kinds of racing sports, from drag racing to harness racing.*

Opposite bottom: *The spread of gaming, throughout America and worldwide, has been a boon for Shuffle Master Inc., which produces mechanized shufflers and other gambling equipment, as well as proprietary table and slot games.*

It was during the Black Monday crash of 1987 that Federal Reserve Chairman Alan Greenspan—then new to the job—first came to the attention of the general public.

The quintessential corporate raider, Carl Icahn often focuses on gaining control of troubled companies. Targets have included TWA, Pan Am, RJR Nabisco, and Phillips Petroleum—the object of a $4.05 billion takeover proposal at the time of this 1985 portrait.

at a profit in order to pay off the debt burden accumulated during the takeover. Corporations that resisted takeover were forced to borrow to leverage their independence. Even failed bids could generate millions of dollars for their perpetrators because of so-called greenmail—the process by which shares acquired at a low price during the early stages of the bid were sold at a far higher price as the battle for control reached a climax.

And while all this was going on, everyone in the market, no matter what their point of view, had to keep an eye on what was happening in Tokyo, London, Frankfurt, and half a dozen other places, knowing that in a world economy a breeze from Hong Kong could blow down a house of cards patiently erected in a Manhattan boardroom.

This new and complex kind of market did not breed complacency, which had been the sin of the 1920s. Rather, it engendered a kind of reckless braggadocio that was summed up by Ivan Boesky's famous dictum, "Greed is all right."

When Boesky, the brigand of risk arbitrage, was accused in 1986 of taking payoffs and indulging in influence peddling, the market not only survived but continued its ascent. Insider trading and other forms of criminal activity were not what would bring about the crash. They were, however, symptomatic of certain attitudes that permeated the bull market of that era, in which it seemed that almost anything was permissible as long as you had the chutzpah to get away with it. These attitudes permitted financial sleight-of-hand artists to create astonishing fiscal illusions while blinding everyone—including the illusionists themselves—to impending collapse.

In the late summer of 1987 the longtime chairman of the Federal Reserve, Paul Volcker, left his post to be replaced by Alan Greenspan. Volcker, a fiscal conservative, had spent most of his term fighting inflation. He had raised the Fed's discount rate on a number of occasions, but it had been standing at a modest 5 percent for more than a year when, on September 4, Greenspan raised it to 6 percent. This had the anticipated effect of putting pressure on the bull market, which nonetheless held fairly steady through September and into the first week of October. Then, on October 6, there was an unexpected sell-off, with the Dow losing 92 points in a single session, and for no clear reason, though many possible theories were bandied about. On the seventh, stocks fell, then recovered, then dropped significantly on the final two trading days of the week. The following week, the steady decline continued, fueled by bad news on both the domestic and foreign fronts. On Friday, October 16, the Dow fell by 108 points—a record—closing at 2,247 on a record volume of 338 million shares.

By opening time on Monday it was a given that the rout was on. Markets in the Far East and Europe had already responded badly to Wall Street's Friday closing, and that added to the general pessimism. Led by Fidelity Investment, money managers for investment funds set out to cover a rapidly deteriorating position by selling equities to raise cash. The major pension funds followed suit, and so did banks, placing sell orders for billions of dollars' worth of stocks and stock options. The size of the blocks being liquidated was huge, and quickly triggered further sell orders that kicked in from computers programmed to respond to precisely this kind of market free fall. As in 1929, the technology could not keep pace with the gathering speed of the disaster. Computers might dictate the sale of large blocks of securities, but these big transactions were handled one by one on the floor of the NYSE, just as they had been for decades, with the result that processing fell so far behind that sell orders were executed after the securities had dropped many points below the level at which the orders had been submitted. Institutional investors and other savvy parties who tried to cover themselves in the options market found that the backup in executing orders there was so bad that it was impossible to maneuver effectively.

By the closing bell, the Dow Jones Industrial Average had lost more than five hundred points. A half a trillion dollars had been shaved from the value of American stocks. Television commentators and newspaper editors alike, few with serious credentials in the financial world,

went ballistic with headlines and leads that made *Variety*'s legendary response to the 1929 crash—"Wall Street Lays an Egg"—seem positively lyrical. But all the pundits in the world appeared unable to explain exactly what had happened. In reality, no pinprick had been needed to pop the bubble. It had simply burst under its own internal pressure.

THE BIG BANG

One way in which the financial markets had changed in the climate created by the eurodollar and options mania was that big investors now thought in global terms—they had to—and this had an unsettling effect upon some long-established financial institutions. The London banking community had benefited from the move to eurodollars, but the once-omnipotent London Stock Exchange had become seriously compromised by its refusal to purge itself of anachronistic practices such as fixed commissions. In 1979 controls on the operation of British securities markets were loosened in the hope that this would make the City more competitive. In fact, the result was the opposite, and the London exchange began to lose business at an alarming rate to overseas competitors. British investors muddled along for a while, frustrated by their inability to share fully in the boom that was beginning to gain momentum on Wall Street. Then, in the mid-1980s, after considerable urging from Margaret Thatcher's Tory government, the LSE decided to try a much bolder experiment.

On October 27, 1986, the day of the "Big Bang," radically new rules were introduced. Among the most important changes were the following:

• Ownership of member firms by a foreign corporation was now permitted, meaning that overseas giants like Merrill Lynch, Goldman Sachs, and Salomon Brothers could (and did) become players in London, greatly enlarging the market's capital base.

• The old division between brokers and dealers was abolished so that all firms could deal with clients directly instead of having to go through a third party.

• Fixed scales of commission were abolished; members were now free to negotiate commissions with clients.

• Instead of the face-to-face trading that had been traditional for hundreds of years, business would now be conducted by way of computer and telephone.

To borrow a word much overused by young British brokers, the initial outcome of these changes was "brilliant." Foreign capital poured into London. In some ways, though, the innovations were too successful. Suddenly the clubhouse was overcrowded as American and Japanese dealers, among others, attempted to muscle their way into the previously exclusive arena. A few thrived. Others quickly bowed out. Then came the crash of 1987, a tidal wave that swept around the globe, sending stock prices tumbling everywhere, London included. For a moment it looked as if the Big Bang might be a big bust, but the basic concept was sound, and as the world market

On October 27, 1986, the London Stock Exchange introduced a new set of rules so far-reaching in its implications that the event was nicknamed "the Big Bang."

recovered, the London Stock Exchange found itself in a healthier situation than it had been in for some time.

So well, in fact, did it fare in the late 1980s and early 1990s that other exchanges instituted similar reforms, eroding much of London's advantage. Soon Europe as a whole had entered the Big Bang era, with even the more conservative countries, like Switzerland, opening their exchanges to foreign participation. London did not grab any absolute long-term advantage, therefore, but it did succeed in reinventing itself and positioning itself to play a major role in a revitalized European securities marketplace.

Meanwhile, Wall Street recovered relatively quickly from the 1987 debacle, and, despite some understandable jitters, the Dow soon began to ascend once more, continuing to do so—with one significant jolt in the late 1990s—through the end of the millennium. During the 1990s the Dow would rise from below 3,000 to above 11,000 points, a phenomenon so unprecedented as to seem almost incredible. Yet the NYSE was not the top Wall Street story of the decade. The stunning performance of stocks on the Big Board was overshadowed by, and perhaps spurred on by, the rise of the Nasdaq, and that success story was itself built on the transformation of the computer from something almost exotic into something taken for granted as a feature of everyday life.

TECHNICALS AND FUNDAMENTALISTS

In his book *Infoculture,*[18] Steven Lubar has suggested that long before the digital revolution, securities exchanges such as the NYSE had become sophisticated information-processing machines that had evolved to determine stock prices based on buyers' and sellers' responses to market pressures. By facilitating both the trading of stock and the exchange of data related to the companies whose shares were being bought and sold there, such institutions "lowered the cost of information, and thus increased the overall efficiency of the economy." This notion can be expanded to perceive stock exchanges as

Following the success of the Big Bang in London, many other European exchanges altered their constitutions in order to admit foreign banks and brokerages as equal partners. Seen here, the bourse in Zurich, Switzerland.

central processing units interacting with other CPUs, such as the Federal Reserve and the financial press.

The Federal Reserve has many duties, which include issuing currency and maintaining the twelve regional Federal Reserve Banks. Above all, though, its job is to monitor the economy for signs of problems such as inflation and deflation, and to step in when required, typically by adjusting interest rates so as to encourage or discourage capital growth. The impact this has on the stock market is very direct—a rise in interest, for example, working against bullish tendencies, and vice versa.

The way the financial press plays into the picture is less clear, since it deals in opinions rather than economic pressure. By the end of the nineteenth century, there were many market gurus offering analysis and advice in scores of newspapers. Later, these pundits were joined by editorial writers for business weeklies and monthlies, publishers of insider newsletters, radio commentators, and television reporters. Some of the "experts" offered opinions based on solid research; a few printed tips leaked by traders bent on making a killing; and others dealt in investment advice based on arcane systems derived from sources ranging from probability theory to astrology. Recently, however, increasingly skeptical investigative reporting and interviewing has helped restore a more objective flow of financial news.

Long before the Internet came into the picture, there was so much information out there that it was difficult not to become confused. Still, there were few investors who did not pay attention to at least some of these media

The bull market of the 1990s gave financial journalism unprecedented visibility. Here, CNNfn's correspondent John Mataxis reports from the Nasdaq Market Site in Times Square, New York, in early 2001.

sources, and it remains true that when a responsible publication such as *Barron's* or *The Economist* prints a story favorable or unfavorable to a given company, it is likely to have an immediate and very concrete effect on that company's stock. (Some sophisticated traders actually buy and sell *against* these media-induced trends because they believe that the market as a whole tends to overreact.)

On top of this, it is important to take into account the research material supplied by industry professionals to their clients, which adds to the total amount of only partially quantifiable information in circulation, and which carries a special weight because of the broker-client relationship. As the sheer number of players has increased, the dynamic of the interchange between clients and bro-

kerage houses has become in some ways as crucial to the overall picture as what happens on the floor of the NYSE.

The complexity of the picture lends itself to as many interpretations of the market as there are investors. Professionals are sometimes divided into bulls or bears (though many are capable of playing both roles), and sometimes into technicals and fundamentalists. Technical traders make their decisions by studying the market itself, watching the ebb and flow of stocks as if they have a life of their own, quite distinct from the physical realities of products and production lines and the financial realities of assets and liabilities that permit a given company to be listed on the exchange. Fundamentalists, by contrast, want to know if the company's new product is performing up to expectations and the extent of the potential market for that product. They are interested in morale at the company's plants and the bonus paid out to the CEO. They might want to talk to customers and to members of the sales force and are likely to study the company's latest annual report with a magnifying glass. They are interested in learning about corporate strategies and in studying the company's performance in comparison to industry rivals. In short, their trading decisions are based on the realpolitik of the business world.

And then there are the traders who buy and sell according to gut feeling.

THE DIGITAL AGE

All of these players and attitudes were in place before the computer made its mark on the investment world, and the same goes for other aspects of the contemporary marketplace. The Medici were venture capitalists, the mutual fund was anticipated by the investment trusts of the nineteenth century, and even a concept such as the program trading of stocks—large-scale institutional buying and selling based on such factors as the spread between currently quoted prices and prices contracted in the futures market—predates the digital age.

The computer did not alter the underlying structure of how business was done, but it speeded everything up in a way that was both exhilarating and terrifying. It changed the very character of the market in that the rapidity with which it processed information seemed to demand split-second decisions on the part of the investor. Its character did not encourage a trading climate in which investors would be satisfied to invest with caution, waiting patiently for dividends to roll in. Instead, it inspired speculation and a greater interest in the riskiest areas of the market, such as options and day trading.

The impact of the computer was not felt overnight, of course. At first it was employed as an auxiliary to the market's conventional machinery. An early use was in the preparation of stock indexes. One reason the Dow Jones Industrial Average had always been confined to a

small number of blue-chip stocks was that, prior to the computer age, it was mathematically impractical to accurately track large numbers of securities on a daily basis. The Standard & Poor's 500 Index, for example, begun in the 1940s, was calculated just once a month until the 1960s, when time-sharing, combined with new multipurpose machines like those in the IBM System/360 family, brought down the price of computing to the point where a daily index based on five hundred stocks was practical.

It was a little earlier than that, in the late 1950s and early 1960s, that Harry Markowitz and his student William Sharpe—future Nobel laureates in economic science—were able to run computer models that demonstrated

(continued on page 250)

In 1952 Harry Markowitz, a 25-year-old graduate student at the University of Chicago, had a brainstorm that would eventually earn him the Nobel Prize. He realized that investors should be as concerned by volatility (he called it "variance") of stocks as by the return on them. In a landmark article, "Portfolio Selection," he enunciated a rule stating that investors would (or should) want to select those portfolios which give rise to efficient combinations of return and volatility. He envisioned a technique for computing the set of attainable efficient portfolios, tailored to each investor's combination of risk tolerance and investment aims, and he derived formulae for return (E) and volatility (V), which allowed him to show, via graphs like the one here, given a hypothetical set of securities, the point of maximum attainable E, or return, which is located at point "b."

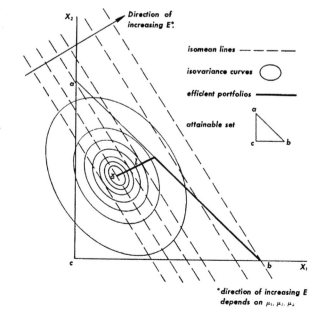

DERIVATIVES:
NATURAL RESOURCES FUTURES

Bulk trading in commodities is concerned primarily with agricultural products, and with natural resources such as timber, coal, petroleum, and metal ores, in which category should be included precious metals and gemstones.

Though not as ancient as agriculture, organized mining and metallurgy are activities that go back to very early phases of civilization. Whole epochs of human evolution are defined by the state of metallurgy in a given era. The Bronze Age, for example—with its enormous advances in terms of tools and weapons—was brought about by the discovery that the smelting of approximately 90 percent copper with 10 percent tin produced an alloy that was much tougher than copper alone, and therefore produced better cutting edges. By the time this discovery was made, in the third millennium B.C., copper had been actively mined and worked into tools and ornaments for a couple of thousand years, and now tin mining became an important activity too. These precious commodities were vital as a stimulus for trade, often being hauled over vast distances under difficult conditions in order to satisfy local demand. Superb Bronze Age artifacts were produced in Scandinavia, but the copper and tin had to be brought from distant parts of Europe, often being exchanged for Scandinavian amber, another highly valued commodity of the period.

Later, one of the prime impulses behind colonialism, especially where the Americas were concerned, was the search for gold and silver, which in turn led to prospecting for other valuable metals. Not surprisingly, then, mining was one of the key activities around which

Copper was first worked by man around 5000 B.C. Today it remains a vital commodity and is mined on a vast scale, as illustrated here by the Bingham Mine, located in Utah, to the southwest of Salt Lake City.

market economies evolved in places such as Canada and various Latin American countries. It was important in the United States, too. The California gold rush of 1849 has been mythologized in books and movies, and for once the reality lives up to the image. The wealth panned from the creeks of Amador County, and hacked from the rocky slopes of the Sierra Nevada, gave rise to an enormous outburst of commercial activity that included the transformation of a trading post named San Francisco into a major city and the construction of the first transcontinental railroad. It helped provide the context for the rise of companies like Wells Fargo that are still major players on today's financial stage.

In the case of South Africa, the discovery of diamonds and then gold in astonishing proliferation was so startling that it brought an entire nation into the commercial mainstream. Elsewhere, natural resources have played a vital if less spectacular role, contributing to major economic developments. The Industrial Revolution, for example, might have evolved in a very different way and elsewhere if it were not for the fact that the British Isles were richly endowed with resources such as coal and iron ore.

The initial exploitation of newly discovered natural resources tends to give rise to several different kinds of financial activity. The California gold strikes of the mid-nineteenth century, for example, spawned scores of small banks, many of which collapsed in the market crash of 1857, sometimes called the "Western Blizzard." The same gold rush also saw the launching of joint stock companies designed

to carry out prospecting and mining work (and in some cases to defraud suckers back east who thought they might make a fortune by investing in any company that had an engraving of a mine entrance on its stock certificates). Other businesses were formed to supply the miners with provisions. Most importantly, though, the gold strikes had a profound impact on the value of gold itself, and hence of many currencies, since they significantly increased the quantity in circulation.

(The concept of a "gold standard"—in which any given nation's currency was pegged to a fixed rate of exchange *vis-à-vis* gold measured in units of weight—had been adopted in Britain in 1821 and was taken up by other countries including France, Germany, and the United States in the 1870s. During the period in which the gold standard prevailed in many parts of the world, gold in effect functioned as the measure of currencies rather than as a true commodity. When, in 1971, during the Nixon presidency, a direct connection between the dollar and gold was finally severed, gold reverted to being just another commodity, however precious.)

Opposite top left: *The Industrial Revolution resulted in a huge increase in the exploitation of natural resources. In this print from about 1805, smoke billows from the chimneys of Colebrook Dale Ironworks, in England, where pig iron was first produced in 1709.*

Opposite top right: *This c. 1852 daguerreotype show four prospectors, one a woman, near the junction of the north and middle forks of the American River during the California Gold Rush that had begun three years earlier.*

Opposite bottom: *In Siberia, in 1961, Soviet drillers celebrate an oil strike.*

Top: *During World War II, coal miners in Bishop, West Virginia, end their long shift underground.*

Left: *At Kharg Island, in the Persian Gulf, pipelines connect a petroleum pumping station with waiting tankers.*

As with agricultural products, fluctuations in supply and demand eventually led to futures trading in a variety of natural resources. Where this kind of commodity is concerned, however, the pressures that influence supply and demand are quite different. Scarcity of a given agricultural product is apt to be caused by a climatic disaster leading to crop failure. Fluctuations in the price of natural resources are more likely to be effected by long-term changes in industrial practices, in market demand for certain products, or even by social pressures. More dramatically, they can also be caused by econo-political decisions on the part of governments.

There is still plenty of coal in the ground in many parts of the world, yet mines have been abandoned from South Wales to West Virginia because, among other reasons, coal is no longer used as a domestic fuel, because it is no longer called upon to power ships and locomotives, and because its burning threatens the environment.

Due to worldwide dependence upon trucks, buses, and automobiles, not to mention ships, trains and airplanes, today's fossil fuel of choice is petroleum. It is no secret that the price of this precious commodity depends greatly upon decisions made by members of the Organization of Petroleum Exporting Countries (OPEC), especially the oil rich states clustered around the Persian Gulf. This has been graphically illustrated during crisis periods such as occurred in 1973 when Arab members of OPEC placed an embargo on oil exports to the United States in retaliation for American support for Israel during the Yom Kippur War. Moments of high drama such as this brought home the fact that there are forces in the world able, because of their wealth in a given natural resource, to control the price of key commodities simply by increasing or decreasing production of that resource.

It is in large part because of this that derivatives trading in the natural resource field is so important—and so difficult to master. Everybody knows what it costs to buy gasoline at the pump today. The secret is to guess accurately what it will be selling for six months or a year from now. ■

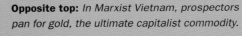

Opposite top: *In Marxist Vietnam, prospectors pan for gold, the ultimate capitalist commodity.*

Opposite bottom: *Offering a contrast between old and new, a large oil tanker glides past the mussel fishermen's marina near Venice.*

Above left: *This ExxonMobil plant is used to convert natural gas into liquid form that can be transported to remote areas not reached by pipe lines.*

Above center: *At a wind farm near Palm Springs, California, a renewable resource is harnessed to produce electricity.*

Top right: *Workers at an open cast mine in Dhanbad, India, carry baskets of coke to load into wagons, each man hauling up to three tons a day.*

Above: *Seams of coal can clearly be seen in this Alaskan escarpment, stratified like a layer cake.*

Left: *During a controlled flooding experiment, water jets from the Glen Canyon Dam on the Colorado River in Page, Arizona, one of the many hydroelectric facilities that supply power to the western United States.*

Inside the Nasdaq 100 stock index futures pit at the Merc, a woman trader shouts an offer as tech stocks begin to slide in April of 2000.

the legitimacy of the former's mathematically based theory about portfolio selection, which revolved around the relationship between diversification and levels of risk. The models conceived by Markowitz, and simplified by Sharpe, provided the prototypes for millions of future computer-generated studies and projections of segments and sections of the securities marketplace.

Soon computers were having an impact on the operations of the exchanges themselves. In 1967 the Chicago Board of Trade became one of the first exchanges to install electronic price displays above the trading floor, so that quotations were available to traders with just a few seconds' delay. By 1970 digital technology had become so vital to CBOT's operations that the Board contracted to install its computer systems in the care of a facilities management agency located more than fifteen miles from the trading floor, a practice that was soon copied by other large exchanges.

The world's first electronic stock market was the Nasdaq, which began operations in 1971. The Nasdaq Stock Market as we know it today was the eventual outcome of a study made by the Securities and Exchange Commission that came to the conclusion that the over-

the-counter securities market needed to reorganize for the protection of investors. The SEC further suggested that the answer to the situation prevailing in the 1960s—described as "fragmented and obscure"—lay in automation. In 1963 implementation of the plan was entrusted to the National Association of Securities Dealers, a loosely knit group of brokers founded in 1939 in response to congressional legislation. The NASD members were not uninterested in the idea of automation, but they lacked the means and organization to do anything about it at the time.

Automation was a hot topic in the business world in the 1960s, and a few entrepreneurs were already working on electronic exchange software. By 1968 a computer designer named Alan Kay had a very basic system called AutEx up and operating. Seated at an AutEx workstation, a broker's representative could transmit what would come to be known as an e-mail, offering to buy or sell specified quantities of named stocks. This would go to all subscribers to the system, and interested parties could respond by telephone. Kay hoped to convince the NYSE of the utility of this idea, but the exchange had already decided that it would shun automation and stick to its traditional ways. Even so, Kay soon found a significant number of subscribers for AutEx, some of them NYSE members.

In 1970 a rival automated system called Instinet went into service. This was the brainchild of Jerome Pustilnik, a former market analyst who headed a company named Institutional Networks Corporation. Instinet was a considerable improvement on AutEx because it permitted orders to be executed entirely within the computer network—no need for telephone calls—thus simplifying the procedure and ensuring privacy for both buyer and seller.

Suddenly, these embryonic systems were threatening to provide an alternative to the three main securities marketplaces—the NYSE, AMEX, and the traditional over-the-counter market—and this prompted the NASD to act. A year before AutEx made its debut, the organization had contracted with an electronics company named Bunker Ramo to begin development of a fully automated marketplace. With the arrival on the scene of competition they stepped up their efforts, and by February 8, 1971, the Nasdaq was ready to go online in the offices of member companies, the flickering black-and-white monitors displaying median quotes for more than 2,500 over-the-counter companies. At the heart of the system, located in Trumbull, Connecticut, was a cluster of UNIVAC mainframes. Scattered elsewhere throughout the network was a motley array of processors, some of which are reputed to have been hardwired to calculate gaming odds for Las Vegas bookies and casino operators.

Few people realized it at the time, but the NYSE now had a serious rival. It would be the 1990s before the potential of the Nasdaq was fully realized, but from the first it began to make its mark, rapidly moving to deal with the kind of teething problems that were to be expected. In 1975, stiffer listings standards were established to provide greater safeguards to the investment community. Starting in 1980, Nasdaq monitors began to display inside quotations—the market's best bid and offer quotes—helping to alleviate suspicions that some Nasdaq brokers were taking advantage of the system by "stretching" the spreads between bid and ask prices to maximize their earnings. In 1982 the top Nasdaq corporations—those able to meet still higher listing standards—split off from the rest to form the Nasdaq National Market. Simultaneously, the exchange began to offer real-time trade reporting for those elite companies, providing brokers and investors with improved service. In 1984 the Nasdaq's Small Orders Execution System was introduced, a service that permitted even the most modest orders to be executed automatically against the best current quotations.

These improvements and innovations made the Nasdaq more reliable and efficient, and hence more competitive with the NYSE, which, as the day of the personal computer arrived, began to resemble a living fossil—a coelacanth-like specimen unique to the depths of Lower Manhattan. It was not just the use of computer networks that separated Nasdaq from the NYSE, however. As noted, the NYSE is a continuous auction market, with market making in specific securities performed by specialists who double as traders and auctioneers. The Nasdaq is a dealer market in which multiple registered market makers compete for customers' orders by providing continuous bid and ask quotations, which they must be willing to back by drawing upon their own pool of cash or securities when necessary. Within this system, a brokerage can act either as a broker, negotiating trades between buyer and seller, or as a dealer-principal, acting as a market maker or selling from its own account. (It is required to disclose which role it is playing in any given transaction, and must be prepared to demonstrate that it made every effort to obtain the best posted price.) Some brokerages, especially discount houses, route trades (NYSE-listed as well as Nasdaq-listed stocks) to satellite market makers who rebate a small percentage of each transaction—seldom more than a couple of cents per share—back to the brokerage. These rebates permit the discount houses to charge smaller commissions.

Stripped to its basics, a Nasdaq-like system might work without computers, but it is the numbers-crunching ability of the microprocessor that has made the Nasdaq so revolutionary, and that has led to the adoption of similar systems all over the world. Appropriately enough, it is the high-tech stocks that have ridden the crest of the Nasdaq's tidal wave, starting with hardware and software giants like Apple, Intel, and Microsoft and continuing with Internet companies from Amazon to Yahoo. Among the latter group are the new online brokerage houses that have, in a sense, completed the loop, bringing the stock market into the home.

The 1998 merger of the NASD and the AMEX brought the Nasdaq and AMEX exchanges together under the auspices of a single marketing group. More significantly, it is now commonplace to buy and sell NYSE-listed stocks over the Internet. The bid and ask process is still completed by specialists and brokers on the floor of the exchange, but as far as the investor is concerned, it begins and ends with the PC workstation. In a sense, then, the NYSE is piggybacking on the success of the Nasdaq, being carried into the electronic age by the success of its rival's technology.

The NYSE is not entirely innocent of electronic aids, of course. The trading floor is retrofitted with all kinds

*A half-point interest rate cut generates a news flash on the Times Square
ticker, next to the Nasdaq marketsite.*

of digital displays—banks of monitors suspended above specialists' heads and quotation crawls flickering against the marble walls—and has direct computer links to other exchanges. The Intermarket Trading System (ITS) was initiated in 1978 as a first step toward developing a computerized national market system. It enabled exchange members to access trading in other markets in search of the best prices. The current SuperDot (Super Designated Order Turnaround) message-switching system is a more advanced electronic tool, handling the majority of NYSE orders with great efficiency and providing links between member firms and the AMEX trading floor. At the time of writing, the NYSE board has approved a plan to install a state-of-the-art electronic communications network (ECN) and to move toward a new "multiplatform market structure." What this means is that the NYSE is seeking to match the efficiency of the Nasdaq and other electronic exchanges but

without giving up its core system of live specialists and traders. (The ECN will, incidentally, provide NYSE floor traders with direct access to Nasdaq stock quotations.) If further competition emerges from other automated exchanges, such improved performance will be all the more crucial.

Meanwhile, in 1999 the NYSE unveiled a three-dimensional virtual trading floor (3DTF), an interactive, high-resolution graphic representation of everything that is going on in the exchange environment at any given moment. Marvelous and efficient though this is, it may never be copied elsewhere for the simple reason that its purpose is to make visible the dynamics of a large and complex trading floor, and there are few others of any significant size left. When one of the largest and most storied, that of the London Stock Exchange, was retired from service, it was sold, ironically, to Knight Securities International, a subsidiary of Knight/Trimark, the U.S.

wholesale market maker in equities and one of the biggest names in the field of online trading. Once gone, such institutions do not return, and certainly it would be a shame to lose the color of the NYSE. (A crash wouldn't be a crash without the displays of emotion on the trading floor behind that imposing façade at 18 Broad Street.) Most people do not doubt that the NYSE has a future. After all, the asking price for membership in the exchange is still around $2 million.

Still, the future is clearly digital, and in the digital age fluidity seems almost as important as liquidity (though this may prove to be an illusion). The ability of the computer to deal with astronomical numbers means that the trends behind market movements can be broken down statistically and analyzed stringently. The right software can take this information and generate models of, say, the evolving market in index options, which can be interpreted in much the way a meteorologist interprets the development of a gathering storm by following Doppler

On January 4, 1999—the first day of trading for the year—bulls stampede past the New York Stock Exchange as part of an annual ritual calculated to bring good fortune to Wall Street. That year, observance of the ritual paid off.

radar patterns. Even the standard electronic communications systems can supply subscribers with vast arrays of information.

When dealing with the Nasdaq, for example, three levels of subscription service are available, catering to brokerage houses (Level 1), institutional investors and traders (Level 2), and registered market makers (Level 3). The retail investor is most likely to be interested in Level 2, which can be accessed by means of the Internet. Among the basic material such a service provides is the following:

• A real-time quote monitor, fed directly from the exchanges, offering quotes on any security. The menu for this monitor can be customized in many ways so that the trader can view stocks currently in his own portfolio, stocks in a given sector, and other data.

• A real-time display of Level 2 data on any stock with market-making information that allows the trader to select the best available deal at any given moment. This is combined with a quick-order module that permits the trader to place his order in much the way that you would purchase a book from Amazon.com.

• An index monitor showing movements of the Nasdaq Composite Index, the Dow, Standard & Poor's 500, and so on.

• A same-day high-and-low monitor, which records the extremes of the upward and downward movements of both individual stocks and indexes for the current trading session.

• Animated graphs showing trends for individual stocks as they have evolved over the past several hours.

• A monitor providing detailed information about positions held in the current market.

• A message monitor offering a real-time display of all entered orders and the current status of each order.

It is thanks to the availability of ECN-routed information that a phenomenon such as day trading has come to prominence. Exchange members of a certain stripe have indulged in day trading since continuous trading became the norm: buying and selling (or selling and buying) blocks of the same stock during the course of a single market session in order to realize quick profits. In the past, though, access to the exchange floor, or at least to a reliable broker, was necessary if you wished to indulge in this kind of speculation. The information explosion has made it possible for anyone who knows how to operate a PC to play the same game. All you need is a line of credit and the ability to delude yourself into believing that you possess the sangfroid and nerves of steel of a veteran risk arbitrageur. That much accomplished, it's a simple matter of interpreting all that color-coded information on the monitor, or else playing a hunch like any sucker whiling away the afternoon with the thoroughbreds at Belmont Park or Epsom Downs.

Day trading may soon be a misnomer. Several exchanges now permit after-hours trading, and by the time this book appears, it's quite possible that 24/7 trading—markets that never close—will be a reality. The day trader will be forced to become a day and night trader, never able to sleep because he cannot afford to close his eyes lest he miss some vital snippet of phosphor-dot information on those ECN monitors.

Already, the stress of the electronic marketplace has contributed to one tragedy. In July 1999 Mark Barton, a forty-four-year-old chemist and sales executive who had lost his shirt day trading, murdered his wife and children before wreaking mayhem in a pair of Atlanta, Georgia, brokerage offices. By the time he finally took his own life, twelve people were dead and thirteen wounded.

Perhaps the oddest quirk about electronic trading is that it may lead back to the very oldest form of transaction. Stu Feldman, director of the Institute for Advanced Commerce,[19] has suggested that, since the computer can calculate the value of securities so precisely at any given moment, there is no technical reason why one block of stock could not be swapped for another without the first being liquidated into cash that is then used to purchase the other. It would involve a relatively simple process of breaking down the values of the two securities into small enough units to allow an exact exchange to be effected.

How the tax authorities will deal with electronic barter is a matter for speculation.

Hedge fund guru George Soros is the principal advisor for the Quantum Fund, which was, for a period of nearly three decades, the best-performing fund in the world.

HARD TIMES AND HEDGE FUNDS

The New Economy euphoria of the 1990s, generated by the perceived success of dot-com and other high-tech stocks, survived into the new millennium, but only for a few months. Professionals claim to have known that the boom must end, yet its momentum continued for a while despite the evidence that price/earnings ratios provided no justification for the value at which New Economy stocks were being traded. The argument offered by optimists was that it was future earning that justified the prices being paid for shares in last week's IPOs (initial public offerings). This optimism proved to be unjustified. Many once highly touted companies disappeared entirely. Others survived, but only after seeing the value of their stock greatly reduced.

In retrospect, though, investors were right to be excited about the New Economy. This was not a situation where people could claim to have been duped (except for those who were taken in by the online bucket shops that promoted fraudulent securities). The problem was that the market in tech stocks became overcrowded. Where only a few companies could succeed, many aspired, and their aspirations were rewarded with lavish financial support until it became apparent—too late for anyone to bail out—that they were redundancies on the financial landscape. Also, some companies, especially in the e-commerce field, found that they were in no position to compete with Old Economy competitors who were far better capitalized and could afford to hire the talent that enabled them to adapt to the new technology.

In the cautious climate that resulted from the deflation of the New Economy, investors turned to risk management, and the public's imagination was caught by a much misunderstood phenomenon known as the hedge fund.

Hedge funds were not new. The concept seems to have been invented as long ago as 1949 by a sociologist named Alfred Winslow Jones. It was only in the 1990s, however, that such funds really began to gain in popularity, following the enormous success displayed by George Soros's Quantum Fund.

Hedge funds are private partnerships (limited in America to a maximum of ninety-nine partners) that, unlike mutual funds, are not subject to regulations that forbid shorting and options trading. Such regulations are applied to mutual funds to protect investors from unnecessary speculative risk. Ironically, it is precisely risk management that attracts wealthy private investors and institutions such as university endowments to entrust their money to hedge funds. (Minimum investment in these funds typically runs between $500,000 and $1 million, amounts that are not shocking to investors who did even moderately well in the last bull market.) At the most basic level, the ability to sell short means that a fund can balance short and long positions in its portfolio in order to hedge and minimize risk. More speculatively, it can short in an aim to make profits during a bear market. In reality, however, every so-called hedge fund has its own way of operating. Some are heavily leveraged; others avoid leverage. Many actually dislike the hedge fund sobriquet and prefer to describe themselves as practitioners of alternative or nontraditional investment strategies. Among the activities such funds may specialize in are merger arbitrage, bankruptcy arbitrage, leveraged loans, distressed security arbitrage, special real estate opportunities, and so forth. Many of these enterprises fall into the category of "event-driven situations" that have little to do with the current overall performance of the financial markets.

Whatever his fund's specialties, every fund manager/general partner has a strong incentive to generate profits, because a very substantial 20 percent of those profits are returned to the fund.

A recent development is "funds of funds" that permit smaller investors to participate in hedge funds by putting money into subsidiary funds that become partners in hedge funds.

Where will it end?

"In the financial world," says the CEO of a major hedge fund, "if you want to make money, you have to reinvent yourself every few years. At the moment, hedge funds are the name of the game, but that will change. Already everyone is trying to get in on the action. I was lucky. I staked my claim early on. I hope I have the sense to get out before it's too late."

At the closing bell on March 29, 1999, traders at the New York Stock Exchange look up at the monitors cantilevered above their heads and celebrate the Dow's lofty perch above the 10,000 mark.

8 : The Global
Marketplace

1990–present

1,453 feet tall, and intended as the world's tallest buildings—but never quite completed—the Petronis twin towers in Kuala Lumpur, Malaysia, were once seen as a symbol of Asia's commercial ascendancy. That was before the economic downturn of the late 1990s.

Difficult though it may be for today's traders to comprehend, this was the entrance to the stock exchange in Karachi, Pakistan, as it appeared in 1958. Even then, the ramshackle nature of the structure was misleading. The exchange was in fact quite active by regional standards. It listed 70 stocks and had 190 members, each of whom paid $2,100—a considerable sum at the time—in order to join.

One of Latin America's busiest exchanges, today's Bolsa Mexicana de Valores towers above the Avenida Reforma in Mexico City.

Historians have argued, with some reason, that a global economy was operating by the end of the fifteenth century. This is true to the extent that there was by then international trade involving Europe, Africa, the Near and Far East, and the Americas. And that trade did have tremendous repercussions, with seagoing European nations placed at a great commercial and strategic advantage. What came into existence at that time, however, was not so much a single global marketplace as the beginnings of a global network made up of interacting but distant, and distinct, marketplaces. Merchants in Amsterdam might trade with their opposite numbers in Java, but the two markets remained isolated from each other in their day-to-day operations.

The situation began to change as communications improved during the nineteenth and twentieth centuries. The laying of the transatlantic cable knit North America more tightly to the European market. Telegraphy, the telephone, and radio helped bring all markets closer together, but it was the computer that really created the possibility of a single global marketplace. Not only could the computer process and transmit information instantly, it had the effect of partially neutralizing the Tower of Babel factor. Prior to the digital age, markets had been separated as much by linguistic and cultural differences as by physical distance. The electronic processor reduces the data needed to complete any given transaction to its essential digital elements, and the Internet flashes those around the world without showing favor to any nation or class of individuals.

In reality, of course, linguistic, cultural, and political differences still have a way of creeping in and messing things up. The computer does nothing to directly undermine tariffs and embargoes. It is unable to rid the marketplace of the legacy of colonialism. It cannot do away with biases based on ethnicity, nor can it transform dictatorships or absolute monarchies into democracies

During the first years of the U.S. military occupation of Japan, after World War II, securities exchanges were closed. In 1949, several were permitted to re-open with modified western-style constitutions. Shown here is the inauguration of the new Tokyo exchange that year.

overnight. Most of all, it is unable to reach into the wretched sinks of poverty that still proliferate around the world, so that the equal opportunity implied by the notion of a global marketplace is somewhat compromised from the start.

Ironically, we can understand progress toward a fully functioning global marketplace only by looking at its potential components one by one.

MODERN JAPAN

A good place to start is Japan, which, despite recent troubles, is home to the financial markets that have made the greatest strides during the past half century, and that hold some of the keys to the future of globalism.

Aside from the relatively brief American occupation of the islands (from 1945 to 1952), Japan has no colonial legacy to shake off. That American intervention was crucial, however, in providing the occasion for a devastating break with the past and the adoption of a body of legislation that influenced everything, including the launching, in 1949, of newly constituted stock exchanges in Tokyo, Osaka, Nagoya, Kyoto, Hiroshima, Fukuoka, Niigata, and Kobe. (The last was closed in 1967.) The Sapporo Securities Exchange was established the following year.

The Japanese Miracle did not happen overnight, nor did the Tokyo Exchange immediately meet the highest international standards. It was not until 1967 that modern auction procedures were put in place and *bakai* trades abolished. (*Bakai* trading had been the practice of making off-floor deals and later reporting them as official exchange contracts.) It was as recently as 1970 that the TSE was admitted to the International Federation of Stock Exchanges.

Since the 1980s, no stock exchange has witnessed more drama than the Tokyo Exchange, a fact that is memorialized in these faces captured in the days—not too long ago—before the Samurai-like traditions of the trading floor gave way to tidy rows of computer work stations.

Top row

Left: *In 1991 a brokerage scandal led to the temporary suspension of trading by Nomura, Japan's leading commission house. Here, a passer by stares up at a quotation board outside a shuttered branch office.*

Center: *In January of 1994, the rejection by the Upper House of Prime Minister Morihiro Hosokawa's controversial political reform bill led to a wild selling spree on the Tokyo exchange.*

Right: *A woman broker—one of the first in Japan to break through the gender barrier—uses hand signals to send in a order.*

Middle row

Left: *Traders react to plummeting stock prices as Tokyo responds to the Wall Street panic of October 1987.*

Center: *A floor trader fights for space during a hectic 1989 session.*

Right: *Squeezed by the surrounding mob, a trader fights for breath towards the end of a two day buying spree, in March of 1989, which saw the Nikkei index shoot up 430.92 points to a record 32,737.28.*

Bottom row

Left: *On August 7, 1990, glum brokers watched as prices tumbled, with the Nikkei index losing more than 1,300 points by midday.*

Center: *Floor traders appear to be caught up in some elaborate dance ritual.*

Right: *Traders collapse onto their desks at the end of a frantic day of trading, February 18, 1991, when hopes of an early end to the Gulf War sent stock prices soaring.*

By that time the Japanese economy had already begun its spectacular ascent. At first, expansion was due largely to the domestic demand for consumer goods as the Japanese people sought a higher standard of living. Later the emphasis began to shift, thanks in part to the terms of the 1951 security treaty that had guaranteed Japanese business access to American markets in return for America's right to maintain military bases in Japan. As the economy strengthened, Japan's exports rose. Initial successes included the heavy manufacturing sector, which saw the Japanese shipbuilding industry, for instance, becoming a world leader. Then came the triumph of Japanese small-consumer goods, especially items such as transistor radios utilizing the new miniaturization technologies. For a while, even Japan's economic crises seemed to have happy endings. The OPEC oil embargo of 1973–74 wreaked havoc within the Japanese economy and reminded the world of Japan's poverty in terms of natural resources. At the same time, it created a market for compact and subcompact cars in the United States, which Japan's auto makers—till then dwarfed by companies like General Motors and Ford—were ready to meet. Cementing these successes was the fact that Japan's exports proved to be of very high quality, eroding the reputation for shoddiness that had dogged Japanese consumer items since the interwar years.

Along with this came the consolidation of the Japanese banking industry into a small cluster of international giants, not dissimilar in style to the trustlike group of New York financial institutions that had dominated the American business world early in the twentieth century. By the mid-1980s, per capita income in Japan was higher than in the United States. Over a period of two decades, from 1970 to 1989, stocks listed on the Tokyo Stock Exchange increased in value by 300 percent.

The boom could not last forever, of course. The admiration that Japanese business had earned abroad in the 1970s and 1980s began to turn to distrust and anger as it became apparent to foreign economists that mounting trade surpluses in Japan owed a great deal to the Japanese government's practice of economic protection-

ism on a disturbing scale, enforcing embargoes against many kinds of imports in a way that was reminiscent of mercantilism in the pre–Adam Smith era. This had seemed reasonable during Japan's rebuilding phase, but hardly made sense to her competitors when the Tokyo Stock Exchange was within an ace of becoming the largest in the world.[20]

At home, meanwhile, Japanese commentators began talking about the "bubble economy" in which readily available credit, combined with speculative euphoria, pushed equity and real estate markets to levels that seemed unrealistically high. (At the same time, the strong yen encouraged big Japanese investors to snap up banks, entertainment companies, and real estate of all kinds abroad, engendering more overseas hostility.) In 1992 the bubble burst and—despite continuing success in the field of exports—Japan slid into recession.

The news since then has been largely bad. Banks and giant brokerage houses have collapsed. Bribery scandals have rocked the Finance Ministry and the Bank of Japan. A fast-track Member of Parliament was accused of accepting payoffs from a major securities company and promptly hanged himself. Humiliating events of this sort point to tensions between the old Japan and the new that have yet to be resolved. Bribery is virtually a tradition in Japan, its roots going back to feudal times. It is not considered shameful until the parties involved are

On December 27, 1973, traders at the Tokyo Stock Exchange use hand signals to signify "buy" orders following reports that the Arab oil exporting nations will relax their restrictions regarding petroleum exports to Japan.

caught—as is much more likely to happen in modern times, when all the social and political connections in the world cannot protect anyone from the scrutiny that comes with the institutions of democracy, even when they are somewhat compromised by backwash from the predemocratic era.

As much as in England in the pre–Big Bang era, a kind of elitism based on old-school-tie connections is commonplace in the Japanese business world, as it is in mainstream Japanese politics. *Zaibatsu*-like clusters of intertwined companies provide one another with patronage on the basis of connections that go back for generations. Bloodlines are accorded exaggerated respect, especially when the great feudal clans or the merchant dynasties connected with the former *zaibatsu* are concerned.

Consequently, the Japanese business world is having to confront the possibility of collapsing under the weight of dubious patronage and obsolete tradition. Moreover, this is occurring just as it becomes apparent that Japan must change its posture in the context of the global economy.

It is probable that in the future many Japanese companies will be obliged to do most of their manufacturing abroad—a trend that has already begun—taking advantage of favorable exchange rates, cheaper labor, and proximity to emerging markets. The Tokyo Stock Exchange and its smaller cousins will serve as the nerve centers for industries that are just as likely to have their physical plants in Brazil or Hungary as in Nagasaki or Yokohama.

Despite changing times, the Asian market panic of the late 1990s, and the lingering stench of corruption, the sleekly automated Tokyo Stock Exchange remains an intimidating presence on the international financial stage—a model and a challenge for the rest of the region. Meanwhile, the importance of the Osaka Securities Exchange has been boosted by an alliance made with the Nasdaq that creates a platform for trading top American Nasdaq stocks and launching Japanese high-tech start-ups.

OTHER ASIAN ECONOMIES

The economy of South Korea is in some ways a reflection of that of Japan, the nation that occupied it as a colonial power during much of the first half of the twentieth century. In South Korea, as in Japan, modernization has been tempered by powerful ties to a past in which hereditary privilege was crucial to advancement.

The Korean Stock Exchange was founded in 1956, three years after the end of the Korean War. In 1962 it was reorganized as a joint-stock company, but the following year it was revamped again as a government-run nonprofit entity. In 1988 it was privatized once more. Whatever the status of the ownership of the KSE, however, the South Korean government—paranoid about its Communist neighbor to the north, and about its own labor unions—has involved itself closely with every aspect of the private sector of the economy, reflect-

In recent years the Seoul Stock Exchange, in South Korea, has been one of the most active in Asia. Here, on the final work day of 1990, clerks and traders throw chits into the air, celebrating the fact that a year in which listed stocks tumbled 23.5% is mercifully over.

A pillar of the South Korean economy has been the automobile industry. This assembly line worker is seen at the Samsung Motor's plant in Pusan.

Recent decades have seen South Korea develop into a major exporting nation. This Korean container ship is docked in Seattle, Washington.

ing the Japanese-style paternalism that permeates the Korean business world. South Korea followed Japan in becoming one of the "Asian Tigers" of the 1970s and 1980s. Even more so than is the case in Tokyo, however, the Seoul bourse is dominated by a tiny group of huge conglomerates—the so-called *chaebol*, the Korean equivalent of the *zaibatsu*. Currently just four corporations—Samsung, Daewoo, Hyundai, and LG (the result of a merger between Lucky and Goldstar)—are responsible for more than half of the nation's exports. Their importance to the economy is such that they are able to function as quasi-monopolies.

At the same time, government-legislated guarantees of full employment have meant that it has been very difficult to dismiss workers. (When these regulations were eased, in 1996, the result was violent labor unrest.) Unable to trim their payrolls, the *chaebol* were forced to diversify into areas in which they had little or no experience in order to find work for employees they were bound by law to keep on the payroll. This made for levels of inefficiency that hurt South Korean business just as the Asian economy as a whole was beginning to sour.

The Korea Stock Exchange itself is a model of efficiency, however, fully computerized and functioning in a floorless

environment. In 1991 membership in the exchange was opened to foreign brokerage houses, and in 1996 overseas entities were permitted to issue and list shares on the KSE. That same year, the KSE spun off its Stock Index Futures Market, followed in 1997 by its Stock Index Options Market. Also in 1997, all ceilings on foreign investment were lifted.

Two of Asia's most vital markets, Singapore and Hong Kong, are located on islands in bustling port cities that

South Korea's Finance and Economy Minister Jin Nyum (center) joins in ceremonies marking the beginning of the trading year, January 2, 2001.

Among Asian economies, Singapore has established a position for itself out of all proportion to its modest size. Even at night the Singapore business district hums with activity.

have strong ties to the London business and banking world. The Republic of Singapore is an independent city-state, which until 1965 was part of Malaysia. It occupies just 225 square miles, including a swarm of tiny islets, and has a total population of approximately 3.5 million. Despite its diminutive size, however, it has become a formidable presence in the Asian economy because it has succeeded in maximizing its own manufacturing infrastructure—especially in high-tech areas. This has provided its entrepreneurs with the wealth to invest in neighboring markets, so that its economic strength has become regional. In addition, just as its port once gave Western ships access to a large segment of Asia, Singapore now forms a favored base for offshore operations on the part of Western financial institutions servicing the Asian dollar market. It is, in short, a money haven of the sort that could come into being only in the age of electronic telecommunications.

The present Singapore Exchange (SGX) was formed in 1999 by the merger of the Stock Exchange of Singapore and the Singapore Futures Exchange. The former was incorporated in 1973 and the latter launched in 1984, making it Asia's first futures exchange; it also became a pioneer in exchange linkages by establishing the world's first mutual offset trading link in partnership with the Chicago Mercantile Exchange. At the time of the merger, the SGX became the first demutualized integrated securities and derivatives exchange in the region.

With a land area of a little over four hundred square miles and a population of five to six million, Hong Kong is a bit larger than Singapore. Its long period of rule by the British came to an end in 1997, when sovereignty reverted to China. Even though the Chinese government promised to leave most of Hong Kong's institutions intact and guaranteed the existence of a capitalist system there for fifty years, this changeover made local businessmen nervous, memories of the Tiananmen Square massacre being fresh in their memories. Some companies moved their operations to other parts of the region, most typically to Singapore. Many more remained, however, and Hong Kong's economy—a quarter the size of the economy of the rest of China—survived more or less intact without sustaining damage from clumsy dragons, at least in the short run.

Hong Kong's first bourse was the Association of Stockbrokers in Hong Kong, established in 1891 and renamed the Hong Kong Stock Exchange in 1914. A second exchange, the Hong Kong Stockbrokers' Association, was incorporated in 1921 and merged with the Hong Kong Stock Exchange in 1947. As the Asian economy began to boom after World War II, other exchanges—including the Far East Exchange (1969), the Kam Ngan Stock Exchange (1971), and the Kowloon Stock Exchange (1972)—came into being. In 1980 the four exchanges agreed to unite in order to consolidate Hong Kong's strength in the securities marketplace. The new bourse, known as the Stock Exchange of Hong Kong and trading by way of a wholly computerized platform, began operations in 1986. In May 2000 it launched a pilot program in partnership with the Nasdaq that permits trading in American stocks with a strong Asian presence, such as Starbucks, Microsoft, and Intel.

By 1995 Hong Kong's stock market was the eighth largest in the world and the second largest in Asia, behind only Japan. In January 2000, two and a half years after the British conceded power to China, it was still the second largest in Asia, although it had dropped to tenth position on world lists—hardly a devastating decline, given the circumstances. There has been little evidence of the kind of heavy-handed interference from the Beijing government that had been feared in some quarters, interference that could throw the famously free-flowing and self-adjusting mechanisms of the Hong Kong exchange out of whack.

Across the border in Mainland China, progress toward a limited market economy, instigated by Deng Xiaoping in the final quarter of the twentieth century, has contin-

The Bank of China towers over Hong Kong's financial district, symbolizing the city's economic vitality.

The Stock Exchange of Hong Kong pictured in 1987, a year after it was created to unite the city's four previous exchanges.

ued to gather momentum, but the stock markets there have been slow to develop into major players on the international scene. Despite lofty plans—including the creation of a new financial district for Shanghai—the Shanghai and Shenzhen exchanges, established in 1992, have displayed a tentative character, as if the Chinese government is still not entirely sure that they are appropriate to its vision of society. Most businesses in China are government-owned and remain unlisted. It is extremely difficult for an entrepreneur to launch a private enterprise of any kind because it's impossible to obtain a bank loan without a guarantor, and such guarantors are almost nonexistent. In any case, the only loans available are extremely short-term. Generally they must be paid off in a matter of months. As for seats on the Shanghai and Shenzhen exchanges, these are not available to private businessmen and are, to all intents and purposes, occupied by party functionaries.

One area in which entrepreneurial Chinese have had some modest success is the dot-com world. This sector of the market requires relatively little start-up capital, making the initial bank loan problem less pressing, and it is of great interest to Western venture capitalists because it offers the possibility of large returns for moderate invest-

ments. At the same time, dot-coms must deal with many of the same political and bureaucratic barriers faced by all Chinese private businesses, and they are formidable.

Companies listed on the mainland exchanges have been divided into Class A shares, for Chinese investors only, and Class B shares, reserved for foreign capital. Overseas corporate investors were quick to enter the market once given access, but soon discovered that it was difficult to obtain the kind of background research information that is taken for granted in the developed world. Worse still, distrust was fueled by a near-farcical series of events in 1996, precipitated by the decision of the Shenzhen exchange to promote the sale of Class B shares by floating loans on behalf of some of the local brokers, and bending the rules regarding the sale of these shares to Chinese citizens. This prompted an artificial market rally, which was quickly snuffed out by government regulators as they realized that the involvement of local speculators in the Class B market was costing China precious capital. In putting an end to this, the government drove down the market, so that foreign investors were badly burned, causing many of them to be far more cautious in their future dealings with Shenzhen and Shanghai.

Given this background, it's hardly surprising that the

Left: The present Shanghai Stock Exchange did not open till 1992. Before that, however, investors managed to do over-the-counter business, with the aid of an abacus, as seen in this 1987 photograph.

Below: In February of 2001, Beijing residents open an account at a brokerage in the Chinese capital in order to take advantage of changed rules that permit Chinese citizens to purchase hard currency B shares, previously reserved for foreign buyers.

This colorful stock market in Calcutta, India, is reminiscent of the many open-air street or curb exchanges that once thrived all over the world.

Asian panic of the late 1990s hit the Chinese exchanges very hard. In 1999 trading was so depressed that the Shanghai bourse closed for three weeks, nominally in celebration of the Chinese New Year. Despite early setbacks on the road to capitalism, however, China remains the greatest underdeveloped market in the world, and, especially now that Hong Kong is its portal to the international financial community, it seems certain that its role in the global economy can only become vastly more important.

Aside from the 1.2 billion people that make up the population of mainland China, it's important to note that tens of millions of people of Chinese descent have long been established in other Asian countries, as well as in Europe and the Americas. Expatriate Chinese merchant clans sometimes have family members in many different major centers—Hong Kong, Shanghai, Singapore, Jakarta, Kuala Lumpur, Hanoi, Manila, Honolulu, San Francisco, New York, London, and

Amsterdam, just to name a few. They are able to form worldwide networks that make nonsense of national or regional boundaries.

Much the same can be said of merchant families of Indian descent. They have been familiar for centuries in parts of Africa and in the Caribbean, as well as in Southeast Asia. Sikh peddlers used to travel around the British Isles on bicycles, and since World War II, Indian tradesmen have become familiar presences in British cities, contributing much to both culture and commerce. The United States is now home to a significant number of citizens and residents of Indian extraction, and they have become prominent in sectors of the economy such as hotel and motel ownership. Indeed, Indians abroad seem to possess a sure knack for finding places for themselves in evolving business environments.

In the mother country, however, Indians do not always fare as well. Many have left for other countries because

The stock exchange in Bombay (known to Indians as Mumbai) is the busiest in India and one of the most important in all of Asia, a product of India's attempt to create a modern economy despite all the problems endemic to a highly traditional society with a vast underclass, much of which remains in deep poverty.

India remains a nation of deeply seated traditions and devout religious observance, but its educated classes have embraced the Internet and the nation's level of computer literacy has added greatly to the strength of the economy.

India has provided so little financial incentive to those who stayed. After attaining independence from Great Britain in 1947, the nation slipped into what might be described as patriarchal (and sometimes matriarchal) socialism, a benevolent but misbegotten attempt to provide an approximation of a welfare state under conditions that were virtually doomed to failure by the size of the population (creeping toward one billion) and pervasive poverty, complicated by the persistence of a caste system that hardly augured well for the implementation of liberal ideals. Punitive taxation of the rich and inefficient public ownership of key industries did nothing to alleviate the situation. Nor did the fact that partially autonomous regional governments, such as Marxist West Bengal, have often been at odds with the central regime in New Delhi.

Until the mid-1990s, Indian politics was dominated by the Congress Party—the party of Jawaharlal Nehru and Indira Gandhi—which, although controlled by upper-class Brahmins, had enjoyed the support of "backward caste" voters and untouchables grateful for the gift of independence. In the 1996 election, however, the support of the masses swung to various alternative groups and the Congress Party was swept from power. The minority coalition government that replaced it was too divided to take decisive action where the economy was concerned, though it made efforts to implement reforms broached by the previous administration in the 1980s and amplified in the early 1990s.

These reforms were an attempt to partially deregulate Indian securities markets and open them to foreign trade, integrating India into the global marketplace. To date, however, they have encountered only partial success, and, despite the country's considerable accomplishments in the Internet and software fields (Bangalore is the region's Silicon Valley), India still faces huge problems, not the least of which is its military standoff with Pakistan. As with China, however, nobody can afford to ignore the potential of the Indian market. Its dozen stock exchanges, of which the Mumbai (Bombay) bourse remains the most important, are sure to figure in any future global picture.

Other Asian exchanges are to be found in Dhaka, Bangladesh; Jakarta and Surabaya, Indonesia; Bangkok, Thailand; Kuala Lumpur, Malaysia; and Islamabad, Lahore, and Karachi, Pakistan. The development of some of these has been inhibited by attitudes that seem designed to discourage foreign investment. In other cases, ambitious plans have been scaled back because of the Asian slump of the late 1990s. Still, there is no lack of enthusiasm for speculative investment in this part of the world, where gambling is an obsession. On July 28, 2000, the Socialist Republic of Vietnam joined the stock market club when the Ho Chi Minh City Securities Trading Center opened for business. Two companies were listed—the Refrigeration Electrical Engineering Company and the Cables and Telecommunications Material Joint Stock Company—and $5,000 worth of stock was traded in the first two-hour session.

AUSTRALIA AND NEW ZEALAND

Well established and capable of considerable resilience are the stock markets of Australia and New Zealand. The present Australian Stock Exchange (ASX) was formed in 1987 by amalgamating smaller bourses located in Melbourne, Sydney, Hobart, Adelaide, and Perth—all

dating back to the nineteenth century—into a single entity, with the different cities linked by the Stock Exchange Automated Trading System (SEATS).

Language and shared cultural traditions have ensured that the Australian securities market retains strong ties with exchanges in England and the United States, but in recent years institutional investors Down Under have increasingly looked to maximizing the advantages of their position with respect to expanding Asian markets. Australia is blessed with a wealth of natural resources, making it a world leader in the export of agricultural products—especially wheat and wool—as well as fish and a variety of mineral ores, from gold and silver to iron and aluminum. All of these commodities are in great demand in Asia, which makes for a healthy Australian economy, reflected in a securities market that is active, diversified, and highly liquid.

Not surprisingly, the Australian Stock Exchange has proven attractive to foreign as well as domestic investors. Americans in particular feel at home dealing with a bourse whose listings include familiar names such as

(continued on page 276)

A busy day on the floor of the Sydney Stock Exchange. With strong links to Europe, America, and South East Asia, Australia has become an important player in world markets.

DERIVATIVES:
AGRICULTURAL COMMODITIES FUTURES

For casual observers of the market, perhaps its most confusing aspect is the world of derivatives—which is to say the trading in contracts such as futures and options, the value of which depends upon the performance of underlying entities such as commodities, securities, or currencies. In simple terms, a futures contract is a promise to buy or sell some entity for a pre-agreed price at some specified date in the future. An option contract gives the right to buy or sell some entity at a pre-agreed price at any time within a set period.

This may make it seem that derivatives trading is a sector of the market tailored to the needs of speculators. Certainly speculators are attracted to the world of derivatives, but that world in fact had its origins in the most conservative of all markets, the trading of agricultural goods. Farmers cannot predict from year to year what their harvest will be like—whether they will be blessed with ideal growing conditions or devastated by flood or drought. The quantity and quality of, say, wheat harvested would determine its price when it reached the grain elevator and the flour mill. To even out the impact of fat and lean years, farmers started to sell their crops for future delivery—in other words, before they were grown, and before the harvest could be accurately predicted—thus passing on some of the risk to the grain dealers with whom they dealt. For their part, the dealers would hedge their bets by placing offsetting high bids and low bids on the coming season's crops. Thus the prudent dealer's position in the market was

Agricultural products, such as the wheat and potatoes growing in these fields in the valley of the Snake River, Idaho, are among the most actively traded entities in world commodity markets.

balanced and, in theory at least, he could protect himself from disaster no matter what kind of harvest came about. Fundamentally, then, futures trading is about risk management, but at the same time it is almost irresistible to the speculator.

The concept of futures trading in agricultural goods reached its apogee in the great Chicago commodity exchanges—the Chicago Board of Trade (CBOT) and the Chicago Mercantile Exchange—which have their roots in the rural Midwest of the nineteenth century but remain strong presences today.

Although CBOT now trades in many kinds of commodities, agricultural and otherwise, it began in 1848 as a grain exchange and dealt exclusively in grain until 1966, at times handling as much as 90 percent of the world's cereal futures. On its main trading floor, the supercharged world of commodity futures comes vividly to life, the scene sometimes resembling a political convention in uproar, the similarity deriving in part from the fact that, like convention delegates, the men and women on the trading floor appear to be in

costume, bedecked with identity tags and favors. In fact, the brightly colored trading jackets they sport, retrofitted with the heraldry of their profession, announce company affiliations and personal specializations, providing them with instant recognizability in a kind of free-form theater that involves thousands of players in bursts of hyperkinetic activity.

Most of this activity centers on the "pits," modular structures, somewhat resembling staggered bleachers surrounding a cock-fighting pit. Each of these areas is devoted to a specific commodity and market-making traders occupy specific positions that indicate the date on which a given futures contract will come due. These traders execute orders brought in by clerk and runner from the hundreds of trading booths that edge the floor. Communication is by "open outcry"—a euphemism for loud and systematic haggling—and hand signals. Fingers held vertically indicate quantity. Extended horizontally, the same digits convey information about price. A deal is confirmed with a nod of the head, then recorded as a scribble on a trading card.

COMBINED HARVESTER NO 1053
PHOTO
BY W A RAYMOND MORO ORE

Opposite left and top: *The great American commodity markets, such as the Chicago Board of Trade and the Chicago Mercantile Exchange, evolved in response to the wealth of agricultural products, from beef to wheat, shipped from the nation's heartland.*

Above: *Although America has been blessed with vast tracts of fertile land, it is also prone to natural disasters of many kinds. One of the worst of the twentieth century was the drought that led to the Dust Bowl, which destroyed millions of arable acres in the 1930s. Such disasters have enormous repercussions in the commodity futures markets.*

Left: *A terrible drought in England in 1934, though less economically damaging than the Dust Bowl, led to this astonishing exercise in labor-intensive agriculture in which 100,000 cabbages were watered by hand.*

Opposite left: *During the New Deal era, WPA artists celebrated the contribution to economic recovery made by agricultural workers, as in this 1934 fresco painted by Maxine Albro for San Francisco's Coit Tower.*

Opposite far left: *Chickens and eggs have long been staples of the commodity futures markets, leading to the growth of such giant concerns as Arkansas-based Tyson Foods. Here, in 1946, John Tyson is seen unloading prime breeding stock chickens from a light airplane.*

Sad to say, the world of commodities trading is changing and the CBOT trading floor, with its gunslinger tradition of High Noon confrontation, may soon give way to the cold efficiency of the computer, which has taken over elsewhere. Already CBOT has had to relinquish its long-held position as the world's largest derivatives market, that honor now belonging to the German-based exchange Eurex, founded as recently as 1998.

Despite the rise of digital trading, the field of agricultural futures remains hectic and nervewracking, even for participants who employ every known form of risk management. The degree of risk varies from commodity to commodity. Egg production, for example, is considered to be a relatively stable field, because chickens can be raised under controlled conditions almost anywhere and thus the steady supply of eggs is not subject to fluctuations caused by variations in climate or localized natural disasters. Even so, there is always the danger of epidemic striking without warning in any agricultural area (one need think only of mad cow disease).

Many agricultural commodities remain subject to extreme market volatility because of their vulnerability to climatic and other natural conditions, a situation that is now complicated by factors such as genetically engineered seed—that can prevent crop failures but may yet cause other problems—and global warming, which is likely to have a huge impact on traditional agricultural patterns in the relatively near future.

Aficionados of the pits at CBOT all have stories of fellow traders whose fortunes were wiped out in a single day—and these were men and women who had spent their entire careers dealing in futures and calculating the risks involved. Of all forms of investment, trading in the derivatives of agricultural commodities is perhaps the most unpredictable. ∎

Top center: *Sheep and other forms of livestock are among the staples of the agricultural commodities market.*

Above: *Constant scientific research is carried out to improve the efficiency of agricultural techniques and hence help stabilize crop prices in the futures markets. Here an experiment to measure photosynthesis is set up in a citrus orchard.*

Near right: *A rancher examines his tangerine crop for freeze damage. Frost in the citrus belt will have repercussions in both commodity exchanges and supermarkets.*

Bottom right: *Wheat fields stretch to the horizon in Parana, Brazil. In a global market, the success or failure of a harvest here will impact markets everywhere.*

Top right: *At the Chicago Mercantile Exchange, two forms of futures trading, new and old. While one block of traders works sedately at computer workstations, another group (below) employs the more dynamic open outcry system associated with the traditional trading floor.*

Below left: *Soy beans constitute a classic commodity futures crop.*

Below: *Every growing season brings it share of catastrophes, such as floods, this one bringing misery to farmers in California's agriculture-rich Central Valley. Disasters such as this make the agricultural futures markets very volatile.*

Bottom: *A good harvest brings satisfaction to farmers, like this one in Paris, Kentucky— and to commodity dealers.*

Foster's Brewing Group (which owns or has interests in Asia, Europe, and North America as well as in Australia) and Rupert Murdoch's News Corporation (parent of the Fox entertainment companies, along with scores of other media and publishing concerns). A strategic alliance between ASX and the Nasdaq, struck in 1999, helped make international investors even more aware of the possibilities inherent in the Australian economy. American companies like Merrill Lynch, Salomon Smith Barney, Morgan Stanley, and Goldman Sachs have become major presences in Oz, and Ord Minnett, one of the most venerable Australian brokerage firms—founded in 1872—was taken over in 2000 by Chase Manhattan.

The Australian Stock Exchange is considerably smaller than the Tokyo Stock Exchange and marginally smaller than the Hong Kong exchange. Australia's natural resources, however, combined with a well-educated population that is small in proportion to the usable land area, make for benefits that neither Japan nor Hong Kong (nor even China) can offer. It is difficult to see how the Australian economy, already strong, can fail to become even more dynamic. The only thing inhibiting growth is that an already high standard of living encourages a healthily laid-back attitude that contrasts with the urgency verging on desperation that drives capitalism in some other Pacific Rim nations. Australians are tough competi-

tors, however, and are not likely to let their advantages slip away. All the signs point to a combination of steady growth and stability that would be hard to match.

The New Zealand Stock Exchange has much in common with its Australian cousin, though inevitably it is smaller and therefore less diversified. The possibility of a merger between the two exchanges must have crossed many minds, but New Zealanders are fiercely independent and slow to embrace change for its own sake. This reflects the fact that the economy of this spectacularly beautiful country is still heavily reliant upon the export of commodities such as meat, dairy products, wool, and timber, the kinds of goods familiar to the merchants of the Middle Ages or the ancient world. Even the industries New Zealand is best known for—food processing and the manufacture of cloth, clothing, and footwear—have a distinctly traditional feel to them.

It was a classic commodity, gold, that provided stock trading in New Zealand with its original impetus back in the 1870s, when significant strikes were made in several locations. In 1872 a dozen brokers formed the Auckland Sharebrokers' Association, which in 1892 evolved into the Auckland Stock Exchange. In 1915 this became the linchpin of the Stock Exchange Association of New Zealand, an organization designed to coordinate the activities of the autonomous regional exchanges. Located

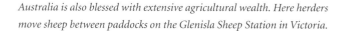

Australia is rich in mineral resources. These stockpiles of iron ore are in Port Hedland, Western Australia.

Australia is also blessed with extensive agricultural wealth. Here herders move sheep between paddocks on the Glenisla Sheep Station in Victoria.

The Prophet Muhammad was himself a merchant, and the merchant tradition is strong throughout the Islamic world where crowded souqs and bazaars—such as this example in Iran—are an integral part of the urban fabric.

in Wellington, Christchurch, Thames, and Dunedin, as well as Auckland, each had its own trading floor, where the "open outcry" style of trading survived until 1991. The five exchanges were officially merged in 1989, but it took another two years before the regional trading floors were closed down as a prelude to the introduction of a nationwide, fully automated electronic platform.

Geographically, New Zealand is probably the most isolated developed country in the world. In the electronic era, however, a sheep farmer in the foothills above the Canterbury Plain can watch his beloved All Blacks rugby team as they scrummage in London or Cape Town. Meanwhile, his broker sits in front of a keyboard and monitor that places him in instant contact with markets in Sydney, Hong Kong, Tokyo, and New York. It's a sure bet that New Zealanders will hang on to their independent spirit, but it's just as certain that today's technology is drawing them into an interactive global economy that has already shrunk the distances that once separated national and regional marketplaces.

OIL STATES AND OTHERS

The Middle East is a region subject to an extreme volatility that threatens the well-being of any possible global marketplace. Much of it is heir to Islamic tradition, in which the market, or souk (*souq* in Arabic), is central to cultural life and merchants have for centuries been treated with respect, partly in recognition of the fact that the prophet Muhammad himself—alone among the founders of major religions—began life as a merchant.

The economic heavyweight of the region is Saudi Arabia. It differs from comparably large markets elsewhere, however, in that it lacks an independent stock exchange; investment there is channeled through the Saudi Arabian Monetary Agency, which also functions as the nation's central bank. This is because Saudi Arabia is an absolute monarchy, its legislature a "consultation council" appointed by the king. Free enterprise and foreign investment receive nominal encouragement, but only within strict parameters established by this council. An overseas institution may invest in a Saudi enterprise, for example, but only on condition that it has a Saudi partner or agent. In reality, Saudi businesses do not need capital from overseas because so much is available locally. Some individual companies actually prohibit foreign investment even to the extent that it is permitted by law. Because of these restrictions on foreign trade, Saudi Arabia has never sought membership in the World Trade Organization, as is also the case with Kuwait and several other Arab countries.

Saudi Arabia's economy is dependent on its enormous reserves of petroleum, which belong to the state in the person of the monarch. Under the guidance of successive rulers, the king's council has attempted to use the revenues derived from this mineral wealth to improve the lot of Saudis as a whole, building highways, investing in education and medical services, and so on. The sons of former desert sheikhs, with close ties to the royal family, have become wealthy as a simple right of heritage. Other Saudis have benefited from the oil boom by making fortunes in businesses ranging from construction to merchant banking to the import of luxury goods. Till now the great majority of these businesses, some of which employ tens of thousands of workers, have been family owned, much as was the case with the Islamic merchant enterprises of the Middle Ages. Many have been dominated by a single patriarchal figure; now, however, a number of such businesses are facing the inevitable transition to leadership by a new generation. Whether sons brought up in pampered luxury will have the same ability to command respect as did their fathers, who scratched for a living on the streets of Riyadh or who arrived from Oman as houseboys, is becoming a matter of some concern to Saudi chambers of commerce. It is commonly thought that it would be healthy for many of these family businesses to go public. This would mean a leap in the number of joint-stock companies that would be very attractive to both the oil sheikhs and foreign investors. Whether or not this would lead to a marketplace less subject to patriarchal control is a matter for speculation.

The wealth of modern Saudi Arabia is built upon the nation's enormous reserves of petroleum and natural gas which have made it the economic powerhouse of the Middle East. By the late 1940s, when these photos were made, Arab technicians began to replace Western workers, as the Saudi government took control of the vast wealth beneath the sand.

At the Kuwait Stock Exchange, dealers in traditional costume relax between sessions.

During the Persian Gulf War, Iraqui demolition teams rigged Kuwait's oil wells for destruction in the event of a forced retreat. By the time the war was over, hundreds of wells blazed furiously, casting a pall that significantly lowered temperatures over parts of Asia.

The relationship between oil and family businesses obtains throughout the Persian Gulf States. This is certainly the case with Kuwait, which was the scene of a major stock market crash in 1982, when tough new trading regulations at the official, government-controlled bourse caused speculators to transfer funds into the Souq al-Manakh, an illegal and unregulated over-the-counter market. The use of postdated checks as a form of credit buying was commonplace in the Souq al-Manakh. One large bounced check prompted a government investigation, which revealed that the Souq was propped up by $94 *billion* in outstand-

ing checks written by a mere six thousand or so investors!

The consequences of this crash were felt throughout Kuwait, with families ruined and all but one bank in the country rendered technically insolvent. The crisis had subsided only slightly by the time of the Persian Gulf war (1991), after which the government stepped in with a plan to buy up the banks' domestic loans in their entirety, removing debt pressure from many of Kuwait's leading families. Since that time, the official Kuwait Stock Exchange has performed reasonably well within the limits set by the fact that it is, in effect, an arm of a highly centralized government.

Investors from other Gulf States lost money in the Souq al-Manakh crash; this encouraged some small neighboring countries to institute official exchanges of their own to provide safer securities markets. The Bahrain Stock Exchange, for example, commenced business in 1989 and, in the following decade, signed a cross-trading agreement with the Kuwait bourse and cross-listing agreements with Oman's Muscat Securities Market and Jordan's Amman Financial Market. Another small securities exchange operates in Oman.

In business since 1978, the Amman Financial Market is a public institution charged with encouraging domestic economic development and helping bring Jordan into the modern world. Until the 1970s, many of the nation's citizens still relied on barter rather than money in their everyday dealings. To remedy this, King Hussein's government embarked on a policy of developing banking services. This was so successful—attracting both domes-

At the Bahrain Stock Exchange, an exchange employee enters figures on a large options board.

At the Baghdad exchange, an employee counts piles of Iraqi dinars. The enlarged $100 bill behind him, with Ben Franklin's face crossed out, is a warning that, because of post–Gulf War restrictions, American currency is no longer legal tender.

This night time view of Tel Aviv epitomizes the vitality of modern Israel. For a variety of reasons, however—most notably political unrest—the Tel Aviv bourse has not yet lived up to its full potential.

tic savings and large deposits from other Arab states— that it tended to divert capital from investment in securities. Tightened banking regulations, instituted in 1984, corrected this situation somewhat, permitting the AFM to function more effectively.

The 1991 Persian Gulf war created serious economic problems for Jordan. Many Jordanians lived and worked in the Gulf States, sending money home to their families. For a while, that cash flow was reduced to a trickle. International sanctions against Saddam Hussein's administration in Baghdad hurt even more, since Iraq had been Jordan's primary trading partner. Wary of excessive dependence upon a few neighbors, the government of King Abdullah, Hussein's successor, took action in the late 1990s to open up Jordan's markets to the world, even though this presented a danger of unprotected competition to its own fledgling companies. Despite many obstacles, this policy seems to be working, and in April 2000 Jordan was accepted into full membership in the World Trade Organization.

As noted earlier, Egypt is served by two of the oldest bourses in the region. In the period following World War II, when King Farouk occupied the throne, the capitalization of the Cairo and Alexandria markets gave them a

combined value that placed them at an astonishing fifth in world rankings. Starting in the mid-1950s, however, the socialist policies of Gamal Abdel Nasser made the exchanges redundant. While still nominally socialist, the regime of his successor, Anwar el-Sadat, was far more sympathetic to capitalist enterprises, but it was not until 1991, a decade after Sadat was assassinated, that the two Egyptian exchanges returned to life.

The reborn exchanges have had to face doubts caused by continued political unrest in the region, the rise of Islamic fundamentalism, and the precarious state of the nation's economy, which has struggled to keep pace with an enormous population explosion, and which has relied heavily on support from wealthier Arab states such as Saudi Arabia. Given these circumstances, the Egyptian bourses have fared well, their market capitalization having risen from 8.8 billion Egyptian pounds in 1991 to 71.3 billion by the end of 1999.

There are three significant non-Arab exchanges in the Middle East still to be considered, located in Iran, Israel, and Turkey. The Tehran Stock Exchange began life under Shah Mohammad Reza Pahlavi in 1968, at first dealing principally in government securities and then, in the 1970s, expanding into the private sector. The Iranian Islamic revolution of 1979 brought a temporary halt to stock market activity as control of the economy came under the direct supervision of the Ayatollah Khomeini's fundamentalist regime. Ten years later the implementation of a five-year plan called for the revival of private-sector investment, which was further encouraged by the privatization of some nationalized businesses. Since then, the Tehran Stock Exchange has shown steady growth and now lists more than three hundred companies.

The Israeli stock market has its roots in British-occupied Palestine, where, in 1935, a consortium of banks and brokerage houses organized an informal but active market known as the Exchange Bureau for Securities. After the founding of Israel in 1948, the government moved to institute an official bourse, resulting in the incorporation of the Tel Aviv Stock Exchange. In 1968 the Knesset introduced securities legislation that established

The Tel Aviv Stock Exchange after a sudden downturn in the market in 1983.

new operating standards for the TASE, aimed at putting it in line with major exchanges in Europe and America by providing investors with a high degree of security. A derivatives market was inaugurated in 1993, and since 1999 all securities and derivatives are traded on a fully automated and integrated trading platform.

Many things make the Tel Aviv market attractive to foreign investors. Israeli business is especially strong, for example, in the kinds of high-tech areas that have been so hot in recent years. Against this must be weighed Israel's position at the unstable center of an unstable region.

In addition, overseas investors with moderately long memories recall past problems in the Israeli private sector, such as the bank scandal of the 1980s. This came about because Israel's four premier private banks, Bank Hapoalim, Bank Leumi, Israel Discount, and United Mizrachi, had been lending their customers money to buy bank shares—those same shares being used as security for the loans! The banks also used their considerable influence within the stock exchange to boost the value of their stock, with the result that over a period of several years it appreciated greatly in market worth. All went well with this chancy scheme until October 1983, when it appeared that the Israeli government was about to devalue the shekel. Investors rushed to divest themselves of their bank shares so they could purchase dollars as a shelter against the expected devaluation. Faced with disaster, the banks began to buy back shares in huge quantities. They succeeded in holding the line so far as

Turkey—the land where coinage was invented—is today home to the very modern Istanbul Stock Exchange, photographed here on February 22, 2001, when a government decision to let the lira float sent stocks surging upwards.

The Istanbul waterfront remains as active today as it was a thousand years ago when the city, then called Constantinople, was among the world's most powerful commercial centers.

share values were concerned, but most of their capital reserves were wiped out in the process. The Israeli banking system found itself on the verge of collapse, and the government was forced to step in to bail out the industry to the tune of almost $7 billion. A Commission of Inquiry found that the banks had put the entire economy at risk by behaving in a way that "came close to fraud."

In recent years, however, Israel has been free of financial scandals on this scale. Should peace come to the Middle East, the Tel Aviv Stock Exchange is likely to become a major player on the international stage.

It was Anatolia, now part of modern Turkey, that gave birth to the first market-driven economy (see chapter 1). Later, as the center of the Byzantine Empire, Constantinople was for a thousand years the financial hub of one of the world's great powers. Turkey, then, has plenty of economic tradition, and in the waning days of the Ottoman Empire—in the period following the Crimean War (1853–56)—the Dersaadet Securities Exchange was established in Istanbul as an entity intended to attract investments from Western Europe. In 1929, following the establishment of the Turkish Republic, the Dersaadet exchange was replaced by the Istanbul Securities and Foreign Exchange Bourse, but the Great Depression and World War II slowed its devel-

opment. After the war, the Turkish marketplace saw steady growth as more and more privately owned firms, often former family concerns, evolved into joint-stock companies. A burst of investment activity in the 1980s led to the setting up of the regulatory Capital Markets Board, based in Ankara, and the inauguration, in 1985, of the new Istanbul Stock Exchange. In 1995 the bourse moved into an architecturally spectacular new complex in the suburb of Istinye.

Geographically, Turkey occupies a pivotal position between Europe and Asia, between West and East. It has been the ambition of recent Turkish governments to exploit this to the fullest, seeking membership in the European Economic Community while retaining traditional ties to the Middle East and beyond. What makes this difficult to achieve is that when outsiders take note of such ongoing issues as suppression of the Kurdish peoples and belligerence toward Greece, they tend to perceive Turkey as belonging to the troubled Middle East rather than to the stable West.

As is the case in other parts of the world, the future probably lies with merger and regional consolidation and in forming partnerships with outside entities. One such entity is the Nasdaq, which has already announced a strong interest in the long-term possibilities of participating in a Middle Eastern stock market, perhaps anchored by Egypt, Israel, and Turkey.

LATIN AMERICA

Mexico is a nation with an economy characterized equally by promise and frustration. Today's Bolsa Mexicana de Valores features a state-of-the-art electronic trading platform and the exchange is among the busiest in Latin America. Past volatility, however, plus political scandals and social unrest, especially the Chiapas revolt, have made some overseas investors cautious about participating in the Mexican arena. Government-sponsored reforms in the 1980s (following a 1982 default on foreign debt) succeeded in bringing down inflation and appeared to be stabilizing the economy, but this did little to ease

Petroleum is one of the strengths of the Mexican economy. Pictured here is a refinery operated by Pemex, one of the nation's leading oil producers.

the plight of the millions living in poverty, and a variety of problems began to surface that led, in 1994, to the devaluation of the peso. Till then, its worth had been pegged for some years to that of the dollar. When the government of Ernesto Zedillo severed this connection, American and other foreign investors in the Mexican market lost their shirts.

The Mexican market operates in the context of a

The old trading floor of the Bolsa Mexicana de Valores was topped with a handsome glass dome. This photograph was taken in 1995, not long before the trading floor was replaced by an all-automatic computerized system.

Despite persistent problems with inflation and poverty, the Brazilian economy has many potential strengths, notably extensive mineral and agricultural resources. Here workers from the Carajas Grande mine load iron ore into freight cars (left), and wranglers herd cattle near Pantanal.

Catch-22 environment in which the financial strictures essential to stabilizing the economy tend to inflict the most pain on the poor, who make up approximately half of the electorate. It's a politician's nightmare, and repercussions on the stock market are inevitable. At the same time, Mexico is a partially industrialized nation with many established companies. Any upturn in the economy would permit some, at least, of the poor to move toward middle-class consumerism, thus creating a huge new market for many kinds of products and bringing special benefits to sectors such as telecommunications. In addition, the Mexican economy's integration with the U.S. economy, by way of the North American Free Trade Agreement, has helped to restore confidence in the Mexican market, as was made apparent by the success of a large government bond offering in January 2000 that was subscribed to by many foreign investors, including normally prudent institutional buyers. The election of Vicente Fox as president later that same year ushered in a new political era that was greeted with initial enthusiasm in international financial circles.

Among South American markets, Brazil is the giant, with vast natural resources, enormous reserves of manpower, and pockets of viable industrialization. Like

Mexico, however, it has formidable internal problems rooted in the gaping chasm between rich and poor, penthouse and shantytown. It has suffered more than its fair share of government corruption, and in the recent past has endured runaway inflation at a level rivaling that found in Germany in the wake of World War I. (So bad was Brazil's inflation that four new currencies were introduced between 1985 and 1994.)

Still, the Brazilian stock exchanges have continued to function with surprising resilience, riding a securities

In 1999, traders at the Sao Paulo exchange make frantic calls in the wake of a government announcement regarding currency policy.

In recent years, one of the most successful exchanges in Latin America has been the handsome Bolsa de Comercio de Santiago, in Chile.

roller coaster that has provided soaring elation at one moment, stomach-churning terror the next. Until recently there were nine of these exchanges, each serving a different region, with the bolsas of Rio de Janeiro (founded in 1845) and São Paulo (founded in 1890) being the most important. The São Paulo exchange was both the volume leader and the chief innovator, introducing automated trading in the early 1970s and an options market later in the decade. As the century ended, it was decided that the nine exchanges should join forces, and in 2000, agreements were signed to set this integration in motion; the Bolsa de Valores de São Paulo was placed in charge of the integration of the domestic commercial securities market, and the Rio exchange was charged with setting up an electronic marketplace for the trading

of government paper. It is hoped that this integration of the exchanges will encourage regional investment and help set the economy on a course that will permit full value to be gained from the country's impressive natural resources. On top of this, collaboration within the continent has been stimulated by agreements with the Santiago and Buenos Aires exchanges that permit trading in one another's blue chips. Additionally, as of March 31, 2000, the Comisión Nacional de Valores—Brazil's securities and exchange commission—removed virtually all restrictions on foreign investment.

Given its resources, it is not surprising that Brazil has long been home to important commodities exchanges. Founded in 1917, the São Paulo Commodities Exchange established itself as a major marketplace for coffee,

(continued on page 292)

UNCOMMON CURRENCIES:
FINANCIAL DERIVATIVES

Although future delivery contracts and the like have been fairly commonplace since the nineteenth century (and probably existed much earlier) the term "derivatives," now used to describe futures and options, did not come into common use until the 1970s. Its introduction corresponded to an enormous expansion of the field that came about because of the de facto devaluation of the dollar in 1971, a misbegotten attempt by the Nixon regime to battle inflation. For a quarter of a century, most of the world's currencies had been pegged to the dollar, which itself was understood to be convertible into gold (though this was rarely put to the test). No longer backed by gold, the dollar remained the benchmark of world currencies but those currencies were now free to float up and down against the dollar and against one another. Since international trade depends upon currency convertibility, this meant, for example, that the price for imported goods in any given domestic market would depend upon the shifting relationship between the currency of that market and the currency of the exporting country.

Suddenly, currency exchange had become as volatile as commodities trading. Not surprisingly, then, it was in Chicago—then in its heyday as the commodities capital of the world—that traders quickly realized that there was a place for a market in currency futures since, in a sense, currencies had become mere commodities. Trading in currency derivatives began under the auspices of the International Money Market (IMM) in 1971. This was soon followed

The trading floor of the London International Financial Futures Exchange (LIFFE) as it appeared in the 1990s when life in the pits was not for the weak of will or the feeble of constitution.

by derivatives trading rooted in various forms of financial instruments such as mortgages, Treasury bills, and bonds.

Most shockingly, for the financial establishment, the Chicago Board of Trade (CBOT) in 1973 spun off a new exchange called the Chicago Board Options Exchange (CBOE), which had the temerity to offer trading in options on stock prices. Stock options (contracts to buy or sell stocks at a given price with a certain time limit) had been traded informally on Wall Street—there were even some small firms that specialized in this kind of activity—but never within the context of an organized exchange. When CBOE came into existence, investors—both institutional and private—who had never considered the advantages of stock options before rushed to participate. As with any kind of derivatives trading, the purpose of most players was risk management through hedging. And, as with any kind of derivatives trading, the new market attracted more than its fair share of speculators, some of whom made fortunes and some of whom lost their shirts.

This was just the beginning. Soon there were futures contracts on interest rates, options contracts on futures, and an ever more complex array of hybrids, some so complex even professionals found them difficult to understand. Wall Street began to get into the act with the American Stock Exchange establishing a thriving market in financial derivatives, as did the New York Futures

Above: *First issued in 1878, silver certificates were the primary currency of the United States for many years. Issued in denominations ranging from $1 to $1,000, they could be redeemed for silver on demand at the U.S. Treasury. The last certificates were issued in 1957.*

Above right: *Like silver, gold has long held a special value as a precious metal, and it still remains an object of speculation on the derivatives markets. Here molten gold cascades towards a crucible at the Lebanon Gold Mine near Johannesburg, South Africa.*

Right center: *The markets in currency derivatives are rooted in the shifting relationships between the currencies of different nations, which become especially volatile in times of inflation or devaluation. Mega-inflation in post–World War I Germany led to a thriving black market in dollars. In this 1922 photograph, two men strike a furtive deal behind the sheltering bulk of an accomplice reading a newspaper.*

Below left and right: *Frantic derivatives trading in London.*

Above left: *On January 24, 1986, Sharon Hayward made a little piece of history as she became the first woman to trade on the floor of the Financial Futures Market at the Royal Exchange in London.*

Top right: *In September 2000, in front of the DAX Index board on the floor of the Frankfurt Exchange, a trader juggles two telephones as the market responds to news that the world's largest central banks were intervening in the currency markets.*

Above: *In January 1981, forecasts that American hostages were to be released by the Iranian government in Tehran led to a busy session at the Frankfurt Currency Exchange.*

Left: *Wearing multi-striped jackets to indicate their company affiliations, traders at the London International Financial Futures Exchange (LIFFE) respond to a run on sterling.*

Left: *A Mexican currency exchange worker adjusts a display showing the rate of the peso against the U.S. dollar.*

Right: *In 1998 money dealers trade under an electronic board quoting the Japanese yen rate against the U.S. dollar.*

Below: *A man counts U.S. dollars he has just bought in Moscow, December 2000.*

Bottom left: *A blackboard in Biskkek, Kyrghizstan—formerly a province of the Soviet Union—displays international currency exchange rates.*

Bottom right: *In a bureau de change booth on a Hong Kong street, money changers count currency.*

Exchange, though both trailed far behind Chicago.

As might be expected, the rest of the world did not ignore all this activity. London became a hub of international derivatives activity, soon followed by Frankfurt and other European centers. Important derivatives markets also sprang up in Singapore, Hong Kong, and Tokyo.

Conservative elements in the financial community were wary of all this mushrooming activity, seeing it as potentially destabilizing on a geo-economic scale. In retrospect, however, it can be seen that trading in derivatives was a response to a situation that had already been destabilized when the Nixon administration abandoned the convertibility of dollars to gold and opened a Pandora's box of currency fluctuation. Certainly the derivatives exchanges became a playground for big time speculators, but they also provided a means for fiscally responsible institutions to protect their investors from the kind of volatility that was an inherent aspect of the financial world from the 1970s onwards.

The ability of the trade in financial instruments to perform corrections within the geo-economy has itself been dependent upon the rapid evolution of information technology. Whereas in the past, traders sometimes took advantage of slow communications to exploit investors in distant markets, today everyone must rely upon the instantaneous transmission of data to make their decisions, and nowhere is this more the case than in the derivatives markets, which become more complex by the day as arcane new forms of contracts are introduced. ■

Left: *On New Year's Day, 1999, a new world currency—the Euro—was launched with all the fanfare and ballyhoo that might ordinarily be called upon to welcome the Miss World Pageant, or the Eurovision Song Contest. During the course of an ice show at the Grand Palais in Brussels, skaters held aloft hoops, one crowned with a war bonnet of fireworks, another framing a shiny Euro symbol, and a third indicating the opening exchange rate of the Belgian franc against the Euro.*

Below: *In late 2000 the Tokyo Stock Exchange and the Chicago Mercantile Exchange, seen here, announced an alliance to develop a globally-linked electronic trading system, knitting together still further international trading in financial and equity futures.*

Coffee remains a crucial crop to the economies of several Latin American countries. Here beans are dried in the sun on the roof a plantation building in Bolombolo, Colombia.

cattle, and cotton, and was the first in Brazil to offer forward transactions. In 1985 it was joined by the Mercantile and Futures Exchange, also located in São Paulo. These markets merged in 1991 and soon absorbed the Brazilian Futures Exchange, which had been operating in Rio since 1983.

A recent South American success story has been the Santiago Stock Exchange. The Bolsa de Comercio de Santiago was founded in 1899 but was not much of a player on the world stage until the 1970s, when the military regime of General Augusto Pinochet Ugarte came to power in Chile. Pinochet's ruthless methods have made his name infamous. Unlike many dictators, however, he did not allow the economy of his country to stagnate and did much to encourage the development of a market-driven commercial environment. With input from American-trained economists, this seemed to work for a while and began to attract foreign investment. The Chilean peso was too weak to keep pace with the dollar, however, and devaluation of the currency in the early 1980s brought on a savage recession.

This proved to be relatively short-lived. In the mid-1980s a new minister of economics, Hernan Buchi, took strong measures to bring the nation's budget under control and permitted the peso to drift downward against the dollar, to the point where it made Chilean exports very attractive in markets such as Western Europe, Japan, and the United States. This triggered a revival of the economy as capital flowed into the bolsa and Chilean entrepreneurs began to reach out into other Latin American countries to extend their base of activities. Today the Chilean economy is among the strongest in South America, and Santiago even has its own version of the Nasdaq, the Bolsa Electrónica de Chile.

The Bolsa Comercio de Buenos Aires suffered serious losses as a consequence of the 1994 Mexican devaluation crisis. For many foreign investors, all of these markets had been tarred with the same brush, and, looking at

Argentina in particular, the currency did seem overvalued. As in Chile during Pinochet's dictatorship, the peso was pegged to the dollar, but there was an important difference. The Argentine currency was backed by substantial gold reserves. Combined with the implementation of some rather stringent penny-pinching on the part of the government, this helped the market revive in the late 1990s. The revival has not matched the Chilean renaissance, however, though privatization of a number of previously state-owned companies has provided foreign investors with opportunities to buy into choice sections of Argentina's economic infrastructure. Improving the Buenos Aires exchange's chances for a healthy future is a legislative climate that is favorable to foreign investors, who are treated, to all intents and purposes, no differently from their domestic counterparts.

Stock exchanges can be found in all the smaller South and Central American countries. It would be tempting to think that, in the near future, they might band together with the larger Latin American exchanges to form a confederation such as seems to be emerging in Europe. With the region's material and labor resources, this could evolve into a formidable economic entity. Before that can happen, however, each national economy has to settle at least some of its own problems, and that is likely to prove far from easy.

St. Paul's Cathedral continues to dominate the skyline of London's financial district. While forced to accommodate to the changes implicit in a global market place, the City of London remains a prime center for banking and financial services of all kinds.

A Frankfurt trader signals "We're number one" as the DAX index reached an all time high on January 3, 2000. DAX is the blue-chip index of the Deutsche Börse, comprising the thirty largest enterprises in Germany.

EUROPE

The latter half of the 1990s saw the forging of merger and trading agreements between various European exchanges, both major and minor. Most dramatically, in 1998 the London Stock Exchange and the Frankfurt Deutsche Börse announced a strategic alliance with the aim of developing a joint electronic trading platform for U.K. and German blue-chip securities. Two years later, this was solidified into a plan to merge the two exchanges, but eventually the deal fell through, demonstrating that international consolidation is not always straightforward.

By then, in 1998, the German and Swiss exchanges had launched Eurex, a joint futures market that extended its influence the following year by signing an agreement with the Chicago Board of Trade to establish a common electronic trading system. In 2000 Eurex overtook CBOT as the world's largest derivatives exchange. A 1999 development was an understanding that the stock exchanges located in London, Frankfurt, Paris, Amsterdam, Brussels, Milan, Zurich, and Madrid would collaborate to create a pan-European blue-chip platform. This was followed, soon after the turn of the millennium, by an announcement that the Paris, Amsterdam, and Brussels

bourses would be amalgamating.

The logical conclusion of all this would be a single European stock market that could hold its own on the world stage as the macroeconomic patterns of the twenty-first century take shape. Logic does not always win out, however, especially given the cultural and linguistic differences that exist within a continent where national traditions reach back a thousand years and more.

During the twentieth century some of those traditions were torn apart by the rise of Communism. Adopted by revolutionary fiat in Russia, Marxist principles were imposed upon most of Eastern Europe in the aftermath of World War II. The collapse of Communism more than four decades later meant that Eastern European nations were free to enter the market economy world. The extent to which they have succeeded in doing so has varied a great deal. So far as securities markets are concerned, those that have been most successful seem to be the ones that have become established in countries with an exploitable supply of natural resources, along with both a significant industrial base and a previous market tradition.

A good example of this is the Prague Stock Exchange. Although no industrial giant, the Czech Republic has reserves of coal and iron ore and is home to internationally viable companies producing a variety of goods, from beer to machine tools to airplanes. There is also a tradition of open-market activity there, dating back to the mid-nineteenth century, when Prague became an important regional center for commodities trading within the Austro-Hungarian Empire. For many years securities trading played a secondary role at the old Prague exchange, but that changed between World Wars I and II, during which period Prague hosted a healthy stock and bond market. This was effectively removed from the international stage when Hitler annexed Czechoslovakia in 1939, and did not return until April 6, 1993, when the first trading session commenced at the newly constituted exchange. Since then, the Prague Stock Exchange has enjoyed steady growth, with every effort having been made to bring its standards into line with those of major Western marketplaces.

The Budapest and Warsaw securities exchanges, too, have been as successful as one could reasonably hope. Like other Eastern European exchanges, the Budapest bourse is subject to downturns when there is unrest in Russia, but increasingly its commercial links are with the West, and this has helped perceptions of its future stability. Much the same can be said about the Warsaw exchange, where recent interest in the high-tech and Internet sectors have led to the proposal of creating a Polish equivalent of the Nasdaq.

Other former Communist countries, such as Bulgaria and Romania, have been less fortunate in their attempts to set up modern securities markets. Foreigners complain about everything from incompetent bookkeeping to outright larceny, and nowhere has the problem of entering the market-driven environment been more apparent than in the former Soviet Union.

The fall of the Iron Curtain has brought former Soviet bloc economies within the free market system. A few, like the Czech Republic, were ready to handle the radical changes involved. Others were not.

Romanians welcomed democracy. This crowd, waiting to vote, is seen through a hole in a flag resulting from the Communist party symbol having been removed. Unfortunately, the passage to capitalism would not prove easy for them.

Even before the Soviet era, the Russian experience of democracy was virtually zero. The revolution of 1917 overturned four centuries of imperial patriarchy and replaced it with a nominal collectivism that in reality was patriarchy in disguise. When the post-Communist era arrived, there was no precedent for free elections, or for the establishment of the infrastructure—legal and otherwise—that would allow the development of a market economy. A concept as basic as "property rights" was almost unknown. Add to this the fact that the Soviets had left industry and the economy as a whole in tatters, and the grimness of the situation begins to become apparent. It was further compounded by political instability and high inflation. In addition, many of the apparatchiks who helped destroy the economy managed to hold on to positions of responsibility, and along with all this came the rise of a new class of criminals willing to exploit whatever opportunities presented themselves.

Such were the conditions under which Russians attempted to enter the sophisticated world of contemporary securities trading. Not surprisingly, there was no overnight success story. Persistence, however—on the part of both domestic entrepreneurs and Westerners who refuse to ignore the vast potential of the nation's natural resources—has paid off, and the Moscow bourse, along with some

An example of northern neo-classicism, the stock exchange building in St. Petersburg, Russia.

smaller cousins, has struggled to gain a position of respectability. The future may lie with a confederation of the Russian stock and currency exchanges with those in former Soviet states such as Georgia, Ukraine, Crimea, Azerbaijan, Belarus, and Uzbekistan. The possibilities inherent in such an idea are currently under serious discussion.

MARKETPLACE EARTH

It is no coincidence that the concept of the market economy can be traced back to the Greek city-states of the first millennium B.C. Those states, and Athens in particular, are credited with the creation of democracy, and it can be argued that democracies and market economies have evolved hand in hand. It is difficult to imagine, in fact, that such economies could have arisen under other circumstances.

Every democracy has its own peculiarities and imperfections. Ancient Athens, the daddy of them all, was a democracy made up of slave owners. Britain, prior to the Second Reform Bill of 1867, was a democracy for property owners and the holders of long-term leases. ("You *rent* this place? Sorry, old chap, no vote for you.") The United States had its own history of slavery and, like most democracies in the developed world, withheld the vote from the female half of the adult population until modern times.

The cultural and social differences between apparently closely related democracies should never be underestimated. Britain and America enjoy a common language and many shared traditions, but the British parliamentary system differs significantly from the equally democratic American congressional system, meaning that similar political problems are routinely dealt with in dissimilar ways. Given the relationship between government and the marketplace, this can have an impact on the way business is done.

There are also considerable dissimilarities—some minor, some major—between the traditions of British democracy and those of other European nations, as has become abundantly clear during the relatively short history of the European Union. And there are even greater

Fireworks light up the Hong Kong skyline in celebration of the Lunar New Year. The former British colony continues to thrive as a financial center despite its changed status as a part of communist China.

disparities between the mechanics of both European and North American democracies and those to be found in Asia and Latin America. However, all these democratic entities sustain market economies to a greater or lesser extent, and these interact with one another reasonably well, though not entirely without tensions.

Disagreements frequently arise out of protectionist behavior on the part of individual governments and the special interests they may represent. For example, Japanese policies designed to safeguard key domestic industries from foreign competition have frequently been a target of complaints by Japan's trading partners. Although

such policies may have been justified when Japan was rebuilding its economy after World War II, it seems clear that today they run counter to the unfettered operation of a global market economy.

However committed to international trade, each country still has its own priorities, traditions, and limitations. India is the world's largest democracy and its high-tech sector rivals America's in the availability of first-class talent, but Indian society provides a very different environment for e-commerce and other aspects of the dot-com economy. Literacy must precede computer literacy, and the vast majority of India's one billion citizens are still in greater need of medical supplies, food, and untainted water than of access to the Internet.

The case of China is even more significant. Moving slowly away from the strictures of Maoism, the Chinese government has given plain indications of wanting to participate in the global marketplace. At the same time, the Chinese Communist Party has not been willing to give up its perceived mandate to supervise a planned economy.

The point of all this is that the idea of a global market economy cannot be looked at objectively without taking into consideration the political and cultural differences that define the national economies of the component nations. The market economy system works better than any other system that has been put into practice, but this does not mean it has been or will be accepted wholesale by all of the world's major powers. Nor does it mean that it can be applied like a poultice to the ailing economies of weaker emerging nations. The possibility of a true global market economy will increase to the extent that its participants demonstrate their willingness to respond to existing market conditions, and to help underdeveloped nations develop the legal, social, and political structures that will permit those nations to eventually participate more equally on the world stage.

Cultural differences aside, what makes this goal even more difficult to achieve is that the world's largest companies have access to intellectual, organizational, and financial resources that far exceed those of many market participants in smaller countries. The evolution of these mammoth commercial entities is due to the fact that market economies in the developed world have encouraged and thrived on fierce competition, meaning that many major corporations have been obliged to grow in order to succeed. And the big multinationals sometimes behave like the corporate equivalents of Sumo wrestlers, determined to triumph over their rivals through sheer size.

This gigantism has its frightening aspect. Bigger often means fewer choices. Even the smaller giants get squeezed out of business, or swallowed up, because they lack the buying and borrowing power of the larger organizations and thus are apt to be losers in a price war. In developed markets this leads to a reduction of choice and sometimes of competition. In emerging markets, it sometimes means that locally based competition has little or no chance, unless it can find a niche catering to domestic tastes beyond the understanding of the giants, or beneath their attention.

There were other giants back at the beginning of the twentieth century. In America the steel trust, the petroleum trust, the money trust, and other cartels were broken up as violators of the Sherman Antitrust Act (1890), and it's tempting to ask why—if it made for good economic policy then—today's giant corporations could not be forcibly dismantled through governmental intervention.

One answer is that today's giants come equipped with legions of lawyers whose job it is to make sure that sufficient competition survives to keep the enforcers of the Sherman Act at bay. In addition, these giants are truly multinational, so the question arises, Which government might have the power to dismantle them, or to prevent them from growing larger in the first instance? There are international agreements touching on antitrust measures, but enforcement has certainly become a great deal more complicated in the twenty-first century.

There is probably very little that can be done to curtail the reach of the multinationals, and it cannot be taken for granted that they will always behave entirely responsibly toward the people of the host countries where their factories, filling stations, and bottling plants are located. They exist primarily, after all, to make money for their investors, and when the scent of profit is in the air they are bound by nature to track the elusive prey to its lair and close in for the kill.

On the plus side, multinationals are becoming truly cosmopolitan in their makeup and more enlightened in the pursuit of their commercial aspirations. A corporation operating in fifty countries will have employees from a hundred. Most, it's true, are likely to have been hired in the more humble capacities, but cultural and linguistic considerations mean that people native to each market must be introduced into the executive chain. To suggest that a manager hired to oversee a Volkswagen spare-parts distribution service in Chad has a good chance of becoming head honcho of the entire Beetle empire would be naïve, but multinationals have proven to be fertile breeding grounds for men of character. At the age of twenty-two, Mexico's president Vicente Fox was a Coca-Cola route manager. Less than ten years later he had become the youngest-ever president of Coke's Mexican operations; from there he went on to lead Mexico, doing so by overturning a party that had been in power for three-quarters of century. What if Fox had aspired to continue his rise through the ranks at Coke? Would he have run into a nationalistic version of the glass ceiling? Or could he have fought his way to the CEO's office at 1 Coca-Cola Plaza in peachy downtown Atlanta? Although such a scenario remains unusual today, it has surely passed the impossibility stage.

In the post–World War II era there was much fear in countries like France and Italy that American business would come to completely dominate the Western European economic arena. Certainly American corporations took root there, but the postwar recovery saw European companies asserting themselves very effectively in America, and eventually a kind of dynamic balance of power came to prevail. The more recent economic relationship between America and Japan has produced similar results, with Japanese bankers a force on Wall Street and American brokers active in Tokyo.

Anticapitalists tend to focus on the American ownership of businesses in other parts of the world, but it is not beside the point that millions of Americans are now working for foreign companies. U.S. influence, while still powerful, is significantly less ubiquitous than it once was, while the fear of homogeneity bred by that influence has also triggered a rebirth of cultural reassertion, as a result of which each nation's unique ethnicity and outlook is celebrated once more. As companies become more internationalized—as opposed to merely international—they will likely become increasingly responsive to the mores of host countries. (After all, McDonald's has always served wine in its French outlets.)

The problem that will not go away quickly, however, is

In this classic example of old meets new, a camel is used to transport solar power panels that will be used to produce electricity for computers in the North African desert.

poverty. Historically, the very rich have turned to charity once they have made their pile. This is all well and good, but if the global marketplace is to grow and thrive, the world's business leaders will have to find ways of utilizing an increasing fraction of their companies' assets to collaborate with like-minded governments and independent agencies to raise and broaden the level of opportunity and wealth creation in the battle against poverty.

Will shareholders tolerate such an idea? Surely, as long as the goal is defined as the long-term development of significant markets for the sale of the corporation's goods and services, and if meaningful profits are still possible, there is no reason to suppose that the great majority of investors would find this untenable.

Thus—recalling Henry Ford's insight that his employees were his customers—there is no question that the elimination or reduction of poverty will actually benefit the development of the global marketplace. If poverty and opportunity are not addressed, on the other hand, this inattention is likely to provide a breeding ground for the very forces that will work to undermine market economies and bring them tumbling down. It would be a tragic irony if the economic system born of democracy should prove, in the end, to be unresponsive to the needs of so many and thus be the cause of democracy's destruction.

Notes

1. William Wordsworth, *The Prelude, or, the Growth of a Poet's Mind: An Autobiographical Poem* (London: Edward Moxon, 1850), vii, 659–87.

2. This occurred more or less contemporaneously with the introduction, by the Lydians, of coinage in the Western world.

3. The history of usury during the Middle Ages is shot through with contradictions. The threat of punishment was very real, but many bankers seem to have been able to circumvent the church's strictures by performing favors for the Vatican, or else by purchasing indulgences. Certainly the levying of interest was so commonplace in the thirteenth century that many cities had laws governing maximum rates. In Genoa and Milan, for example, these stood at 15 percent per annum. In cities with weaker economies the rates were far higher. In London, the top permissible rate was 43⅓ percent.

4. Although its laws against usury were even stricter than those in place in Europe, Islam had developed a sophisticated market economy during the Middle Ages. The prophet Muhammad had begun his life as a merchant, so it is hardly surprising that merchant culture was encouraged among the faithful, and it seems likely that Crusaders and other Westerners visiting the Middle East adopted some of the commercial customs of the Islamic world.

5. The mottling of these so-called Rembrandt tulips was actually caused by a kind of virus. Examples dating back to the sixteenth century can be seen at the bulb museum (Hortus Bulborum) in Limmen, Holland.

6. John Stow, *The Survey of London*, Everyman's Library (1956), p.173.

7. Interestingly, the London business community, fired by the libertarian rhetoric of John Wilkes, seems to have been sympathetic to the colonial cause until war actually broke out, interfering with commerce.

Fossil fuels remain crucial to the world economy. Here coal is piled up for transportation in Provodeniya, Siberia.

8. A similar but more extensive system was used in France during the Napoleonic period, bringing news of victories and defeats (as well as winning lottery numbers) to the French provinces.

9. Among other achievements, Belmont introduced thoroughbred racing to the United States; the Belmont Stakes—the last of the three summer classics—is named for him.

10. George G. Foster, *New York by Gaslight, and Other Urban Sketches* (Berkeley, Calif.: University of California Press, 1990), pp. 220–24.

11. Allan Nevins and Milton Halsey Thomas, eds., *The Diary of George Templeton Strong, 1835–1875*, vol. 4 (New York: Macmillan, 1952), pp. 493–94.

12. The Chinese had developed paper money independently during the T'ang dynasty (A.D. 618–907). Its use was commonplace under the Mongol emperors (1260–1368), but it was withdrawn from circulation by the end of the fourteenth century.

13. To a large degree it is the world created by these city merchants—very distinct from the rural environment inhabited by farmers, peasants, and samurai—that one finds portrayed in the ukiyo-e woodblock prints that eventually found their way to the West, influencing artists like Whistler, Toulouse-Lautrec, and van Gogh.

14. In the negative sense, a trust can be defined as a cartel of companies whose stock is controlled by a small number of common trustees who are thus in a position to influence prices and discourage competition.

15. Robert Sobel, *Panic on Wall Street: A Classic History of America's Financial Disasters, with a New Exploration of the Crash of 1987* (New York: E. P. Dutton, 1988), pp. 355–56.

16. Although the term bourgeois-bohemian is enjoying a vogue today, it is not entirely new, having first been used by the artist, novelist, and critic Percy Wyndham Lewis in about 1930.

17. Sobel, *Panic on Wall Street*, pp. 454–57.

18. Steven Lubar, *Infoculture: The Smithsonian Book of Information Age Inventions* (Boston: Houghton Mifflin, 1993), p. 300.

19. Quoted by Chip Bayers, "The Bot.Com Future," *Wired* 8 (March 2000): 216.

20. The Tokyo Stock Exchange itself cannot be considered protectionist. Foreign brokerage houses have been admitted to membership since 1986.

As the global economy adjusts to a new millennium, the search for new sources of power has become crucial. This plant in Paracicaba, Brazil, produces gasohol from sugarcane to use as an alternative to gasoline.

100 SHARES

NUMBER

F 281784

THE PENNSYLVANIA

INCORPORATED UNDER THE LAWS OF THE C

This Certifies that Marion C. Holle

entitled to ~~ONE H~~

Capital Stock of The Pennsylvania R

Attorney on the books of the said C

Witness the Seal of the Company and

[signature] SECRETARY

REGISTERED IN NEW YORK

IRVING TRUST COMPANY.

REGISTRAR

ASSISTANT SECRETARY

COUNTERSIGNED

TRANSFER AGENT.

THIS CERTIFICATE MAY BE PRESENTED FOR TRANSFER IN PHILADELPHIA, NEW YORK, BOSTON, CHICAGO, LONDON.

SHARES

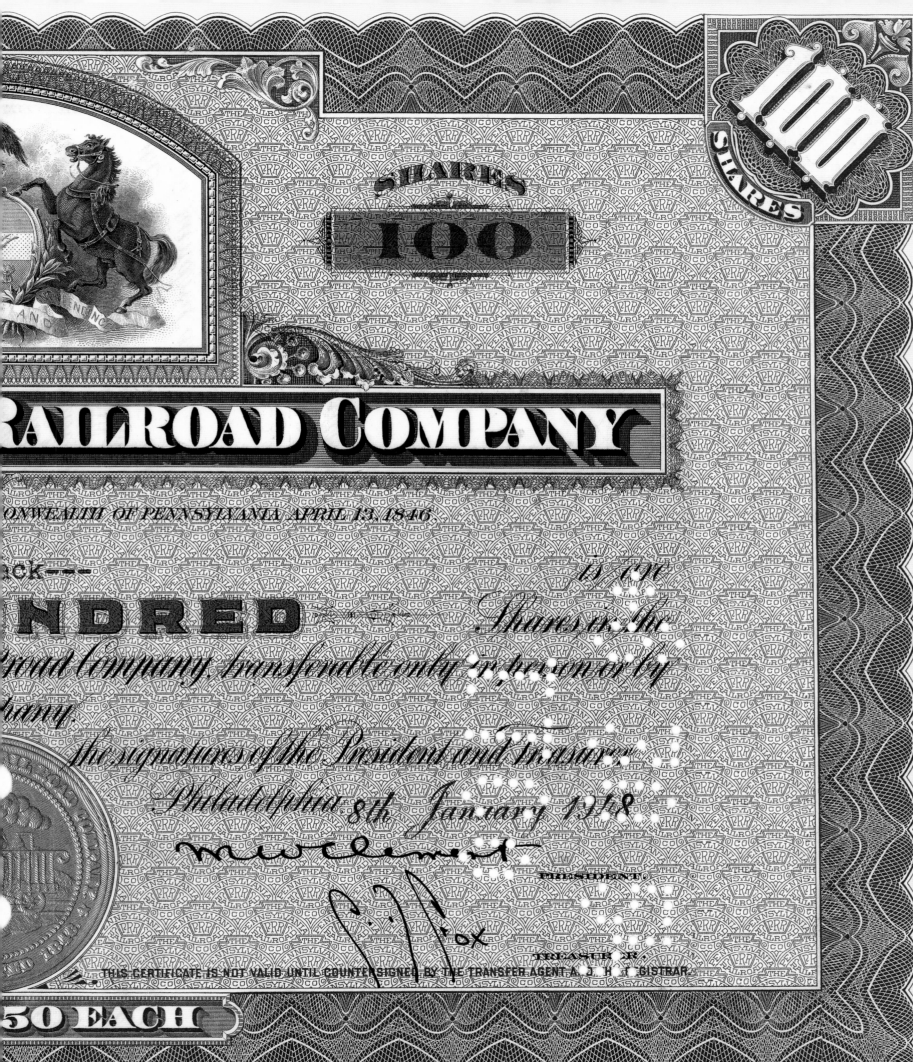

RAILROAD COMPANY

ONWEALTH OF PENNSYLVANIA APRIL 13, 1846.

SHARES 100

100

SHARES

ck---

NDRED

Shares in the

road Company transferable only transferable by

pany.

the signatures of the President and Treasurer

Philadelphia 8th January 1948

M W Clement

PRESIDENT.

G. J. Fox

TREASURER.

THIS CERTIFICATE IS NOT VALID UNTIL COUNTERSIGNED BY THE TRANSFER AGENT AND THE REGISTRAR.

50 EACH

PANY, PHILADELPHIA.

NOTICE: THE SIGNATURE TO THIS ASSIGN
OF THE CERTIFICATE, IN EVERY PARTIC

... of the above-named assignee, to make and execute all necessary acts of assignment and transfer of the said stock on the books of the said Company, and Attorneys one or more to substitute with like full power for the purposes aforesaid, hereby ratifying and confirming all that said Attorney, or his substitute or substitutes, shall lawfully do by virtue hereof.

In Witness Whereof, ... have hereunto set .... hand and seal, this .... day of .... one thousand nine hundred and ....

.... L.S.

Signed, Sealed, and Delivered in presence of

....

It is hereby certified that the transfer of the attached shares is made under such circumstances as to come within one of the exemptions specified in section 1802 of the Internal Revenue Code and section 270-5 of the Tax Law of the State of New York and that evidence in proof of the exemption is maintained by the undersigned and is available for inspection by Internal Revenue officers and representatives of the New York State Tax Commission.

JOHN MUIR & CO.

N.Y.-FED. TAX DUE PAID
THRU STK. CLN. CPN.

AUG 26 1954

MONTGOMERY SCOTT & CO.

Contents

A Few Men and Women Who Helped Shape the World Marketplace

GIOVANNI AGNELLI 1921–
Giovanni Agnelli (generally called Gianni) is the grandson of the principal founder of the Fiat automobile company (also named Giovanni), who might be described as the Henry Ford of Italy. After World War II service and a dolce vita period, Gianni took control of the Agnelli's ball-bearing company before becoming managing director of Fiat in 1963, then its chairman and CEO in 1966. From that time on, he was as dominant a force in the Italian corporate world as his grandfather had been.

As head of Fiat SpA, Agnelli controlled not only one of the world's premier automobile manufacturers but also financial institutions such as the Banca di Roma and Sanpaolo IMI, along with newspapers, hotels, shipping companies, oil refineries, industrial plants, and sports franchises like Juventas—one of the world's great soccer clubs—and the Ferrari grand prix racing team.

At the beginning of the twenty-first century, Fiat had 221,000 employees worldwide. By then Agnelli had officially retired, but he remained a powerful influence as honorary chairman of Fiat and head of IFI and IFIL, the family holding companies that own close to a third of Fiat stock. In March 2000, Agnelli was instrumental in the decision that permitted General Motors to acquire 20 percent of Fiat's automobile division, thus helping transform a family-style business, however large, into a company that is better positioned to function in the new global marketplace.

BERNARD ARNAULT 1949–
Sometimes called the Pope of Fashion, Bernard Arnault is a leading example of the new kind of French business magnate, unapologetically progressive yet able to build on one of France's traditional commercial strengths, the marketing of name-brand chic.

Born in Roubaix, a northern town hardly associated with fashion, Arnault graduated from the École Polytechnique in Paris, then spent some time in Florida selling real estate. The chutzpah he honed during this American interlude served him well on his return to France, though it raised more than a few eyebrows in the conservative French business world.

Starting in the 1980s, Arnault began to put together a formidable stable of internationally famous companies associated with the upper echelons of conspicuous consumerism. His aggressive takeover campaigns for such celebrated fashion houses as Dior and Givenchy shocked the world of haute couture, as did his decision to dump the venerable Hubert de Givenchy—the man who made Audrey Hepburn an icon—and replace him with John Galliano.

This kind of audacity characterizes the way Arnault has handled all the components of his LVMH conglomerate, under which umbrella are to be found, along with the houses of Dior and Givenchy, such recognizable names as Kenzo, Christian Lacroix, Tag Heuer, and Dom Perignon, as well as the com-panies that lend the group its initials—Louis Vuitton, Moët, and Hennessy. The prestige of the brand name is preserved and Arnault finds a way to reshape the product to suit changing markets.

Recently, Arnault has been using his personal fortune to enter another and very different field, the world of cyberspace. He has invested more than $200 million in American dot-coms such as Datek Online and eBay, and far more than that in LibertySurf, a French Internet access service, and Europ@Web, an Internet holding company.

JOHN JACOB ASTOR 1763–1848
The richest man in America at the time of his death, John Jacob Astor was born in the German city of Waldorf. Aboard the ship on which he emigrated to the United States in 1783, he fell in with employees of the Hudson's Bay Company, who convinced him that a good living could be made in the fur business. By 1786 he was in a position to open a retail furrier's store in New York City, which he used as the launching pad for the American Fur Company. By 1800 he had become the nation's largest fur trader, having proved himself capable of making shrewd but fair deals with both the Native Americans who supplied him with pelts and with the British officials who controlled access to the Asian ports established by the East India Company. This enabled Astor's agents to ship furs to China as well as to the

East Coast and to Europe. The American Fur Company's control of the industry was so complete that it is generally accepted to have been the nation's first monopoly.

Astor built on this initial success by investing in New York City real estate, erecting more than seven hundred buildings and buying up the land that is now known as Greenwich Village (for which he paid $75,000 in 1805). He also had a sharp eye for good values in the securities markets. When, for example, the federal government could not find subscribers for all of the bonds it had floated to finance the War of 1812, Astor was one of three businessmen who bought up the $10 million surplus, and subsequently resold it at a considerable profit. The archetypal self-made immigrant millionaire, Astor was one of the founders of New York society and a somewhat grudging philanthropist whose greatest gift to the city was a bequest of $400,000 for the founding of a public library.

SEWELL AVERY 1873–1960

Born in Saginaw, Michigan, Sewell Avery was a retail industry executive who, from 1931 to 1956, served as president of Montgomery Ward. He would be largely forgotten today if it were not for two acts of stubbornness and one of generosity.

He first earned a degree of popular notoriety during the Depression when he adamantly refused to go along with some aspects of FDR's New Deal legislation and, for his trouble, was removed from his post by court order and literally carried out of his office, still in his chair, by a couple of burly Feds. When the Supreme Court decided that the legislation in question was unconstitutional, Avery got his job back.

At the end of World War II, Montgomery Ward was second only to Sears, Roebuck as America's leading retail chain. Avery, a history buff, had noted that most wars were followed by depressions. While Robert E. Wood of Sears saw a booming postwar economy and expanded his company's operations as rapidly as possible, Avery—stubbornly certain that depression was just around the corner—actually closed stores despite the fact that Montgomery Ward operations were firmly in the black.

In response to Avery's reactionary attitudes, an ambitious investor named Louis Wolfson decided to make a bid for the company. He put together a block of $500,000 worth of Montgomery Ward's 6.5 million shares and made his move, but was turned down. Not easily repulsed, Wolfson decided to try something that at the time—1955—was still a relatively novel approach in the world of takeovers: he would exploit the proxy system by which directors are elected annually.

First Wolfson, acting as a major stockholder, went to court to demand that all nine seats on the board of directors should be up for grabs that year, instead of just three as was usually the case. Then he began to lobby the shareholders. When the stockholders' meeting was held, Wolfson and his forces were able to win three seats on the board. It was enough to force Avery to resign a few weeks later.

Avery's act of generosity had occurred several years earlier. As is well known, *Rudolph the Red-Nosed Reindeer* originated in 1939 as a children's book thought up by a Montgomery Ward employee named Robert May. It was issued as a promotional item for the store, and by 1946 more than 3.6 million copies had been given away. The copyright belonged to Montgomery Ward, but in 1947 Avery learned that May was heavily in debt due to medical bills contracted during his wife's long and eventually fatal illness. Avery had the rights made over to May, who, shortly after, asked his brother-in-law Johnny Marks to help develop a song based on the Rudolph character. The

result caught the attention of Gene Autry's wife and she persuaded the cowboy star to record it as the flip side of a holiday single. The rest is history.

JULES BACHE 1861–1944

Jules Bache was born in Germany in 1861 and came to America in the 1870s. In 1880, at the age of nineteen, he joined the staff of his uncle's brokerage firm, Leopold Cahn & Co. Quickly proving his capabilities, Bache was shortly promoted to treasurer, and within three years he was a partner. Leopold Cahn & Co. capitalized on the late-nineteenth-century American economic expansion and Bache himself established important relationships with influential businessmen including John D. Rockefeller, Edward H. Harriman, and Jay Gould.

Bache's influence was reflected by a firm-wide restructuring in 1892, after which the company was known as J. S. Bache & Co. Under his leadership the firm extended its reach both nationally and internationally. Secure in its leading position on Wall Street, with seats on all the major exchanges nationwide, the firm was able to participate actively in the business dealings of World War I's Allied powers. In the postwar years and through the Depression, J. S. Bache & Co. continued to expand across the United States, Asia, and Europe, until World War II instigated the closing of all Asian and European offices except London's. As during World War I, J. S. Bache & Co. participated actively in the American war effort, selling government bonds and expanding employment policies to allow women to fill jobs vacated by men in the military.

A noted art collector, Bache helped found the theater-focused Escholier Club in 1941 and was a charter member of the National Arts Club, established in 1898 to stimulate public interest in the arts across disparate disciplines, one of the few such organizations open to women as well as men.

WALTER BAGEHOT 1826–77
Editor, literary critic, political historian, and economic theorist, Walter Bagehot (pronounced Badge-ut) was one of the finest essayists of the nineteenth century and the founder of modern business journalism. Born in Langport, in the west of England, he graduated from University College, London, then studied law. He became a writer by chance, as a consequence of being in Paris in 1851 at the time of Louis Napoleon's coup d'état, which he reported for a weekly of the period.

After this experience, Bagehot took a job in his uncle's bank—which provided him with practical experience of the financial world—writing in his spare time essays on literary topics and studies of political figures of the recent past. He also wrote occasional pieces on economics that attracted the attention of James Wilson, who in 1843 had founded *The Economist.*

Bagehot married Wilson's eldest daughter and, in 1860, took over control of *The Economist* when Wilson died while on a government mission to India. Until his own relatively early death, Bagehot wrote the lead articles for the magazine—displaying a keen grasp of market psychology—and reshaped the publication into the prototypical modern business journal, emphasizing both the statistical analysis of financial trends and the importance of the political and social context.

Bagehot's books include *The English Constitution* (1867), an investigation of the distribution of power within the English political system, and *Lombard*

Street (1873), a study of the Bank of England that has been seen as anticipating twentieth-century concepts of the importance of central banking and exchange control. Although Bagehot is hardly a household name, his influence is still felt in the pages of *The Economist* and every other financial journal.

GEORGE FISHER BAKER 1840–1931
George Baker, the son of a U.S. State Department official, was just twenty-three years old when the national banking system was established in 1863, at the height of the Civil War. He was prescient enough to join with several brokers in becoming a founding stockholder in the First National Bank of New York City. He began his career there as little better than a teller, but rose quickly to become the de facto CEO.

During the Panic of 1873, the bank found itself embroiled in the failure of Jay Cooke & Co. There was a run on First National, and Baker's principal partners were ready to close the doors. Baker refused to go along with them, saying he would continue to honor depositors' withdrawals until the money gave out. This display of good faith restored confidence in the bank, and four years later Baker was named its president.

For the next two decades, First National grew enormously in stature under Baker's essentially conservative leadership. By the turn of the century, he was acknowledged as one of the big guns of American finance, along with men like J. P. Morgan and James Stillman of National City Bank. Increasingly, Baker found himself allied with Morgan and other members of the banking elite in engineering mergers and corporate restructuring on a mammoth scale. Their

control over the nation's credit led to Baker's finding himself a target of the Pujo Committee's 1912 congressional antitrust hearings.

Baker emerged unscathed from these hearings and continued to play a prominent role in the financial realpolitik of Wall Street until after the 1929 crash. As a philanthropist, he made large gifts to the Metropolitan Museum of Art and the American Red Cross, but one of his most significant contributions was his $6 million endowment of Harvard's Graduate School of Business Administration.

BERNARD BARUCH 1870–1965
Although he is principally remembered as an adviser to U.S. presidents and for his elder statesman role at the United Nations, Bernard Baruch was one of the most successful Wall Street speculators and stock manipulators of his generation.

Born in Camden, South Carolina, he graduated from New York's City College in 1899 and, after a brief spell as an office boy in the linen business, found employment on Wall Street. His talent was soon noticed and he rose quickly to become a member of the New York Stock Exchange, where he became a legendary figure, inspiring awe because of his seemingly sure instinct for playing both bull and bear markets.

Baruch himself was not given to awe, and on more than one occasion remarked that Wall Street was home to more overrated men than any other place in the world. He explained his success by saying that he had the common sense to get out of the market on the way up, before the inevitable crash arrived.

Having already accumulated a considerable fortune, Baruch became, during World War I, the chairman of the

War Industries Board. In 1919 he was a personal adviser to President Wilson at the Versailles Peace Conference. Between the wars, he was frequently called upon by occupants of the White House to offer opinions on subjects ranging from farm policy to military preparedness. During World War II he was a key member of President Roosevelt's brain trust, and in the postwar era he devoted much of his time to working with the United Nations formulating policy pertaining to the control of nuclear energy.

AUGUST BELMONT 1816–90

August Belmont was born into a prosperous Jewish family in Rhenish Prussia. At the age of fourteen, he was accepted into the Frankfurt branch of the Rothschild banking house. He showed great promise and was rapidly promoted to an important position in the bank's Naples office. Belmont decided in 1837 to strike out on his own in the United States, doing so with the blessings of his former employers, who commissioned him to act as their agent in New York. Since the Rothschilds were the world's preeminent bankers at the time, this gave Belmont access to the highest financial circles in New York. He soon opened his own bank, which, thanks to his fiscal savvy and powerful European connections, quickly became one of the largest in America.

Belmont took an active role in politics, becoming chairman of the national committee of the Democratic party and serving as U.S. minister at The Hague. He was a fervent opponent of slavery and was instrumental in winning European support for the Union cause during the Civil War. A prominent social figure in New York, Washington, and Europe, Belmont was an enthusiastic art collector and introduced thoroughbred horse racing to the United States, lending his name to the Belmont Stakes, the oldest of America's classic races.

Married to Caroline Slidell Perry, the daughter of Commodore Matthew Perry, Belmont founded a dynasty that continued to be prominent in banking and political affairs for four generations. His son, August Belmont Jr. (1853–1924), was a crusader for public transportation who played a leading role in financing the building of the New York City subway system.

NICHOLAS BIDDLE 1786–1844

Early in his career, Nicholas Biddle, who had been born into a Philadelphia Quaker family, was the editor of America's first literary magazine and author/editor of the classic *History of the Expedition of Captains Lewis and Clark*, based on the explorers' notes. He served as a member of the Pennsylvania state senate and came to national prominence after James Monroe became president in 1817. Biddle had been Monroe's secretary while the latter was minister to the United Kingdom. In 1819 the president made Biddle a director of the Second Bank of the United States, which he headed from 1823 to 1836.

Biddle proved himself an able, practical economist, using his position to promote fiscal responsibility by taking a tough stance on supplying credit to the private sector of the banking industry. His influence was felt in many quarters, including the stock market, which benefited from the stability he brought to the economy as a whole.

The bank had powerful opponents, however, both among business leaders who resented Biddle's personal power and among members of the Democratic party who were opposed on philosophical grounds to the very idea of a central bank. When Andrew Jackson became

president the campaign against the bank was stepped up, and in 1833, Jackson ordered all federal deposits withdrawn from its coffers. From that point on the bank's days were numbered, and in 1836 its charter was revoked.

Without a strong central bank as a stabilizing force, the economy faltered; within a year there was a wave of private bank and business failures, leading to a prolonged recession. Biddle, meanwhile, became president of the Bank of the United States of Pennsylvania before retiring to the life of a literary lion, hosting salons attended by famous writers of the day at his country home.

MICHAEL R. BLOOMBERG 1942–

Raised in Medford, Massachusetts, in modest circumstances, Michael Bloomberg graduated from Johns Hopkins University in 1964 and established himself as a significant Wall Street player during the fifteen years, from 1966 to 1981, that he spent at Salomon Brothers, where he rose to the position of general partner. In 1981 Bloomberg left Salomon Brothers to found Bloomberg Financial Markets, a company that would set new standards for the distribution of financial information, in America and at least one hundred other countries.

The new company set up in business with a handful of clients connected to its communications web. Bloomberg had the insight to see what the computer could do for the marketplace, dispensing information and advice at lightning speed, and soon he was proving the value of the service his company had to offer. Scores and then thousands of proprietary data terminals—quickly dubbed "Bloomberg Boxes"—were installed in the offices of banks, brokerage houses, and other subscribing financial institutions.

From that start, Bloomberg succeeded in building a global media empire that came to include magazines, radio and television stations, Internet services, and book publishing houses. It is the "Bloomberg Boxes," however, that pump the lifeblood of the empire. As of July 2001, more than 150,000 of them were in service.

At the time of writing, Mr. Bloomberg is a candidate for the office of mayor of New York City.

IVAN BOESKY 1937–

Long after the details of his crimes have been forgotten, Ivan Boesky will be remembered as the warped embodiment of 1980s go-go Wall Street—the man who infamously told the world, "Greed is all right."

Boesky began his career as a Detroit tax accountant. He shifted his attention to the stock market and in 1966 arrived in New York, where he quickly established himself, displaying a knack for arbitrage and a steely nerve that made him a man to be watched. His reputation was not acquired without hints of controversy, though; in 1975 he was fined $10,000 for violation of short-selling rules.

Later that year he founded his own company, specializing in arbitrage. This thrived until 1981, when Boesky made the mistake of becoming entangled in the Hunt brothers' attempt to corner silver. That almost ruined him, but he soon launched a new company, CX Partners Ltd., which—along with London-based Cambrian & General Securities—attracted many investors and gave him the means to generate a sizable personal fortune in a rather short period of time.

Boesky's ability to identify takeover targets before they became apparent to other professionals made him a public figure—an unofficial but much-quoted spokesman for the yuppie traders and investors swept along by the momentum of the 1980s' bull market. In 1986, however, a federal investigation uncovered the fact that Boesky had been purchasing insider information from an employee of Drexel Burnham Lambert, Inc. Realizing that his position was untenable, Boesky agreed to cooperate with authorities in return for a reduced sentence. He paid a fine of $100 million and served two years at a federal prison camp plus six months in a halfway house. He was released in 1990, still a wealthy man.

There is little doubt that Boesky was guilty of the crimes he was accused of. Some observers suspect, however, that he did nothing that other, less high-profile traders have not indulged in. His biggest mistake, so this theory goes, was to flaunt his success, thus arousing the ire of the establishment.

JOHN C. BOGLE 1929–

John Bogle is known as a thrifty man, but he is quite adept with large sums of money: as the founder and long-time chairman of The Vanguard Group, Bogle was responsible for the creation of what has grown to become a $550 billion–plus giant.

Often declared the father of index fund investing, John Bogle has inspired nearly cultlike adoration among the legions of investors who subscribe to his theories—"Bogleheads," as his fans call themselves in chat rooms across the Internet. Bogle's investment principles didn't always inspire such praises; when he created the world's first index fund—

the Vanguard 500, which debuted in 1976—it was referred to by some as "Bogle's Folly." Based on Nobel prize-winning work of the 1960s on the concept of indexing, the fund operates on the tenet that a market-tracking index fund will earn better returns in the long run than an actively-managed mutual fund whose possibly greater gains will be offset by high management and trading expenses.

Bogle was born in 1929 in Montclair, New Jersey. His college training at Princeton culminated in a groundbreaking senior thesis, written in 1951, that analyzed the then-obscure field of mutual-fund investing. This thesis launched a successful career in both finance and writing, and Bogle is now a media commentator for print and television as well as the author of innumerable articles and several books. Cajoled into stepping down as Vanguard CEO by an enforced retire-at-seventy policy, Bogle maintains an active public speaking schedule, continues to write, and serves as president of the Vanguard-supported Bogle Financial Markets Research Center.

WARREN BUFFETT 1930–

Perhaps the most famous American investor of the final quarter of the twentieth century, Warren Buffett established his reputation by bucking the trends of the period. Rather than riding the bull markets, Buffett has been a believer in investing for the long term. And although in recent years the markets have been swept along by the momentum of high-tech stocks, Buffett has nourished the peerless reputation of his Berkshire Hathaway Corporation by trusting to his knowledge of the "old economy."

Born in Omaha, Nebraska, Buffett is said to have been investing in the stock market by the time he was eleven. In high school he started a pinball machine business with a friend and a little later began to acquire real estate. While studying for his master's degree at Columbia University, he came under the influence of Benjamin Graham, an economist who believed that an investor should look for undervalued companies that will prosper in the long run.

It is this philosophy that Buffett has implemented with a combination of analytical insight and creativity. To give a single example, in 1963 American Express became involved in a scandal and the word on the street was that the company might fold. Buffett took note that Amex cards were still being flashed in every restaurant he dined in. Convinced that the company would rebound, he bought 5 percent of its stock. Before the decade was out its value had increased fivefold.

Buffett, who has shared his outlook on investing in a number of best-selling books, remains modest about his success: "I don't try to jump over seven-foot bars," he once said. "I look around for one-foot bars I can step over."

ROBERTO CALVI 1920–82

When Roberto Calvi was found hanging by the neck from Blackfriars Bridge, his handmade shoes dangling above the River Thames a stone's throw from London's financial district, the verdict of the coroner's court was suicide. Some of those who had followed Calvi's career closely were not convinced by the court's conclusion.

Shortly after World War II, Calvi had joined the modest, Milan-based Banco Ambrosiano. Italy was developing an industrialized economy and Calvi was instrumental in steering the bank toward lucrative investments that soon made it one of the country's most important financial institutions. By the time he took full control of the bank, in the early 1970s, the Italian economy was slowing down and he began to look abroad—especially to Latin America—for new sources of profits.

Secretive and devious, Calvi used his overseas connections to set up nominally independent businesses in other countries, thus making it possible for his bank to circumvent Italy's strict laws against exporting capital. In this capacity, he frequently found himself collaborating with, or acting on behalf of, the Vatican's private bank, the Instituto per le Opere di Religione. Calvi's baroque fiscal schemes sometimes involved sending billions of lire bouncing around the globe like pinballs. The profits that accrued permitted him to channel substantial quantities of money to the Vatican and to the Catholic newspaper *Corriere della Sera*, which returned his favors by massaging his public image. Cynical observers dubbed him "God's banker."

At the same time, though, Calvi became deeply involved with a cloak-and-dagger Masonic group called P2, led by a neo-Fascist guru, Licio Gelli, whose admirers included high-ranking members of the Italian military and secret-service, operatives reputed to be behind schemes to overthrow the government. Calvi may well have helped finance this organization, possibly with money surreptitiously funneled from the Vatican.

This did nothing to slow the Banco Ambrosiano's growth, and by the early 1980s it had become Italy's largest private bank. In 1981, however, Calvi was convicted of illegal currency transactions. Soon after, he disappeared and rumors began to circulate. Banco Ambrosiano's stock fell sharply. When Calvi's body was found, the news triggered panic selling that forced the Milan Stock Exchange to close for three days.

It was discovered that the Banco Ambrosiano had accumulated bad debts totaling $1.3 billion, and an additional $400 million was missing. Calvi's operations had become so convoluted that they have never been satisfactorily explained, and his last days remain a mystery.

ANDREW CARNEGIE 1835–1919

Andrew Carnegie's stature as an industrialist—the nabob of steel—is familiar to anyone who has a passing acquaintance with American history, as is his later role as a philanthropist. Less well known is that his career was built in large part upon shrewd investment.

Born in Scotland, Carnegie was brought to America as a twelve-year-old and was immediately set to work, educating himself by reading and attending night school. At fourteen he found employment in a telegraph office, which led to a job as secretary and private telegrapher to a superintendent for the Pennsylvania Railroad Company. By the time he was twenty-three, Carnegie had himself attained the rank of superintendent.

It was at this point, enjoying some disposable income, that he began to invest. One of his first investments was in the Woodruff Sleeping Car Company, the forerunner of the Pullman Company. He was in a position to give the enterprise a boost by introducing sleeping-car service on his line, and he soon began to invest in other businesses such as the Pittsburgh Locomotive Works and a Pennsylvania oil field. He also made a number of trips to Europe, selling American railroad securities.

Several of the companies in which he had invested were connected with steel. In 1865 he took over the management of one of these, the Keystone Bridge Company, which provided him with a springboard for his assault on the steel industry. Throughout the final quarter of the century, the Carnegie Steel Company was dominant in its field. In 1900 its profits were $40 million, of which Carnegie himself pocketed $25 million. The following year, he sold the company to J. P. Morgan's United States Steel Corporation for $250 million, and subsequently devoted himself to various charitable foundations, giving away an estimated $350 million.

RONNIE CHAN 1950–

Ronnie Chan was raised in Hong Kong but came to America to attend college, earning both bachelor's and master's degrees in biology from California State University. Growing disillusioned with science, he switched to business, receiving his M.B.A. from the University of Southern California in 1976.

A leading example of the entrepreneurial Chinese businessman, Chan serves as chairman of the Hang Lung Development Company, a group of Hong Kong–listed companies dealing in real estate and property investment, development, and management. He founded and manages the Morningside/Springfield Group, which owns and oversees industrial and service companies throughout the United States, Europe, and Asia, and is a director for Enron Corp., Motorola Inc., and Standard Chartered PLC. He also serves on the boards of several publicly traded companies and is a non–executive director of the Securities and Futures Commission of Hong Kong and a director of the Hong Kong Real Estate Developers Association.

Besides his considerable business achievements, Chan has prioritized open discussion of cultural differences within the international community, and has been quoted as saying that "culture is more emotive than cognitive." Meetings with government officials and business leaders from around the world have served to reinforce what Chan learned in his early years in America: one of the most important building blocks of success in today's world is the ability to negotiate and appreciate foreign cultures.

JAY COOKE 1821–1905

Jay Cooke was descended from a pioneer family that arrived in Massachusetts in 1630. Cooke himself—whose father served one term as a U.S. congressman—was born in Sandusky, Ohio. While still in his teens he moved to Philadelphia, where he found employment with E. W. Clark and Company, a merchant banking enterprise that also traded in securities on a fairly ambitious scale, advertising aggressively and maintaining an office in New York.

This environment suited Cooke's entrepreneurial spirit as well as his somewhat magisterial manner, and within three years he was made a partner. In 1861 Cooke opened his own bank. During the Civil War he was engaged first by the state of Pennsylvania and then by the federal government to sell bonds with a face value of more than a billion dollars, intended to fund the Union cause. Cooke made a spectacular success of meeting this challenge by setting up a network of agents in large cities and small towns throughout the northern states, supervising their activities by means of the telegraph.

By the end of the war Cooke was recognized as the king of bond retailers. Shortly after, though, he made a serious miscalculation when he became involved in the financing of the Northern Pacific Railroad and his company collapsed. Eventually, Cooke discharged all his personal obligations and was able to rebuild his fortune, but he never regained the glory he had enjoyed during the Civil War period.

CHARLES HENRY DOW 1851–1902 and EDWARD DAVIS JONES 1856–1920

Possessor of what was to become one of the most famous names in the annals of finance, Charles Dow was born in a Connecticut farmhouse, and an archetypal New England rectitude clung to him throughout his life. He was curious about the world and intelligent, and in 1872 found work as a journalist at the *Springfield Daily Republican*. Not long after, the *Providence Journal* sent him west to report on a silver strike. This proved to be a turning point in his life, as he became fascinated with the grass-roots economics of life in a boomtown.

Dow turned his attention to Wall Street and, in 1882—in partnership with an old friend, Edward Davis Jones, and Charles M. Bergstresser, a stock market reporter who had the means to finance the project—launched the *Customer's Afternoon Letter*, which in 1889 became *The Wall Street Journal*. The three men made a good team. Aside from backing the project, Bergstresser was a hard-nosed reporter with excellent connections on the Street. Jones ran the newsroom like a boot camp, and Dow sat quietly in his cubicle planning new features.

One of these was the stock average. Starting in 1884, the newsletter would publish indexes diagramming the performance of various stocks, especially those of railroad companies. It was in 1896 that Dow arrived at something rather more sophisticated that came to be known as the Dow Jones Industrial Average. (Jones, in fact, had no part in the concept, but Dow Jones was the company name.)

It was Dow's idea that a sense of the economy as a whole could be achieved by tracking the performance of a limited number of industrial stocks, and viewing them in conjunction with a similar average of transportation stocks. (After all, he argued, industrial products have to be transported to their destination.) The first Dow Jones Industrial Average followed the fortunes of just twelve companies. (General Electric is the only one of these that remains in the expanded index at the time of writing.) Modest in scale, it nonetheless caught the imagination of investors and forever changed the way stock markets around the world would be interpreted.

DANIEL DREW 1797–1879

Daniel Drew was born in Putnam County, New York. Lanky and cadaverous, he never bothered to acquire much book learning but received an education in the legendary school of hard knocks, spending time as a tavern owner, a cattle driver, a moneylender, and even a circus roustabout. Eventually he gained control of several steamship lines, then entered the brokerage business in 1844 as senior partner in the firm of Drew, Robinson and Company. Along the way, he was smitten with a hellfire-and-brimstone form of Methodism that did not preach forgiveness of debts or find anything sinful about coveting another man's railroad.

It was as a predatory raider of other men's railroads that Drew achieved notoriety. He would zero in on a line with financial problems and lend it money secured by the company's physical assets—land, locomotives, et cetera. In return for this generosity, he would become an officer of the company, preferably its treasurer, thus putting himself in a position to manipulate the stock to his enormous profit, generally by stock watering or selling short. Most famously he took control of the Erie Railroad, turning it into a cash cow that generated millions of dollars for his company.

After the Civil War, Drew joined forces with two younger speculators, James Gould and Jim Fisk, and they fought a fierce campaign—it lasted from 1866 to 1868—against Cornelius Vanderbilt for control of the Erie. For almost two decades Drew was the most feared man on Wall Street, but by the early 1870s he had grown tired and dispirited and no longer had the stomach for the takeover battles and glorified shell game schemes that had won him his unenviable reputation. He suffered major losses in the Panic of 1873 and in 1876 was forced to file for bankruptcy.

PIERRE SAMUEL DU PONT 1870–1954

The E. I. du Pont de Nemours Company was founded in Wilmington, Delaware, in 1802 by Éleuthère Irénée du Pont, producing black powder and other explosives for both military and mining purposes; during the course of the nineteenth century it became one of America's industrial giants.

In the twentieth century, Du Pont (the name of the company was compressed to DuPont in 1995) would become increasingly involved in the production of chemicals, plastics, synthetic fibers, and motion picture film. Early in the century the company also acquired large holdings of stock in emerging companies such as General Motors.

The firm was headed by members of the du Pont family until 1940. Among the most influential was Pierre, a graduate of the Massachusetts Institute of Technology, who chaired not only the family business but also, for a while, GM. He was at the helm when Du Pont developed such important products as nylon, synthetic rubber, and Duco enamel paints, which enabled GM to market inexpensive, brightly colored cars that helped make the Model T Ford seem an anachronism by the late 1920s.

In addition, Pierre was active in such lobbying groups as the Association Against the Prohibition Amendment, an organization dedicated to repealing the Eighteenth Amendment. It was not that Pierre was a "wet" in the normal sense of the word; rather, he was devoted to the cause of reducing income taxes (as was befitting of someone who paid more of them than almost anyone else alive). He advocated repeal of the Prohibition laws on the grounds that the government could then place a heavy tax on alcohol sales, thus making it possible to cut assessments on personal income.

ALFRED ESCHER 1819–82

Born in Zurich, Alfred Escher was one of two figures who dominated Swiss politics and business during the middle decades of the nineteenth century. The other, Jakob Stämpfli, was a man of radical ideas who was often ahead of his time. Escher, by contrast, was a moderate with an instinct for smoothing ruffled feathers. Much smoothing was needed during the two major diplomatic crises of the period, one involving Prussia's claim to sovereignty over the canton of Neuchâtel, the other the cession of Savoy to France.

As a businessman, Escher was very much the archetype of the modern Swiss capitalist, founding Credit Suisse in 1856. Had Stämpfli had his way—and he enjoyed considerable support—Switzerland might have become a decidedly different place. In the 1860s, for example, Stämpfli was a powerful advocate for nationalization of the Swiss railway system. Escher, who was head of a railroad company, was the principal spokesman for the development of privately owned rail lines, which were to prove a powerful stimulus to the Swiss economy, though they were in fact nationalized in 1898.

Among Escher's greatest achievements was the establishment of the famous Gotthard rail line linking Zurich with Milan via the Alps; its creation involved many feats of both engineering and diplomacy and cost well over 150 lives. Escher was four times president of the Swiss national assembly.

JAMES FISK 1834–72

Flamboyant and unscrupulous, "Jubilee Jim" Fisk was the clown prince of Wall Street in the years following the Civil War.

Born in Bennington, Vermont, Fisk tried his luck at a variety of jobs—peddler, waiter, carnival hand—before he discovered that there were easier ways of making money. During the War Between the States, he smuggled cotton through Confederate and Union lines to capitalize on the shortage in the North.

After the war he came to Wall Street and soon teamed up with Daniel Drew, the old master of the bear market, and Jay Gould. The three of them participated in the infamous war with Cornelius Vanderbilt over control of the Erie Railroad, a campaign in which political bribes fluttered down like autumn leaves along the Hudson. Later, Fisk was involved with Gould in the latter's attempt to corner the market in gold.

Even without these events, however, Fisk would be remembered for his Barnum-like flamboyance. A corpulent man, he was fond of wearing musical comedy–style uniforms and riding in his matched coach and six with a French showgirl on each arm. To maintain a supply of the latter, he used corporate funds to become the owner of Pike's Opera House, home to some of the more risqué shows of the period, above which he maintained an office.

His steady girlfriend (not counting his wife, who was kept under wraps in Boston) was Josie Mansfield, a well-known buxom beauty of the period. Eventually, though, they quarreled and she took up with a less talented speculator named Edward Stokes. Attempting blackmail, Stokes threatened to release letters Fisk had written to Josie. Fisk paid up for a while, but finally decided to risk the scandal that would be involved in taking Stokes to court. The case made Fisk a laughingstock in the yellow press, but it had a far more ruinous impact upon Stokes, who responded by shooting his tormentor to death on the stairway of a New York hotel.

MALCOLM FORBES 1919–90

One of America's most eccentric and unusual millionaires, publisher Malcolm Forbes left an indelible impression on the business world. Born in New Jersey in 1919, Forbes was the third son of a Scottish immigrant who had founded *Forbes* magazine in 1917. Malcolm attended Princeton University, graduating in 1941, and assumed control of the magazine upon his father's death in 1954. With Malcolm at the helm, *Forbes* became a household name as one of the top general-interest business magazines, boasting a circulation of 735,000. The success of the magazine enhanced Forbes's public visibility, and he used his media presence—which included *Forbes*, numerous books, and other publications—as a bully pulpit to promote his belief in the virtues of laissez-faire capitalism. Forbes was fairly hands-off with his staff, avoiding micromanagement and allowing their skills to shine through. He was the mastermind behind hits such as the annual list of the four hundred richest Americans, and he encouraged investigative stories. As former staff member Steve Quickel has written, "Malcolm did turn *Forbes* into a huge business success, but not by sacrificing editorial integrity on the cross of commerce."

Forbes embraced the capitalist spirit—the corporate jet was dubbed the "Capitalist Tool." He loved spending money as much as earning it; an avid motorcycle aficionado, Forbes was reputed to have biked to work in Manhattan from New Jersey, following a limousine to block the wind. Another great passion was ballooning, and to this day the Forbes family hosts events such as the Rassemblement des Ballons at their château in Normandy, France. He owned a private island in the Fiji archipelago, the Château de Balleroy in France, and a Moroccan palace. In addition to acquiring property, Forbes amassed collections of paintings, Fabergé eggs, and over one hundred thousand military miniatures. Spirited and gregarious, Forbes threw famously lavish parties throughout his life, and ran with the rich and famous. His legendary seventieth birthday party at the Moroccan retreat was reported as featuring six hundred belly dancers, two hundred Berber horsemen, three jets to bring guests, and his friend Elizabeth Taylor in attendance.

Virtually the only arena in which Forbes was unsuccessful was government. With two failed runs for governor, public office remained an unfulfilled dream. Perhaps it is family fate: his son, Malcolm Stevenson Forbes Jr., better known as Steve, made two unsuccessful bids for president after his father had passed away.

HENRY FORD 1863–1947

Henry Ford did not invent the automobile, but he certainly did more than anyone else to make car ownership a way of life. He achieved this by identifying a niche market of staggering potential, then building a vast industrial empire while largely ignoring the conventional ways of organizing and financing such an enterprise.

Ford was a farm boy whose knack for working with machinery brought him into contact with the internal combustion engine. In 1896 he built his first "horseless carriage" and in 1899 launched the Detroit Automobile Company, which soon was renamed the Henry Ford Company. During the next three years Ford gained public recognition as his cars broke several speed records. He risked his own life by driving one special to a world record on a frozen lake. He also antagonized his backers and, in 1902, left the company (which became the Cadillac Motor Car Company) to start a new business, the Ford Motor Company.

Now Ford was forced to take on the Association of Licensed Automobile Manufacturers, which tried to put him out of business on grounds of patent infringement. But Ford—the "little man"—won victory in court over the giants of the industry, which helped make him a popular hero and provided a boost when it came to marketing the Model T, the first example of which was built in 1908.

It was Ford's idea to make the Model T a car that almost anyone could afford, yet one that was tough enough to withstand the roughest conditions. In order to build it in quantity he introduced production-line techniques, paying his workers an unheard of $5.00 a day (more than double the industry standard). This worked so well that he embarked on an expansion plan so ambitious that it frightened his shareholders. Ford owned 58 percent of his company's stock, and in 1919 he bought out the seven minority shareholders for a total of a little over $125 million. For the next thirty-seven years—until the company finally went public—only Ford family members were permitted to own stock, making Ford at its peak the largest family-held company in the world, with interests in thirty-three countries on five continents.

Almost seventeen million Model Ts were produced during Ford's glory period, which lasted from 1908 to 1927. By the late 1920s other companies, such as General Motors, were stealing some of that glory, and Ford never succeeded in regaining its position of absolute leadership. During the 1930s and 1940s Ford's problems were compounded by its founder's tendencies toward megalomania and paranoia, which had an impact on everything from labor relations to styling decisions. When Henry Ford died, his stock holdings went to the Ford Foundation, which then became the world's wealthiest private foundation.

BENJAMIN FRANKLIN 1706–90

Benjamin Franklin is universally celebrated for his public service, his experiments with electricity, and such utilitarian inventions and innovations as bifocal eyeglasses, the lightning rod, and a highly efficient type of stove that is still in production more than two hundred years later.

Despite the importance of his diplomacy and the usefulness of his inventions—not to mention his part in writing the Declaration of Independence—school history books and Hollywood movies have tended to present Franklin as a kind of benign prototype of the nutty professor—brainy but impractical. Anything but impractical, Franklin was in fact one of America's pioneer capitalists. A recent historical survey concluded that, by the time of the War of Independence, Franklin, like George Washington, was one of the wealthiest men in the thirteen states.

The basis of Franklin's fortune was his printing business. In 1729 he published a treatise entitled *A Modest Enquiry into the Nature and Necessity of a Paper Currency*. This helped him win a lucrative contract to print banknotes for the state of Pennsylvania, which led to similar contracts with Delaware, Maryland, and New Jersey. He then went on to profitable publishing ventures such as the *Pennsylvania Gazette* and, especially, *Poor Richard's Almanac*, a pioneering self-help book published annually from 1732 to 1757. The money he made from these business enterprises he invested wisely in real estate and partnerships with printers in other parts of the country, and even in the British West Indies. It is only appropriate, then, that Franklin's likeness embellishes today's $100 bill.

MILTON FRIEDMAN 1912–

Although modest about his considerable personal accomplishments, Milton Friedman is one of the most passionate economists of our time, with an almost evangelical belief in the power of the free market. A 1976 Nobel Prize in economics capped an influential career in academia and government.

Friedman was born in 1912 in Brooklyn, New York, and raised in New Jersey in a financially strained household. Reliant upon scholarships to finance his education, Friedman attended the undergraduate program at Rutgers University, rounding out his tuition aid with the typical slate of odd jobs—waiting tables, retail clerking, and summer employment. His initial interest was in mathematics, with an eye toward becoming an actuary. He simultaneously studied economics and eventually won a full scholarship to the University of Chicago to pursue graduate work in that discipline.

Friedman's graduate-school years were fruitful for both his studies and love, for it was there that he met his future wife and lifelong professional partner, Rose Director. He received his master's degree from Chicago in 1933 and joined the research staff at the National Bureau of Economic Research, a position he held in various forms for forty-four years. Friedman spent the early 1940s engaged at the U.S. Treasury Department and as a mathematical statistician with a Columbia University group that tackled issues of wartime tax policy, weapon design, military tactics, and metallurgical experiments. He earned his Ph.D. from Columbia in 1946.

After World War II, Friedman settled into a combination of academia— primarily at the University of Chicago, which he has dubbed his intellectual home—and government. Increasing interest in the public arena in the 1960s led to him serve as an economic adviser to Barry Goldwater (1964) and Richard Nixon (1968) in their quests for the presidency, a role to which he returned during Ronald Reagan's 1980 campaign. In England, Friedman's scientific work influenced Margaret Thatcher's Tory government to adopt monetarist policies upon her election to the post of prime minister in 1979.

In 1966 Friedman began writing a triweekly current affairs column for *Newsweek* magazine. This began a prolific career as a writer and media interpreter of economics, which included a 1980s television series, *Free to Choose,* several pivotal books, and countless articles.

Since his official retirement from the University of Chicago in 1977, Friedman has continued to pursue writing, lecturing, and research, dividing his time between his home in Vermont and the Hoover Institution of Stanford University, where he is a senior research fellow. In 1988 Friedman was awarded both the Presidential Medal of Freedom and the National Medal of Science. In 1998 he and Rose D. Friedman cowrote *Two Lucky People,* a memoir about their experiences and contributions to economics.

THE FUGGER FAMILY

Although less well known to today's readers than the Medici, the Rothschilds, or the Morgans, the Fuggers belong among the banking families that dominated their respective eras.

Like many great banking families of the Middle Ages and the Renaissance, the Fuggers had their beginnings among the textile guilds, in their case in the German city of Augsburg. During the fifteenth century, two branches of the family emerged—the Fugger vom Reh (Fuggers of the Doe) and the Fugger von der Lilie (Fuggers of the Lily), names that derived from their coats of arms. Both established international trading networks, but the Fugger vom Reh went bankrupt in 1499 and thereafter it was the von der Lilie branch, founded by Jakob I (d. 1469), that thrived. By the end of the fifteenth century, its members were handling such important responsibilities as collecting remittances for the Vatican. For several years they ran the papal mint.

Jakob II (1459–1525)—who would become known as Jakob the Rich—was the youngest son of Jakob I. At first he was intended for a career in the church, but after studying bookkeeping in Venice, he was placed in charge of the family's Innsbruck office, where he made shrewd investments in the silver mines of the neighboring Tyrol. These led to further sorties into mining, including a major investment in the

copper fields of Slovakia, which under Jakob's guidance became enormously productive. The Fuggers also became involved in many other kinds of ventures including the spice trade, real estate, and precious stones.

Since 1490 the Fuggers had been the chief bankers of Maximilian I, who in 1508 had become the Holy Roman Emperor; in 1514 Maximilian elevated Jakob to the nobility with the rank of count. Later Jakob financed the election of Charles V as Maximilian's successor. Another royal figure who turned to Jakob for financial aid was Henry VIII of England.

Jakob had his portrait painted by Albrecht Dürer, and he commissioned many fine buildings to house the Fugger enterprises. He was ably succeeded by his nephew Anton (1493–1560), who used the resources of the House of Fugger to support the cause of the Catholic emperors and kings in their wars against the Protestant states. He also involved the family in a variety of new enterprises, ranging from mining ventures in Scandinavia to participation in the Atlantic slave trade.

Anton lacked a successor of real ability, but the Fugger banking enterprises remained in business until the mid-seventeenth century. The name is still borne by three houses of German nobility that owe their current wealth to the immense real estate investments of Jakob II and Anton.

BILL GATES 1955–
The Bill Gates story can be summed up as the saga of a kid from the great Northwest who went from pioneer computer buff to world's richest man in a matter of two decades. Born in Seattle,

he attended Harvard but dropped out to found Microsoft along with his friend Paul Allen. They adapted the BASIC programming language for the Altair 8800, which many point to as the first personal computer. This led to IBM's asking Microsoft to provide the operating system for its PC, to be released in 1981. Gates and Allen purchased Q-DOS from a small Seattle company and rejigged it to fit the PC specs. They also retained the rights to the software.

As PC clones appeared, DOS beat out other, more sophisticated systems—including the windows-and-mouse combination developed by Xerox programmers several years earlier—and, against the odds, became the industry standard. Even when Apple released the Macintosh in 1984, with its state-of-the-art operating system, DOS not only survived but actually thrived, holding off its rivals until Microsoft could come out with Windows in 1990.

By then Microsoft had been a listed company for just four years, but Gates and Allen (who had gone his own way) were already multimillionaires.

Microsoft has seldom been at the cutting edge of software development. Rather, it has succeeded as a hard-working concern that, through a combination of luck and judgment, has managed to stay abreast of users' familiarity with the evolving world of software. Bill Gates's genius has been for marketing Microsoft, displaying a keen instinct for zeroing in on consumer needs and backing this up with packaging, promotion, and all the other tools of effective salesmanship.

Whatever happens in the wake of antitrust lawsuits, Microsoft will stand forever as the ultimate example of the so-called New Economy's ability to generate enormous sums of money in very short periods of time. History is likely to see Bill Gates as symbolizing American commercial progress in the final decades of the twentieth century in much the way Henry Ford did between 1910 and 1930.

STEPHEN GIRARD 1750–1831

Stephen Girard is one of the forgotten pioneers of banking in the United States. Born in France, he went to sea in his early teens and eventually became the skipper of a ship that plied its trade between the American colonies and various Caribbean ports. During the War of Independence, British blockades interfered with his business and he settled in Philadelphia. After the war he used contacts he had made there to finance a fleet of vessels that made him one of the largest shipowners in the country.

In 1811, when Congress refused to renew the charter of the First Bank of the United States, Girard bought out its assets and modestly renamed it the Bank of Stephen Girard. He continued to operate it almost as if it were a federally sponsored central bank, providing much-needed credit during the War of 1812. When the government floated war bonds that were hopelessly undersubscribed, it was Girard, along with John Jacob Astor and banker David Paris, who bought up the balance of the issue at a discount. They profited handsomely from reselling the bonds to the public, but had these financiers not stepped in when they did, the government would have been hard-pressed to continue the war.

JAY GOULD 1836–92

Born in upstate New York, Jason "Jay" Gould—the man who would one day be dubbed "the Mephistopheles of Wall Street"—attended local schools and then became a surveyor. He saved up enough money to go into the tanning business along with a partner named Zadoc Pratt. After a short time Pratt discovered that Gould was cooking the books, but instead of bringing charges he allowed the young embezzler to buy him out.

Gould had been using his ill-gotten gains to play the futures market in hides. He had made enough money to buy into another tannery, this time in partnership with a successful leather merchant named Charles Leupp. Soon Gould was up to his old tricks, filching company money to play the futures market. By the time he was twenty, his worth on paper was more than a million dollars.

When the market in hides collapsed, most of that fortune was lost. Leupp was ruined and committed suicide. Undeterred by this turn of events, Gould began speculating in railroad stocks and before long was in a position to buy and reorganize a couple of smaller lines. This brought him to the attention of Daniel Drew and Jim Fisk. He became their partner in the Erie Railroad war, and was the mastermind behind the 1869 scheme to corner the market in gold.

Much of Gould's initial clout derived from his knowledge of which palms to grease in the New York political machine headed by Boss Tweed. When the Tweed Ring was driven out of office, Gould turned his attention elsewhere and, in alliance with Russell Sage, began to acquire western railroads, putting together what was at the time the nation's most extensive railroad empire, which included such prize holdings as the Union Pacific. He also took over the Western Union Telegraph Company, bought the New York *World* newspaper, and gained a monopoly of elevated rail service in New York City.

Although Gould maintained his knack for making enemies and remained a pitiless dealmaker, he finally became something of an establishment figure. He died worth close to $80 million.

BENJAMIN GRAHAM 1894–1976

Benjamin Graham was a partner in a Wall Street investment house that was ruined in the 1929 crash. Luckily, he had recently started another career, teaching in the graduate school of business at Columbia University. In 1934 he published his book *Securities Analysis* (written with David Dodd), which was immediately recognized as a classic and is now looked on as the bible of "value-oriented investment," the first work to deal with the fundamentals of financial markets.

Greatly moved by the tragic events of the Depression, Graham followed *Securities Analysis* with *Storage and Stability* (1937), suggesting, among other things, the creation of a sort of central commodities bank that would stockpile essential goods in preparation for future crises. This book also attacked the gold standard, which Graham believed to be a dangerous anachronism.

His own Graham-Newman Fund proved the efficacy of his fundamental analysis theories by averaging a 17 percent annual return over a twenty-year period during which the Standard & Poor's 500 index produced a 14 percent return. Among Graham's Columbia students were many star money managers of the future, most notably Warren Buffett.

HETTY GREEN 1834–1916

In 1998 *American Heritage* published a list of the forty richest Americans of all time. The only woman to find a place on that list, ranking number thirty-six, was Hetty Green—sometimes known as the Witch of Wall Street—whose fortune was estimated to have amounted to more than $17 billion as expressed in late twentieth-century money. Yet Green was so cheap she would walk to the local grocery store to buy broken biscuits in bulk, and is said to have once spent hours searching for a two-cent stamp she had mislaid. When her son injured his leg, Green refused to pay a doctor to treat the wound, with the consequence that the leg had to be amputated.

Born Hetty Robinson, this future mistress of the stock market came from wealthy New Bedford whaling stock. Her mother's family, the Howlands, had crossed the Atlantic on the Mayflower, and Hetty was brought up in a distinctly Puritan atmosphere. By the time she was six, she was reading the financial pages to her father and grandfather, both of whom suffered from poor eyesight. This aroused an early interest in the workings of the stock market.

When she was twenty-one, Hetty inherited almost $8 million and decided to take on Wall Street. Frugal by inclination but ready to risk capital when it came to investment, she plunged into the financial world at the time it was dominated by ruthless men like Cornelius Vanderbilt, Daniel Drew, and Jay Gould. Hetty proved to be as astute as any of them and proceeded to increase her already considerable fortune into one of the largest of the day.

At the same time, while in New York she ate her meals in Trinity Place greasy spoons where a slice of mutton, a slab of bread, and a mug of milk set the diner back fifteen cents. She moved from lodging to lodging with great frequency, as if afraid that someone might be stalking her. As for suitors, she suspected them of being more interested in her bank account than in her other assets.

That changed, however, when she met Edward Henry Green, handsome, self-assured, and—best of all—independently wealthy. Hetty and Edward were married in 1867, had two children,

Ned and Sylvia, and eventually made their primary home in Bellows Falls, Vermont, though Hetty returned to New York after her husband's death, continuing to live as frugally as ever.

ALAN "ACE" GREENBERG 1928–

Alan Greenberg, commonly called Ace, was born in Wichita, Kansas, and raised in Oklahoma City during the years when the Midwest was ravaged by the deprivations of the Great Depression and the tragic economic and social consequences of the Dust Bowl. He attended the University of Oklahoma on a football scholarship, later transferring to the University of Missouri, from which he graduated with a business degree. In 1949 Greenberg headed for Wall Street and was hired as a clerk by the investment banking firm Bear Stearns, receiving $32.50 a week in salary. He was soon given the chance to prove himself as a trader—an activity he relished—then, despite a life-threatening brush with cancer, rose quickly through the ranks, becoming the company's chief executive in 1978 and remaining in that post till 1993. From 1993 till 2001, he served as Bear Stearns's chairman. Known as one of the most astute executives on Wall Street, Greenberg piloted Bear Stearns through the tricky period that followed the abolition of fixed commissions on the New York Stock Exchange, and oversaw the company's 1985 IPO.

A passionate bridge player and amateur magician, Greenberg has long been recognized for his extensive charitable activities. While CEO at Bear Stearns, he instituted a policy requiring employees to donate 4 percent of their income to charity.

ALAN GREENSPAN 1926–

It may come as a surprise to some readers to learn that Alan Greenspan's first job after leaving college was as a jazz musician. Certainly, given his later reputation for circumspection, it is difficult to picture him as—if only briefly—a member of the bebop generation.

After earning an M.A. in economics Greenspan spent several years as a consultant, during which period he fell under the influence of Ayn Rand, absorbing the principles of her objectivist philosophy. During the 1970s he held several government posts under the Nixon and Ford administrations. In 1987 he was appointed chairman of the Federal Reserve, replacing Paul Volcker, who had established a solid reputation as a tough inflation fighter.

At first Wall Street was skeptical of Greenspan, and he was immediately put to the test by the Black Monday crash. Greenspan came through this crisis unscathed, demonstrating that he was capable of handling pressure without cracking, and he soon began to win the respect of the Street.

Leaving his objectivist-inspired laissez-faire principles behind, Greenspan took to intervening decisively in the marketplace, adjusting interest rates to control growth rates and curb inflationary trends. Any original doubts about his ability to manage the Fed were quickly dispelled, and a collective sigh of relief greeted his reappointment to the chairmanship by President Clinton.

Only in the late 1990s did Greenspan begin to encounter criticism again, chiefly from new-wave bulls who felt that the boom in technology stocks represented a kind of market so radically different from anything that had preceded it as to invalidate traditional analysis.

Within that context, it was thought that some of Greenspan's interventions were excessively conservative, placing a damper on market growth. Subsequent events, indicating an apparent return to a "normal" pattern of market cycles, silenced most of the grumbling.

SIR THOMAS GRESHAM 1518–79

Thomas Gresham was England's most important financier and merchant during the first two decades of Queen Elizabeth I's reign. Born into a well-to-do family of Londoners, Gresham attended Cambridge University and then studied law. Thanks to good connections he was sent by the government to the Netherlands and Flanders, where he engaged in diplomacy, smuggling, and espionage. His greatest and most useful skill, however, was his ability to negotiate currency exchange dealings.

In that period, the British crown often borrowed considerable sums of money from foreign bankers. When these bankers were repaid, with appropriate interest, the amounts involved could set off fluctuations in international exchange rates, usually to the lender's benefit. It was Gresham's job to minimize his government's disadvantage, a task to which he brought both economic and diplomatic finesse.

One problem he had to contend with was that Henry VIII had debased English currency. When Elizabeth succeeded to the throne, Gresham advised her to remove the debased coins from circulation and issue new ones. His reasoning was that if two coins of the same face value were available, but one contained a greater quantity of precious metal, then people would tend to hoard the specie with the greater gold or silver content. The way this principle came to be expressed was "bad money drives out good," and in time it came to be known as Gresham's law.

Gresham did not devote all of his time to serving the government and royal family. He also traded skillfully and aggressively on his own behalf, so that when he died he was the wealthiest commoner in England. Among his legacies to the people of his native city were the Royal Exchange, a gathering place for bankers and merchants, and Gresham College.

ALEXANDER HAMILTON 1755–1804

The first secretary of the Treasury of the United States, Hamilton was a champion of both centralized government and the idea of a central bank. He was born in the British West Indies on the island of Nevis, where he became apprenticed to New York merchants; this eventually led to his being sent to the American colonies on the eve of the Revolutionary War. He studied at King's College in New York (the future Columbia University), then displayed leadership and bravery during the war, becoming George Washington's aide-de-camp.

With the assistance of James Madison and John Jay, Hamilton wrote the Federalist Papers, arguing for the proposed Constitution, which he further defended at the ratifying convention in the summer of 1788. Appointed secretary of the Treasury in 1789, Hamilton continued to argue for the ascendancy of the central government over the states, and for the federal assumption of debts that had accrued to the states during the Revolution. He was able to get legislation passed regarding the retirement of these debts only at the cost of a famous compromise with Thomas Jefferson that led to the nation's capital being built on the banks of the Potomac, a site regarded as part of the South, for which Jefferson was the spokesman.

In his *Report on a National Bank*, submitted to Congress in 1790, Hamilton advocated the establishment of a central bank. In 1791 Congress did establish the Bank of the United States, but its charter was withdrawn twenty years later due to opposition from commercial and states' rights advocates. In 1791 Hamilton made another insightful presentation to Congress titled *Report on Manufactures*, in which he proposed ways to encourage American industry, using ideas based on the then-revolutionary proposals of the Scottish author and economist Adam Smith, whose *Wealth of Nations* had been published in 1776.

In 1804, Hamilton was killed during the course of a duel instigated by Aaron Burr.

EDWARD HENRY HARRIMAN
1848–1909 **and** JAMES HILL 1838–1916
The names E. H. Harriman (left) and Jim Hill (right) will always be linked in the annals of American business thanks to their titanic struggle over the control of the Northern Pacific Railroad, which led to a major financial crisis in 1901.

Harriman was a clergyman's son who became a broker's clerk and then a member of the New York Stock Exchange with a special interest in railroads. In 1898 he put together a syndicate that gained control of the Union Pacific Railroad. Having turned that company around, he did the same with the Southern Pacific and then shifted his attention to other prizes that brought him into conflict with Hill—the so-called Little Giant— a legendary, Canadian-born railroad man who controlled the Great Northern and the Northern Pacific.

Like Harriman's Union Pacific, these lines linked the Midwest with the West Coast, but neither man controlled a right of way that gave him access to Chicago, the key hub in any transcontinental service. Aiming to remedy this, both went after the Chicago, Burlington & Quincy Railroad Company, with Hill, aided by J. P. Morgan, winning the financial duel. Infuriated and bent on revenge, Harriman turned to Kuhn, Loeb's Jacob Schiff to assist him in implementing a plan to corner Northern Pacific stock.

Carefully timed, the plan was put into operation while Hill was in Seattle and his banker, Morgan, was in Europe. When he sensed what was happening from telegraphed stock reports, Hill ordered a special train to carry him to New York. By the time he got there, Harriman had come within an ace of accumulating enough Northern Pacific stock to take control. Morgan's underlings had been caught napping, but after a brief period of intensive scrambling, Hill just managed to hold on to his line. The hectic financial maneuverings— involving Morgan, Kuhn, Loeb, and Rockefeller interests—caught many investors off guard and caused a sizable market panic.

Ironically, Harriman and Hill, having fought to a virtual standoff, became allies. With Morgan serving as peacemaker, Harriman was given representation on the boards of both the Northern Pacific and the C.B.&Q., and Union Pacific trains were permitted trackage rights within Hill's empire.

JOHNS HOPKINS 1795–1873
Johns Hopkins was born to a Quaker family in Maryland, where his father was a tobacco farmer. When the family, as an act of conscience, emancipated its slaves, Hopkins—then age twelve—left school to help with the chores. In 1812 he moved to Baltimore to be apprenticed to an uncle in the grocery business. He was soon given much of the responsibility for running the enterprise but fell out with his uncle over the latter's refusal to allow farmers to barter whisky for provisions.

Hopkins then set up his own wholesale grocery concern, eventually bringing in three of his brothers as partners. Their business expanded throughout the Middle Atlantic states and into the Midwest. Not only did the brothers gladly accept whisky as payment, they also resold it as Hopkins' Best.

With the capital he had accumulated in the grocery business, Hopkins began to invest in real estate and in a variety of businesses including banks, insurance brokerages, shipping lines, and the Baltimore & Ohio Railroad, in which he became the largest private stockholder. Despite his involvement with advances in transportation, however, Hopkins never traveled far from his modest Baltimore home. Nor did he ever marry, but he did accumulate a large fortune and left much of it to endow an orphanage for black children and two major institutions, Johns Hopkins University and Johns Hopkins Medical Center.

THE HUNT FAMILY
Born in Ramsey, Illinois, H. Lamar Hunt (1889–1974) began his career rather inauspiciously, trading in cotton properties. In his early thirties, he used a borrowed stake to speculate in oil leases, which brought him enough money to invest in a 1930 East Texas oil strike that turned out to be one of the richest ever. That placed him in a position to make further oil investments, both in the United States and abroad. He expanded into other businesses as well—from publishing to health food—and by the 1950s was one of the wealthiest men in America.

An archconservative, Hunt used his fortune to fund a foundation called Facts Forum, which produced radio and television shows devoted to the defeat of Communism and a variety of extreme right-wing causes. Hunt was a major supporter of Senator Joseph McCarthy and of the House Un-American Activities Committee.

After he died, the businesses he had set up remained privately held. In 1980 two of his sons, Nelson Bunker Hunt (born 1926, right) and W. Herbert Hunt (born 1929, left), engaged in an extraordinary attempt to corner the world market in silver. In retrospect their move seems foolhardy, but it was undeniably bold and the consequences were devastating. On March 27 of that year, silver prices fell from $21.62 per ounce to $10.80 per ounce—a drop of more than 50 percent in a single day. (Just over two months earlier, the price had stood at $52.) Since almost everyone involved in silver, including the Hunts, had positions in the stock market too, Wall Street took a major hit, entering a precipitous slide that saw 16 percent eroded from the Dow Jones Industrial Average during the next two months.

The biggest losers were the Hunts. It has been estimated that the failure of their attempted corner cost the family two-thirds of its wealth, amounting to billions of dollars.

SAMUEL INSULL 1859–1938
One of the most conspicuous victims of the 1929 crash was Samuel Insull, who for two decades had been the monarch of Midwestern utilities companies. Born in England, Insull had begun his career in London as an assistant to one of Thomas Edison's agents there. Attracting the great man's attention, he moved to the United States and became Edison's private secretary. He was appointed

a vice president of the Edison General Electric Company and then, in 1892, moved on to become president of the Chicago Edison Company. By 1907 Insull had a monopoly on supplying power to the city of Chicago, which he systematically extended to much of Illinois and parts of surrounding states.

During the 1920s Insull's regional empire continued to expand, due largely to his cunning use of holding companies in which his family held large blocks of shares. The corporations gathered under the umbrellas of these holding companies were organized according to a pyramid system. A company at the base of the pyramid would be capitalized with 50 percent bonds, 20 percent preferred nonvoting stock, and 30 percent common voting stock. All the common voting stock was held by a company on the next level up in the pyramid, which was financed in exactly the same way, and so on. By holding the voting stock at the top of the pyramid, Insull was able to maintain control of all the companies below. For relatively little personal outlay, he would reap most of the profits, while a small surplus was used to pay just enough interest on the bonds and nonvoting stock to keep his investors happy.

It was a clever scheme but the structure was fragile. If there was a default on bonds at the base of the pyramid, the whole thing could come tumbling down.

At the height of the bull market that led up to the crash, Cyrus Eaton, a Cleveland investment banker, saw the vulnerability of Insull's empire and began to plan a hostile takeover bid. Insull responded by consolidating his five principal holding companies into two that now carried a considerable debt burden, which made them far less attractive as takeover targets. Then came the crash, and when stock prices plummeted Insull was stuck with the crippling debt, which now had to be met from the reduced revenues that hit utility companies during the Depression.

Worse was to come. Investigators for a Senate subcommittee came to the conclusion that, prior to the crash, Insull appeared to have played fast and loose with the way his holding companies had been financed. Rather than deal with prosecution, Insull fled to Europe, but returned to face the music two years later. Ironically, he was exonerated, but was never able to regain his previous pinnacle of power.

IWASAKI YATARO 1835–85
Iwasaki Yataro was born into a provincial samurai family. Known for their achievements as warriors, samurai were also often employed as administrators of feudal estates, and this was the case with Iwasaki, who became the business manager for a small fiefdom.

When, in 1868, the Meiji government abolished the feudal domains, Iwasaki was able to gain control of the fief's shipping concerns. In 1873 he named his company Mitsubishi Shokai. The business thrived, in large part because the government was encouraging the expansion of the Japanese shipbuilding industry and helped Iwasaki acquire a state-of-the-art shipyard in Nagasaki.

This became the beginning of the Mitsubishi *zaibatsu* ("financial coterie," approximately), one of the great family-owned, cartel-like Japanese combines with interests that ranged from banking to heavy industry.

JOSEPH P. KENNEDY 1888–1969
Long before he became known as the patriarch of one of America's greatest political dynasties, Joseph Kennedy was a man to be reckoned with on Wall Street. The grandson of an Irish immigrant, Kennedy graduated from Harvard,

married the daughter of a Boston mayor, and launched a business career that saw him president of a bank by the age of twenty-five.

After World War I he took over the stock operations of Hayden, Stone & Co., a merchant banking concern, where he acquired the skills necessary to play the market with the big boys. In 1925 he set up business on his own. During the next five years, as the market climbed to what were then considered dizzying heights, he made a considerable fortune, indulging in all the speculative practices of the day. Like a few others—Bernard Baruch and Charles Merrill, for example—he had the prescience to bail out before the crash and thus kept the bulk of his capital intact. (Legend has it that Kennedy decided to sell when a boot-black told him to buy. "If I start taking the advice of a bootblack," he reasoned, "I'm in trouble.")

Kennedy then had a fling with the movies, becoming head of RKO. Later he became top man at the Securities and Exchange Commission (1934–37), with a mandate from President Roosevelt to clean up Wall Street's speculative excesses—presumably on the assumption that he was familiar with these from the inside. He later served as ambassador to Great Britain (1937–40), resigning because he found himself at odds with the president over the probable outcome of the struggle between Britain and Nazi Germany. He devoted much of the rest of his life to promoting his sons' political careers.

JOHN MAYNARD KEYNES 1883–1946
John Maynard Keynes has been called the key economist of the twentieth century, and certainly he was among the most influential. The son of a Cambridge University scholar and administrator, he excelled academically at Eton and King's College, Cambridge. During his undergraduate years, he fell under the influence of Alfred Marshall, an authority on the inner workings of corporations and competitive markets, and also came into contact with young intellectuals like Duncan Grant and Lytton Strachey, who drew him into the circle that became known as the Bloomsbury Group.

After Cambridge, Keynes became a civil servant attached to the India Office, a position that enabled him to produce a highly regarded study of Indian finance and currency. He then taught at Cambridge before being engaged, during World War I, by the British Treasury, which he advised on such matters as foreign exchange. At the time of the Versailles Peace Conference, he was called upon to counsel the British prime minister, Lloyd George, but resigned because he came to believe that the terms of restitution being imposed upon the defeated Germans were preposterous and could only result in ruin.

It was his treatise *The Economic Consequences of the Peace* (1919) that brought Keynes to the attention of the general public, the text being notable both for its economic cogency and for the vitriolic portraits of Lloyd George, Woodrow Wilson, and other world leaders that gave life to the author's arguments. In the following decade he returned to Cambridge and, in a characteristic burst of iconoclasm, debunked the return to the gold standard being proposed by then Chancellor of the Exchequer Winston Churchill.

In 1935–36 Keynes produced the work that would ensure his place in history. This was *The General Theory of Employment, Interest, and Money*, which attacked conventional ideas about the causes of unemployment and suggested that in extreme circumstances, such as a great depression, government intervention in the form of subsidies and public work programs was not only justified but necessary. Quickly accepted by most economists, Keynes's theories were soon being put into practice by governments around the globe, as World War II and the postwar period provided ample opportunities to test its validity. By the late 1960s, even once skeptical politicians were taking Keynes's principles for granted.

Keynes himself was a liberal with strong socialist sympathies. A regular contributor to leftist publications such as *The New Statesman*, he nonetheless had no qualms about putting his economic knowledge to work through investment in the stock market. And if he was not wealthy by the standards of the great speculators, he became, to employ a British understatement, comfortably well off.

IVAR KREUGER 1880–1932
Ivar Kreuger's life began ordinarily enough, then became increasingly baroque before ending in tragedy. Born in Kalmar, Sweden, he studied engineering in Stockholm and, upon graduation, spent several years as a civil engineer in South Africa and the United States. Back in Sweden he launched a company that produced safety matches. World War I gave him the opportunity to gain control of virtually the entire Swedish match industry, and after the war he conceived a scheme to extend his monopoly to as much of the world as possible.

At this time many countries were short of foreign currency, especially dollars. Kreuger employed borrowed capital, most of it from American investors, to make long-term loans to governments in exchange for exclusive rights to the local production of matches. At the onset of the Depression the companies belonging to his trust manufactured half of the world's matches.

After the 1929 crash, however, capital for expansion was hard to come by. Kreuger was already greatly overextended and his empire began to fall apart. In 1932 he shot himself. After his death it became apparent that he had been covering up a variety of fraudulent practices, habitually reporting profits that were in fact nonexistent.

ROBERT KUOK 1923–

Robert Kuok grew up in Malaysia, where his father had settled before World War I. He became a commodities trader, and by the 1970s was one of the world's largest sugar merchants. Now based in Hong Kong, Kuok has moved into other fields, entering into partnership with Coca-Cola in its expansion into mainland China and building Beijing's World Trade Center.

Often described as a man of mystery, Robert Kuok has parlayed a shrewd business instinct and complete fearlessness into a successful career that has spanned continents and industries. Ethnically Chinese, raised in Malaysia, and currently based in Hong Kong, Kuok attended a Chinese school until he went to Singapore at age eighteen to study English, history, and economics at Raffles College, part of the National University of Singapore. The plan was quickly interrupted by the Japanese bombing of Singapore and declaration of war late in 1941, at which point Kuok returned to Johor Baharu to work in the local office of the Japanese trading company Mitsubishi Corporation.

Kuok first achieved large-scale success as Malaysia's "Sugar King" in the 1950s and 1960s, simultaneously cornering the markets for flour and palm oil. Unsatisfied with the fortune he amassed in the process, Kuok continued to expand into commodities trading, hotels, financial services, and other industries, acquiring

Rupert Murdoch's *South China Morning Post* and becoming Coca-Cola's Chinese bottling partner along the way, creating the multibillion-dollar empire he oversees today.

Throughout his career Kuok has had a reputation for acting on instinct, making bold moves, and maintaining unpopular positions—strategies that have almost uniformly paid off. An important element of his business style, seen among other successful *huaqiao* (Southeast Asia's overseas Chinese) and perhaps springing from his experiences as an ethnic minority, is keeping his empire closed to all but those he trusts the most, usually members of his large family. Equally well-known is his management style, dubbed "Confucian": perhaps a bit opaque, but always achieving results. By spreading his ventures across several countries and diversifying industries, Kuok has offset long-term risk and managed to maintain a relatively stable financial position despite Asia's uncertain economy of the past several years.

Kuok's name appears frequently in the international business press, yet little is known about him other than what is demonstrated by his actions. Legend has it that several years ago an international investigative agency nosed around the Kuok empire and revealed the following in its final report: Name: Robert Kuok; Political Affiliation: unknown; Adversaries: none identified; Litigation: nothing known; Ambitions: not known.

JOHN LAW 1671–1729

Remembered as the man behind the Mississippi Bubble, John Law was part serious economic theorist and part speculator on the grandest of grand scales. His contemporaries—especially those who lost money due to his schemes— ended up seeing him as a villain. From a present-day perspective, it's possible to view his career with a certain amount

of sympathy, not to mention awe.

Scottish by birth, Law found himself in trouble early in life when he killed a man in a duel. He took refuge in Amsterdam, where he learned a good deal about the financial world. Back in Scotland he wrote *Money and Trade Considered, with a Proposal for Supplying the Nation with Money* (1705).

Stated in its simplest form, Law's theory was that public debt could be reduced by putting more money into circulation. Since a nation's holdings of gold and silver were finite, this would entail circulating banknotes that were not backed by precious metals. In Law's estimation, these should be issued by a central bank.

The Scottish Parliament had no interest in his plan, but in 1716 he was given permission to try it out in France, where the treasury was heavily in debt because of recent military adventures. With sublime chutzpah, Law not only founded the quasi-governmental Banque Générale, with the authority to issue paper money, but also managed to tie that bank to the Compagnie des Indes—which he also headed—a highly speculative enterprise intended to exploit France's colonies in North America. The national debt was to be paid off from investments in these companies. Meanwhile, Law also took over tax collection throughout France and assumed control of the French mint.

For a couple of years, John Law was the sole keeper of the French economy. Then it became apparent that the Compagnie des Indes was not generating anything like the returns that had been anticipated, and the whole scheme began to unravel. Many investors, in France and elsewhere, were ruined and Law was forced to flee the country, dying in Venice several years later.

In retrospect it is difficult to think of him as a criminal. Rather, he was a flawed visionary whose chief failing was his inability to recognize his own limitations.

NICHOLAS LEESON 1967–

Pedigree may still count for something in the financial world, but it is no guarantee against disaster. This was demonstrated in 1995 when Barings PLC, Britain's most venerable merchant bank, with roots going back to the days when stocks were traded in the coffeehouses of 'Change Alley, was forced into receivership by the actions of one employee.

There was nothing outstanding about Nicholas Leeson except perhaps that he lacked the upper-class background that would have been essential for advancement at Barings a generation earlier. He was talented enough to be appointed, at age twenty-seven, to a responsible post in the derivatives division of the company's Singapore office. There he managed to accumulate losses in excess of $1 billion in the Asian futures markets. Barings officials later claimed that Leeson had been trading without authority and hiding his losses in a secret account. Singapore investigators came to a different conclusion, believing that Leeson's employers had actually encouraged him in the naïve belief that he was generating large profits.

Whatever the truth, Leeson panicked and skipped town, finally surfacing weeks later in Frankfurt, on a plane about to leave for London. He was arrested and extradited to England, where he was sentenced to a six-year prison term on reduced charges.

Barings (which was subsequently acquired by a Dutch banking group) had been especially vulnerable because of its relatively small size, and perhaps because of its overeagerness for quick profits. Just seven months after the story broke, it became apparent that much larger and more conservative institutions were subject to similar problems when it was revealed that Toshihide Iguchi, a New York–based bond trader for the Daiwa Bank, one of Japan's financial giants, had managed to conceal more than a billion dollars' worth of losses accumulated over more than a decade.

FERDINAND, VICOMTE DE LESSEPS 1805–94

Ferdinand de Lesseps was responsible for one of the great speculative triumphs of the nineteenth century, as well as one of its great speculative failures. Born into a politically well-connected family, he entered the French diplomatic service in 1825. One of his postings was to Alexandria, Egypt, and it was there, in 1832, that he had the opportunity to study a plan, drawn up by one of Napoleon's engineers, to connect the Mediterranean with the Gulf of Suez and the Red Sea by means of a canal cut through the Isthmus of Suez.

Although fascinated by this scheme, Lesseps was in no position to do anything about it at the time. Instead, he pursued his diplomatic career with growing success until, in 1849, he was dispatched to Rome to deal with a difficult situation. The patriot and revolutionist Giuseppe Mazzini had declared Italy a republic and the pope had been forced to flee the Vatican. Lesseps attempted to mediate between the church and the republicans, but it was a hopeless task. He was recalled to France and censured for his efforts, which effectively brought his time as a diplomat to a premature end.

In 1854, however, an old friend, Sa'id Pasha, now viceroy of Egypt, sent for Lesseps with the idea of having him carry out the scheme to create a canal through the Isthmus of Suez. Plans were drawn up and in 1858 Lesseps opened the subscription lists for his Compagnie Universelle du Canal Maritime de Suez. The company was to be capitalized to the tune of 200 million francs in 400,000 shares of 500 francs each. Most of the world looked on, but Lesseps had succeeded in arousing the enthusiasm of the French people and also the citizens of the Ottoman Empire. Well over three-quarters of the shares were spoken for in less than a month and work on the canal was begun the following year.

In 1879 the success of the Suez Canal led the International Congress of Geographical Sciences to turn to Lesseps to carry out the construction of the proposed Panama Canal. Lesseps was now in his mid-seventies, and this time he bit off more than he could chew. Tropical diseases and the topography of Panama defeated him, and the company that had been enthusiastically subscribed to was forced to liquidate in humiliating circumstances. Worse, an inquiry by the French government came to the conclusion that bribes had been offered to political figures and others in positions of power. Lesseps and his son Charles were both sentenced to jail, though only Charles served time; in a matter of weeks an appeals court overturned the original verdict.

GUS LEVY 1910–76

Gustave Levy, born in New Orleans and educated at Tulane University, took his first job on Wall Street in 1928 and went on to become a partner at Goldman Sachs in 1946.

In the early 1970s, informed market observers began to take note of an innovative trading philosophy that had become the specialty of a subspecies of Wall Street fauna recently graced with the sobriquet "institutional investor." There was nothing novel about companies investing on the behalf of institutional clients, such as pension funds or college endowments, but the approach of money managers in these areas had tended till then to be somewhat conservative. What was different about the new institutional investors was that they were far more aggressive about making money for their clients. The advent of negotiated commissions (which began in 1971 for trades involving more than $500,000) rendered it practical for fund investors and the like to begin trading in huge units of stock—ten thousand shares or more—a practice that came to be called "block trading."

Names associated with this kind of activity included Tubby Burnham, Bob and Don Stott, Sy Lewis, and Bunny Lasker. The originator among these pioneers, however, is generally conceded to have been Gus Levy. Not only did Levy help introduce block trading—a key feature of major stock markets ever since— he is also credited with inventing the concept of risk arbitrage, a chancy but potentially profitable strategy that involves buying up large blocks of stock in a company rumored to be on the verge of traumatic change (targeted for takeover, for example). In the 1980s Goldman Sachs was able to capitalize on the arbitrage expertise Levy had brought to the company to counter the ambitions of the junk bond-fueled leveraged-buyout raiders of the period.

Gus Levy is also remembered for coining the phrase "long-term greedy," perhaps foreshadowing fellow risk arbitrager Ivan Boesky's infamous dictum some years later that greed is all right. It is polite to assume that by "long-term

greedy" Levy was proposing that it's appropriate to accumulate money slowly and judiciously. At least one former associate, however, has suggested that by "long-term" Levy meant "this afternoon rather than this morning."

LIEM SIOE LIONG 1917–

Indonesian tycoon Liem Sioe Liong enjoyed the friendship of a very powerful man: former president Suharto. A business connection established when Suharto was a young army lieutenant colonel and Liem was an obscure merchant grew to benefit both of them, aiding Suharto's consolidation of power and Liem's rise to become one of Indonesia's richest citizens.

Born into a poor family in the Fujinan province in China, Liem received no more than a junior high school education before his family fled from Communist rule to Indonesia in 1937. Liem was selling cloves, peanuts, and bicycle parts in central Java when he began, in the 1950s, supplying the military base run by Suharto. In 1952 Liem moved to Jakarta to set up what later became Bank Central Asia, but the two men maintained their relationship over the succeeding years. When Suharto forced out President Sukarno in 1966, Liem was one of the chosen few in Suharto's mission to expand the Indonesian economy. Aided by government monopoly licenses, Liem soon dominated entire industries—cloves, coffee, rubber, sugar, wheat, flour, noodles, and so on. His mutually beneficial relationship with Suharto meant that when the president wanted Indonesia to expand into certain industries, Liem complied; in exchange, favors were granted that helped make Liem's Salim Group one of the biggest conglomerates in Asia. By the early 1990s the Salim Group accounted for 5 percent of Indonesia's economic output. In 1992 Liem's son Anthony Salim became CEO and president of the company,

allowing Liem to retire from the limelight yet still maintain sizable influence in the firm.

Liem's relationship with Suharto turned into a liability when the latter was ousted from the presidency. Marked by both his economic success and ethnic Chinese background, Liem was a prime target for the violence that ravaged Indonesia in 1998. Liem's opulent house was burned to the ground by rioters, and withdrawals from his Bank Central Asia forced a $3 billion government bailout.

LI KA-SHING 1928–

Li Ka-shing is Hong Kong's most celebrated businessman and a classic example of the ethnic Chinese family tycoon.

Li began his ascent to power in the 1950s by selling plastic flowers, using the earnings he was able to save from this modest enterprise to invest in real estate and a variety of other fields, eventually gaining control of publicly traded companies worth 10 percent of the total value of the Hong Kong stock market. By 1979 he was in a position to purchase Hutchison Whampoa, a British trading house that had been a major symbol of colonial power in Hong Kong, and in 1987 took over another British institution, Hongkong Land, the real estate division of Jardine Matheson. It is rumored that Li was able to put together the multibillion-dollar deal for this takeover at a single overnight session with his wealthy mah-jongg-playing cronies.

Ties of family and friendship are still crucial in the Asian business world. Li Ka-shing's sons, Victor and Richard, both educated in America, have been brought into the company. Richard had a considerable coup in 1993 when the Star-TV satellite network he had launched for his father's company was sold to Rupert Murdoch for a reported profit of $425 million.

JACOB LITTLE 1796–1865

Starting his career in the days when deals were consummated at Tontine's Coffee House, Jacob Little was one of the first Wall Street masters of stock manipulation. By the standards of the day he was not actually dishonest, but he quickly learned to take advantage of all the then current tricks of the trade, while sometimes also profiting from the kind of inside information that today might put a speculator behind bars. He was the pioneer of the slyly orchestrated short sale, a technique that involved selling shares he didn't yet own for delivery at some future date at a fixed price. He would then set about depressing the market value of those shares by spreading rumors about the sorry state of the company that had issued them so that he could snap up the quantity needed at a bargain rate, thus making a profit on his original contract.

By the mid-1830s Little held significant positions in a number of enterprises, and rising stock values enabled him to lead pools intent on gaining control of major companies. His biggest single triumph came when he gained a corner on a market in Morris Canal & Banking stock, forcing its price up from $10 to $185 in a matter of weeks.

Having earned the sobriquet "the Great Bear of Wall Street," Little went on to other adventures but was ruined during the "western blizzard" panic of 1857. He ended his life bankrupt, dependent on the financial support of David Groesbeck, a prominent broker of the post–Civil War period who had been a Little protégé.

JESSE LIVERMORE 1877–1940

Dubbed the King of Speculators, Jesse Livermore operated with such a lack of flamboyance that his face was hardly known outside the financial community. Even within the Wall Street world he was almost invisible, sometimes working out of a secret office connected to the floor of the NYSE by telephone. Yet the influence of his market strategies was felt everywhere.

Before becoming a member of the exchange, Livermore had run a bucket shop—an unlicensed brokerage—which gave him the opportunity to study the way the market could be manipulated, both aboveboard and below. A bear by instinct, he went short during the panic of 1907, making a substantial profit. During World War I he turned bullish, but, anticipating the postwar depression, he liquidated his stock holdings at the height of the market, went short again, and garnered a fortune.

During the bull market of the 1920s he became bullish once more. Some historians date the beginning of that notorious bull market from Livermore's 1923 intervention in a feud between Clarence Saunders, president of the Piggly-Wiggly supermarket chain, and a bear pool that was trying to force down Piggly-Wiggly's stock price. Saunders asked Livermore to head a rival bull pool to push the stock up. Livermore succeeded so brilliantly that the governors of the NYSE illegally suspended trading in the stock, precipitating a scandal.

Later in the 1920s, Livermore's fame was increased by a notorious series of stock duels in which he was pitted against Arthur W. Cutten. Cutten was a former grain speculator who brought his skills to Wall Street just as Livermore took temporary leave of the NYSE in favor of

commodity trading, at which he excelled. By 1926 both men were operating in the Wall Street arena, where it became understood that if one was bullish on a stock, the other would be bearish, and each would be working assiduously behind the scenes to manipulate that stock in any way he thought he could get away with. When word of one of these duels got out, lesser speculators would hurry to take sides.

Like Bernard Baruch and Joseph Kennedy, Livermore belonged to the last generation of speculators that was able to take outrageous advantage of the lack of supervision existing in the markets prior to the 1929 crash. His curious career ended in suicide.

SAMUEL JONES LOYD, FIRST BARON OVERSTONE 1796–1883

The future Lord Overstone was the son of a Welsh nonconformist minister. Displaying considerable precocity, he became a Liberal member of Parliament by the time he was twenty-three years old and was a founding partner of Jones Loyd & Company, a privately held banking concern that later was incorporated as the London and Westminster Bank.

Raised to the peerage in 1850, Overstone was recognized as one of the mid–nineteenth century's great authorities on banking and banking law. He made many appearances before committees of the House of Commons, during which he presented his opinions on sound banking policy. The evidence he gave was considered so important that it was published and remains in print today. Overstone is generally held to have been the chief architect of the Bank Charter Act of 1844.

PETER LYNCH 1944–

Peter Lynch has a very simple claim to fame. In the thirteen years he spent as portfolio manager of Fidelity Investments' Magellan Fund, he established a record that led others in the industry to call him the most successful stock picker of his generation.

Lynch grew up in Massachusetts and became interested in the stock market because, while caddying at a local golf club, he would hear members chatting about share prices. While at Boston College he did research in the air freight industry, made an investment in a company called Flying Tiger, and had his first ten bagger (to use his own terminology, borrowed from baseball, meaning his investment increased tenfold in value).

After doing graduate work at the Wharton School, Lynch began working at Fidelity in the late 1960s, having caddied for its president for several years. In 1977 he was placed in charge of the Magellan Fund, which then had $20 million in assets. He retired in 1990, after building Magellan into an investment fund with more than one million shareholders and assets exceeding $14 billion. Under Lynch's stewardship, Magellan had generated an astonishing average annual return of almost 30 percent.

Since his retirement from Magellan, Lynch has remained a considerable presence through best-selling books such as *Beating the Street*, regular articles for *Worth* magazine, and frequent appearances on radio and television.

HARRY MARKOWITZ 1927–

Described by his colleagues at Baruch College as bookish and possessed with an intellectual fervor, Harry Markowitz transformed his lifelong intellectual curiosity into a career in economics crowned by the Nobel Prize.

Markowitz was born and raised in Chicago, an only child whose parents owned a modest grocery store. During his tenure as a student at the University of Chicago, where he earned his bachelor's and Ph.D. degrees, Markowitz was a member of the Cowles Commission for Research in Economics. It was at Chicago that he began to investigate the need to account for risk—the beta factor—in stock market investing. The theory Markowitz first presented in a 1952 article, "Portfolio Selection," and developed throughout his career became modern portfolio theory and laid the foundation for investment diversification as it is now practiced.

Markowitz spent much of the 1950s and 1960s at the RAND Corporation, and subsequently as an I.B.M. researcher and a consultant to the Japanese investment house Daiwa Securities. In these years he worked primarily on two areas of research besides portfolio theory: sparse matrix techniques and the SIMSCRIPT programming language that is used to write economic analysis programs. For these three areas of research, he received the John von Neumann Prize in Operations Research Theory in 1989. The following year he shared with William Sharpe and Morton Miller the 1990 Nobel Memorial Prize in Economic Science.

ROBERT MAXWELL 1923–91

Former employees of Robert Maxwell's various publishing and media enterprises report that he had a talent for posing as one of the lads, joining reporters and photographers in Fleet Street pubs for a pint of wallop. In reality, he was anything but the boy next door.

Born in Czechoslovakia, his original name was Jan Ludvick Hoch. In 1939, on the eve of the Holocaust, he escaped from Budapest and joined the British army, where he earned a commission and was awarded the Military Cross for conspicuous bravery.

After the war Maxwell established Pergamon Press, which soon became Britain's premier scientific publishing house. In 1964 he was elected to the House of Commons as a Labour member of Parliament. In the early 1980s he took over the troubled British Printing Corporation, which became the Maxwell Communications Corporation. In 1984 Maxwell became chairman of Mirror Group Newspapers—one of Britain's largest publishing concerns—and over the next half-dozen years built up a vast media empire that included broadcasting and movie as well as publishing interests and gave him a presence on several continents.

The problem was that very few of his properties managed to generate much in the way of profits. By 1991 Maxwell was attempting to divest himself of some of his less auspicious acquisitions, and later that year he mysteriously disappeared from his yacht off the Canary Islands. His body was found some days later but the circumstances of his death remain a mystery.

It transpired that Maxwell's businesses were approximately $720 million in the red, and an investigation concluded that he had indulged in embezzlement on a grand scale. Those employees who had once enjoyed a beer with their boss discovered that he had been picking up the tab with the aid of cash misappropriated from their pension fund.

EDWARD T. McCORMICK 1911–91

In 1951 the old New York Curb Exchange hired Edward McCormick, formerly with the Securities and Exchange Commission, to be its president.

A CPA with a doctorate in economics, McCormick was both well qualified and well liked in the financial community and seemed an ideal choice to improve the image of the exchange, which had become somewhat tarnished.

McCormick quickly displayed a knack for promotion, lobbying to have the venerable institution's name changed to the American Stock Exchange, which came with the sexy AMEX acronym. He was also determined to increase the number of stocks listed, and here he was less rigorous that he might have been, allowing in some companies that should perhaps have been excluded. Worse still, McCormick appears to have turned a blind eye to illegal trading practices by exchange members, some of whom were brought to trial. When an SEC investigation implicated him in the scandal, McCormick resigned in disgrace, though he continued to protest that he had not known of any criminal activities. He could not claim ignorance of the law, however. Not only had he served as an SEC commissioner, he had even written a book entitled *Understanding the Securities Act and the SEC.*

THE MEDICI FAMILY

The Medici family constituted the greatest of all Italian banking dynasties at a time when Italian banking was a dominant force in the evolution of European society. Its members virtually ruled the city of Florence for nearly four centuries, during which time the Medici produced two queens of France and four popes.

All this from a family that had barely escaped its peasant roots when, in 1397, Giovanni di Bicci de' Medici founded the bank that bore his name. It thrived for close to a hundred years, establishing branches in many European cities, collecting tithes for the Vatican, and financing the wars and grand estates of kings and princes from England to Austria. Along with other Italian bankers, such

as the Bardi and Peruzzi, the Medici employed many of the methods of modern banking, from double-entry bookkeeping to the use of bills of exchange to facilitate the transfer of funds from one country to another. In the manner of the era, they also used the money deposited with their scattered branches to engage in various forms of merchant adventuring, often related to the cloth trade, the business in which the family had grown wealthy before entering the banking field.

The two most outstanding members of the family were Cosimo the Elder (1389–1464) and Lorenzo the Magnificent (1449–92), both of whom were major political figures, distinguished scholars, and patrons of the arts on a scale that has rarely if ever been matched.

HARSHAD MEHTA 1955–

In 1978 Harshad Mehta wrote an article predicting that India would be transformed over the next twenty-five years as it evolved toward a modern market-driven economy. A large and imposing man popularly known as Big Bull, Mehta acted on his vision with a boldness that shocked many people in the rather staid Indian financial world, which was then dominated by a distinctly Anglophile banking community.

As an entrepreneurial investor Mehta had an unparalleled record in the 1980s, a period during which Rajiv Gandhi's administration did much to liberalize the Indian economy, especially the operation of the stock markets. Some observers, however, did not care for Mehta's methods, suggesting that he was manipulating stock in much the way that American rogue speculators had done back in the bad old days prior to strict supervision and regulation. In short, he was accused of behaving like someone who was determined to get his hands on a ton of money no matter whom he had to push out of the way to grab it.

In 1992 Mehta and some of his associates were accused of perpetrating a securities scam involving millions of rupees. The case dragged on for seven years, during which time Mehta, through his Damayanti Group, attempted to make several comebacks, engaging, according to his accusers, in further rounds of irregularities. Despite his problems, Mehta remained for many people a symbol of the New India and continued to have ardent admirers, some of whom believed he was the victim of powerful and jealous enemies in establishment circles.

In September 1999 the Mumbai (Bombay) High Court sentenced Mehta and three others to five years in jail for criminal conspiracy to engage in securities fraud. Mehta took the case to India's Supreme Court and his sentence was suspended pending appeal.

ANDREW W. MELLON 1855–1937

The son of a Pittsburgh banker, Andrew Mellon entered the family business when he graduated from college, and by 1882 had become head of the concern. Pittsburgh was a hotbed of technological innovation—the Silicon Valley of the late Victorian era—and Mellon displayed a knack for investing in companies that were at the cutting edge. He was, for example, instrumental in the foundation of the Aluminum Company of America (Alcoa) and Gulf Oil, and he was William Clay Frick's partner in the creation of the Union Steel Company, which was later absorbed into the United States Steel Corporation. By the end of World War I Mellon had accumulated one of America's great fortunes.

At that point Mellon turned to public life. In 1921 President Warren Harding appointed him to head the U.S. Treasury, a post he held until 1932. During World War I federal taxation had been increased to unprecedented levels. There were those who believed these levels should be maintained in order to reduce the national debt, but Mellon thought otherwise, and in his tenure at the Treasury taxes were reduced to stimulate investment. To a considerable extent, then, Mellon was responsible for creating the climate that encouraged the bull market of the 1920s. He was still at the Treasury when the market crashed; justly or not, he absorbed a good deal of the blame for the events of 1929 and the Great Depression that followed.

Like his sometime partner Frick, Mellon was one of the great art collectors of his generation. His donations were in large part responsible for the establishment of the National Gallery of Art in Washington, D.C.

KARL MENGER 1840–1921, FRIEDRICH VON WIESER 1851–1926, and EUGEN VON BÖHM-BAWERK 1851–1914

These three men were the founders of the influential Austrian school of economics. Menger, the eldest, was the first to come to prominence through his 1871 book *Principles of Economics*. In that treatise he sought to throw light on the intertwined relationships among utility, value, and price, which he saw as having strong subjective elements.

Von Wieser and von Böhm-Bawerk (the latter Austria's minister of finance from 1889 to 1904) built on Menger's thought, and their joint achievements were an important influence on the evolution of what is sometimes called the classic theory of economics, which held that economic trends were to a large degree governed by internal checks and controls. This had significant implications for bankers, investors, and businessmen of all kinds, since it suggested that the marketplace was best left

to its own devices and would not benefit from governmental interference.

It was this viewpoint that was called into question by John Maynard Keynes.

CHARLES MERRILL 1885–1956

Destined to change the entire character of the stock market, Charles Merrill was born in Florida and forced to drop out of college for lack of funds. He made his way to New York and found employment in the investment banking world, where he quickly established his reputation by recognizing the emerging importance of chain stores. On the eve of World War I, he made his first fortune by underwriting S. S. Kresge (the future Kmart) and Safeway supermarkets.

Merrill was far from unique in thriving during the bull market of the 1920s. He was, however, one of a small group of major Wall Street players, including Bernard Baruch and Joseph P. Kennedy, who saw that the bubble was likely to burst and acted accordingly, liquidating his company's entire stock portfolio months before the 1929 crash.

The idea that would make Charles Merrill a key figure in the financial world of his generation was simple but revolutionary. He believed that the future of the stock market lay in opening up the world of investment to the millions of middle-class Americans who had, till then, thought that investment was for the rich. Conventional wisdom warned that this was precisely what had happened in the 1920s, with disastrous results. Merrill did not accept this point of view. Small investors had suffered in the 1920s, he believed, because they had been misled and exploited by an irresponsible brokerage industry.

What Merrill had in mind was something completely different. Through the Teletype machine and the telephone, he would bring Wall Street to Main Street, setting up a web of "wire houses" that could provide small investors with the kind of in-depth research tools that were taken for granted by the big-time professionals.

By the time of his death, he had succeeded to the extent that Merrill Lynch had more than 400,000 clients and was the largest brokerage house in the world. Still, he was disappointed that Wall Street as a whole had not followed his example. Had he lived just a few years more, he would have been delighted to see the growth of the mutual fund specialists and discount brokerages that were reshaping the investment world along the lines he had envisioned.

MICHAEL MILKEN 1946–

If you had spotted him in an airport departure lounge during his 1980s heyday, you might have taken Michael Milken for a middle-management type from the Midwest. Call him on the phone—he generally picked up himself—and he would regale you with the kind of cookie-cutter sales slogans you would expect to hear from a mutual funds salesman in some suburban branch office. While his contemporaries were busy embarrassing themselves at this month's A-list disco, meeting the opening bell on Wall Street with hangovers as big as the national debt, Milken eschewed the pleasures of the flesh and avoided the media. He didn't need publicity or hype; he was the King of Junk Bonds.

There are many who still believe that Michael Milken was a financial genius, and for a while, at least, that seemed to be the case. As head of Drexel Burnham Lambert's high-yield bond department, he revolutionized the use of junk bonds as leverage for corporate takeovers. Junk bonds offer high returns but traditionally have been considered risky—sub-investment grade—even when issued by well-established companies. It was Milken's premise that the risk involved was greatly exaggerated. He encouraged his clients to use junk bonds to help finance a number of major takeovers, with targets including companies like Metromedia and the food giant Beatrice.

At his peak, Milken was taking home half a billion dollars a year. Once he had shown the way, however, other people could and did put junk bonds to the same use. At this point, it seems, Milken turned to illegal activities as a way of restoring Drexel's fortunes. His fate was jail time, a record fine, and a lifetime ban from the securities markets.

JEAN MONNET 1888–1979

More than any other single person, Jean Monnet was responsible for the creation of the European Union. Born into a family that produced brandy in the Cognac region, he chose a career in public service and after World War I became deputy secretary general of the League of Nations. In 1925 he entered the financial world as European partner of a New York merchant banking concern, thus gaining practical knowledge of international finance.

At the outset of World War II, Monnet worked with the British on planning economic coordination in the struggle against Hitler. After the fall of France he was able to make his way to the United States, remaining there until

1943, when he was posted to Algiers as a senior member of the "Free France" administration.

Following the war, Monnet was placed in charge of the committee appointed to develop a plan to put French industry and commerce back on a peacetime footing. His ideas for modernization were well received and he was asked to supervise their implementation. This in turn led to a proposal—made by Monnet and French foreign minister Robert Schuman—to form a European Coal and Steel Community in order to place the production of these commodities on a more rational basis. This came into being in 1952, with France, West Germany, Belgium, the Netherlands, Luxembourg, and Italy as signatories to the pact and Monnet as first president of the organization. It was due in large part to the success of the European Coal and Steel Community idea that the European Common Market was launched in 1957.

Monnet continued to fight for a unified Europe for the rest of his life, serving from 1956 to 1975 as president of the Action Committee for the United States of Europe.

JOHN PIERPOINT MORGAN 1837–1913

The most celebrated of all American bankers, J. P. Morgan was a towering presence on the financial scene on both sides of the Atlantic from the 1880s until his death in 1913.

Morgan's father, Junius Spencer Morgan, was himself a formidable figure who came to prominence as the partner of George Peabody, an American financier who had established himself in London just as American capital

was beginning to play a significant role in European markets. When Peabody retired, Peabody & Co. became J. S. Morgan & Co.

In New York the younger Morgan became a partner in Drexel, Morgan & Company, acting as the American representative of his father's bank. In the 1880s he began to make a name for himself by becoming involved in the takeover and restructuring of railroads—a popular activity of the era—and by the turn of the century he controlled close to five thousand miles of rights of way.

In 1893, under J. P. Morgan's guidance, Drexel, Morgan bailed out the U.S. government by putting together a syndicate that restored credibility to the nation's gold reserves. Two years later the company was reconstituted as J. P. Morgan & Co. Soon after, Morgan underwrote the Federal Steel Company, which he subsequently merged with Carnegie Steel and other producers to create U.S. Steel, the first company to have billion-dollar capitalization. He was already responsible for the mergers that had led to the creation of General Electric, and in 1902 he oversaw the combining of several large agricultural equipment manufacturers to create International Harvester.

During the last fifteen years of his life, Morgan headed an informal syndicate of large banks that acted on occasion almost as a government-sponsored central bank, providing a reserve of liquidity that could be called upon in crisis situations such as the Panic of 1907. This did not protect Morgan and his allies from the scrutiny of trust-busting politicians, who were disturbed to find a small group of commercially interconnected people monopolizing the boards of the nation's top financial houses. Not long before the end of his life, Morgan was called upon to testify before Congress's Pujo Committee, which was investigating the possible existence of an illegal banking cartel. He and his colleagues emerged unscathed, but these hearings marked the beginning of the end of an era in which powerful bankers could ride roughshod across the financial landscape.

Morgan's son, J. P. Morgan Jr., usually called Jack, was a prominent figure in the banking world during the 1920s and 1930s.

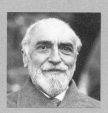

MONTAGU COLLET NORMAN, FIRST BARON NORMAN of ST. CLERE 1871–1950

Montagu Norman was governor of the Bank of England from 1920 to 1944, giving him control of England's central bank for an unprecedented length of time. He was in fact one of the great advocates of the idea of central banking, famously defining the role of such an institution as attempting to be "at all times in . . . as complete harmony as possible [with the government]." He added, however, that it was the bank's "unique right to offer advice and to press such advice even to the point of 'nagging.'"

With his white goatee and his trademark soft-brimmed hats, Norman looked more like a Bloomsbury dandy than a prince of banking. He was also notoriously secretive, to the extent that when traveling outside the country he would go by the name of Professor Clarence Skinner.

During his long tenure at the Bank of England, Norman regularly nagged the government about what he perceived as the importance of the gold standard. He was, therefore, a strong supporter of Chancellor of the Exchequer Winston Churchill when, in 1925, the latter announced a return to the previously abandoned standard by which a pound

sterling was valued at 123.27 grains of fine gold. This move proved disastrous, making British exports so costly abroad that unemployment became rampant, accompanied by social unrest that culminated in the General Strike of 1926, which had to be put down by military force.

Norman escaped blame for this, however, largely because so many other voices had joined in the clamor for a return to the gold standard. It was considered to be in Norman's favor that—especially through his alliance with Benjamin Strong, president of the Federal Reserve Bank of New York—he had been able to effect a number of measures that were thought at the time to be beneficial to the British economy, though many historians have questioned the reality of these perceived benefits.

NICOLE D'ORESME C. 1325–82

Possessed of one of the most remarkable minds of the Middle Ages, Nicole d'Oresme studied theology in Paris, then ascended through the Catholic hierarchy to become chaplain to Charles V (known as Charles the Wise). Later he was appointed to the bishopric of Lisieux.

Oresme's translation of Aristotle was an important influence on the development of the modern French language. His mathematical studies presaged the discovery of analytical geometry; he was a pioneer in the field of kinetics; and almost a century and a half before Copernicus, he theorized that Earth was not at the center of the universe.

As if this was not enough, Oresme can also lay claim to having been one of the greatest medieval economists. During his period of service to Charles he advised the king on matters of taxation and coinage, firmly advocating the importance of specie of a face value that precisely reflected the weight of the precious metal from which it was minted. It was his further opinion that coins belonged to the people who used them,

not to the feudal lord who issued them, so that no prince or king had the right to debase the currency (as was all too common a practice at the time). His treatise *De Moneta* (c. 1360) was considered the standard text on the philosophy of coinage and was reprinted many times during the next three hundred years.

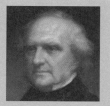

GEORGE PEABODY 1795–1879

Born in Massachusetts, George Peabody was apprenticed into the grocery business. While still a young man he became a partner in a dry-goods company that was headquartered first on the outskirts of Washington, D.C., and later in Baltimore, with branches in other northeastern cities.

In Baltimore he was the contemporary of another successful merchant, Johns Hopkins. Unlike Hopkins, however, Peabody was something of a traveler. In 1837 he moved to England, settling in London, where he negotiated a loan on behalf of the state of Maryland, which had been on the brink of bankruptcy. In 1851, still in London, Peabody set up a merchant banking company that bore his name. Soon after, he recruited a Boston banker named Junius Morgan as a partner. On its founder's retirement, Peabody & Co. became J. S. Morgan & Co., which was to be the launching pad for the career of J. P. Morgan.

Peabody was a notable philanthropist, funding extensive slum clearance schemes in his adopted city as well as endowing many educational institutions in the United States, including the Peabody Museum of Archaeology and Ethnology at Harvard and the Peabody Museum of Natural History at Yale.

RONALD PERELMAN 1935–

Born into a business family, Ronald Perelman is said to have sat in on his first board meeting when he was eleven years old. He attended the University of Pennsylvania and the Wharton School before joining the family firm, Belmont Industries. In 1978 he set up his own holding company, McAndrews & Forbes, becoming a client of Drexel Burnham Lambert during the period of Michael Milken's rise to power there.

Perelman was a principal or a major participant in several of the Milken-orchestrated junk bond–leveraged takeovers of the 1980s, gaining a reputation as a turnaround specialist who was ruthless in his reorganization of companies, liquidating unprofitable divisions and restructuring the core components. His biggest coup was the acquisition of the cosmetics giant Revlon, which he still controls at the time of writing.

Unlike some leveraged takeover mavens, Perelman has succeeded as both a speculator and an executive. One of the wealthiest men in America, he has made extensive gifts to academic institutions and Jewish causes.

CECIL RHODES 1853–1902

The son of a British clergyman, Cecil Rhodes first visited South Africa as a teenager. His elder brother Herbert operated a cotton plantation in Natal, and the young Cecil arrived just in time for the first big diamond strike in the Kimberley diamond fields. The brothers staked a claim and soon found themselves wealthy.

For a while Rhodes shuttled between South Africa and England, where he had enrolled at Oxford University. Eventually he received his degree, but more and more of his attention was focused on his diamond-producing interests, and in 1880 he formed the De Beers Mining Company. By now he had a considerable power base, which he used to manipulate native African leaders into granting him more mining concessions. By 1888, Rhodes and his former rival Barney Barnato had joined forces as De Beers Consolidated Mines to monopolize production in the Kimberley diamond fields.

Remarkable though it was, Rhodes's success as a businessman was eclipsed by his career as a politician and his role as an advocate of British colonialism. As a young man he had developed a vision of a British South Africa that was certain to bring him into violent conflict with the Boers, descendants of the Dutch settlers who originally colonized the region. Rhodes was elected to the Cape Colony Parliament in 1881 and became prime minister in 1890. He used his position to conspire against the Boer-dominated Transvaal government of Paul Kruger. This culminated in the notorious Jameson raid, a botched 1895 attempt to overthrow Kruger, which led to censure from London that forced Rhodes's resignation.

During the Boer War, Rhodes commanded the British garrison at Kimberley. For the most part, though, he spent his last years encouraging the development of Rhodesia, the colony named after him that has been known, since independence, as Zimbabwe. He bequeathed part of his wealth to endow the scholarships that bear his name, intended to bring students from the British Commonwealth and the United States for three years of postgraduate study at Oxford University.

JULIAN ROBERTSON 1933–

One of Wall Street's more volatile figures, Julian Robertson has seen his career swing from high to low and back again.

After an unremarkable childhood in North Carolina and lackluster years as a student at the University of North Carolina, Robertson served time in the Navy and then moved to New York, joining the investment firm of Kidder, Peabody & Co. Over his twenty years at Kidder, Robertson progressed from sales to stockbroker to head of a money-management unit, demonstrating considerable skill with mathematics and great stock-picking acumen. In 1980 Robertson left Kidder to start Tiger Management, a global investing firm with a simple mandate: to provide partners with an investment vehicle that concentrated on fundamental stock picking. Modeled on a classic hedge-fund structure, Tiger remained fairly small throughout the 1980s, although it demonstrated early success in 1981, when it delivered a post-fees return of almost 20 percent in a year when the S&P 500 declined 5 percent. Expanding throughout the postcrash 1980s and 1990s, Tiger delivered a compound rate of return averaging 32 percent. However, an average rate is somewhat inaccurate in the case of Tiger, as it masks years such as 1997, when Tiger investors enjoyed a post-fees return of 56 percent, and years like 1995, when numerous investors defected and Tiger's pre-fees returns were twenty points below the S&P 500. Devastated by the technology-driven market of the late 1990s, Robertson closed Tiger in 2000, stating that he "frankly did not understand" the current state of the market.

Robertson himself is often as contradictory as his company was; known for irascibility and a tendency to snap at employees, he has demonstrated a more charitable side by actions such as launching the Tiger Foundation in 1989 to support organizations serving disadvantaged youths and their families in New York City.

JOHN D. ROCKEFELLER 1839–1927

The phrase "rich as Rockefeller" is woven into the American psyche. No other name is so irrevocably linked to the idea of fabulous wealth.

Born in upstate New York, John D. Rockefeller and his younger brother William moved with their family to Cleveland in 1853. Both became produce merchants dealing in grains, meats, and other commodities. In the 1860s John became interested in the oil business and built a refinery in the Cleveland area. Soon he was shipping petroleum to the East Coast and beyond, and he asked William to become his export agent in New York. In 1870 John founded Standard Oil and began to buy out other companies until, by the early 1880s, he had achieved a virtual monopoly. At that point he set up a board of nine trustees to control the company, with himself as chairman and William playing an important role as head of the New Jersey and New York divisions. Standard Oil thus became the prototypical "trust"—the term being synonymous with exclusion of competition—on which all others were modeled. When the trust ran into legal difficulties because of an Ohio antimonopoly law, the Rockefellers employed various strategies to circumvent the problem, culminating in the formation of Standard Oil (New Jersey) as a trustlike holding company.

It was largely to counter the Standard Oil monopoly that the Sherman Antitrust Act was passed in 1890. In 1911, armed with that far-reaching legislation, the Supreme Court dissolved the holding company. By then, John D. Rockefeller had been devoting himself for more than a decade to philanthropic activities such as the endowment of the University of Chicago and the Rockefeller Institute for Medical Research in Manhattan. In 1913, along with his son John D. Rockefeller Jr., he established the Rockefeller Foundation.

THE ROTHSCHILD FAMILY

Along with the Medici and the Fuggers, the Rothschilds are among the greatest of the European banking families. The House of Rothschild was founded in Frankfurt am Main by Mayer Amschel Rothschild (1744–1812). Joined in the business by his five sons, Mayer started out as a dealer in rare coins, jewelry, and securities. Soon the family expanded into banking on a large scale, taking advantage of the upheavals caused by the Napoleonic wars to forge links with the mighty of Europe, many of whom were in dire need of funds to raise armies and wage campaigns.

The eldest son, Amschel (1773–1855), remained with his father in Frankfurt, which served as the command post for a growing empire. Salomon (1774–1875) opened an office in Vienna, Nathan (1777–1836, right) did likewise in London, Karl (1788–1855) established himself in Naples, while Jakob (1792–1868, left), also known as James, made Paris his base. In addition to making loans and performing other standard banking functions, the Rothschilds capitalized on Napoleonic unrest to carry on less conventional activities. They dealt on a huge scale in many kinds of commodities, including armaments. They also provided the means for British merchants to continue doing business in mainland Europe despite Napoleon's efforts to enforce an embargo.

After Waterloo the Rothschilds invested heavily in railroads and other expanding industries, and served as well as agents for both government bonds and blue-chip securities. Some historians have expressed surprise that the family did not establish an office in the United States, which might have proved an effective way of expanding their power base. In fact they were ably represented there by August Belmont, a Rothschild protégé.

By the end of the nineteenth century the Rothschilds were no longer the overwhelmingly dominant force they had been a few decades earlier. They remained a formidable dynasty, however, prominent not only in banking but also in such fields as art patronage and winemaking.

ROBERT E. RUBIN 1938–

Born in New York, Robert Rubin graduated summa cum laude from Harvard, then received a degree from Yale Law School before attending the London School of Economics. He joined Goldman Sachs & Co. in 1966, rising through the ranks to become co–senior partner and co–senior chairman while establishing a reputation for putting together complicated financial deals under tough circumstances.

In 1993 President Bill Clinton brought him to the White House to direct the National Economic Council. Two years later he became the seventieth secretary of the Treasury and immediately made an impression by orchestrating the United States's bailout of the Mexican economy, which entailed $40 billion in public funds.

If this bailout seemed risky at the time (the loan was in fact repaid ahead of schedule), Rubin's four-year tenure at the Treasury was marked by circumspection, and he is credited with having contributed much to the planning that enabled the president to implement his vision of balancing the federal budget for the first time in three decades. During Clinton's second term, Rubin spent much energy in attempting to devise rescue schemes for troubled Asian economies.

Upon leaving the Treasury, Rubin returned to the commercial world as chairman of Citigroup, the world's largest financial company.

RUSSELL SAGE 1816–1906

Like a number of other nineteenth-century American financiers, Russell Sage began his career in the grocery business, in his case in the city of Troy in upstate New York. He enjoyed early success and graduated to the banking business, in which, thanks to underhanded practices and old-fashioned bribery, he prospered. He served a term in Congress and then, in his late forties, moved to New York City, where he displayed great prowess and chicanery as a stock speculator.

Together with another crafty and rapacious investor, Jay Gould, Sage staged successful raids on a number of railroads, chiefly in the West. The pair also gained control of the New York elevated railroad system and the Western Union Telegraph Company.

In 1891 Sage survived an assassination attempt. Following his death fifteen years later, his wife, Margaret, made large gifts to a variety of philanthropies and established the Russell Sage Foundation, devoted to "the improvement of social and living conditions."

MARCUS SAMUEL, VISCOUNT BEARSTED 1853–1927 and SIR HENRI W. A. DETERDING 1866–1939

In 1878 Marcus Samuel became manager of a London-based business that imported seashells and other items from the Far East and used them to create popular decorative objects. While traveling on company business, Samuel became aware of the growing importance of kerosene as a commodity. This led him to form the Shell Transport and Trading Company, which, thanks to the rising demand that created a booming market for petroleum products, soon owned a fleet of tankers and was operating oil wells and refineries in Borneo, Sumatra, Russia, Romania, and even Texas.

Among Shell's rivals was the Royal Dutch Company, which began drilling and refining in Sumatra in 1892. Four years later, Henri W. A. Deterding was called in to run the business and built up a fleet of tankers capable of competing with Shell's. In 1903 the two companies decided to rationalize their operations by amalgamating their sales and distribution forces in certain markets. In 1907 the former rivals merged to form the Royal Dutch/Shell Group, with Deterding as managing director.

Without abandoning its roots in the world of petroleum, Shell (the registered name since 1949) would become one of the world's largest conglomerates, with interests ranging from consumer products to nuclear energy.

PAUL SAMUELSON 1915–

Paul Samuelson has characterized himself as "the last 'generalist' in economics" in an age of specialization—a reference to his economic theories that could just as well apply to his career, which has broadly spanned academia and govern-

ment with remarkable success. One of the most prolific writers in the field, Samuelson has produced a large body of work, including the best-selling economics textbook of all time, *Economics: An Introductory Analysis* (1948), and the seminal *Foundations of Economic Analysis* (1947), which reinvigorated neoclassical economics and kicked off an era of emphasizing mathematics in economics.

Born in Gary, Indiana, in 1915, Samuelson received a B.A. from the University of Chicago in 1935 and an M.A. (1936) and Ph.D. (1941) from Harvard. Legend has it that Samuelson's understanding of economic theory was so prodigious that at the end of his dissertation defense one of his professors turned to another—both of whose theories Samuelson had discussed— and asked, "Well, have we passed?" After his stint at Harvard, Samuelson embarked on a long and distinguished career at the Massachusetts Institute of Technology, rising from assistant professor in 1940 to Institute professor, a rank reserved for few, in 1966. In 1991 M.I.T. created in his honor the Paul A. Samuelson Professorship in Economics. Additionally, he has received over two dozen honorary degrees in both America and abroad.

Samuelson's groundbreaking work in economics garnered him the distinction of being the first American to receive the Nobel Prize in Economic Sciences, which he won in 1970. In 1996 he was granted the National Medal of Science. His government work has included serving as a valued adviser to Presidents John F. Kennedy, Lyndon Johnson, and Jimmy Carter, and holding a top spot on President Richard Nixon's "enemies list," along with several colleagues at M.I.T. Indeed, Samuelson was quoted as saying in 1975, "If you turn this recession upside down, you will read clearly on its bottom, 'Made in Washington.'"

JACOB SCHIFF 1847–1920

Born into a prosperous Jewish family in Frankfurt am Main, Jacob Schiff came to the United States at the age of eighteen. He soon established himself in the brokerage business and came to prominence a few years later as the result of a chance encounter while visiting Germany on the occasion of his father's death. During the course of this trip he met Abraham Kuhn, a partner in Kuhn, Loeb, then the leading Jewish investment bank in the United States. Schiff was invited to join the firm and in 1885 became its head.

During the last part of the nineteenth century, Schiff emerged as J. P. Morgan's greatest rival. Each employed the same tactic of using his position as primary creditor to reorganize insolvent companies in such a way as to take over controlling interest. Both applied this method in particular to the reorganization of railroads, 192 of which were in receivership in 1894 alone.

Occasionally Schiff and Morgan cooperated on a deal. More often, though, they were fierce competitors, Morgan's determination to best Schiff reputedly being fueled by more than a hint of anti-Semitism. Their most famous confrontation came in 1901, when Schiff and E. H. Harriman contended with Morgan and Jim Hill for control of the Northern Pacific Railroad. In that instance there was a virtual standoff, though technically Morgan could claim victory. The rest of Wall Street was obliged to suffer through a panic.

CHARLES SCHWAB 1937–

Charles Schwab is well known as the publicly visible head of the world's largest discount brokerage firm. Born in Sacramento, California, Schwab showed his entrepreneurial spirit at a young age, collecting walnuts, selling eggs door-to-door, and caddying at the local golf course. He went on to attend Stanford University, from which he received a B.A. in economics in 1959 and an M.B.A. in 1961. In 1967 he and several associates founded a no-load mutual fund called Investment Indicators. Although the fund quickly achieved success, with assets of $20 million, an administrative filing blunder caused the SEC and the federal government to essentially shut down the firm. Schwab was left with more than $100,000 in debt and a dissolved marriage.

In 1971, with funds borrowed from an uncle, he started what became the present-day Charles Schwab & Co. The firm got off to a rocky start, and within a few years all of the initial investors sold their shares back to Schwab, making him the sole owner of the company. In 1973 the first signs of an upturn began and Schwab opened a second office in Sacramento.

In mid-1975, critical legislation was passed: commissions on all trades by stockbrokers became negotiable, paving the way to Schwab's establishment of a discount brokerage. Believing from the start that average investors could make good decisions if they were educated, Schwab eliminated the costs associated with individualized investment advice. Charles Schwab & Co. continued to grow steadily throughout the 1970s and 1980s, and seized on the birth of the Internet

as a chance to expand the company's customer base. Through Internet trading and dissemination of information, Schwab's vision of putting investing in the hands of investors was taken to a new level. In 1998 Charles Schwab & Co. managed 2.2 million online accounts, making it the leader in the field, and the company's market value reached $25.5 billion, surpassing that of Merrill Lynch.

WILLIAM F. SHARPE 1934–

William Sharpe is a man concerned with risk: over the course of his fifty-plus-year involvement with economics, Sharpe has developed primary economic theories and computational tools to aid in the quantification of risk for both money managers and individual investors.

Born in Massachusetts and raised in Boston, Texas, and California, Sharpe went to college intending to study science as a step toward pursuing a degree in medicine. After his initial year at the University of California at Berkeley, he realized that this was not the right course for him and transferred to the Los Angeles campus of the U.C. system to pursue business administration and then economics, receiving his Ph.D. in 1961. While earning his doctorate, he also worked as a researcher for the RAND Corporation. It was there that Sharpe, influenced by the research of his colleague Harry Markowitz on risk and return, began to develop the Capital Asset Pricing Model (CAPM), which measures the relationship between risk and return of financial assets. His work with CAPM was largely computer-based, utilizing FORTRAN, punch cards, and room-size mainframes to execute algorithms to test his theories.

Formal acknowledgement of Sharpe's work have included a Nobel Memorial Prize in Economic Sciences in 1990, shared with his one-time mentor, Harry Markowitz, and Merton Miller.

MURIEL SIEBERT 1932–

Muriel Siebert has the distinction of being the first woman to breach the walls of what had been one of America's most solid bastions of the masculine ego, the New York Stock Exchange. Born in Cleveland, she came to New York City in 1954 and for the next dozen years worked as a financial analyst, becoming a partner in three different companies. In 1967 she became the first woman to buy a seat on the NYSE, and two years later she founded Muriel Siebert & Co., Inc.

In 1977 Siebert entered public service, becoming superintendent of banking for the state of New York. Simultaneously, she was director of both New York City's Urban Development Corporation and its Job Development Authority, after which, in 1982, she ran unsuccessfully for the U.S. Senate. She then returned to the brokerage world.

ADAM SMITH 1723–90

Few people would dispute that Adam Smith is the progenitor of modern political economy. Born in a small Scottish town, Smith studied at the University of Glasgow, then a notable center of philosophical inquiry, and Balliol College, Oxford. Upon returning to Glasgow he taught logic and moral philosophy at the university, becoming a close friend of the philosopher David Hume.

Smith's first important published work was *The Theory of Moral Sentiments* (1759), in which he attempted to come to grips with problems surrounding the origins of ethical judgments. After traveling in Europe from 1763 to 1767, he spent some years in London, where he was elected a fellow of the Royal Society. By then he had probably begun work on his most famous book, *The Wealth of Nations*, published in 1776.

In this seminal work, Smith turned his back on the simpleminded mercantilism that had dominated European economic thought for hundreds of years and embraced the concept of free enterprise. He traced the evolution of society through historical stages that began with hunting and foraging and ended with a situation in which interdependent market forces shape the economic life of the community. He saw the wealth of a nation as being expressed in terms of its annual production of goods and services, ultimately dependent upon what he believed to be the nation's greatest resource, its workforce. Beyond this, he discussed how the wealth of a nation is divided among property owners, manufacturers, and the laboring classes, with competition serving as a regulating mechanism that controls prices.

Smith's arguments are too complex to summarize adequately here, but it can reasonably be said that he broached most of the major themes taken up by later economists, from Karl Marx to John Maynard Keynes.

GEORGE SOROS 1930–

Born in Hungary, George Soros made his way to England in 1947, where he studied at the London School of Economics. Nine years later he moved to the United States. In 1970 his Soros Fund Management was placed in charge of the Quantum Fund, an international investment fund. For more than a quarter of a century Quantum outperformed virtually all of its rivals, making Soros a legend among money managers.

He is equally famous as a philanthropist: Soros's efforts and gifts have spawned a network of cultural and educational foundations operating in the United States, South Africa, and in central and eastern Europe. Most notably, perhaps, he was instrumental in founding Central European University, which offers postgraduate studies in Budapest, Prague, and Warsaw in economics, history, political science, social science, and art history.

SERGE ALEXANDRE STAVISKY 1886–1934

Serge Stavisky was the mysterious figure at the center of what became known as "*l'affaire Stavisky*," a political crisis that led to violent riots and forced the resignation of two French prime ministers. Before becoming involved in the scandal that brought him to the world's attention, the Russian-born Stavisky had been a café singer, a nightclub manager, a gambler, the owner of a striptease theater, a drug runner, and the operator of a sleazy bucket shop, selling worthless securities to the unwary. During the course of this unsavory career he became well connected in political circles, which enabled him to embark on more grandiose swindles and pyramid schemes.

After serving a brief prison term due to his carelessness while engaged in embezzling bonds, Stavisky was issued a false passport bearing the surname Alexandre. Apparently under the protection of the police—for whom he may have been an informer—he was permitted to continue his life of white-collar crime and even became something of a social figure, living in grand style and owning highly regarded racehorses.

In the early 1930s he gained control of the municipal credit union—a kind of glorified pawnshop licensed by the local authorities—in the southwestern city of Bayonne. This position enabled Stavisky to float semiofficial bonds, which he marketed to various insurance companies with considerable success, probably with the assistance of political figures, a couple of whom held ministerial positions. When these bonds proved to be worthless, Stavisky disappeared and was found dead in Chamonix in January 1934. The police said it was suicide. Far-right-wing agitators belonging to royalist and fascist groups such as Action Française and the Croix de Feu spread the rumor that Stavisky had been murdered to cover up his involvement with members of the Radical Socialist government headed by Camille Chautemps.

The government made the mistake of trying to sweep these accusations under the rug. This gave conservative extremists in Paris an excuse to stir up riots, during which fifteen people were killed in the shadow of the Chamber of Deputies. Chautemps was forced to resign, as was his successor, Édouard Daladier. For a few days it appeared that the very existence of the republic was threatened, but stability was restored when a centrist government was installed under former president Gaston Doumergue.

MICHAEL STEINHARDT 1941–

Known for his philanthropy and the impressive returns of his hedge-fund investment company, Michael Steinhardt made his entrée into Wall Street as a research analyst and he founded his own firm in 1967, at the age of twenty-six.

Years of stellar investing choices in the high-stakes arena of hedge funds yielded an average annual return of 24 percent until 1995, when Steinhardt, like some other hedge-fund managers, closed his company's doors rather than operate in the unpredictable late-1990s market.

Steinhardt has devoted recent years to sharing his wealth with the goals of infusing American society with secular Jewish values, preserving wildlife, and promoting the arts. Steinhardt collects Greek and Roman art, and his estate in Mount Kisco, New York, includes a private zoo complete with free-range zebras, an ostrich, wallabies, antelope, and a golden spider monkey.

JAMES STILLMAN 1850–1918

One of the key banking figures of the J. P. Morgan period, James Stillman was the son of a wealthy businessman, becoming a partner in his father's firm when he was just twenty-one. A decade later he began to collaborate with Moses Taylor, president of National City Bank, on the reorganization of bankrupt railroads. At about the same time, he met William Rockefeller, one of the original partners in the Standard Oil Company, and the two became lifelong friends.

In 1891 Stillman became head of National City and immediately began to use his Rockefeller connections to further the bank's interests, winning the right to market many Standard Oil securities. On occasion Stillman also collaborated with Jacob Schiff of Kuhn, Loeb, but it was the Rockefeller connection that permitted National City to grow, by 1905, into the nation's largest bank.

BENJAMIN STRONG 1872–1928

In 1913 the U.S. government created the regional Federal Reserve banks, the most important of which was in New York. Its first president was Benjamin Strong, a man with close ties to the House of Morgan.

As head of the Federal Reserve Bank of New York, Strong was able to play a significant role in both domestic and international financial matters. An ally of Montagu Norman, governor of the Bank of England, Strong provided financial support for the 1925 British return to the gold standard, which proved disastrous. On the plus side, however, he helped both British and American economies by cooperating with Norman to control interest rates and keep London markets closed to foreigners, which offered the battered British economy protection while sending foreign investors to burgeoning American markets. Strong later provided the same kind of protection to the French and German economies.

Contributing to the bubble-like expansion that typified American markets in the mid- to late 1920s was that the Federal Reserve banks, led by Strong, continued to make money available at low interest rates. He thus played a role in encouraging the mood of reckless optimism that preceded the 1929 crash, apparently believing that he could apply the brakes to the runaway bull market simply by raising interest rates. When he did so, in 1928, it was too late, but Strong did not live to see the consequences.

JAMSETJI NUSSERWANJI TATA 1839–1904

Born into an upper-caste Parsi family, Jamsetji Nusserwanji Tata was educated at Elphinstone College in Bombay, then joined his father's successful export-import company, traveling widely to set up branch offices in China, Japan, Europe, and the United States. In the 1870s he began to build a chain of modern cotton mills, quickly establishing a reputation for both quality and enlightened labor relations. He consolidated his textile empire by introducing the production of raw silk to the subcontinent and then expanded into utilities, as well as iron and steel.

Under the leadership of Tata's sons, Sir Dorabji Tata (1859–1933) and Sir Ratanji Tata (1871–1918), the empire was enlarged still further to include the manufacture of chemicals, cement, and commercial vehicles. A third generation continued the family tradition, with one member founding the company that became Air India.

NILS TAUBE 1928–

Estonian by birth, Nils Taube has been a fund manager in London for close to half a century. His name has long been associated with J. Rothschild Assurance, which remains the largest single client of Taube Hodson Stonex, the company through which Taube oversees the Partners Fund, the Partners European Fund, International Growth and Value, and other entities.

Known for entrusting his own money to the funds he manages, Taube has established an enviable record of annual returns over a sustained period that places him in the same league as celebrated American stock pickers like Peter Lynch and George Soros.

SIR JOHN TEMPLETON 1912–

When Germany invaded France in the summer of 1940, John Templeton hit on an interesting investment strategy. Sensing that the war would revitalize American industry, he borrowed $10,000 and invested in 104 American companies whose shares were selling for a dollar or less. It was his guess that at least a majority of them would benefit from the international situation. In fact, all but four of the companies went up in value by V-J Day—many of them spectacularly so—and Templeton pocketed a handsome profit.

This illustrates the unconventional thinking of a man who has been called

the greatest global stock picker of the century. In 1954 he launched the Templeton Growth Fund—specializing in international investment fields where he felt bargains were to be found—which eventually could boast returns that averaged 15 percent annually for thirty-eight years. He sold the business in 1992. As a long-term manager he has a record comparable to other legends such as Warren Buffett, Nils Taube, and Peter Lynch.

Intensely religious, and notoriously frugal except where his own extensive charitable foundations are concerned, Templeton was born in Tennessee and now lives in the Bahamas. He is one of the few men born in America who have been granted a British knighthood.

CORNELIUS VANDERBILT 1794–1877

The name Vanderbilt is so synonymous with wealth that it comes as a shock to realize that the man who made it famous grew up in poverty on the waterfront of Staten Island, New York. But by the time he was sixteen, Cornelius Vanderbilt had bought his first small boat and was using it to ferry passengers between Staten Island and Manhattan. Soon after, during the War of 1812, he expanded his modest fleet and leased it to the government.

In 1818 he became a steamship captain, and over the next decade saved enough capital to start his own line, which quickly dominated traffic on the Hudson River. When his competitors bought him out, he used the money to start similar operations between New York and cities such as Boston and Providence. By the time of the California gold rush, Vanderbilt had established

a lucrative transport business linking New York and New Orleans with San Francisco by way of Nicaragua.

It wasn't until the 1850s that Vanderbilt turned his attention to the railroads, the field of endeavor for which he is best remembered. Above all, he is associated with the development of the New York Central, but in his day he was one of the great stock manipulators and takeover virtuosos, using a variety of strategies to gain control of railroad companies and other enterprises. A rogue of the first water, his place in history is due as much to his epic battles with fellow reprobates as to any lasting achievements of his own. In particular, Vanderbilt's struggle with Daniel Drew, Jay Gould, and Jim Fisk over control of the Erie Railroad is the stuff of legend.

HENRY VILLARD 1835–1900

Born in Germany (and originally named Ferdinand Hilgard), Villard came to the United States in his late teens and became a newspaper correspondent, gaining considerable renown for his reports of the Lincoln-Douglas debates and his coverage of various aspects of the Civil War.

After a successful journalistic career he began to deal in railroad securities and soon became involved in financing western railroads, forming the Oregon Railway and Navigation Company and gaining control of the Northern Pacific. More than one entrepreneur had been defeated by the physical and financial challenges posed by the Northern Pacific, and Villard was bankrupted by the cost of driving the line through the Rocky Mountains. He found new backers, however, and regained control of the company, then went on to form General Electric and to revive his newspaper interests by taking control of the New York *Evening Post*.

NINA WANG 1938–

Flamboyant in dress and one of the richest women in the world, Nina Wang's status stems in part from tragedy. In 1990 her husband, Teddy Wang, was abducted. A ransom was paid but he was never returned, and everyone but Nina believes him to be dead. In his absence she became, in her terminology, "chairlady" of the Chinachem Group, and has continued the successful dealings of Hong Kong's largest private property developer.

A legal feud with her father-in-law, who founded Chinachem, has not prevented her from expanding into broadband, pharmaceutical, and importing ventures. She heads a private investment firm, Veron International, and is vice president and director of the Real Estate Developers Association of Hong Kong. Known for her generous financial support of organizations at home and abroad, Wang has created the Chinachem Charitable Foundation Limited. Contributions have included a sizable gift, in 1996, to Harvard University's Kennedy School of Government to encourage research and teaching about China's growing role in international affairs and to promote closer relationships between the United States and China.

THE WARBURG FAMILY

The Warburg family took its name from Warburgum, the German town where it became established in the sixteenth century. Over the next three hundred years branches of the family settled in other parts of Germany as well as in Sweden, Denmark, England, and the United States.

In 1798 Moses Marcus Warburg and his brother Gerson founded a bank in Hamburg. The family banking tradition continued there and in America, where Moses' grandsons Paul Moritz (1868–1932) and Felix Moritz (1871–1937, above) both became partners in Kuhn, Loeb & Co. The former was an advocate of a central bank, along the lines long established in many European countries, and was one of the architects of the Federal Reserve Board, refusing its chairmanship but serving for several years as a director. In the late 1920s his was among the few voices raised in warning of an impending stock market crash. His son James (1896–1969) was a banker and economist who was often called upon for advice by President Franklin D. Roosevelt.

RICHARD WHITNEY 1888–1974

On the morning of October 24, 1929, as the New York Stock Exchange tottered on the brink of the biggest crash in its history, a patrician figure was seen striding across the trading floor. Everyone recognized Richard Whitney, several times president of the exchange, who was understood to be acting as the proxy for the House of Morgan, where his brother was a partner. He arrived at the U.S. Steel post and placed a strong bid for ten thousand shares. He then moved on to other stations, placing orders for more than $20 million worth of stock. As the word spread a little of the tension drained from the vast room. The big boys, it seemed, were ready to buttress the market.

It was a dramatic gesture, but it did little good in the long run as stocks continued their free-fall. It did, however, help cement Whitney's position as a leading representative of the financial establishment, and in the wake of the crash he became a spokesman for fiscal responsibility in high places, while leading the conservative group that opposed reform of the exchange's constitution.

Then, in 1938, came a bombshell as irregularities were discovered in the business practices of Richard Whitney & Co. In March of that year, Whitney himself was charged with theft. It emerged in court that he had made unconscionably reckless investments that forced him to seek loans amounting to almost $30 million. When the loans were exhausted, he had stolen securities from the New York Yacht Club and various clients, and had even pilfered close to a million from the NYSE itself.

Whitney became the first member—or ex-member—of the NYSE to serve time in a maximum-security prison. A matter of weeks after he had been suspended by the exchange, a new constitution was introduced.

VICTORIA CLAFLIN WOODHULL 1838–1927 and TENNESSEE CELESTE CLAFLIN 1845–1923

To say that Victoria and Tennessee Claflin were among the most remarkable women of the nineteenth century is almost an understatement. Born into a large Ohio family, they began traveling with a medicine show at a very young age, giving spiritualist performances. At fifteen Victoria married Dr. Canning Woodhull, with whom she had two children. She continued to astonish Midwesterners with her amazing talent for communicating with the beyond, but Dr. Woodhull took to drink and in 1864 they were divorced.

In 1866 Victoria was married "by the spirits" to Colonel James Harvey Blood, whom she divorced two years later, though they continued to live together and even remarried, only to be divorced once again. (For some of this period they shared their household with Dr. Woodhull.) Colonel Blood then disappeared under mysterious circumstances.

In 1868 Victoria and Tennie C. (as she now signed herself) moved to New York, where they made the acquaintance of Cornelius Vanderbilt, a devotee of spiritualism. In 1870, with Commodore Vanderbilt's guidance, they opened a bank and a brokerage office, the first Wall Street institutions to be run by women. Perhaps thanks to Vanderbilt's advice, these businesses prospered. Also in 1870, the sisters launched *Woodhull & Claflin's Weekly*, which advocated women's suffrage and free love.

From that point on Victoria and Tennie were much in demand on the lucrative lecture circuit, delivering addresses on a variety of feminist themes. In 1871 Victoria precipitated a scandal by denouncing a prominent clergyman of the period, Henry Ward Beecher, as a hypocrite, since he preached against free love despite having had an affair with the wife of a journalist named Theodore Tilton. (Tilton, as it happens, may well have been Victoria's lover at the time.)

While remaining a champion of suffrage—and becoming, in 1872, the first woman to be nominated as a presidential candidate—Victoria later modified her views, renouncing free love. When Cornelius Vanderbilt died, leaving almost all of his fortune to one son, there was a move to challenge his will on grounds of mental incompetence. His involvement with spiritualism made Victoria and Tennie potentially damaging witnesses and they were spirited away to England, their relocation presumably financed with Vanderbilt dollars.

Both sisters took to the British way of life and married into the higher ranks of society. Victoria's husband, a member of a prominent banking family, met

a premature end, and she spent her waning years as a country dowager whose salon attracted tarot card readers, palmists, astrologers, numerologists, and spiritualists from all parts of the known universe and beyond.

WALTER WRISTON 1919–
Among the most influential bankers of recent decades, Walter Wriston became president and CEO of New York–based Citibank in 1967. This was a time when banking practices were undergoing radical changes, and Wriston was among the leaders in an era when credit, once firmly anchored to verifiable equity, became increasingly available to those for whom equity was largely a matter of potential. (College students, for example, could obtain credit cards on the assumption that their degrees would provide them with the means to meet at least the minimum payments on their monthly bills—and to keep paying interest on the running balance for the rest of their lives.)

It was possible to make consumer debt available on this apparently risky basis because the federal government had provided safety nets to protect both banks and bank depositors. Wriston built Citibank into an international giant by facilitating the handling of consumer debt, and corporate debt too, through technological advances such as the introduction of automated teller machines for ordinary depositors, and sophisticated software that gave the bank's largest and most important clients an edge in the management of their portfolios.

Wriston also committed Citibank funds to extensive overseas loans, especially in Third World countries. These were not always repaid, but Wriston, who retired in 1984, has argued that these loans did much to shore up economies in parts of the world that at the time were vulnerable to destabilization.

Certainly, Wriston was a prophet of the directions finance would take in the digital age. It is he who came up with the dictum "Information about money has become almost as important as money itself," now inscribed in the lobby of the New York Library of Science, Industry and Business.

YASUDA ZENJIRO 1838–1921
Born into extreme poverty, Yasuda Zenjiro was the founder of one of the four principal *zaibatsu*, the family-controlled financial and industrial combines that dominated Japan's business scene from the last quarter of the nineteenth century until World War II—at which time it is said that fifteen families handled 80 percent of Japanese capital. After the war, during the period of the American occupation, legislation was introduced to break up the *zaibatsu*. It is commonly believed, however, that their spirit survived and still flourishes in the form of undeclared trusts.

Running away from home, Yasuda made his way to Tokyo, where he found work as a clerk in a retail store. He became a broker of commodities and securities, accumulating a large fortune that enabled him to found a banking house that was one of the main financial underpinnings of the Meiji government. Later, Yasuda expanded into railways, shipping, and manufacturing, among other businesses. In 1921 Yasuda was assassinated by a right-wing fanatic who saw him as a symbol of commercial corruption.

Timeline: 3500 B.C.—A.D. 2001

C. 3500 B.C.

The first cities appear on the floodplains of the Euphrates River.

2000 B.C.

By this date, markets and long-distance trade routes are firmly established in Mesopotamia, Egypt, the Indus Valley, China, and Peru. It is unlikely that any of these civilizations supported free markets in anything close to the modern sense of the term. The evidence suggests that most commerce was tightly controlled by priestly bureaucracies in the service of rulers who in many places were thought of as gods.

C. 1800 B.C.

King Hammurabi of Babylon establishes laws governing credit, interest charged on loans, and collateral.

C. 1800 B.C.—1000 B.C.

The Shang dynasty rules China. The cowrie shell is used as money.

640 B.C.

The first European coins are minted in the Anatolian kingdom of Lydia. The Lydians, the most famous of whom was King Croesus, are also credited with giving birth to the free-market system. In their cities, areas are set aside as marketplaces in which bargaining is actively encouraged as a flexible way of establishing prices on a day-to-day basis.

SIXTH CENTURY B.C.

During the Chou period, a form of coinage is introduced in China and Chinese silks appear in the Mediterranean region.

550 B.C.

Greek city-states build on the Lydian example, striking their own coins and evolving a civilization that is centered on the marketplace—the agora—which becomes a focus for political and philosophical discussion. Free trade becomes the dominant force in the Greek economy.

479–323 B.C.

This is Greece's classical period, marked by the rise of a fully democratic government, market-driven economies, and a flourishing of the arts.

332 B.C.

Aristotle describes usury as a crime against nature, an opinion perpetuated in later Christian and Moslem prohibitions against the taking of interest.

At around this time, the first Roman coins are struck.

250 B.C.

By this date, there is evidence of trade between the Greek world and China.

206 B.C.—A.D. 220

The Han dynasty rules China. The period is marked by increased contact with the West and India, and trade within China begins to thrive.

A.D. 33

Christ drives the money changers out of the temple at Jerusalem.

A.D. 54–68

Nero rules Rome. He debases the empire's coinage, which causes inflation; debasement becomes commonplace and contributes to the empire's collapse at the end of the fourth century.

161–180

Marcus Aurelius rules the Roman Empire. During his reign Rome reaches its greatest extent, controlling most of Europe and the Middle East and trading with India, China, and sub-Saharan Africa. The Roman economy has become very sophisticated, giving rise to concepts such as banking and insurance, but throughout the empire trade is governed by imperial fiat rather than by the give-and-take of the marketplace. Prices are set by law or convention.

324

Constantine I comes to power and makes Christianity the official state religion. By this time the Roman Empire's economy is in ruins.

330

Constantine moves the capital of the Roman Empire east to Byzantium, which he renames Constantinople (present-day Istanbul).

410

Rome is sacked by Visigoths, precipitating the end of the western Roman Empire. Western Europe enters the so-called Dark Ages, during which European economies revert to barter as the basis of trade.

618–907

The T'ang dynasty rules China. During this time a market economy begins to develop there.

622

The prophet Muhammad flees Mecca for Medina, the event that traditionally marks the beginning of Islam, the only major world religion founded by a merchant. Not surprisingly, Islam will be well disposed toward market activity. Although usury is condemned, profit from trade is explicitly encouraged.

800–1600

Islamic merchants engage in trans-Saharan trade that brings gold north from West Africa in exchange for commodities such as salt. Some of this gold reaches Europe, where it is crucial to the evolution of a new market-based economy in the late Middle Ages.

1022

The government of Szechwan begins to print paper money. It does so in response to the breakdown of a system of privately issued paper money that proved susceptible to forgery and fraud.

1066

The Normans conquer England. Following this, Jews are permitted to settle in the British Isles, by which time they have established colonies in most parts of Western Europe. Forced to function outside the feudal system, they have little opportunity of acquiring land. They are also prevented, by the rising urban merchant class, from engaging in many forms of commerce. The one advantage the Jews have is that they are not subject to the Christian church's edicts against usury. From the eleventh century to the thirteenth century, they are the principal moneylenders and bankers in many European cities. This comes to an end when one European monarch after another—beginning with Edward I of England in 1290—expels the local Jewish communities.

1096–1291

The Crusades, a series of wars instigated by Christian leaders to regain the Holy Land from the Muslims, bring feudal Europe in contact with the Middle East. Trade with Arab cultures opens new markets and reintroduces capitalism.

EARLY TWELFTH CENTURY

Bills of exchange are invented in northern Italy.

1118

The order of the Knights Templars is founded. In 1202 the Knights become treasurers for the French crown. For the next hundred years the order serves as banker to the kings and princes of Europe. Its power is destroyed c. 1310 by King Philip IV of France, who, with a view to seizing the Templars' assets, accuses members of the order of a variety of heinous crimes and has their leaders burned at the stake.

1141

Louis VII of France centralizes trading in bills of exchange on a bridge over the Seine that is henceforth known as the Pont-au-Change.

1183

The Karimi, a loose association of powerful merchants, build a great warehouse in Fustat, Egypt. They have grown rich through the spice trade, maintaining branch offices as far away as India, and employ such commercial devices as limited partnerships long before these are known in the West.

EARLY THIRTEENTH CENTURY

All over Europe, urban areas are attaining a level of power and independence not known for almost a thousand years. Towns form alliances for mutual protection and trading rights. Cathedrals rise as pilgrimage sites; this encourages rulers to offer travelers protection, which helps reestablish trade routes and encourages the growth of great commercial fairs.

Banking and other modern forms of business practice begin to emerge in the burgeoning cities of northern Italy. Italian merchant bankers become established in London and elsewhere. Investment bankers and merchants adopt the use of Arabic numerals.

1204

The Crusaders sack Constantinople; Venice then takes over the commercial interests of the Byzantine Empire, including its profitable spice routes.

1250–1350

This is an era of world trade on a scale never seen before. A united Mongol empire means that commercial caravans can cross central Asia with relative impunity. Oceangoing vessels connect Africa and the Far East with the Middle East and Europe. The trade in luxury goods is becoming global. Florence, Genoa, and Venice mint gold coins, the first important examples to be struck in the West since Roman times.

1271–95

Venice's Marco Polo claims to have traveled through Asia with his merchant father and uncle.

1290

Edward I of England expels all Jews who refuse to convert to Christianity.

LATE THIRTEENTH CENTURY

In Italy, successful trading families form banks; prominent among them are the Bardi and Peruzzi of Florence.

EARLY FOURTEENTH CENTURY

Flanders, especially the cities of Ghent and Bruges, is now a major center of commerce. Bruges becomes the site of the world's first stock exchange.

1327

The London goldsmiths' guild is chartered by the Crown and given the right to inspect all gold and silver for purity and workmanship.

1337–1453

Hundred Years' War between England and France.

1341

Edward III of England defaults on war loans from Italy's Bardi and Peruzzi banking houses, which are thus ruined.

1348

The Black Death (bubonic plague) wipes out much of Europe's population.

1350

Florence institutes long-term municipal debt, which is traded on an active secondary market.

1397

Giovanni di Bicci de' Medici founds a bank in Florence; the Medici dynasty rules that city for most of the fifteenth century.

1407

Genoa founds the Casa de San Giorgio, the first public clearing bank. Although it fails in 1444, it serves as a model for future central clearing banks.

1430

The Chinese, whose great cannon-carrying ships have dominated trade in the Indian Ocean, largely withdraw from long-distance ocean commerce. The power vacuum this creates opens up routes to India and the Far East for European merchant adventurers.

1450–1550

The Fuggers of Bavaria are dominant merchant bankers.

1487

Vessels of many nations begin to ply the Indian Ocean.

1492

Columbus discovers (or rediscovers) America, providing merchant adventurers with another and hitherto unexploited source of potential wealth.

SIXTEENTH CENTURY

In Japan, fortified castle towns (*jokamachi*) begin to evolve into commercial centers.

1509

The combined Indian and Egyptian fleets are routed by the Portuguese at Diu, in the Persian Gulf, a key event in establishing European supremacy in world trade.

1521

Martin Luther is excommunicated.

1529

Captured in battle by the Spanish, Francis I of France is forced to pay a ransom of twelve million escudos. Counting and testing the money takes four months, and forty thousand coins are rejected by the Spaniards as substandard.

1542

Charles V's wartime effort to raise funds in the Hapsburg Netherlands helps create a large and growing market for government annuities.

1553

Chartered by the Crown, the Muscovy Company—trading with Russia—becomes Britain's first joint-stock company.

C. 1560

Antwerp is one of Europe's busiest market towns.

1567

An indoor exchange is erected in London's Cornhill.

1576

Spanish mercenaries raid Antwerp in an anti-Protestant move; this "Spanish Fury" starts the city on a downward spiral.

1577–80

Sir Francis Drake captains the first British ship in the Indian Ocean.

MID-1580s

Amsterdam is now the chief marketplace of the Low Countries.

SEVENTEENTH CENTURY

Amsterdam becomes Europe's financial center. It has the world's most active securities market, but a lack of organization and regulation impedes its evolution, and by the end of the century it is being overtaken in importance by the London market.

1602

The Dutch East India Company is formed, a joint-stock company licensed by the government to act as a quasi-military organization, permitted to establish fortified colonies in Asia and to engage in naval warfare in order to protect Dutch overseas commercial interests. During its almost two centuries of existence, the company averages annual dividends of close to 18 percent.

1637

The Dutch mania for rare kinds of tulips leads to runaway speculation that ends with a market crash—the first of modern times.

1652

The Dutch establish a colony at the Cape of Good Hope.

C. 1662

The British acquire Bombay.

1663

Britain strikes gold coins, setting the stage for the rise of the gold standard. For centuries, slivers of metal have been shaved from the edges of coins. The British government counters this by introducing coins with milled edges.

1666

A great fire devastates London.

1673

France's Compagnie des Indes Orientales, competing with the Dutch, Portuguese, and English around the coasts of India, establishes a beachhead on the Bay of Bengal.

C. 1680

Thomas Lloyd opens a London coffeehouse where traders, shipowners, and sea captains gather to make agreements on pooling risk. These informal meetings will lead to the formation of the Lloyd's of London insurance market.

1681

In Denmark, a government ordinance on commerce establishes official ground rules for securities trading. That same year, the first known printed stock quotes are published in England.

1689–1713

Wars throughout Europe lead to great increases in national debt, especially in France and Britain. The resulting financial crises generate greatly increased activity in the trading of government securities.

1694

The Bank of England is founded. At about the same time, a group of stock-jobbers is banned from the Royal Exchange for rowdy behavior. They respond by shifting their business to the coffeehouses that cluster around the exchange, the most famous of these being Garraway's—already well known for its auctions of commodities—and Jonathan's.

1717

In his day job as master of the Mint, Sir Isaac Newton determines that Britain's pound sterling will exchange for precisely 123.274 grains of gold. This undervalues gold relative to silver, so that silver coins become worth more for their metallic content than for their face value. They soon disappear from circulation and Britain moves decisively toward a pure gold standard.

1720

Almost simultaneously, Britain's South Sea Bubble and France's Mississippi Bubble burst, ruining tens of thousands of speculators. Both crashes are the result of gullible investors believing that fortunes can be made from plausible but unproven schemes involving distant colonial markets.

1724

In France, Louis XV officially recognizes the Paris Bourse; it will take on modern form in 1801 and move into the Palais de la Bourse in 1808.

1726

The Bank of England begins to issue 3 percent annuities. The British government follows suit during the War of Austrian Succession (1740–48). In reaction to the disastrous "bubble economy" of the recent past, trade in these issues, and in other conservative interest-bearing securities, makes up the bulk of business on the London Stock Exchange for the next hundred years.

1757

England's General Robert Clive defeats French forces in the Battle of Plassey, leaving stockholders of the British East India Company de facto rulers of Bengal. Britain becomes the supreme colonial force in India.

1771

The Vienna stock exchange is founded by Hapsburg imperial decree. It will remain the main capital market for Eastern and Central Europe until World War II.

1773

In London, on June 14, New Jonathan's Coffee House is renamed the Stock Exchange.

1776

The drawing up and signing of America's Declaration of Independence comes about in significant part because Britain's American colonists demand the right to trade with whatever nations they choose, free of the restrictions placed on them by Parliament in London.

That same year, Adam Smith publishes his influential book *The Wealth of Nations*, advocating free trade.

1776–83

America wages its Revolutionary War. During this period, the already existing financial markets in New York and Philadelphia become established as independent entities, trading primarily in war bonds.

1777

Attempting to head off the fiscal crisis that will help precipitate the French Revolution, France's director general of Finance, Jacques Necker, follows the example of other European finance ministers by selling large numbers of annuities guaranteed to pay a fixed rate of interest for the life of the bearer. Consortiums of investors hit on the scheme of buying large quantities of these annuities in the name of individual young girls who have been selected by doctors as having good prospects for long and healthy lives. The theory is that the interest will be paid to these girls, then divided up among the investors, with each girl's family taking a small share for the use of her name. The popularity of this scheme wanes, however, when it is learned that a Geneva consortium has lost millions of livres in anticipated income because its designated recipient, Pernette Elizabeth Martin, has thoughtlessly died, age eight.

1789

The U.S. Treasury Department is established.

1790

U.S. Treasury Secretary Alexander Hamilton persuades the federal government to assume the war debt of the various states, and to repay all government debt at its full value. This is good news for speculators who have bought most of these bonds, typically at deep discounts, from war veterans (or their widows), who originally received them in lieu of pay.

The first organized American stock exchange is established in Philadelphia.

1791

The First Bank of the United States is founded (it will be dissolved in 1811).

1792

A group of New York brokers meets under a buttonwood tree on Wall Street and agrees to found a securities exchange that will have at least a modicum of self-regulation, shunning the rigged auctions that are common at the time.

1798

Nathan Mayer Rothschild moves to London and establishes a branch of his father's Frankfurt-based bank; by 1815 he will be the principal financier of the British and other governments. The Rothschild family plays a dominant role in the European financial world throughout the nineteenth century, giving rise to the saying, "No government in Europe goes to war without consulting the Rothschilds."

1801

The London Stock Exchange is incorporated as a joint-stock company.

That same year, Napoleon founds the Brussels Stock Exchange, an organization that has its roots in the Flemish curb exchanges of the late Middle Ages.

1807

In France, the Napoleonic Commercial Code makes it easy to form limited-liability corporations. Its influence will be felt throughout Europe.

1812–15

The War of 1812 between the United States and Great Britain is financed partly by government bonds, informally underwritten by John Jacob Astor, among others.

1816–17

In the wake of the Napoleonic Wars comes a major European depression. Ninety British banks fail.

1817

The Berlin Börse is formed; the New York Stock & Exchange Board is formally established.

1819

The British East India Company establishes Singapore as a trading post.

1822

The Societé générale pour favoriser l'industrie nationale is established in Belgium. This is a new type of bank that not only finances commercial enterprises but also actively participates in them. It serves as a model for the bank-centered financial systems that will develop in Germany and elsewhere, in which banks replace the capital markets and become the chief instruments of industrial development.

1824

The first daily stock price listings are published by James Westenhall in the *British and Foreign Share List*.

1828

Australia's first stock exchange is established in Sydney. Initially, just one stock is listed.

1830s

The rapid expansion of the British railway system is financed largely through the stock market. This creates a considerably larger pool of shareholders and provides impetus for the opening of regional stock markets.

1839–42

The British force China to import opium from Crown colonies, the opium being sold to capitalize the purchase of Chinese goods. This prompts the first Opium War; China's defeat results in the Treaty of Nanking (1842), by which several ports are opened to British trade and Hong Kong is ceded to Britain.

1843

The Economist is founded in London, providing a lively mixture of hard business news and free-trade advocacy and setting a standard for financial journalism that has never been surpassed.

1844

The telegraph is invented; its ability to transmit information instantly over long distances will revolutionize the stock market.

1844–62

In Britain, a succession of acts of Parliament establishes the legal basis for the modern limited-liability corporation.

1845

Brazil's first stock exchange is founded in Rio de Janeiro.

1848

The Chicago Board of Trade begins business over a flour store on South Water Street.

1848–51

Major gold strikes in California and Australia lead to a significant increase in the world's supply of the precious metal, encouraging a number of countries to adopt the gold standard.

1852

The vogue for American railroad stocks begins to gather steam, and the Toronto Stock Exchange is founded. In France, Crédit Mobilier is established as a universal bank on the model of the Belgian Societé Générale. For a dozen years, it is wildly successful, but in 1867 it fails and the Paris Bourse begins to reassert its preeminence among French financial markets.

1853–54

U.S. Commodore Matthew Perry arrives in Japan to negotiate opening up the country to commerce with the West; a treaty is signed in 1854, granting the United States trading rights.

1855

Creditanstalt is founded in Vienna; it functions as a classic universal bank.

1857

Having been carried sky-high by speculators, many American railroad stocks crash. The Panic of 1857 (also known as the "western blizzard") results from inflation precipitated by the 1848 California gold rush.

1861–65

The Civil War is waged in America. The first "greenbacks" are issued as legal tender in the North. The Philadelphia banker and broker Jay Cooke does his part to preserve the Union by setting up a network of agents to market federal war bonds.

1863

The New York Stock & Exchange Board changes its name to the New York Stock Exchange.

1863–64

The National Banking Act creates an American national currency, putting an end to the era when any state-chartered bank could issue banknotes. The act also establishes the two-tier system of state- and national-chartered banks.

1866

The first transatlantic telegraph cable is in place.

1867

The first ticker-tape machine appears on Wall Street.

1867–68

Jay Gould, Jim Fisk, and Daniel Drew battle Cornelius Vanderbilt for control of the Erie Railroad.

1868

In Japan, the shogunate that has ruled the country for hundreds of years is overthrown by the Meiji government, which restores the emperor to an active role in politics. Impressed by the technical superiority of the advanced European powers and the United States, the new Japanese leaders actively foster the development of industry and a modified form of Western-style capitalism.

1869

The New York Stock Exchange and its Government Bond Department merge with the rival Open Board of Stock Brokers. On September 24 of that year (Black Friday), Jay Gould's attempt to corner the U.S. gold market fails, causing a major crash.

1873

The collapse of the eminent Wall Street house of Jay Cooke & Co.—which has become overextended in its position on railroads—is the most spectacular feature of a Wall Street panic that sees many institutions fail. A six-year-long depression follows with disastrous effects for Reconstruction in the American South.

1874

The Chicago Mercantile Exchange is founded as a market for farm produce. A century later, it will become a major market for currency and precious metal futures.

1877

The London Metal Exchange is founded to trade in lead, copper, tin, and zinc. Its three-month-forward delivery contract, which becomes the world standard, is initially based on the transit time for copper from Chile to Britain.

1878

Stock exchanges are founded in Tokyo and Osaka.

The first telephone is installed on the trading floor of the New York Stock Exchange.

1879

The United States returns to the gold standard, abandoned during the Civil War. This marks the beginning of a period in which every major country's currency is linked to gold.

C. 1880

Mexico City's *bolsa* is established with sidewalk trading in shares and commodities.

1880–1914

The late Victorian and Edwardian eras see British industrial and commercial supremacy at its peak.

1880s

Paris and Amsterdam join London as important centers for foreign listings. American railway stocks remain a staple for both the London and the New York exchanges.

1882

The Nippon Ginko (Bank of Japan) is founded.

1884

Charles Henry Dow publishes the first Dow Jones Index in the *Customer's Afternoon Letter*. It traces eleven stocks, nine of them railroads. That same year, J. P. Morgan helps avert a financial disaster brought on by a market crash caused by Ferdinand Ward.

1886

A stock exchange is established in Nagoya, Japan.

1887

The Johannesburg Stock Exchange is founded in South Africa.

1888

A stock exchange opens in Alexandria, Egypt.

The Financial Times is founded in London.

1889

Charles Henry Dow, Edward Davis Jones, and Charles M. Bergstresser launch *The Wall Street Journal* in New York.

1890

Baring Brothers, a leading London merchant banking concern, is unable to place Argentine bonds it has underwritten and faces insolvency. The Bank of England and the British government provide an emergency loan. This marks the first time the British government has stepped in to save a failing bank.

An exchange is founded in São Paulo, Brazil.

In the United States the Sherman Antitrust Act is passed to prohibit monopolies.

1892

Chile's first stock exchange is founded in Valparaiso; the Santiago Stock Exchange follows a year later.

1893

At the head of a hastily organized consortium of bankers, J. P. Morgan steps in, with government support, to stem a major Wall Street panic that threatens the entire American financial system.

1896

The Dow Jones Industrial Average first appears in *The Wall Street Journal*, May 26; twelve stocks are listed.

1898–1904

This period sees the first great wave of mergers in America. One cause of this is the Sherman Antitrust Act, which, while outlawing collusive agreements between companies, permits consolidation through merger. The outcome will be the modern giant corporation, often with multinational components.

1901

The Bolsa Popular de Medellín becomes Colombia's first stock exchange.

1903

A stock exchange opens in Cairo.

1907

Once again, a J. P. Morgan–led consortium bails out Wall Street, which is caught in a panic that some observers believe has been deliberately brought on by the activities of Morgan and his allies. This crisis will force the government to move toward creating the Federal Reserve system.

1908

The Bolsa de Valores de México is founded.

1909

John Moody publishes the first bond ratings.

1913

The Federal Reserve Act creates the Federal Reserve as lender of last resort and regulator of the nation's money supply.

Personal income tax is signed into law in the United States. Shortly after its introduction, stock options are first used as a form of compensation.

1914–18

World War I sees the European participants deplete their financial reserves and run up foreign debt on an unprecedented scale.

1919

According to the Treaty of Versailles, Germany is required to pay reparations to the victorious Allies of 132 billion gold marks, in addition to a 26 percent tax on its exports for the next forty-two years—an estimated $40 billion in total. Germany eventually pays about one-tenth of this amount, most of the money coming from American loans.

1919–23

Under the pressure of war reparations and internal political chaos, the German government prints money in an attempt to meet its expenses. The consequence is hyperinflation. By November 1923, it takes 4 trillion marks to purchase a single dollar.

1924–29

One of the greatest bull markets in American history sees stocks quadruple in value over a five-year period.

1925

The British government returns the pound to the gold standard with disastrous results, triggering the 1926 General Strike and widespread unemployment.

1929

For much of the year the American bull market continues, fueled by the growing public belief that it's easy to get rich by speculating in stocks. Buying on margin becomes commonplace and a bubble situation begins to develop, ignored by all but a few shrewd, veteran investors. The Dow reaches a high of 381.4 before crashing on October 28. It will be a quarter century before the Dow surpasses that 1929 high.

1929–33

In the United States the 1929 crash is followed by the Great Depression. Industrial production drops by a third and unemployment reaches 27 percent.

1931

Britain suspends gold convertibility, ending the nation's brief and disastrous return to the gold standard.

1933–41

Franklin Delano Roosevelt's New Deal policies trigger a slow recovery in the U.S. economy.

1933

The Glass-Steagall Banking Act creates the Federal Deposit Insurance Corporation to provide security for American bank accounts. It also establishes a clear legal distinction between commercial and investment banks.

1935

The *Financial Times* commences publication of its thirty-listing Industrial Ordinary Share Index, the most widely quoted British index for the next half century.

1936

John Maynard Keynes publishes *The General Theory of Employment, Interest and Money*, his revolutionary and influential thesis suggesting that the way to end a recession is for governments to increase demand through deficit spending.

In Hitler's Germany, deficit spending— specifically aimed at rebuilding the nation's military infrastructure—helps restore an economy that has been in a state of chronic recession since the conclusion of World War I. Also crucial to this recovery is an extreme form of protectionism in which severe restrictions are placed on commerce with former trading partners.

1939

The German invasion of Poland precipitates World War II. Once again, Britain and her allies will be reliant upon loans from America for their defense. To avoid a debt repayment crisis such as that which followed World War I, FDR masterminds the lend-lease system,

in which military aid can be sent to the European democracies on the understanding that the industrial outlay involved will some day be repaid "in kind."

1940–47

In German-occupied Europe, and subsequently in Allied-occupied Germany, cigarettes become a major currency, at times effectively replacing official currencies.

1941

America's entry into the war sees the country's industries working at full capacity, bringing an end to the lingering depression.

1943

Women are first admitted to the NYSE trading floor.

1944

At Bretton Woods, New Hampshire, an international conference establishes the parameters of postwar monetary policy. The outcome is a system of currencies pegged to the dollar, which is itself pegged to gold. This will prove extremely stable for the next thirty years.

1947

India gains independence and a new stock exchange is opened in New Delhi, joining those that already exist in Mumbai (Bombay) and Bangalore.

1948

The American authorities in occupied Japan rewrite the country's financial regulations. The goal is to break up the *zaibatsu*—the trustlike conglomerates that have dominated Japanese industry and commerce—and establish a U.S.-style system with a broad base of shareholders. The Americans succeed in changing the letter of the law, but the spirit of the *zaibatsu* is not entirely crushed.

The United States establishes the Marshall Plan to aid postwar Europe in its economic recovery.

1950s

The Soviet Union and its Eastern European satellites begin to place their dollar deposits in London to avoid the possibility of freezing or seizing of funds by the United States. This helps lay the foundation for the eurocurrency market that will boom a decade later as eurodollars take on a heightened importance in the world of international finance.

1950

The German Börse resumes operation.

The NYSE's daily business volume is never below a million trades.

The American Stock Exchange (AMEX) adopts its present name.

1957

The Bundesbank is established as postwar West Germany's central bank.

The Soviet Union launches *Sputnik I*, causing a downturn in Western markets.

1960s

The increasing expatriation of economic activity and the growth of multinational corporations lead to the growth of offshore banking centers in the Caribbean, the British Channel Islands, the Isle of Man, the Persian Gulf, Far Eastern city-states, and elsewhere.

In the United States, a series of far-reaching mergers creates giant—and sometimes unviable—conglomerates out of groups of unrelated businesses.

1961

The Securities and Exchange Commission rules that insider trading—based on privileged information available to executives or employees of a corporation, but not to the general public—is illegal.

The Paris Bourse is reorganized, abolishing the antiquated Parquet and Coulisse divisions.

1962

The Cuban Missile Crisis triggers a temporary downturn in the American economy.

1964

The Voluntary Credit Restraint Program restricts overseas lending by U.S. banks, but not by their foreign affiliates or subsidiaries. This encourages banks to open foreign branches, a development that fosters the growth of the eurodollar market.

1967

The first woman is admitted to membership in the NYSE.

1971

The Nixon administration closes the Treasury's gold window, meaning that dollars can no longer be exchanged for gold. Efforts to maintain a fixed rate of exchange between the dollar and Europe's most stable currency, the German mark, are abandoned. This marks the end of the Bretton Woods system, which will be formally abolished two years later, subjecting the exchange values of almost all the world's major currencies to the vagaries of the market.

In New York, the National Association of Securities Dealers (NASD) announces the launching of an automated trading system, to be known as Nasdaq.

1972

The Dow Jones Industrial Average passes the 1,000 mark for the first time.

1973–75

A fierce bear market drives down the value of U.S. stocks by some 40 percent.

1973

With the dollar and most other currencies free floating, foreign exchange options are traded for the first time, in Chicago. Amsterdam will launch the first European financial futures market in 1978, to be followed by London, Paris, and Frankfurt.

1974

Franklin National Bank goes broke due to massive losses in foreign exchange trading. It is the largest bank failure in American history. Foreign exchange

speculation gone sour is also the reason for the closure of I. D. Herstatt, a Cologne-based German bank.

OPEC countries cut crude-oil production and quadruple prices. The efforts made by industrialized nations to use monetary policy to defuse the crisis leads to runaway inflation. When OPEC precipitates another oil crisis in 1979, the industrialized nations make no attempt to defuse the situation, which leads to severe recession.

The Dow Jones Industrial Average falls below 600.

In Washington, the Employment Retirement Income Security Act is passed, transforming the American pension system and creating Individual Retirement Accounts (IRAs).

1975

The SEC abolishes fixed brokers' commissions on trades.

The federal government guarantees loans to help New York City avoid bankruptcy.

1977

Drexel Burnham Lambert begins underwriting "junk bonds"—high-yield, high-risk bonds issued by companies with low credit ratings. Business is initially slow, but takes off after 1984 as junk bonds are increasingly used to finance corporate takeovers. By the late 1980s, high-risk bonds account for nearly one-quarter of the corporate bond market, the vast majority of these issues being used for acquisitions, takeovers, and leveraged buyouts.

1978

The Amman Financial Market is established in Jordan.

1979

The Islamic revolution in Iran brings a temporary halt to stock-market activity.

1980

The Stock Exchange of Hong Kong is formed by the merger of four separate exchanges.

1981

IBM introduces the personal computer. Within a few years, it will have transformed the way the world's markets do business.

1982

On Friday, August 13, Mexico suspends payment on its foreign debt. This starts what becomes known as the Third World debt crisis and it takes frantic action on the part of creditor governments to provide a temporary solution to the problem.

A major bull market begins to take hold on Wall Street.

Top Nasdaq corporations split off to form the Nasdaq National Market.

The Israeli banking system is on the verge of collapse, due to a scandal involving the country's four premier banks; the government is forced to bail out the industry.

1985–90

Japan develops a bubble economy that sees stock and land prices soar in value during the latter half of the 1980s, only to tumble in the 1990s.

1985

With commercial banks reluctant to extend new loans to heavily indebted Third World countries, Treasury Secretary James Baker III proposes a plan in which further loans will be arranged for on the understanding that the recipients will pursue a policy of economic growth rather than austerity. The loans will come from the World Bank, which can provide long-term debt, rather than from the International Monetary Fund. The crisis continues unabated.

The Dow Jones Average passes 1,500 in December.

1986

In Margaret Thatcher's England, the London stock market is transformed by the massive deregulation that is commonly referred to as the Big Bang. The old distinction between brokers and jobbers (market makers) is eliminated, and trading shifts from the floor to a computerized platform. Most importantly, membership in the exchange is made available to foreigners, a situation that major American and Japanese brokerage houses are quick to take advantage of.

In America, Ivan Boesky pleads guilty to insider trading and pays a record $100 million fine.

1987

In January the Dow Jones index breaks 2,000, but on October 19 the New York stock market falls by 23 percent, the largest one-day decline ever. Newly installed Federal Reserve chairman Alan Greenspan moves quickly to support the market with injections of liquidity and guarantees against loss for banks that buy stocks. Thanks in large part to this swift response, the greater economy sustains little damage and the stock market recovers quickly, making up its losses in less than two years.

The Australian Stock Exchange (ASX) is formed by combining bourses in Melbourne, Sydney, Hobart, Adelaide, and Perth.

1988

Drexel Burnham Lambert pleads guilty to six criminal counts related to insider trading and pays a fine of $650 million. It is required to fire Michael Milken, head of its junk bond department, who is later barred from the securities markets. Two years later Drexel declares bankruptcy, marking the end of Wall Street's infatuation with high-risk bonds.

In the Soviet Union, the All-Union Conference of the Communist Party approves Mikhail Gorbachev's plans for *perestroika*, or restructuring. Within a few years, the U.S.S.R.'s planned economy will be history, along with the U.S.S.R. itself.

1989

Treasury Secretary Nicholas Brady announces a new plan to deal with Third World debt. For the first time debt reduction, however modest, replaces new loans as the focus of the proposed solution.

In the United States a great wave of mergers and acquisitions reaches its peak.

The Bahrain Stock Exchange is established.

1990s

The beginnings of a world economy can be traced back to the 1490s. Five hundred years later, a full-fledged global economy is coming into existence as multinational conglomerates establish bases on every continent, while computers and modern communications technology permit the instantaneous transmission of information from one side of the world to the other.

In the United States, stocks enjoy the greatest bull market in decades; the Dow index rises from below 3,000 to above 11,000 points. The automated Nasdaq exchange becomes a force to be reckoned with, and stocks of the emerging high-tech companies it lists soar in value, prompting fears of an approaching "correction." Millions of Americans refuse to take these fears seriously. More and more people are investing in the stock market, either directly or through indirect instruments such as mutual funds and 401(k)s.

1990

Long shuttered by the Chinese Communist government, the Shanghai Stock Exchange reopens for business, as does the bourse in Budapest. By the end of the decade, there will be hardly a country in the world without its own stock market.

1991

Representatives of the twelve nations belonging to the European Economic Community meet in Maastricht and agree on a program of monetary union. The plan calls for Europe to end the decade with a single currency—the euro—and a single central bank.

Stock exchanges in Alexandria and Cairo, dormant since the mid-1950s under socialism, return to life.

The New Zealand Stock Exchange closes regional trading floors, implements its Screen Trading System, and abolishes the open-outcry style of trading.

Membership in the Korea Stock Exchange is opened to foreign brokerage houses.

1992
In an attempt to compete with the NYSE and the Nasdaq, the American Stock Exchange (AMEX) creates the Emerging Company Marketplace. The ECM is quickly caught up in scandal, however. (One of the first companies that it lists, a manufacturer of flame retardants, turns out to be owned by an admitted stock manipulator who also happens to be a convicted arsonist.) In 1998 AMEX will become the junior partner in a merger with the Nasdaq.

In Europe, attacks by speculators—especially those involved in hedge funds—force several currencies, including the once mighty pound, to drop out of the exchange-rate mechanism that has been created in anticipation of monetary union.

Japan's bubble economy bursts and the country slides into a recession.

In China, exchanges are established in Shanghai and Shenzhen.

1993
A newly reconstituted Prague Stock Exchange resumes activity.

1994
Mexico's emergency devaluation of the peso wreaks havoc on the country's financial system and reawakens frighten-

ing memories of the 1980s debt crisis.

In the United States, the Nasdaq surpasses the NYSE in daily volume for the first time.

The Federal Reserve raises interest rates for the first time in five years, toppling rickety financial structures around the country. California's wealthy Orange County is among the victims; its fund manager had bet that rates would fall. Rather than raise taxes, the county declares bankruptcy.

1996
The SEC rules that Nasdaq dealers have illegally colluded to boost spreads in the market-making process, enriching themselves at the expense of their customers.

1997
Stock markets throughout Asia crash and currencies are devalued, setting off what will be known as the Asian Crisis. The economies of what had been the world's fastest-growing region are brought to a virtual standstill, raising questions about the stability of the global financial system.

Hong Kong reverts from British to Chinese rule.

1998
The Russian government's decision to devalue the ruble and suspend payment on foreign debts leads many observers to conclude that the country's attempt to become a market economy has failed.

Long-term Capital Management, a hedge fund run by, among others, two Nobel Prize–winning economists, collapses after betting the wrong way on interest-rate movements. The Federal Reserve Bank of New York hastily orchestrates a bailout.

Chrysler merges with Daimler-Benz, an early instance of the kind of multinational merger between giant companies that will spread throughout the automobile industry, the communications industry, and elsewhere.

Exchanges in Germany and Switzerland launch Eurex, a joint futures market.

1999
The Singapore Exchange (SGX) is formed by a merger of the Stock Exchange of Singapore and the Singapore Futures Exchange.

The Shanghai Stock Exchange closes for three weeks due to depressed trading.

2000
The merger trend extends to major stock markets as the London and Frankfurt exchanges announce their intent to merge, as do the Paris, Brussels, and Amsterdam bourses. The Nasdaq, meanwhile, signs a number of important partnership agreements with exchanges in Europe, Asia, and Australia.

Vietnam establishes a stock market, the Ho Chi Minh Securities Trading Center.

Jordan is accepted into full membership in the World Trade Organization.

The Mexican market gains investor confidence due to the North American Free Trade Agreement.

Brazil's nine exchanges integrate in an effort to gain full value of the country's natural resources.

2001
The so-called New Economy—rooted in high-tech stocks—continues the decline that had set in the previous year.

The U.S. economy and the economies of Western Europe attempt to stave off recession.

Selected Bibliography

Abu-Lughod, Janet. *Before European Hegemony: The World System A.D. 1250–1350*. Oxford: Oxford University Press, 1989.

Aldcroft, Derek H. *From Versailles to Wall Street, 1919–1929*. Berkeley, Calif.: University of California Press, 1977.

Arditti, Fred D. *Derivatives: A Comprehensive Resource for Options, Futures, Interest Rate Swaps, and Mortgage Securities*. Boston: Harvard Business School Press, 1996.

Armstrong, Philip, Andrew Glyn, and John Harrison. *Capitalism Since 1945*. Oxford: Basil Blackwell, 1991.

Austen, Ralph. *African Economic History*. London: James Currey, 1987.

Bagehot, Walter. *Lombard Street: A Description of the Money Market*. New York: Wiley Investment Classics, 1999.

Baruch, Bernard. *My Own Story*. New York: Holt, Rinehart & Winston, 1957.

Bernstein, Peter L. *Capital Ideas: The Improbable Origins of Modern Wall Street*. New York: Free Press, 1992.

Boltho, A. *Japan, An Economic Survey*. Oxford: Oxford University Press, 1975.

Braudel, Fernand. *The Wheels of Commerce*. Berkeley, Calif.: University of California Press, 1992.

Brezinski, Horst, and Michael Fritsch, eds. *The Emergence and Evolution of Markets*. Cheltenham, England, and Northampton, Mass.: Edward Elgar, 1997.

Bruck, Connie. *The Predators' Ball: The Inside Story of Drexel Burnham and the Rise of the Junk Bond Raiders*. New York: Simon and Schuster, 1988.

Buchan, James. *Frozen Desire: The Meaning of Money*. New York: Farrar, Straus & Giroux, 1997.

Buffett, Warren, with Janet C. Lowe. *Warren Buffet Speaks*. New York: John Wiley, 1997.

Carosso, Vincent. *Investment Banking in America: A History*. Cambridge, Mass.: Harvard University Press, 1970.

Chancellor, Edward. *Devil Take the Hindmost: A History of Financial Speculation*. New York: Farrar, Straus & Giroux, 1999.

Chaudhuri, K. N. *Asia Before Europe: Economy and Civilization of the Indian Ocean from the Rise of Islam to 1750*. Cambridge: Cambridge University Press, 1990.

———. *Trade and Civilization in the Indian Ocean: An Economic History from the Rise of Islam to 1750*. Cambridge: Cambridge University Press, 1985.

Chernow, Ron. *The House of Morgan: An American Banking Dynasty and the Rise of Modern Finance*. New York: Atlantic Monthly Press, 1990.

Collins, Frederick L. *Money Town, the Story of Manhattan Toe: That Golden Mile That Lies Between the Battery and the Fields*. New York: G. P. Putnam, 1946.

Eames, Francis L. *The New York Stock Exchange*. New York: Thomas G. Hall, 1964.

Ferguson, Niall. *The House of Rothschild*. New York: Viking, 1998.

Finley, M. I. *The Ancient Economy*. Berkeley, Calif.: University of California Press, 1973.

Frantz, Douglas. *Levine & Co.: Wall Street's Insider Trading Scandal*. New York: Henry Holt & Co., 1987.

Friedman, Milton, and Anna Jacobson Schwartz. *A Monetary History of the United States*. Princeton, N.J.: Princeton University Press, 1963.

Galbraith, John Kenneth. *The Great Crash, 1929 (50th Anniversary Edition)*. Boston: Houghton Mifflin, 1979.

———. *A Short History of Financial Euphoria*. New York: Whittle Books, in association with Viking, 1993.

———. *A Journey Through Economic Time: A Firsthand View*. Boston: Houghton Mifflin, 1994.

Geisst, Charles. *Wall Street: A History*. New York: Oxford University Press, 1997.

Gordon, John Steele. *The Great Game: The Emergence of Wall Street as a World Power, 1653–2000*. New York: Scribner, 1999.

———. *The Scarlet Woman of Wall Street: Jay Gould, Jim Fisk, Cornelius Vanderbilt, the Erie Railway Wars, and the Birth of Wall Street*. New York: Weidenfeld & Nicholson, 1988.

Grant, James. *Money of the Mind: Borrowing and Lending in America from the Civil War to Michael Milken*. New York: Farrar, Straus & Giroux, 1992.

Gresing, David, and Laurie Morse. *Brokers, Bagmen, and Moles: Fraud and Corruption in the Chicago Futures Markets*. New York: John Wiley, 1991.

Haynie, Henry. *Paris Past & Present*. New York: F. A. Stokes, 1902.

Henwood, Doug. *Wall Street: How It Works and for Whom*. London: Verso, 1997.

Herera, Sue. *Women of the Street: Making It on Wall Street—The World's Toughest Business.* New York: John Wiley, 1997.

Inwood, Stephen. *A History of London.* New York: Carroll & Graf, 1998.

Jansen, Marius B. *The Making of Modern Japan.* Cambridge, Mass.: Belknap Press of Harvard University Press, 2000.

Kaliski, Burton S., ed. *Encyclopaedia of Business and Finance.* New York: Macmillan Reference USA, 2001.

Keynes, J. M. *The General Theory of Employment, Interest and Money.* New York: Harcourt, Brace & World, 1936.

Kindleberger, Charles. *Manias, Panics, and Crashes: A History of Financial Crises.* New York: Basic Books, 1989.

———. *A Financial History of Western Europe.* Oxford: Oxford University Press, 1993.

Kurtz, Howard. *The Fortune Tellers: Inside Wall Street's Game of Money, Media, and Manipulation.* New York: Free Press, 2000.

Lewis, Michael. *Liar's Poker: Rising Through the Wreckage on Wall Street.* New York: W. W. Norton, 1989.

Lillywhite, Bryant. *London Coffee Houses: A Reference Book of Coffee Houses of the Seventeenth, Eighteenth, and Nineteeth Centuries.* London: G. Allen and Unwin, 1963.

Lowy, Martin. *High Rollers: Inside the Savings and Loan Debacle.* New York: Praeger, 1991.

Mackay, Charles. *Extraordinary Popular Delusions and the Madness of Crowds.* New York: Harmony Books, 1980.

Naisbitt, John. *Megatrends Asia: Eight Megatrends That Are Reshaping Our World.* New York: Touchstone, 1997.

Newman, Peter, Murray Milgate, and John Eatwell, eds. *The New Palgrave Dictionary of Money and Finance.* New York: Stockton Press, 1992.

Odean, Kathleen. *High Steppers, Fallen Angels, and Lollipops: Wall Street Slang.* New York: Dodd, Mead, 1988.

Partnoy, Frank. *FIASCO: Blood in the Water on Wall Street.* New York: W. W. Norton, 1997.

Prestbo, John A., ed. *The Market's Measure.* New York: Dow Jones, 1999.

Rohwer, Jim. *Asia Rising.* New York: Touchstone, 1996.

Simmel, George. *The Philosophy of Money.* Boston: Beacon Press, 1978.

Smith, Adam. *An Inquiry into the Nature and Causes of the Wealth of Nations.* Oxford: The Clarendon Press, 1976.

Sobel, Robert. *Inside Wall Street: Continuity and Change in the Financial District.* New York: W. W. Norton, 1977.

———. *The Rise and Fall of the Conglomerate Kings.* New York: Stein & Day, 1984.

———. *The Curbstone Brokers: The Origins of the American Stock Exchange.* New York: Macmillan, 1970.

———. *AMEX: A History of the American Stock Exchange, 1921–1971.* New York: Weybright and Talley, 1972.

———. *The Big Board: A History of the New York Stock Exchange, 1935–1975.* New York: Weybright and Talley, 1975.

Soros, George. *The Alchemy of Finance: Reading the Mind of the Market.* New York: Simon and Schuster, 1987.

———. *Soros on Soros: Staying Ahead of the Curve.* New York: John Wiley, 1995.

———. *The Crisis of Global Capitalism: Open Society Endangered.* New York: BBS/Public Affairs, 1998.

Stewart, James B. *Den of Thieves.* New York: Simon and Schuster, 1991.

Strieder, Jacob. *Jacob Fugger the Rich, Merchant and Banker of Augsburg, 1459–1525.* Translated by Mildred L. Hartsough. Hamden, Conn.: The Adelphi Co., 1931.

Tamarkin, Bob. *The Merc: The Emergence of a Global Financial Powerhouse.* New York: HarperBusiness, 1993.

Thomas, Dana Lee. *The Plungers and the Peacocks: An Update of the Classic History of the Stock Market.* New York: Morrow, 1989.

Weatherford, Jack. *The History of Money: From Sandstone to Cyberspace.* New York: Three Rivers Press, 1997.

Werner, Walter, and Steven T. Smith. *Wall Street.* New York: Columbia University Press, 1991.

Wood, Christopher. *Boom and Bust.* New York: Atheneum, 1989.

Zweig, Phillip L. *Wriston: Walter Wriston, Citibank, and the Rise and Fall of American Financial Supremacy.* New York: Crown Publishing Group, 1996.

Glossary

A

ACTIVE MARKET A well-functioning market in which transactions are frequent, volume is high, spreads are narrow, and price swings are moderate.

AMEX The American Stock Exchange. Evolving from the New York Curb Agency, the AMEX started as the home of small over-the-counter companies, eventually becoming a serious alternative to the New York Stock Exchange (NYSE). In 1998, the AMEX entered into a merger with the Nasdaq.

ANNUITY An investment that, in return for a one-time payment, pays a fixed annual amount until the purchaser dies. Relatively unimportant today, annuities were at one time a major form of government borrowing.

ARBITRAGE Simultaneously buying a security in one market and selling it in another to take advantage of price differences. (At any given moment, the price for a particular stock may be fractionally higher or lower in Singapore, say, than it is in Hong Kong.)

AUCTION MARKET A market such as the New York Stock Exchange in which buyers vie with other buyers and sellers with other sellers to establish the most advantageous price. (This is sometimes called a continuous auction market.)

AVERAGES Published averages, such as the Dow Jones Industrial Average, that are statistical expressions of trends in securities prices. The Dow, for example, indexes the movements of thirty stocks, each of which is chosen to represent a significant sector of the economy.

B

BASIS POINT One one-hundredth of a percentage point; a common unit of interest rates.

BEAR MARKET A market in which prices are generally falling. A bear is someone who expects prices, or the price of a particular stock, to fall, and perhaps acts on this expectation by selling short. The term's origins are not entirely clear, but it is believed to have been borrowed from the practice of bear hunters, who accepted payment for skins before they had trapped the animals.

BED-AND-BREAKFAST DEAL Selling a security—usually a block of shares—one day and buying it back the next. This is typically done at the end of the year, for tax purposes.

BID AND ASK The bid is the highest price anyone is willing to pay for a stock. The ask is the lowest anyone will sell it for. The two together are called a quote, and the difference between them is the spread.

BILL OF EXCHANGE A transferable IOU given as payment by a buyer to the seller. The use of bills of exchange became widespread in Europe, beginning in the Late Middle Ages, because they permitted merchants to avoid the dangerous necessity of transporting large quantities of coins or other valuables. They were often resold many times before finally being redeemed, or else canceled out against each other, at periodic bill-of-exchange fairs.

BLUE-CHIP STOCKS Safe, dependable stocks of well-established companies. The term comes from poker, where blue chips are the highest denomination.

BLUE-SKY LAWS Laws established by individual American states to protect the rights of stockholders.

BOND A debt instrument in which the issuing authority, usually a government or a corporation, promises to repay the principal on a certain date and interest on a fixed schedule. Among government issues, a bond conventionally refers to an instrument with a maturity of ten years or more. Government bonds issued in foreign markets are often given cute names: samurai bonds in Japan, bulldog bonds in Great Britain, Rembrandt bonds in the Netherlands, matador bonds in Spain, etc.

BOOK VALUE The value of a stock arrived at by analyzing a company's records and weighing its assets against its liabilities to arrive at its worth. That worth is then divided by the number of outstanding common shares, and the result is the book value of a single share, which may or may not be reflected in the stock's market performance.

BOURSE French for stock exchange. In modern French the word means "purse," but in the context of financial markets the name is thought to have originated in thirteenth-century Bruges, where merchants gathered in front of a house belonging to the commercially prominent van Buerse family to trade bills of credit and other commercial papers.

BROKER An intermediary who executes the public's buy and sell orders.

BUCKET SHOP An unauthorized brokerage, of a sort once common in New York and elsewhere, known for underhanded and outright fraudulent practices. Typically, for example, the operator of a bucket shop would accept a customer's order for a trade but delay executing it until the stock concerned was at a price more favorable to himself. Today the term is sometimes casually applied to smaller brokerages that employ overly aggressive sales tactics.

BULL MARKET The opposite of a bear market—that is, one in which prices are generally rising. This term, in use since at least the eighteenth century, is of unknown origin.

BUSINESS CYCLE Alternating expansions and contractions in the economy. Business cycles typically run seven to ten years from peak to peak or trough to trough. There is no real consensus on the causes of business cycles, but they have been a universal feature of market economies since the early nineteenth century.

BUY, HOLD, AND SELL Standard terms used by financial analysts to recommend for or against owning a given stock. Since a "sell" recommendation is considered overly aggressive, except in extreme circumstances, most analysts stick to "buy" and "hold."

C

CALLS AND PUTS A call is an option to buy. A put is an option to sell. If you sell a call, for example, you are granting the buyer the right to buy a good or security from you at a certain price at any time between now and the call's expiration date.

CAPITAL From the Latin *caput*, or head, this term was first used in thirteenth-century Italy to refer to funds, a stock of merchandise, or money lent at interest. Interestingly, a competing term was *corpo*, from the Latin for body. But the metaphor of a head was ultimately more compelling, and by the seventeenth century capital was being used in more or less its modern sense, while *corpo* had disappeared. Today the word is the subject of semantic disagreements. To Marxists, for instance, it really refers to the social relation between the capitalist and the worker.

CAPITAL GAIN OR LOSS Profit or loss resulting from the sale of an asset.

CAPITALIZATION The total amount of bonds, stocks, and other securities issued by a given corporation.

CASH Not only the stuff in your wallet but any highly liquid reservoir of value. For a large American corporation, "cash" typically means short-term government debt.

COMMERCIAL PAPER Short-term debt instruments issued by companies to raise working capital.

COMMODITY In a financial context, commodities are goods such as crude oil and soybeans available in identical form from a number of producers and not yet branded. Minerals and agricultural products account for the majority of important commodities, which are normally traded on exchanges specializing in futures.

COMMON STOCK Two types of stock, preferred and common, are issued. As the name suggests, common stock is the most numerous type. An investor who purchases common stock is not guaranteed dividends but has a residual claim on the assets of a corporation after taxes, wages, bondholders, other creditors, and preferred stock owners (in that order) have all been paid. Ownership of common stock does, however, give the investor voting rights at the issuing company's stockholders' meetings, providing a say in the control of management that is proportionate to the number of shares held.

CONVERTIBILITY A currency is convertible if it can be freely exchanged for other currencies at the going exchange rate. A convertible currency is often essential to attract foreign investment, but it can create wild swings in the securities and foreign exchange markets as foreign money moves in and out of the country.

CONVERTIBLE SECURITY In the United States a convertible security is a bond, debenture, or preferred stock that gives the owner the right to exchange it for another class of security, usually common stock. In British usage, a convertible security is a government bond that can be exchanged for another of a different maturity.

CORNER An effort, illegal in most markets, to make a profit by gaining control of all the available supply of some commodity.

CORPORATION An association chartered by a government (in the United States, usually a state government) to conduct business. Its major function is to limit the personal liability of the owners for the debts of the organization. Historically, corporations were specially chartered to perform some necessary function—building and maintaining a bridge, say—in which they were often granted a monopoly. Their evolution into the freewheeling profit-making enterprises of today was complete by the late nineteenth century.

CORRECTION A euphemistic term for a sharp decline in stock prices, conventionally of 10 percent or more, that interrupts the upward momentum of a bull market.

COUPON BOND A type of bond issued with detachable coupons along the side. The owner of the bond cuts these off and mails them to the issuer as various interest payments come due (hence the traditional description of the idle rich as "coupon clippers").

D

DAY TRADER A term for a speculator who takes positions in a security or commodity, then liquidates them before the end of the day. The rise of the Internet has made day trading a viable, though very risky, activity for anyone with suitable credit and access to a personal computer.

DEALER An individual or securities company buying and selling stocks and bonds as a principal rather than as an agent.

DEALER MARKET A market in which members of the public trade with professional dealers rather than with each other. The Nasdaq is a dealer market.

DEBENTURE An unsecured bond backed only by the general credit rating of the issuing company.

DEFLATION The reverse of inflation, defined as the economic situation caused by a general decline in prices or an increase in the value of money.

DERIVATIVES Financial instruments whose worth is based on the value of underlying instruments or goods (such as stocks, bonds, commodities, and so on). Options and futures are examples of derivatives.

DIVIDEND A portion of a company's profits paid out to shareholders. In the past, dividends were typically the main source of income from stock ownership, but today returns from capital gains are usually more important.

E

ECONOMIC INDICATOR A statistic drawn from analysis of the national economy that provides professional observers with information that can be factored into predictions of future stock market performance.

EMERGING MARKETS Optimistic designation for underdeveloped countries in general and their stock exchanges in particular. When prices in these exchanges are heading down rather than up, wits sometimes call them submerging markets.

EQUITIES Securities that represent a share of ownership in a company—in other words, common and preferred stocks.

EXCHANGE RATE The ratio at which two currencies exchange. The floating-rate system, under which exchange rates are determined on a day-to-day basis by private markets, is relatively recent. Until 1974 exchange rates were fixed by governments under the Bretton Woods system established at the end of World War II, and for much of the hundred years before that, currencies were strictly pegged to gold.

F

FEDERAL FUNDS RATE The interest rate banks charge each other for overnight loans (so called because what's being loaned comes from the reserves that banks are required to keep on deposit with the Federal Reserve). This is the only interest rate the Fed sets directly, and is its main lever for regulating the economy. The British equivalent is the LIBOR (London Interbank Offered Rate.)

FEDERAL RESERVE The central banking system of the United States, legally responsible for restraining inflation and attempting to maintain full employment—though which of those mandates is a higher priority varies from time to time. The Federal Reserve is also the lender of last resort, charged with providing emergency loans. Often referred to simply as the Fed.

FLOOR BROKERS Brokers who work on the trading floor of a stock exchange, such as the NYSE.

FORMULA INVESTING An investment practice that calls for the shifting of funds from one instrument to another (from common stock to preferred stock, for example) when a given market indicator ascends or descends to a specific point.

FREE MARKET A market in which prices are established by the laws of supply and demand.

FUTURES Contractual agreements to buy or sell specific quantities of a commodity or financial instrument at a specific price at a specific date in the future. Futures attract both speculators and institutional investors seeking to hedge against unfavorable price shifts.

FUTURES MARKET A marketplace where futures are traded.

G

GOING NAKED Selling a call against an asset one doesn't own. Like short-selling, "going naked" exposes the seller to theoretically unlimited losses if the price of the asset rises.

GOING PUBLIC The term used when a company first issues shares for sale to the public in order to raise capital.

GOLD FIX The setting of the price of gold by commodity dealers, especially in London, where meetings take place twice on every trading day.

GOLD STANDARD The system prevailing through much of the nineteenth century and into the twentieth in which all major currencies were linked to gold. Under the gold standard, countries did not have the freedom to devalue their currencies, thus a persistent trade deficit inevitably led to high interest rates and recession.

GREENMAIL One of many takeover-related terms coined during the 1980s. When a company is the object of a takeover threat, it may retaliate by making an emergency buyback of shares, rendering itself less vulnerable but at the same time inevitably pushing up the price of the stock. Even if the would-be "raider" should fail in his takeover bid, he is assured of making a handsome profit on the stock he has already bought to give his bid plausibility.

GRESHAM'S LAW Named for Sir Thomas Gresham, who warned Queen Elizabeth I that bad money drives out good. This sensible rule of thumb went back to the Greeks, but Gresham had in mind a specific situation in which two currencies were in circulation, one minted from pure gold, the other from adulterated gold. People would spend the debased currency as quickly as possible, he insisted, and hoard the other for the intrinsic value of its metal content.

GROWTH STOCK A share of a company whose prospects for growth are considered strong. Typically, these stocks are not good investments by conventional value criteria such as price-earnings ratios.

H

HEDGE FUND An investing group in private partnership (in the United States, restricted by law to fewer than one hundred partners) that, unlike a mutual fund, is allowed to employ such devices as short-selling and complex option strategies to hedge against risks. The minimum investment in a hedge fund is typically $1 million.

HEDGING A way of reducing risk that, to all intents and purposes, is like betting on both horses in a two-horse race. Whichever horse finishes first, the bettor avoids serious losses.

HORIZONTAL INTEGRATION The takeover of one company by another involved in the same kind of business.

HOSTILE TAKEOVER The act of acquiring control of a company that does not wish to be acquired.

I

INCOME STOCK Common stock that pays substantial dividends.

INDEX A statistical tool based on the market movements of a group of stocks whose performance is considered a good indicator for the broader market or economy. The best-known index in the

United States is the Dow Jones Industrial Average. Other major American examples include Standard & Poor's 500 and the Nasdaq Composite Index. The most important British index is the FTSE 100 (Financial Times Stock Exchange, popularly known as "footsie"). Germany has the DAX Index (Deutscher Aktienindex), France the CAC 40 (Compagnie des Agents de Change), Japan the Nikkei 225, Hong Kong the Hang Seng, and Singapore the Straits Times Index.

INFLATION An increase in prices or, equivalently, a decline in the value of money. Depending on the circumstances (and the economist you ask), inflation may be due to excessive printing of money by the government, excessively low interest rates, low unemployment, rapid rises in commodity prices (as with the oil crises of the 1970s), or political unrest.

INSTITUTIONAL INVESTOR An organization such as a bank, insurance company, pension fund, or mutual fund that invests large sums of money in the securities markets.

IN THE MONEY Said of an option whose exercise price is at or near the current price of the underlying security.

INVESTMENT BANK A bank engaged in making long-term loans to industry, in underwriting security issues, in financing merger and acquisition activity, and so forth.

IPO Initial public offering. A privately held company's first issue of shares on the stock market. Making an IPO is often referred to as "going public."

J

JUNK BOND A bond considered below investment grade by the major bond-rating agencies (that is to say, not a rock-solid bet for Junior's college fund). Because of the degree of risk implicit in acquiring these bonds, they are obliged to offer high returns to the speculator;

hence their advocates call them high-yield bonds. Junk bonds (sometimes shortened to "junk") have often been issued to finance corporate takeovers.

K

KEYNESIANISM Named for John Maynard Keynes, the view that markets, especially labor markets, are not always self-regulating, and that government policies of deficit spending and low interest rates may be necessary to achieve full employment.

L

LAISSEZ-FAIRE A policy favoring free or minimally regulated markets. It comes from the slogan of the eighteenth-century Physiocrats, *"laisser faire, laisser passer"* ("leave them alone, let their goods pass"). The Physiocrats were referring specifically to farmers, believing that agriculture was the source of all wealth and that restrictions on agricultural exports should be abolished.

LEVERAGE A function of the ratio of debt to equity in a given company or transaction. A company with a heavy debt load is described as highly leveraged. Likewise, a leveraged buyout is an acquisition of a company in which nearly all the funds used to make the acquisition are borrowed.

LIQUIDITY (1) The ease with which an asset can be converted into cash. (2) In the context of securities markets, liquidity specifically refers to the possibility of buying or selling large amounts of a security without causing major price changes.

LISTED STOCK A stock traded on a registered stock exchange. In order to be listed, a stock must meet the standards of that exchange with regard to capitalization, etc.

"LONG" AND "SHORT" (1) Applied to loans, shorthand for long-term and short-term. (2) Applied to securities, a long position is one in which one owns a security and hopes its price will go up. A short position is one in which one has sold a security, or owes it to someone else, and hopes its price will go down. In this second sense, the terms can be used as verbs, as in, "I am long 100 Yahoo," meaning "I own 100 shares of Yahoo." Traders also talk of "going long" or "going short," as in "X is going short on Microsoft."

M

MARGIN The amount paid by a client (of a bank or brokerage) who uses credit to buy a security. Current U.S. law says the client must pay at least 50 percent.

MARGIN CALL A legally enforceable demand for more money from a client who has used credit to buy a security that has subsequently dropped in value.

MARKET MAKER A dealer who is ready (or sometimes obliged) to buy or sell a given stock on his or her own account on a continuous basis. Market makers are important to maintain market liquidity, ensuring that a would-be buyer or seller can always find someone to trade with.

MERGER The uniting of two or more companies.

MUNICIPAL BONDS Debt instruments issued by cities and other local governments. In the United States their main importance is that income from them is tax-exempt. (Until 1988, taxing municipal bonds was considered unconstitutional. This is no longer the case, but they are still not taxed, ostensibly to provide a subsidy to local governments.)

MUTUAL FUND An open-end investment company that is capitalized by the continuous sale of its stock.

N

NASD National Association of Securities Dealers.

NASDAQ Short for National Association of Securities Dealers Automated Quotation System. The country's largest over-the-counter stock market and second-largest market overall, after the NYSE. The Nasdaq's listing requirements are less stringent than the NYSE's, and companies that trade there tend to be smaller—though many of the largest high-tech companies, such as Microsoft and Sun Microsystems, also trade on the Nasdaq.

NYSE New York Stock Exchange.

O

OPTION A financial instrument that conveys the right to buy or sell a given security at a given price. In the United States, options can be exercised at any time before their expiration date. In Britain they can be exercised only on that date.

OVER-THE-COUNTER STOCKS Originally, the stocks of small companies insufficiently capitalized to be listed on the NYSE or on one of the American regional exchanges. With the growth of AMEX and especially the Nasdaq—both considered over-the-counter markets— the term has come to seem patronizing and almost meaningless.

P

PASS THE BOOK Shift trading from one financial center to another. The conventional itinerary for a global firm begins in Tokyo, shifts to London when that market opens at 4:00 P.M. Tokyo time, and then to New York at 1:00 P.M. London time.

PENNY STOCK A low-priced, often speculative issue, usually trading at less than a dollar a share.

PINK SHEETS At the opposite end of the financial spectrum from blue chips, these are over-the-counter stocks that are too small even to be listed on the Nasdaq. They trade, in effect, by appointment only. The term refers to a price list that is distributed daily to brokers.

PREFERRED STOCK Shares that carry dividends at fixed rates that must be paid before any dividends are paid to common shareholders. Today, preferred stock accounts for less than 2 percent of the shares traded on the New York Stock Exchange, and an even smaller percentage of those listed by the Nasdaq.

PRICE-EARNINGS RATIO Frequently used value measure for stocks: a common stock's market price divided by the company's annual earnings. Traditionally, a p/e ratio of 20 is considered high. At the peak of the 1990s technology boom, however, many stocks reached p/e ratios of 50 and higher.

PRIMARY MARKET When a corporation's stock is issued for the first time, it is said to be sold on the primary market.

PROFIT-TAKING The sale of securities that have appreciated in value. When many investors indulge in profit-taking at the same time, it is apt to cause a downturn in the market.

PROXY A form used by the owner of stock in a company to delegate the voting rights of that stock to someone else. Somewhat confusingly, the same term is also used for the person delegated, and for the vote itself.

R

RECESSION A period of negative economic growth.

S

SEAT A membership in an exchange, allowing the holder to buy and sell securities without paying a commission. Until 1885 it referred to the physical seat that each exchange member was assigned.

SECONDARY MARKET The buying and selling of existing securities. The secondary market accounts for the overwhelming bulk of securities trading.

SECURITIZATION Conversion of financial obligations, usually debt, into tradable instruments. Mortgage-backed securities, for example, are a way for banks to securitize mortgages.

SECURITY A financial instrument that represents ownership (in the case of stocks) or creditorship (in the case of bonds).

SHORT-SELLING Selling borrowed stock in hopes that the price will fall, allowing the short-seller to buy the stock back at a lower price and take the difference as profit.

SPECIALIST On the trading floor of the NYSE (but not in dealer markets like the Nasdaq), a member responsible for ensuring an orderly market in the stock or stocks assigned to him. Specialists maintain "the book" containing current bids and asks, and act as market makers.

SPECIE Coined money.

SPOT The price of goods for immediate delivery.

T

TECHNICAL TRADER A trader who looks for patterns in stock movements to predict future movements. In the opposing camp are fundamental traders, who focus on the economic realities underlying stock prices. Some technical traders, referred to derisively as "chartists," talk about signs like "pennants," "rising wedges," "heads and shoulders," and "saucer bottoms" hidden in price movements. Other technical traders focus on more rigorous indicators like trading volume and price momentum.

3-6-3 RULE The rule said to be followed by bankers during the staid 1950s and '60s: borrow money from your depositors at 3 percent, lend it to your customers at 6 percent, and be on the golf course by 3:00 P.M.

TREASURYS Shorthand for federal debt. Treasury bonds are debt instruments with a maturity of ten years or more. Bills have maturities running from three months to one year, while notes run from one year to ten. The market in Treasurys is by far the largest in the world, dwarfing any stock market.

TRIPLE WITCHING HOUR The final trading hour of the third Friday in March, June, September, and December. Triple witching hours mark the concurrent expiration dates for options and futures on stock indexes.

U

UNDERWRITER (1) A financial institution that acts as an intermediary for a company issuing shares or bonds. It buys the securities from the company, then sells them to the public. (2) In the insurance world, an employee who assesses risk when a policy is being issued.

UP TICK A trade made at a price higher than the previous trade; a "down tick" is a trade made at a lower price.

V

VOLUME Quantity of trading on a market, often stated in terms of the number of shares changing hands daily.

W

WARRANT Similar to an option to buy, but longer-term; sometimes permanent until exercised.

WATERING STOCK Issuing excessive numbers of new shares, thereby devaluing those held by current stockholders.

Y

YIELD Dividends or interest returned to investors on a given security, expressed as a percentage of the present price of that security.

YO-YO STOCK Stock subject to extreme volatility.

Z

ZERO COUPON BOND Literally, a bond to which no coupons are attached (see "coupon bond"). It pays no interest but is priced at a discount when issued so that a profit results when it is redeemed.

Acknowledgments

As described in the foreword, this book derives from an idea suggested by John Angelo, a graduate of Wall Street's bond trading pits, formerly senior managing director of L. F. Rothschild, and now CEO of Angelo, Gordon & Co., a prominent New York firm specializing in nontraditional asset management. Mr. Angelo also gave freely of his time and made many valuable suggestions that have enriched the text.

The concept was nurtured by Robert Abrams, publisher of Abbeville Press, who has shown a commitment to this project that goes far beyond the norm. His own Wall Street background, combined with his long experience in the art book field, enabled him to provide insights and suggestions based on practical experience that have left their mark on every page.

This book had the benefit of being developed under the guidance of two first-rate editors. Nancy Grubb oversaw the early stages of its evolution, before leaving to take charge of the art list of one of the nation's premier university presses. After her departure, it fell to Christopher Lyon to help shape the book into its final form, a task that he undertook with a combination of intelligence, imagination, enthusiasm, and doggedness, along with unflagging good humor that proved invaluable as due dates loomed.

There were others, too, who managed to keep creative juices flowing while the hounds of publishing deadlines snapped at their collective heels. In particular, I would like to thank art director and designer Julietta Cheung, and members of her staff, including Cheryl Peterka, Misha Beletsky, and John Joseph McGowan; production manager Louise Kurtz; picture editors Lisa Barnett and Robin Raffer; as well as Ashley Benning, Kerrie Baldwin, and Sarah Nitterauer of the Abbeville editorial department. Josh Mason made important contributions to the preparation of the timeline, the glossary, and the biographies, and Marian Appellof was a model of diligence, not only copyediting the text but also performing many additional tasks such as transforming the timeline into the "ticker tape" strip that runs at the foot of every page of the historical chapters. I also thank Laure Lion and Donna Daley, who helped to make accessible the rich pictorial resources of Corbis Images.

Among those in the financial community who were generous with their time, I would like to offer my special gratitude to two distinguished Wall Street veterans, Peter J. Solomon and Peter Cohen, each of whom was able to provide me with an insider's perspective on the financial world as it has evolved during the past three tumultuous decades.

Thanks, too, to Kate Hirson, Sam and Martha Peterson, and Joan Rosenbaum for kindnesses that did much to ease my research. As always, my wife Linda lent her considerable editing skills to the project and was supportive in a hundred different ways.

Photo Credits

Jeffrey Aaronson/Network Aspen: 153; Abby Kelley Foster Regional Charter School, Worcester, Ma/Advantage Schools: 71 (center); © AFP/CORBIS: 20, 68-69 (bottom), 69 (bottom), 112, 136-37 (top), 148-49, 187 (center left), 188 (bottom left), 189 (top right), 216-17 (bottom), 252, 253, 254, 255, 263 (top left), 268 (bottom), 279 (top), 282 (top), 284 (bottom), 290 (bottom right, top right), 290 (center), 291 (both), 324 (left), front cover, half-title spread; Agricultural Research Sevice, USDA: 274 (top); © Nubar Alexanian/ CORBIS: 334 (right); Alinari/Art Resource, NY: 26 (top); © Paul Almasy/CORBIS: 186 (center right); Courtesy of American Express Corporate Archives: 186 (center left, top left); Amsterdam Stock and Options Exchange: 98; Courtesy John M. Angelo: 19; AOL Time Warner Inc.: 89 (center left); © AP/Worldwide: 310 (right), 318 (right); © Adrian Arbib/CORBIS: half-title spread, 286-87; © Archivo Iconografico, S.A./CORBIS: 36, 56, 58 (right), 60, 73, 177 (bottom); Art Resource, NY: 45; © Yann Arthus-Bertrand/CORBIS: 12, 16-17, 34 (top right), 151 (bottom), 152-53 (top), back cover; © Asian Art & Archaeology, Inc./CORBIS: 162; © Craig Aurness/CORBIS: 51 (bottom left), 70 (left), 234-35 (bottom); © Margot Balboni: 107 (bottom left); Bank of England Museum: 90 (top); © Dave Bartruff: 266 (left); Bayer AG: 212-13, 214-15 (center), half-title spread, back cover; © Tom Bean/CORBIS: 248-49 (bottom); Bechtel: back cover; © Morton Beebe, S.F./CORBIS: 174-75 (top); © Annie Griffiths Belt/CORBIS: 121 (bottom); Benetton: 216 (center left); © Patrick Bennett/CORBIS: 275 (left); © Bettmann/CORBIS: 14, 18, 48-49 (both), 49 (center), 68 (top left, top right), 86-87 (both), 87 (top left), 88 (top), 91, 105 (top left), 116-17, 118 (top), 122, 124 (bottom left), 128, 129 (both), 133 (bottom left, bottom right), 136-37 (bottom), 142 (bottom left, right, and center), 144, 145, 154-55, 161 (bottom), 166, 172-73 (top), 173 (top), 177 (top), 181, 182, 186-87, 189 (bottom left), 191, 192 (both), 193, 194, 196, 199 (all), 202-203 (top), 206, 207 (both), 209, 210 (right), 219 (top), 224, 225 (right), 228 (both), 230 (both), 231, 235 (center, center left), 238 (both), 246 (bottom), 247 (top), 258 (top), 261, 278 (both), 279 (bottom), 288 (bottom), 300, 307 (left), 308 (right), 310 (left), 313, 314 (left), 318 (top left), 320 (right pair), 321 (both), 322 (both), 324 (right), 326 (left), 328, 329 (both), 330 (left), 331 (left), 333 (left), 335 (left), 336 (top left), 337, 338, 339 (right), 340, back cover, front cover, half-title spread; © Jonathan Blair/CORBIS: 42 (bottom), 63, 215 (bottom), 248 (bottom), 301; Blauel/Gnamm-ARTOTHEK: 65 (right), 72 (top); Boeing: 172 (center), 174; Reuters/Yun Suk Bong/Hulton/Archive by Getty Images: 262; © Barnabas Bosshart/CORBIS: 285; © Marilyn Bridges/CORBIS: 217 (top); © Copyright The British Museum: 40 (bottom), 42 (top), 55; Bureau of Reclamation photo courtesy of Bechtel: 46-47; Courtesy of the California History Room, California State Library, Sacramento, CA: 246 (top right); Courtesy of Caltrans Library: 104 (bottom); © Reuters/Andre Camara/Hulton/Archive by Getty Images: 288-89; Caterpillar Inc.: 174-75 (bottom); Image courtesy of Circus World Museum, Baraboo, Wisconsin with permission from Ringling Bros. and Barnum & Bailey® THE GREATEST SHOW ON EARTH®: 84-85; Courtesy of Clinton Hollins (www.clintonhollins.org): 302-304; The Coca-Cola Company: 172 (top); © W. Cody/CORBIS: 107 (top right); © Michael Collier: 244-45, 270-71; © Dean Conger/CORBIS: 150-51; © CORBIS: 27, 48 (bottom right, top left, top right), 86, 93, 94 (bottom left, top), 104 (top left), 107 (bottom right), 108, 120-21 (top), 124 (bottom right, top), 136, 164, 167 (both), 168 (bottom), 169 (top), 172 (bottom), 176 (all), 178-79, 183 (bottom), 190, 197 (bottom right, top), 272-73, 309 (left), 311, 317 (both), 318 (bottom), 320 (far left), 324 (center), 334 (left), back cover, half-title spread; © The Corcoran Gallery of Art/CORBIS: 315 (right); Cowles Foundation: 243; Culver Pictures: 142 (top), 87 (top right); Douglas Curran: 35 (center), half-title spread; DaimlerChrysler Corporate Archives: 88 (bottom left); © Araldo de Luca/CORBIS: 44 (top); © Leonard de Selva/CORBIS: 214 (bottom right), 222; Howard Pyle, *The Rush from the New York Stock Exchange on September 18, 1873*, from "A History of the Last Quarter Century" by E. Benjamin Andrews, *Scribner's Magazine*, July 1895, Oil on canvas; Delaware Art Museum: 132 (top); John Sloan, *Philadelphia Stock Exchange*, c. 1897-98, Oil on canvas; Delaware Art Museum, Gift of Helen Farr Sloan: 157 (top); © DPA Deutsche Presse-Agentur GmbH: 289 (right center); Walt Disney/Photofest: 232-33; Courtesy of The Dow Chemical Company: 189 (bottom right); Competitive Advertisements Collection (Pre-1955 files), J. Walter Thompson Company Archives, Hartman Center for Sales, Advertising & Marketing History, Rare Book, Manuscript and Special Collections Library, Duke University, Durham, North Carolina. © The Procter & Gamble Company. Used by Permission: 173 (center); Courtesy of Dupont Company: 173 (bottom), 188 (top left, top right); These materials have been reproduced with the permission of eBAY Inc. COPYRIGHT © EBAY INC. ALL RIGHTS RESERVED: 34 (top left); © Ed Eckstein/CORBIS: 240; © Ecoscene/CORBIS: 189 (top left); © Macduff Everton/ CORBIS: back cover; Exxon Mobil Corporation: 205 (top), 249, front cover; © Eye Ubiquitous/CORBIS: 220, 248 (top), half-title spread; Federal Reserve Bank of San Francisco: 113, 131, 132 (bottom), 288 (top left); Fidelity: 327 (left), 203 (top center, top right); © Jack Fields/CORBIS: 78 (top right); © Kevin Fleming/CORBIS: 121 (top), 236-37 (bottom), 274 (bottom left); © Natalie Fobes/CORBIS: 236-37 (top); © Owen Franken/ CORBIS: 23, 34 (top center), half-title spread; © Robert Garvey/CORBIS: 276 (left); Photos courtesy of General Electric: 175 (bottom right), 204 (bottom right), 205 (bottom right); Genessee & Wyoming/Photo © Robert M. Reynolds: 234-35 (top); © Bill Gentile/CORBIS: 150 (right); Courtesy George Eastman House: 68 (top center); © Lowell Georgia/CORBIS: 37 (left); © Mitchell Gerber/CORBIS: 332 (top); © Mark E. Gibson/CORBIS: 229 (bottom right); © Shai Ginott/CORBIS: 280 (bottom); © GlaxoSmithKline Inc.: 89 (bottom right); © Philip Gould/CORBIS: 35-36; © Jeff Greenberg/Unicorn Stock Photos: 296; © Farrell Grehan/CORBIS: 76-77, 79; Photo by Warren Gretz, courtesy of DOE/NREL: 249 (top left); Handspring: 71 (bottom right); © Lindsay Hebberd/CORBIS: 78 (bottom), half-title spread; © John Heseltine/CORBIS: 293 (left); © Historical Picture Archive/CORBIS: 26 (bottom), 80, 83; © 2001 ROBERT HOLMES: 268 (top left, top right); © Jeremy Horner/ CORBIS: 292; © Hulton-Deutsch Collection/CORBIS: 33 (top), 49 (top), 87 (bottom), 89 (top right), 92, 101, 109, 156 (bottom), 179, 180, 208, 246 (top left), 273 (bottom), 288 (center), 327 (right), 332 (bottom), 336 (bottom left); Hulton/Archive by Getty Images: 308 (left), 312, 326 (right), 333 (center left, center right), 336 (right); © Zen Icknow/CORBIS: 249 (top right); Courtesy of Intel Corporation: 170-71; © Peter Johnson/CORBIS: 37 (right); Galerie de Jonckheere, Paris, France/Bridgeman Art Library: 15; © Josse/Abbeville Press: 29, 94 (bottom right), 99, 126; © Wolfgang Kaehler/CORBIS: 43, back cover, half-title spread; © Ed Kashi/CORBIS: 203 (bottom), 204 (center right), 335 (right); © David Katzenstein/CORBIS: 284 (top right), half-title spread; © Douglas Kirkland/ CORBIS: 229 (bottom left); Photographs courtesy of Koch Industries, Inc.: 137 (bottom); © Earl & Nazima Kowall/CORBIS: 264; © Bob Krist/CORBIS: 223, 314 (right); Kymata: 70-71 (bottom); The LaGuardia and Wagner Archives, LaGuardia Community College/The City University of New York: 104-105 (top); © Lake County Museum/CORBIS: 186 (bottom), 105 (top right); © Dan Lamont/CORBIS: 229 (top); © Larry Lee Photography/CORBIS: 256; © David Lees/CORBIS: 306 (left), 218 (bottom), 59 (left); © Danny Lehman/CORBIS: 283 (bottom, top), front cover; © Charles & Josette Lenars/CORBIS: 28, 38-39, back cover; Erich Lessing/Art Resource, NY: 44 (bottom), 53 (bottom), 62; Library of Congress: 32-33 (top), 33 (center), 48 (bottom left), 49 (bottom), 114 (left), 118 (bottom), 118-19 (bottom), 120 (bottom), 168 (top), 259, 272 (top), 273 (top); Photo by Lito/Courtesy of Masha Zakheim: 272 (bottom right); © James Marshall/ CORBIS: 96, 237 (bottom); Used with permission of Martha Stewart Living/Omnimedia, Inc. © 2001 Martha Stewart Living/Omnimedia, Inc. All Rights Reserved: 71 (top); © Gunter Marx Photography/CORBIS: 66-67, 106 (top); © Michael Maslan Historic Photographs/CORBIS: 110-11, 163 (left, right); © Francis G. Mayer/CORBIS: 319 (right); © Stephanie Maze/CORBIS: 274 (bottom right), 284 (top left); © Wally McNamee/CORBIS: 150 (left); © Matt Mendelsohn/CORBIS: 319 (left); Mercedes-Benz USA: 88 (bottom right); Reproduced by courtesy of the Mercers' Company, *Thomas Gresham, aged 26*, oil on panel, Flemish School, 1544: 82; Merrill Lynch Archives: 202, 202-203 (bottom), 203 (center); R. Merritt, Alaska Division of Geological and Geophysical Surveys: 249 (right bottom); Military Stock Photography: 235 (center right); Minnesota Historical Society: 32 (right), 32-33 (bottom), 120-21 (bottom); © Gail Mooney/CORBIS: 24, 34 (bottom); TORU MORIMOTO/Galbe.com: 13 (both); © Motorola, Inc.: 216 (center right); © David Muench/CORBIS: 50-51 (top); Museo d'Arte Moderno di Ca Pesaro, Venice, Italy/ Bridgeman Art Library: 41; © Museum of Flight/CORBIS: 175 (top), 197 (bottom left); © Museum of the City of New York/CORBIS: 147 (top); NASA: 50 (bottom), 51 (top right), back cover, half-title spread; National Archives and Records Administration: 119 (bottom, top), 221; National Maritime Museum, Antwerp, Belgium, Photo by Joris Luyten: 75; Courtesy of Nestlé S.A.: 214 (top); New York City Housing Authority Photo Unit: 105 (bottom center); William Holbrook Beard, *The Bulls and Bears in the Market*, 1879, Oil on canvas, accession no. 1971.104, © Collection of the New York Historical Society: 130-31; New York Stock Exchange Archives: 114 (right), 123 (bottom, top), 133 (top), 140, 169 (bottom), 198, 226; Courtesy of Fox News: 216-17 (top); © Richard T. Nowitz/CORBIS: 265 (left), 282 (bottom), half-title spread; © Charles O'Rear/CORBIS: 21, 152 (both), 175 (bottom left), 214 (bottom left), 235 (top), 288 (top right); The Ohio State University: 104-105 (bottom); © Takashi Okamura/Abbeville Press: 72 (bottom); © Gianni Dagli Orti/CORBIS: 81; Bildarchiv, Österreichische NationalBibliothek, Vienna: 65 (left); Tingqua, *Canton Hongs*, c. 1855, Gouache on paper, Photograph courtesy Peabody Essex Museum, photograph by Jeffrey Dykes: 160; Photodisc: 10; Photofest: 138-139 (all); © Robert Pickett/CORBIS: 235 (bottom); Port Authority of New York and New Jersey: 102-103; Porterfield/Chickering: 267; © Neil Rabinowitz/CORBIS: 263 (top right); © Enzo & Paolo Ragazzini/CORBIS: 218 (top), 219 (bottom); © Vittoriano Rastelli/CORBIS: 64, half-title spread; © Steve Raymer/CORBIS: 61, half-title spread; René-Jacques © Ministère de la Culture-France: 210 (left); © Roger Ressmeyer/CORBIS: 68-69 (top), 89 (top left), 187 (bottom); © Reuters/CORBIS: 260 (bottom left, center, center left, bottom center, center right, top center, top right), 265 (right), 269, 289 (bottom, top left), 297, 333 (right); © Reuters NewMedia Inc./CORBIS: 22, 68 (bottom), 69 (center), 71 (bottom left), 89 (bottom left), 107 (right center), 188 (bottom right), 215 (top), 242, 250, 260 (bottom right, top left), 263 (bottom), 266 (right), 275 (top), 280 (top), 289 (top right), 290 (top left), 294, 306 (center), 309 (right), 325, 336 (bottom), back cover, front cover, half-title spread; © Jim Richardson/CORBIS: 137 (top); © Lynda Richardson/CORBIS: 275 (bottom right), half-title spread; © David Samuel Robbins/CORBIS: 290 (bottom left); © Joel W. Rogers/CORBIS: 217(bottom right); © Fulvio Roiter/CORBIS: 152-53 (bottom); © Bill Ross/CORBIS: 211, half-title spread; © Galen Rowell/CORBIS: 275 (right center); © David Rubinger/CORBIS: 281; Sandia National Laboratories: 50-51 (bottom); Scala/Art Resource, NY: 40 (top); © Schenectady Museum, Hall of Electrical History Foundation/ CORBIS: 172-73 (bottom), 330 (right); © Phil Schermeister/CORBIS: 35 (top); © Joseph Schwartz Collection/CORBIS: 120 (top); © Michael T. Sedam/CORBIS: 51 (bottom right), back cover; Shell International Ltd.: 214-15 (bottom); Seimens Solar/DOE/NREL: 299; Singer Sewing Company: 68 (top left, silo); Photo by Walter Smalling: 70-71 (center); © Joseph Sohm, ChromoSohm Inc./CORBIS: 70-71 (top), 121 (center), 200-201, 204-205, 225 (left), half-title spread; Sonic, America's Drive-In: 236; Courtesy of Sony Pictures Classics Inc.: 216 (bottom); © Hubert Stadler/CORBIS: 274-75; Standard & Poor's: 204 (bottom left); Courtesy of STAR: 217 (right center); The Stock Exchange: 157 (bottom); Stock Exchange Luncheon Club: 115, 125; © Patrick W. Stoll/CORBIS: 234; U.S. Navy photo by Photographer's Mate Airman Christopher B. Stoltz: 50 (top); © Keren Su/CORBIS: 54; © James A. Sugar/CORBIS: 184-85, 205 (bottom left), back cover; © Jim Sugar Photography/CORBIS: 105 (bottom right); Tate Gallery, London/Art Resource, NY: 90 (bottom); Tokyo Stock Exchange: 161 (top); Courtesy of Trex Company: 237 (top); © David & Peter Turnley/CORBIS: 151 (top); © Peter Turnley/ CORBIS: 277, 295 (both); Tyson Foods Inc.: 272 (bottom left); © Underwood & Underwood/CORBIS: 32 (left), 118-19 (top), 158, 183 (top), 307 (right), 308 (center); Union Pacific Historical Collection: 141, 147 (bottom); Uniphoto: 293 (right); © Robert van der Hilst/CORBIS: 279 (center); Courtesy The Vanguard Group: 310 (center); © Vanni Archive/CORBIS: 52; © Gian Berto Vanni/CORBIS: 268 (top center); © Sandro Vannini/CORBIS: 58 (left); © Bill Varie/CORBIS: 204 (top); Volkswagen: 214-215 (top); © Baldwin H. Ward & Kathryn C. Ward/CORBIS: 156 (top); © Nik Wheeler/CORBIS: 30-31, 53 (top), 78 (top left), 107 (top left), half-title spread; © Oscar White/CORBIS: 306 (right), 315 (left), 320 (next left), 331 (right), 339 (left); © Doug Wilson/CORBIS: 69 (top), 316; © Peter M. Wilson/CORBIS: 258 (bottom), front cover; © Roger Wood/CORBIS: 247 (bottom); © Adam Woolfitt/CORBIS: 59 (right), 106 (bottom); Courtesy of Xerox Corporation: 187 (right); © Michael S. Yamashita/CORBIS: 100, 276 (right), 290 (center); Zurich Stock Exchange: 241.

Index

■ ■ IN BRAZIL, THE REAL PLAN BRINGS SOME STABILITY TO DOMESTIC PRICES; ITS AUTHOR, FERNANDO HENRIQUE CARDOSO, IS THEN ELECTED PRESIDENT

■ ■ SEC RULES THAT NASDAQ DEALERS ILLEGALLY COLLUDED TO BOOST SPREADS IN THE MARKET-MAKING PROCESS ■ **1997:** STOCK MARKETS THROUGHOUT

■ ■ KSE INAUGURATES STOCK INDEX OPTIONS MARKET AND LIFTS ALL CEILINGS ON FOREIGN INVESTMENT ■ HONG KONG REVERTS FROM BRITISH TO CHINES

■ ■ LONDON STOCK EXCHANGE AND FRANKFURT DEUTSCHE BÖRSE TRY TO FORM STRATEGTIC ALLIANCE ■ GERMAN AND SWISS EXCHANGES LAUNCH EUREX,

■ ■ CHRYSLER MERGES WITH DAIMLER-BENZ, STARTING TREND THAT WILL SPREAD THROUGH AUTO, COMMUNICATIONS, OTHER INDUSTRIES ■ AMEX BECOME

■ ■ **1999:** SINGAPORE EXCHANGE (SGX) FORMED BY MERGER OF THE STOCK EXCHANGE OF SINGAPORE AND SINGAPORE FUTURES EXCHANGE ■ SHANGHAI STO

■ ■ **2000:** LONDON AND FRANKFURT STOCK MARKETS ANNOUNCE INTENT TO MERGE, AS DO PARIS, BRUSSELS, AND AMSTERDAM BOURSES ■ NASDAQ ENTE

■ ■ JORDAN IS ACCEPTED INTO FULL MEMBERSHIP IN WORLD TRADE ORGANIZATION ■ MEXICAN MARKET GAINS INVESTOR CONFIDENCE THROUGH THE NOR